Frank Wood
BSc(Econ),FCA

FOURTH EDITION

Business Accounting 1

Pitman

PITMAN PUBLISHING
128 Long Acre, London WC2E 9AN

© Frank Wood 1967
© Longman Group Limited 1972, 1979, 1984

Fourth edition first published in Great Britain 1984
Reprinted 1985, 1986, 1987, 1988

British Library Cataloguing in Publication Data

Wood, Frank
  Business accounting.—4th ed.
  1.
  1. Accounting
  I. Title
  657   HF5635

ISBN 0-273-02629-1

Printed in Great Britain by
Richard Clay Ltd, Bungay, Suffolk

VOLUME ONE

Contents

Preface to Fourth Edition

1	The Accounting Equation and the Balance Sheet	1
2	The Double Entry System for Assets and Liabilities	11
3	The Asset of Stock	22
4	The Double Entry System for Expenses and Revenues. The Effect of Profit or Loss on Capital	33
5	Balancing Off Accounts	42
6	The Trial Balance	49
7	Trading and Profit and Loss Accounts: An Introduction	54
8	Balance Sheets	64
9	Trading and Profit and Loss Accounts and Balance Sheets: Further Considerations	69
10	Accounting Concepts and Statements of Standard Accounting Practice	80
11	The Division of the Ledger	88
12	The Banking System	93
13	Two Column Cash Books	99
14	Cash Discounts and the Three Column Cash Book	105
15	The Sales Journal	114
16	The Purchases Journal	121
17	The Returns Journals	125
18	Value Added Tax	133
19	Depreciation of Fixed Assets: Nature and Calculations	145
20	Double Entry Records for Depreciation	153

21 Bad Debts, Provisions for Bad Debts, Provisions for Discounts on Debtors   171

22 Other Adjustments for Final Accounts: Accruals, Prepayments etc.   183

23 A Fully Worked Exercise   198

24 Capital and Revenue Expenditure   221

25 Modern Methods of Processing Data   228

26 Bank Reconciliation Statements   233

27 The Journal   246

28 The Analytical Petty Cash Book and the Imprest System   253

29 Errors Not Affecting Trial Balance Agreement   261

30 Suspense Accounts and Errors   267

31 Control Accounts   277

32 Introduction to Accounting Ratios   287

33 Single Entry and Incomplete Records   296

34 Receipts and Payments Accounts and Income and Expenditure Accounts   318

35 Manufacturing Accounts   331

36 Departmental Accounts   343

37 Columnar Day Books   351

38 Partnership Accounts: An Introduction   359

39 Goodwill   373

40 Partnership Accounts Continued: Revaluation of Assets   388

41 An Introduction to the Final Accounts of Limited Liability Companies   396

42 Purchase of Existing Partnership and Sole Traders' Businesses   412

43 Funds Flow Statements: An Introduction   424

44 The Calculation of Wages and Salaries paid to Employees   433

45 An Introduction to the Analysis and Interpretation of Accounting Statements   440

Appendix I   *Examination Techniques*   446

Appendix II   *Answers to Exercises*   453

Index   472

Preface to the Fourth Edition

This textbook has been written so that a very thorough introduction to Accounting is covered in two volumes. The fact that this task has been split between two volumes is a recognition of the fact that, for many students, their grounding in the subject will not have to be as exhaustive as those who will carry on with professional examinations. Volume 1 fully covers the requirements of the General Certificate of Education at Ordinary level, as well as the first year examinations for many other examining bodies.

The questions set at the end of the relevant chapters are either from the examination papers of the above or have been specially devised. I have regarded it as a duty to ensure that all questions set can be answered by students who have worked through the text up to the chapter concerned. Questions involving needless complications have been avoided, emphasis being given to those which bring out a basic understanding of accounting.

Emphasis has been laid on the 'why' of accounting rather than merely to explain 'how'. In doing this the uses which management and others make of the accounting information are discussed. At the same time out-of-date methods have been mentioned but have not been used.

This edition varies from the third edition in various ways. Because of the changes in examination syllabuses some items have been moved from volume one to volume two. These are mainly the chapters on Bills of Exchange, Partnership Dissolution, Joint Ventures and Consignment Accounts. Conversely some new chapters have been added, these refer to Funds Flow Statements and Interpretation of Accounts. In addition chapters which I now consider were too long in the third edition have been broken down into shorter chapters, this makes assimilation of the information that much easier. In addition over 100 multiple choice questions are now included. These are now a basic ingredient in quite a few accounting examinations.

Anyone who has studied book-keeping or accounting previously may well question the validity of having assets on the left-hand side of the balance sheet and capital and liabilities on the right-hand side, as previously they used to be the opposite to that. However, the current Companies Act lays it down that in two-sided balance sheets assets must be shown on the left-hand side of the balance sheet and capital and liabilities on the right-hand side. In the interest of standardisation, and to avoid confusion, the balance sheets for sole traders and partnership will also be drawn up in the same way. In fact the new method does make book-keeping and accounting much easier to learn than previously. It is however a point to bear in mind when looking at other textbooks which have not been updated.

Generally, the figures used for exhibits and for exercises have been kept down to relatively small amounts. This has been done deliberately to make the work of the user of this book that much easier. Constantly handling large figures does not add anything to the study of the principles of accounting, instead it simply wastes a lot of the student's time, and he/she will probably make far more errors if larger figures are used. It could lead to the author being accused of not being 'realistic' with the figures given, but I believe that it is far more important to make learning easier for the student.

I would like to extend my sincere thanks to my former colleagues Eddie Cainen, A.C.C.A. and Joe Townsley, B.Com., F.C.A., for putting up with me for so many years, and for letting me pick their brains from time to time. Their help and encouragement has certainly improved the book. I also wish to acknowledge the permission to use past examination papers granted by the University of London, the Associated Examining Board, the London Chamber of Commerce, the Joint Matriculation Board, the Chartered Association of Certified Accountants, the Chartered Institute of Management Accountants, the Association of Accounting Technicians, the Institute of Chartered Secretaries and Administrators, the Association of Business Executives, and the Chartered Institute of Bankers.

Frank Wood
Stockport

1

The Accounting Equation and the Balance Sheet

Accounting is often said to be the language of business. It is used in the business world to describe the transactions entered into by all kinds of organizations. Accounting terms and ideas are therefore used by people associated with business, whether they are managers, owners, investors, bankers, lawyers, or accountants. As it is the language of business there are words and terms that mean one thing in accounting, but whose meaning is completely different in ordinary language usage. Fluency comes, as with other languages, after a certain amount of practice. When fluency has been achieved, that person will be able to survey the transactions of businesses, and will gain a greater insight into the way that business is transacted and the methods by which business decisions are taken.

The actual record-making phase of accounting is usually called book-keeping. However, accounting extends far beyond the actual making of records. Accounting is concerned with the use to which these records are put, their analysis and interpretation. An accountant should be concerned with more than the record-making phase. In particular he should be interested in the relationship between the financial results and the events which have created them. He should be studying the various alternatives open to the business, and be using his accounting experience in order to aid the management to select the best plan of action for the business. The owners and managers of a business will need some accounting knowledge in order that they may understand what the accountant is telling them. Investors and others will need accounting knowledge in order that they may read and understand the financial statements issued by the business, and adjust their relationships with the business accordingly.

Probably there are two main questions that the managers or owners of a business want to know: first, whether or not the business is operating at a profit; second, they will want to know whether or not the business will be able to meet its commitments as they fall due, and so not have to close down owing to lack of funds. Both these questions should be answered by the use of the accounting data of the firm.

The Accounting Equation

The whole of financial accounting is based on the accounting equation. This can be stated to be that for a firm to operate it needs resources, and that these resources have had to be supplied to the firm by someone. The resources possessed by the firm are known as Assets, and obviously some of these resources will have been supplied by the owner of the business. The total amount supplied by him is known as Capital. If in fact he was the only one who had supplied the assets then the following equation would hold true:

$$\text{Assets} = \text{Capital}$$

On the other hand, some of the assets will normally have been provided by someone other than the owner. The indebtedness of the firm for these resources is known as Liabilities. The equation can now be expressed as:

$$\text{Assets} = \text{Capital} + \text{Liabilities}$$

It can be seen that the two sides of the equation will have the same totals. This is because we are dealing with the same thing from two different points of view. It is:

$$\text{Resources: What they are} = \text{Resources: Who supplied them}$$
$$\text{(Assets)} \qquad \text{(Capital} + \text{Liabilities)}$$

It is a fact that the totals of each side will always equal one another, and that this will always be true no matter how many transactions are entered into. The actual assets, capital and liabilities may change, but the equality of assets with that of the total of capital and liabilities will always hold true.

Assets consist of property of all kinds, such as buildings, machinery, stocks of goods and motor vehicles, also benefits such as debts owing by customers and the amount of money in the bank account.

Liabilities consist of money owing for goods supplied to the firm, and for expenses, also for loans made to the firm.

Capital is often called the owner's equity or net worth.

The Balance Sheet and the Effects of Business Transactions

The accounting equation is expressed in a financial position statement called the Balance Sheet. It is not the first accounting record to be made, but it is a convenient place to start to consider accounting.

The Introduction of Capital

On 1 May 19-7 B. Blake started in business and deposited £5,000 into a bank account opened specially for the business. The balance sheet would appear:

B. Blake

Balance Sheet as at 1 May 19-7

Assets	£		£
Cash at bank	5,000	Capital	5,000
	5,000		5,000

The Purchase of an Asset by Cheque

On 3 May 19-7 Blake buys a building for £3,000. The effect of this transaction is that the cash at bank is decreased and a new asset, buildings, appears.

B. Blake

Balance Sheet as at 3 May 19-7

Assets	£		£
Buildings	3,000	Capital	5,000
Cash at bank	2,000		
	5,000		5,000

The Purchase of an Asset and the Incurring of a Liability

On 6 May 19-7 Blake buys some goods for £500 from D. Smith, and agrees to pay for them some time within the next two weeks. The effect of this is that a new asset, stock of goods, is acquired, and a liability for the goods is created. A person to whom money is owed for goods is known in accounting language as a creditor.

B. Blake

Balance Sheet as at 6 May 19-7

Assets	£	Capital and Liabilities	£
Buildings	3,000	Capital	5,000
Stock of goods	500	Creditor	500
Cash at bank	2,000		
	5,500		5,500

Sale of an Asset on Credit

On 10 May 19-7 goods which had cost £100 were sold to J. Brown for the same amount, the money to be paid later. The effect is a reduction in the stock of goods and the creation of a new asset. A person who owes the firm money is known in accounting language as a debtor. The balance sheet now appears as:

B. Blake
Balance Sheet as at 10 May 19-7

Assets	£	Capital and Liabilities	£
Buildings	3,000	Capital	5,000
Stock of goods	400	Creditor	500
Debtor	100		
Cash at bank	2,000		
	5,500		5,500

Sale of an Asset for Immediate Payment

On 13 May 19-7 goods which had cost £50 were sold to D. Daley for the same amount, Daley paying for them immediately by cheque. Here one asset, stock of goods, is reduced, while another asset, bank, is increased. The balance sheet now appears:

B. Blake
Balance Sheet as at 13 May 19-7

Assets	£	Capital and Liabilities	£
Buildings	3,000	Capital	5,000
Stock of goods	350	Creditor	500
Debtor	100		
Cash at bank	2,050		
	5,500		5,500

The Payment of a Liability

On 15 May 19-7 Blake pays a cheque for £200 to D. Smith in part payment of the amount owing. The asset of bank is therefore reduced, and the liability of the creditor is also reduced. The balance sheet now appears:

B. Blake
Balance Sheet as at 15 May 19-7

Assets	£	Capital and Liabilities	£
Buildings	3,000	Capital	5,000
Stock of goods	350	Creditor	300
Debtor	100		
Cash at bank	1,850		
	5,300		5,300

Collection of an Asset

J. Brown, who owed Blake £100, makes a part payment of £75 by cheque on 31 May 19-7. The effect is to reduce one asset, debtor, and to increase another asset, bank. This results in a balance sheet as follows:

B. Blake
Balance Sheet as at 31 May 19-7

Assets	£	Capital and Liabilities	£
Buildings	3,000	Capital	5,000
Stock of goods	350	Creditor	300
Debtor	25		
Cash at bank	1,925		
	5,300		5,300

It can be seen that every transaction has affected two items. Sometimes it has changed two assets by reducing one and increasing the other. Other times it has reacted differently. A summary of the effect of transactions upon assets, liabilities and capital is shown below.

Example of Transaction

1.	Buy goods on credit.	Increase Asset (Stock of Goods)	Increase Liability (Creditors)
2.	Buy goods by cheque.	Increase Asset (Stock of Goods)	Decrease Asset (Bank)
3.	Pay creditor by cheque.	Decrease Asset (Bank)	Decrease Liability (Creditors)
4.	Owner pays more capital into the bank.	Increase Asset (Bank)	Increase Capital
5.	Owner takes money out of the business bank for his own use.	Decrease Asset (Bank)	Decrease Capital
6.	Owner pays creditor from private money outside the firm.	Decrease Liability (Creditors)	Increase Capital

Each transaction has therefore maintained the equality of the total of assets with that of capital and liabilities. This can be shown:

Number of transaction as above	Assets	Liabilities and Capital	Effect on balance sheet totals
1	+	+	Each side added to equally.
2	+ −		A plus and a minus both on the assets side cancelling out each other.
3	−	−	Each side has equal deductions.
4	+	+	Each side has equal additions.
5	−	−	Each side has equal deductions.
6		− +	A plus and a minus both on the liabilities and capital side cancelling out each other.

Notes:

(i)   Anyone who has studied book-keeping or accounting previously may well question the validity of having assets on the left-hand side of the balance sheet and capital and liabilities on the right-hand side, as previously they used to be the opposite to that. However, the Companies Act 1985 lays it down that in two-sided balance sheets assets must be shown on the left-hand side of the balance sheet and capital and liabilities on the right-hand side. In the interests of standardisation, and to avoid confusion, the balance sheets for sole traders and partnerships will also be drawn up in the same way.

In fact the new method does make book-keeping and accounting much easier to learn than previously. It is however a point to bear in mind when looking at other textbooks which have not been updated.

(ii)   Generally, the figures used for exhibits and for exercises have been kept down to relatively small amounts. This has been done deliberately to make the work of the user of this book that much easier. Constantly handling large figures does not add anything to the study of the principles of accounting, instead it simply wastes a lot of the student's time, and he/she will probably make far more errors if larger figures are used.

It could lead to the author being accused of not being 'realistic' with the figures given, but I believe that it is far more important to make learning easier for the student.

Exercises

At the end of most chapters you will find several multiple choice questions. They can be identified by the use of the prefix MC before each question, followed by the number of that particular question.

Each multiple choice question has four suggested answers letter (A), (B), (C), (D). You should read each question and then decide which choice is best, either (A) or (B) or (C) or (D). On a separate piece of paper you should then write down your choice. Unless the textbook you are reading belongs to you, you should not make a mark against your choice in the textbook.

ANSWERS TO MULTIPLE CHOICE QUESTIONS ARE GIVEN ON PAGE 453 OF THIS BOOK.

MC1 Which of the following statements is incorrect?
(A) Assets − Capital = Liabilities
(B) Liabilities + Capital = Assets
(C) Liabilities + Assets = Capital
(D) Assets − Liabilities = Capital.

MC2 Which of the following is not an asset?
(A) Buildings
(B) Cash balance
(C) Debtors
(D) Loan from K. Harris.

MC3 Which of the following is a liability?
(A) Machinery
(B) Creditors for goods
(C) Motor Vehicles
(D) Cash at Bank.

MC4 Which of the following is incorrect?

	Assets £	Liabilities £	Capital £
(A)	7,850	1,250	6,600
(B)	8,200	2,800	5,400
(C)	9,550	1,150	8,200
(D)	6,540	1,120	5,420

MC5 Which of the following statements is correct?

		Effect upon Assets	Liabilities
(A)	We paid a creditor by cheque	− Bank	− Creditors
(B)	A debtor paid us £90 in cash	+ Cash	+ Debtors
(C)	J. Hall lends us £500 by cheque	+ Bank	− Loan from Hall
(D)	Bought goods on credit	+ Stock	+ Capital

Exercises (other types of questions)

Note: **Questions with the letter A shown after the question number do NOT have answers shown at the back of the book. Answers to the others are shown on pages 453 onwards.**

1.1 You are to complete the gaps in the following table:

	Assets	Liabilities	Capital
	£	£	£
(a)	12,500	1,800	?
(b)	28,000	4,900	?
(c)	16,800	?	12,500
(d)	19,600	?	16,450
(e)	?	6,300	19,200
(f)	?	11,650	39,750

1.2A. You are to complete the gaps in the following table:

	Assets	Liabilities	Capital
	£	£	£
(a)	55,000	16,900	?
(b)	?	17,200	34,400
(c)	36,100	?	28,500
(d)	119,500	15,400	?
(e)	88,000	?	62,000
(f)	?	49,000	110,000

1.3. Distinguish from the following list the items that are liabilities from those that are assets:
(i) Office machinery
(ii) Loan from C. Shirley
(iii) Fixtures and fittings
(iv) Motor vehicles
(v) We owe for goods
(vi) Bank balance.

1.4A. Classify the following items into liabilities and assets:
Motor vehicles
Premises
Creditors for goods
Stock of goods
Debtors
Owing to bank
Cash in hand
Loan from D. Jones
Machinery.

1.5. State which of the following are shown under the wrong classification for J. White's business:

Assets	Liabilities
Loan from C. Smith	Stock of goods
Cash in hand	Debtors
Machinery	Money owing to bank
Creditors	
Premises	
Motor vehicles.	

1.6A. Which of the following are shown under the wrong headings:

Assets	Liabilities
Cash at bank	Loan from J. Graham
Fixtures	Machinery
Creditors	Motor vehicles
Building	
Stock of goods	
Debtors	
Capital	

1.7. A. Smart sets up a new business. Before he actually sells anything he has bought Motor Vehicles £2,000, Premises £5,000, Stock of goods £1,000. He did not pay in full for his stock of goods and still owes £400 in respect of them. He had borrowed £3,000 from D. Bevan. After the events just described, and before trading starts, he has £100 cash in hand and £700 cash at bank. You are required to calculate the amount of his capital.

1.8A. T. Charles starts a business. Before he actually starts to sell anything he has bought, Fixtures £2,000, Motor Vehicles £5,000 and a stock of goods £3,500. Although he has paid in full for the fixtures and the motor vehicle, he still owes £1,400 for some of the goods. J. Preston had lent him £3,000. Charles, after the above, has £2,800 in the business bank account and £100 cash in hand. You are required to calculate his capital.

1.9. Draw up A. Foster's balance sheet from the following as at 31 December 19-4:

	£
Capital	23,750
Debtors	4,950
Motor vehicles	5,700
Creditors	2,450
Fixtures	5,500
Stock of goods	8,800
Cash at bank	1,250

1.10A. Draw up Kelly's balance sheet as at 30 June 19-2 from the following items:

	£
Capital	13,000
Office machinery	9,000
Creditors	900
Stock of goods	1,550
Debtors	275
Cash at bank	5,075
Loan from C. Smith	2,000

1.11. Complete the columns to show the effects of the following transactions:

Effect upon
Assets   Liabilities   Capital

(a) We pay a creditor £70 in cash
(b) Bought fixtures £200 paying by cheque
(c) Bought goods on credit £275
(d) The proprietor introduces another £500 cash into the firm
(e) J. Walker lends the firm £200 in cash
(f) A debtor pays us £50 by cheque
(g) We return goods costing £60 to a supplier whose bill we had not paid
(h) Bought additional shop premises paying £5,000 by cheque.

1.12A. Complete the columns to show the effects of the following transactions:

Effect upon
Assets   Liabilities   Capital

(a) Bought a motor van on credit £500
(b) Repaid by cash a loan owed to P. Smith £1,000
(c) Bought goods for £150 paying by cheque
(d) The owner puts a further £5,000 cash into the business
(e) A debtor returns to us £80 goods. We agree to make an allowance for them.
(f) Bought goods on credit £220
(g) The owner takes out £100 cash for his personal use
(h) We pay a creditor £190 by cheque.

1.13. C. Sangster has the following items in his balance sheet as on 30 April 19-4:

Capital £18,900; Loan from T. Sharples £2,000; Creditors £1,600; Fixtures £3,500; Motor Vehicle £4,200; Stock of Goods £4,950; Debtors £3,280; Cash at Bank £6,450; Cash in Hand £120.

During the first week of May 19-4 Sangster:
(i)   Bought extra stock of goods £770 on credit.
(ii) One of the debtors paid us £280 in cash.
(iii) Bought extra fixtures by cheque £1,000.

You are to draw up a balance sheet as on 7 May 19-4 after the above transactions have been completed.

2

The Double Entry System for Assets and Liabilities

It has been seen that each transaction affects two items. To show the full effect of each transaction, accounting must therefore show its effect on each of the two items, be they assets, capital or liabilities. From this need arose the double entry system where to show this twofold effect each transaction is entered twice, once to show the effect upon one item, and a second entry to show the effect upon the other item.

It may be thought that drawing up a new balance sheet after each transaction would provide all the information required. However, a balance sheet does not give enough information about the business. It does not, for instance, tell who the debtors are and how much each one of them owes the firm, nor who the creditors are and the details of money owing to each of them. Also, the task of drawing up a new balance sheet after each transaction becomes an impossibility when there are many hundreds of transactions each day, as this would mean drawing up hundreds of balance sheets daily. Because of the work involved, balance sheets are in fact only drawn up periodically, at least annually, but sometimes half-yearly, quarterly, or monthly.

The double entry system has an account (meaning details of transactions in that item) for every asset, every liability and for capital. Thus there will be a Shop Premises Account (for transactions in shop premises), a Motor Vans Accounts (for transactions in Motor Vans), and so on for every asset, liability and for capital.

Each account should be shown on a separate page. The double entry system divides each page into two halves. The left-hand side of each page is called the debit side, while the right-hand side is called the credit side. The title of each account is written across the top of the account at the centre.

It must not be thought that the words 'debit' and 'credit' in book-keeping mean the same as the words 'debit' or 'credit' in normal language usage. Anyone who does will become very confused.

This is a page of an accounts book:

Title of account written here	
Left-hand side of the page. This is the 'debit' side.	Right-hand side of the page. This is the 'credit' side.

If you have to make an entry of £10 on the debit side of the account, the instructions could say 'debit the account with £10' or 'the account needs debiting with £10'.

In Chapter 1 transactions were to increase or decrease assets, liabilities or capital. Double entry rules for accounts are:

Accounts	To record	Entry in the account
Assets	an increase	Debit
	a decrease	Credit
Liabilities	an increase	Credit
	a decrease	Debit
Capital	an increase	Credit
	a decrease	Debit

Once again look at the accounting equation:

	Assets	=	Liabilities	and	Capital
To increase each item	Debit		Credit		Credit
To decrease each item	Credit		Debit		Debit

The double-entry rules for liabilities and capital are the same, but they are exactly the opposite as those for assets. This is because assets are on the opposite side of the equation and therefore follow opposite rules.

Looking at the accounts the rules will appear as:

Any asset account		Any liability Account		Capital account	
Increases	Decreases	Decreases	Increases	Decreases	Increases
+	−	−	+	−	+

There is not enough space in this book to put each account on a separate page, so we will have to list the accounts under each other. In a real firm at least one full page would be taken for each account.

The entry of a few transactions can now be attempted:
1. The proprietor starts the firm with £1,000 in cash on 1 August 19-6.

Effect	Action
(a) Increases the asset of cash in the firm	Debit the cash account
(b) Increases the capital	Credit the capital account

These are entered:

Cash

19-6	£		
Aug 1	1,000		

Capital

		19-6	£
		Aug 1	1,000

The date of the transaction has already been entered. Now there remains the description which is to be entered alongside the amount. This is completed by a cross reference to the title of the other account in which double entry is completed. The double entry to the item in the cash account is completed by an entry in the capital account, therefore the word 'Capital' will appear in the cash account. Similarly, the double entry to the item in the capital account is completed by an entry in the cash account, therefore the word 'Cash' will appear in the capital account.

It always used to be the custom to prefix the description on the debit side of the books with the word 'To', and to prefix the description on the credit side of the books with the word 'By'. These have now fallen into disuse in modern firms, and as they serve no useful purpose they will not be used in this book.

The finally completed accounts are therefore:

Cash

19-6	£		
Aug 1 Capital	1,000		

Capital

		19-6	£
		Aug 1 Cash	1,000

2. A motor van is bought for £275 cash on 2 August 19-6.

Effect	*Action*
(a) Decreases the asset of cash	Credit the cash account
(b) Increases the asset of motor van	Debit the motor van account

Cash

	19-6	£
	Aug 2 Motor van	275

Motor Van

19-6	£	
Aug 2 Cash	275	

3. Fixtures bought on credit from Shop Fitters £115 on 3 August 19-6.

Effect	*Action*
(a) Increase in the asset of fixtures	Debit fixtures account
(b) Increase in the liability of the firm to Shop Fitters	Credit Shop Fitters account

Fixtures

19-6	£	
Aug 3 Shop Fitters	115	

Shop Fitters

	19-6	£
	Aug 3 Fixtures	115

4. Paid the amount owing in cash to Shop Fitters on 17 August 19-6.

Effect	*Action*
(a) Decrease in the asset of cash	Credit the cash account
(b) Decrease in the liability of the firm to Shop Fitters	Debit Shop Fitters account

Cash

	19-6	£
	Aug 17 Shop Fitters	115

Shop Fitters

19-6	£
Aug 17 Cash	115

Transactions to date

Taking the transactions numbered 1 to 4 above, the records will now appear:

Cash

19-6	£	19-6	£
Aug 1 Capital	1,000	Aug 2 Motor van	275
		" 17 Shop Fitters	115

Motor Van

19-6	£
Aug 2 Cash	275

Shop Fitters

19-6	£	19-6	£
Aug 17 Cash	115	Aug 3 Fixtures	115

Fixtures

19-6	£
Aug 3 Shop Fitters	115

Capital

		19-6	£
		Aug 1 Cash	1,000

A Further Worked Example

Now you have actually made some entries in accounts you are to go carefully through the following example. Make certain you can understand every entry.

	Transactions	Effect	Action
19-4			
May 1	Started an engineering business putting £1,000 into a business bank account.	Increases asset of bank.	Debit bank account.
		Increases capital of proprietor.	Credit capital account.
,, 3	Bought works machinery on credit from Unique Machines £275.	Increases asset of machinery.	Debit machinery account.
		Increases liability to Unique Machines.	Credit Unique Machines account.
,, 4	Withdrew £200 cash from the bank and placed it in the cash till.	Decreases asset of bank.	Credit bank account.
		Increases asset of cash.	Debit cash account.
,, 7	Bought motor van paying in cash £180.	Decreases asset of cash.	Credit cash account.
		Increases asset of motor van.	Debit motor van account.
,, 10	Sold some of machinery for £15 on credit to B. Barnes.	Decreases asset of machinery.	Credit machinery account.
		Increases asset of money owing from B. Barnes.	Debit B. Barnes account.
,, 21	Returned some of machinery value £27 to Unique Machines.	Decreases asset of machinery.	Credit machinery account.
		Decreases liability to Unique Machines.	Debit Unique Machines.
,, 28	B. Barnes pays the firm the amount owing, £15, by cheque.	Increases asset of bank.	Debit bank account.
		Decreases asset of money owing by B. Barnes.	Credit B. Barnes account.
,, 30	Bought another motor van paying by cheque £420.	Decreases asset of bank.	Credit bank account.
		Increases asset of motor vans.	Debit motor van account.
,, 31	Paid the amount of £248 to Unique Machines by cheque.	Decreases asset of bank.	Credit bank account.
		Decreases liability to Unique Machines.	Debit Unique Machines.

In account form this is shown:

Bank

	£		£
May 1 Capital	1,000	May 4 Cash	200
,, 28 B. Barnes	15	,, 30 Motor van	420
		,, 31 Unique Machines	248

Cash

	£		£
May 4 Bank	200	May 7 Motor van	180

Capital

			£
		May 1 Bank	1,000

Machinery

	£		£
May 3 Unique Machines	275	May 10 B. Barnes	15
		,, 21 Unique Machines	27

Motor Van

	£
May 7 Cash	180
,, 30 Bank	420

Unique Machines

	£		£
May 21 Machinery	27	May 3 Machinery	275
,, 31 Bank	248		

B. Barnes

	£		£
May 10 Machinery	15	May 28 Bank	15

Abbreviation of 'Limited'

In this book when we come across our transactions with limited companies the use of letters 'Ltd' is used as the abbreviation for 'Limited Company'. Thus we will know that if we see the name of a firm as F. Wood Ltd, then that the firm will be a limited company. In our books the transactions with F. Wood Ltd will be entered the same as for any other customer or supplier. It will be seen later that some limited companies use PLC instead of Ltd.

Exercises (Multiple Choice Questions)

For answers to multiple choice questions see page 453.

MC6 Which of the following are correct?

	Accounts	*To record*	*Entry in the account*
(i)	Assets	an increase	Debit
		a decrease	Credit
(ii)	Capital	an increase	Debit
		a decrease	Credit
(iii)	Liabilities	an increase	Credit
		a decrease	Debit

(A) i and ii
(B) ii and iii
(C) i and iii
(D) None of them.

MC7 Which of the following are correct?

		Account to be debited	*Account to be credited*
(i)	Bought office furniture for cash	Office Furniture	Cash
(ii)	A debtor, P. Sangster, pays us by cheque	Bank	P. Sangster
(iii)	Introduced capital by cheque	Capital	Bank
(iv)	Paid a creditor, B. Lee, by cash	B. Lee	Cash

(A) i, ii and iii only
(B) ii, iii and iv only
(C) i, ii and iv only
(D) i and iv only.

MC8 Which of the following are incorrect?

		Account to be debited	*Account to be credited*
(i)	Sold motor van for cash	Cash	Motor van
(ii)	Returned some of Office Equipment to Suppliers Ltd.	Office Equipment	Suppliers Ltd.
(iii)	Repaid part of Loan from C. Charles by cheque	Loan from C. Charles	Bank
(iv)	Bought Machinery on credit from Betterways Ltd.	Betterways Ltd.	Machinery

(A) ii and iv only
(B) iii and iv only
(C) ii and iii only
(D) i and iii only.

Exercises (other Questions)

Note: Questions with the letter A shown after the question number do NOT have answers shown at the back of the book. Answers to the others are shown on pages 453 onwards.

2.1. Complete the following table showing which accounts are to be credited and which to be debited:

	Account to be debited	Account to be credited
(a) Bought motor van for cash		
(b) Bought office machinery on credit from J. Grant & Son		
(c) Introduced capital in cash		
(d) A debtor, J. Beach, pays us by cheque		
(e) Paid a creditor, A. Barrett, in cash.		

2.2. The following table is also to be completed, showing the accounts to be debited and credited:

	Account to be debited	Account to be credited
(a) Bought machinery on credit from A. Jackson & Son		
(b) Returned machinery to A. Jackson & Son		
(c) A debtor, J. Brown pays us in cash		
(d) J. Smith lends us money, giving it to us by cheque		
(e) Sold office machinery for cash.		

2.3A. Complete the following table:

	Account to be debited	Account to be credited
(a) Bought office machinery on credit from D. Isaacs Ltd		
(b) The proprietor paid a creditor, C. Jones, from his private monies outside the firm		
(c) A debtor, N. Fox, paid us in cash		
(d) Repaid part of loan from P. Exeter by cheque		
(e) Returned some of office machinery to D. Isaacs Ltd		
(f) A debtor, N. Lyn, pays us by cheque		
(g) Bought motor van by cash.		

2.4A. Complete the following table showing which accounts are to be debited and which to be credited:

		Account to be debited	Account to be credited
(a)	Bought motor lorry for cash		
(b)	Paid creditor, T. Lake, by cheque		
(c)	Repaid P. Logan's loan by cash		
(d)	Sold motor lorry for cash		
(e)	Bought office machinery on credit from Ultra Ltd		
(f)	A debtor, A. Hill, pays us by cash		
(g)	A debtor, J. Cross, pays us by cheque		
(h)	Proprietor puts a further amount into the business by cheque		
(i)	A loan of £200 in cash is received from L. Lowe		
(j)	Paid a creditor, D. Lord, by cash.		

2.5. Write up the asset and liability accounts in the records of D. Coy to record these transactions:

19-2

May	1	Started business with £1,000 cash
,,	3	Bought a motor lorry on credit from Speed & Sons for £698
,,	14	Bought office machinery by cash for £60
,,	31	Paid Speed & Sons the amount owing to them, £698, in cash.

2.6. Write up the asset and liability and capital accounts to record the following transactions in the records of G. Powell.

19-3

July	1	Started business with £2,500 in the bank
,,	2	Bought office furniture by cheque £150
,,	3	Bought machinery £750 on credit from Planers Ltd
,,	5	Bought a motor van paying by cheque £600
,,	8	Sold some of the office furniture − not suitable for the firm − for £60 on credit to J. Walker & Sons
,,	15	Paid the amount owing to Planers Ltd £750 by cheque
,,	23	Received the amount due from J. Walker £60 in cash
,,	31	Bought more machinery by cheque £280.

2.7. You are required to open the asset and liability and capital accounts and record the following transactions for June 19-4 in the records of C. Williams.

19-4

June	1	Started business with £2,000 in cash.
,,	2	Paid £1,800 of the opening cash into a bank account for the business
,,	5	Bought office furniture on credit from Betta-Built Ltd. for £120
,,	8	Bought a motor van paying by cheque £950
,,	12	Bought works machinery from Evans & Sons on credit £560
,,	18	Returned faulty office furniture costing £62 to Betta-Built Ltd
,,	25	Sold some of the works machinery for £75 cash
,,	26	Paid amount owing to Betta-Built Ltd £58 by cheque
,,	28	Took £100 out of the bank and put it in the cash till
,,	30	J. Smith lent us £500 − giving us the money by cheque.

2.8. Write up the various accounts needed in the books of S. Russell to record the following transactions:

19-4

April 1 Opened business with £10,000 in the bank

,, 3 Bought office equipment £700 on credit from J. Saunders Ltd

,, 6 Bought motor van paying by cheque £3,000

,, 8 Borrowed £1,000 from H. Thompson — he gave us the money by cheque

,, 11 Russell put further capital into the firm in the form of cash £500

,, 12 Paid £350 of the cash in hand into the bank account

,, 15 Returned some of the office equipment costing £200 — it was faulty — to J. Saunders Ltd

,, 17 Bought more office equipment, paying by cash £50

,, 19 Sold the motor van, as it had proved unsuitable, to R. Jones for £3,000. R. Jones will settle for this by three payments later this month

,, 21 Received a loan in cash from J. Hawkins £400

,, 22 R. Jones paid us a cheque for £1,000

,, 23 Bought a suitable motor van £3,600 on credit from Phillips Garages

,, 26 R. Jones paid us a cheque for £1,800

,, 28 Paid £2,000 by cheque to Phillips Garages Ltd

,, 30 R. Jones paid us cash £200.

2.9A. Write up the asset, capital and liability accounts in the books of C. Walsh to record the following transactions:

19-5

June 1 Started business with £5,000 in the bank

,, 2 Bought motor van paying by cheque £1,200

,, 5 Bought office fixtures £400 on credit from Young Ltd

,, 8 Bought motor van on credit from Super Motors £800

,, 12 Took £100 out of the bank and put it into the cash till

,, 15 Bought office fixtures paying by cash £60

,, 19 Paid Super Motors a cheque for £800

,, 21 A loan of £1,000 cash is received from J. Jarvis

,, 25 Paid £800 of the cash in hand into the bank account

,, 30 Bought more office fixtures paying by cheque £300.

2.10A. Write up the accounts to record the following transactions:

19-3

March 1 Started business with £1,000 cash

,, 2 Received a loan of £5,000 from M. Chow by cheque, a bank account being opened and the cheque paid into it

,, 3 Bought machinery for cash £60

,, 5 Bought display equipment on credit from Better-View Machines £550

,, 8 Took £300 out of the bank and put it into the cash till

,, 15 Repaid part of Chow's loan by cheque £800

,, 17 Paid amount owing to Better-View Machines £550 by cheque

,, 24 Repaid part of Chow's loan by cash £100

,, 31 Bought additional machinery, this time on credit from D. Smith for £500.

3

The Asset of Stock

Goods are sometimes sold at the same price at which they are bought, but this is not usually the case. Normally they are sold above cost price, the difference being profit; sometimes however they are sold at less than cost price, the difference being loss.

If all sales were at cost price, it would be possible to have a stock account, the goods sold being shown as a decrease of an asset, i.e. on the credit side. The purchase of stock could be shown on the debit side as it would be an increase of an asset. The difference between the two sides would then represent the cost of the goods unsold at that date, if wastages and losses of stock are ignored. However, most sales are not at cost price, and therefore the sales figures include elements of profit or loss. Because of this, the difference between the two sides would not represent the stock of goods. Such a stock account would therefore serve no useful purpose.

The Stock Account is accordingly divided into several accounts, each one showing a movement of stock. These can be said to be:

1. Increases in the stock. This can be due to one of two causes.
(a) By the purchase of additional goods.
(b) By the return in to the firm of goods previously sold. The reasons for this are numerous. The goods may have been the wrong type, they may have been surplus to requirements, have been faulty and so on.

To distinguish the two aspects of the increase of stocks of goods two accounts are opened. These are:
(i) Purchases Account − in which purchases of goods are entered.
(ii) Returns Inwards Account − in which goods being returned in to the firm are entered. The alternative name for this account is the Sales Returns Account.

2. Decreases in the stock of goods. This can be due to one of two causes if wastages and losses of stock are ignored.
(a) By the sale of goods.
(b) Goods previously bought by the firm now being returned out of the firm to the supplier.

To distinguish the two aspects of the decrease of stocks of goods two accounts are opened. These are:
(i) Sales Account—in which sales of goods are entered.

(ii) Returns Outwards Account—in which goods being returned out to a supplier are entered. The alternative name for this is the Purchases Returns Account.

Some illustrations can now be shown.

Purchase of Stock on Credit

1 August. Goods costing £165 are bought on credit from D. Henry.

First, the twofold effect of the transactions must be considered in order that the book-keeping entries can be worked out.

1. The asset of stock is increased. An increase in an asset needs a debit entry in an account. Here the account concerned is a stock account showing the particular movement of stock, in this case it is the 'Purchases' movement so that the account concerned must be the purchases account.

2. An increase in a liability. This is the liability of the firm to D. Henry in respect of the goods bought which have not yet been paid for. An increase in a liability needs a credit entry, so that to enter this aspect of the transaction a credit entry is made in D. Henry's account.

Purchases

	£
Aug 1 D Henry	165

D. Henry

	£
Aug 1 Purchases	165

Purchases of Stock for Cash

2 August. Goods costing £22 are bought, cash being paid for them immediately.

1. The asset of stock is increased, so that a debit entry will be needed. The movement of stock is that of a purchase, so that it is the purchases account which needs debiting.

2. The asset of cash is decreased. To reduce an asset a credit entry is called for, and the asset is that of cash so that the cash account needs crediting.

Cash

	£
Aug 2 Purchases	22

Purchases

	£
Aug 2 Cash	22

Sales of Stock on Credit

3 August. Sold goods on credit for £250 to J. Lee.
1.   The asset of stock is decreased. For this a credit entry to reduce an asset is needed. The movement of stock is that of a 'Sale' so the account credited is the sales account.
2.   An asset account is increased. This is the account showing that J. Lee is a debtor for the goods. The increase in the asset of debtors requires a debit and the debtor is J. Lee, so that the account concerned is that of J. Lee.

Sales

		£
	Aug 3 J. Lee	250

J. Lee

	£	
Aug 3 Sales	250	

Sales of Stock for Cash

4 August. Goods are sold for £55, cash being received immediately upon sale.
1.   The asset of cash is increased. This needs a debit in the cash account to show this.
2.   The asset of stock is reduced. The reduction of an asset requires a credit and the movement of stock is represented by 'Sales'. Thus the entry needed is a credit in the sales account.

Sales

		£
	Aug 4 Cash	55

Cash

	£	
Aug 4 Sales	55	

Returns Inwards

5 August. Goods which had been previously sold to F. Lowe for £29 are now returned by him.
1.   The asset of stock is increased by the goods returned. Thus a debit representing an increase of an asset is needed, and this time the movement of stock is that of 'Returns Inwards'. The entry therefore required is a debit in the returns inwards account.

2. A decrease in an asset. The debt of F. Lowe to the firm is now reduced, and to record this a credit is needed in F. Lowe's account.

Returns Inwards

	£
Aug 5 F. Lowe	29

F. Lowe

	£
Aug 5 Returns Inwards	29

An alternative name for a Returns Inwards Account would be a Sales Returns Account.

Returns Outwards

6 August. Goods previously bought for £96 are returned by the firm to K. Howe.

1. The asset of stock is decreased by the goods sent out. Thus a credit representing a reduction in an asset is needed, and the movement of stock is that of 'Returns Outwards' so that the entry will be a credit in the returns outwards account.

2. The liability of the firm to K. Howe is decreased by the value of the goods returned to him. The decrease in a liability needs a debit, this time in K. Howe's account.

Returns Outwards

	£
Aug 6 K. Howe	96

K. Howe

	£
Aug 6 Returns outwards	96

An alternative name for a Returns Outwards Account would be a Purchases Returns Account.

A Worked Example

May	1 Bought goods on credit £68 from D. Small
,,	2 Bought goods on credit £77 from A. Lyon & Son
,,	5 Sold goods on credit to D. Hughes for £60
,,	6 Sold goods on credit to M. Spencer for £45
,,	10 Returned goods £15 to D. Small
,,	12 Goods bought for cash £100
,,	19 M. Spencer returned £16 goods to us
,,	21 Goods sold for cash £150
,,	22 Paid cash to D. Small £53
,,	30 D. Hughes paid the amount owing by him £60 in cash
,,	31 Bought goods on credit £64 from A. Lyon & Son.

Purchases

19-5		£
May	1 D. Small	68
,,	2 A. Lyon & Son	77
,,	12 Cash	100
,,	31 A. Lyon & Son	64

Sales

			19-5		£
			May	5 D. Hughes	60
			,,	6 M. Spencer	45
			,,	21 Cash	150

Returns Outwards

		19-5	£
		May 10 D. Small	15

Returns Inwards

19-5	£
May 19 M. Spencer	16

D. Small

19-5		£	19-5		£
May 10 Returns outwards		15	May	1 Purchases	68
,,	22 Cash	53			

A. Lyon & Son

		19-5		£
		May	2 Purchases	77
		,,	31 Purchases	64

D. Hughes

19-5		£	19-5		£
May	5 Sales	60	May 30 Cash		60

M. Spencer

19-5		£	19-5		£
May	6 Sales	45	May 19 Returns inwards		16

Cash

19-5		£	19-5		£
May 21 Sales		150	May 12 Purchases		100
,,	30 D. Hughes	60	,,	22 D. Small	53

Special Meaning of 'Sales' and 'Purchases'

It must be emphasized that 'Sales' and 'Purchases' have a special meaning in accounting when compared to ordinary language usage.

'Purchases' in accounting means the purchase of those goods which the firm buys with the prime intention of selling. Obviously, sometimes the goods are altered, added to, or used in the manufacture of something else, but it is the element of resale that is important. To a firm that deals in typewriters for instance, typewriters constitute purchases. If something else is bought, such as a motor van, such an item cannot be called purchases, even though in ordinary language it may be said that a motor van has been purchased. The prime intention of buying the motor van is for usage and not for resale.

Similarly, 'Sales' means the sale of those goods in which the firm normally deals and were bought with the prime intention of resale. The word 'Sales' must never be given to the disposal of other items.

Failure to keep to these meanings would result in the different forms of stock account containing something other than goods sold or for resale.

Comparison of Cash and Credit Transactions for Purchases and Sales

The difference between the records needed for cash and credit transactions can now be seen.

The complete set of entries for purchases of goods where they are paid for immediately needs entries:

1. Credit the cash account.
2. Debit the purchases account.

On the other hand the complete set of entries for the purchase of goods on credit can be broken down into two stages. First, the purchase of the goods and second, the payment for them.

The first part is:

1. Debit the purchases account.
2. Credit the supplier's account.

While the second part is:

1. Credit the cash account.
2. Debit the supplier's account.

The difference can now be seen in that with the cash purchase no record is kept of the supplier's account. This is because cash passes immediately and therefore there is no need to keep a check of indebtedness to a supplier. On the other hand, in the credit purchase the records should reveal the identity of the supplier to whom the firm is indebted until payment is made.

A study of cash sales and credit sales will reveal a similar difference.

Cash Sales
Complete entry:
  Debit cash account
  Credit sales account

Credit Sales
First part:
  Debit customer's account
  Credit sales account
Second part:
  Debit cash account
  Credit customer's account

Exercises

MC9 Which of the following BEST describes the meaning of 'Purchases'.
(A) Items bought
(B) Goods bought on credit
(C) Goods bought for resale
(D) Goods paid for.

MC10 Which of the following should not be called 'Sales'.
(A) Office Fixtures sold
(B) Goods sold on credit
(C) Goods sold for cash
(D) Sale of items previously included in 'Purchases'.

MC11 Of the following, which are correct?

		Account to be debited	Account to be credited
(i)	Goods sold on credit to R. Williams	R. Williams	Sales
(ii)	S. Johnson returns goods to us	Returns Inwards	S. Johnson
(iii)	Goods bought for cash	Cash	Purchases
(iv)	We returned goods to A. Henry	A. Henry	Returns Inwards

(A) i and iii only
(B) i and ii only
(C) ii and iv only
(D) iii and iv only.

MC12 Which of the following are incorrect?

		Account to be debited	Account to be credited
(i)	Goods sold for cash	Cash	Sales
(ii)	Goods bought on credit from T. Carter	Purchases	T. Carter
(iii)	Goods returned by us to C. Barry	C. Barry	Returns Outwards
(iv)	Motor Van bought for cash	Purchases	Cash

(A) i and iii only
(B) iii only
(C) ii and iv only
(D) iv only.

Other Exercises

Note: **Questions with the letter A shown after the question number do NOT have answers shown at the back of the book. Answers to the other questions are shown on pages 453 onwards.**

3.1. Complete the following table showing which accounts are to be credited and which are to be debited:

	Account to be debited	Account to be credited
(*a*) Goods bought, cash being paid immediately		
(*b*) Goods bought on credit from E. Flynn		
(*c*) Goods sold on credit to C. Grant		
(*d*) A motor van sold for cash		
(*e*) Goods sold for cash.		

3.2. Similarly, complete this next table:

	Account to be debited	Account to be credited
(*a*) Goods returned to H. Flynn		
(*b*) Goods bought on credit from P. Franklin		
(*c*) Goods sold on credit to S. Mullings		
(*d*) M. Patterson returns goods to us		
(*e*) Goods bought being paid for by cheque immediately.		

3.3A. Complete the following table showing which accounts are to be credited and which are to be debited:

	Account to be debited	Account to be credited
(*a*) Goods bought on credit from J. Reid		
(*b*) Goods sold on credit to B. Perkins		
(*c*) Motor vans bought on credit from H. Thomas		
(*d*) Goods sold, a cheque being received immediately		
(*e*) Goods sold for cash		
(*f*) Goods we returned to H. Hardy		
(*g*) Machinery sold for cash		
(*h*) Goods returned to us by J. Nelson		
(*i*) Goods bought on credit from D. Simpson		
(*j*) Goods we returned to H. Forbes.		

3.4A. Complete the following table:

		Account to be debited	Account to be credited
(a)	Goods bought on credit from T. Morgan		
(b)	Goods returned to us by J. Thomas		
(c)	Machinery returned to L. Jones Ltd		
(d)	Goods bought for cash		
(e)	Motor van bought on credit from D. Davies Ltd		
(f)	Goods returned by us to I. Prince		
(g)	D. Picton paid us his account by cheque		
(h)	Goods bought by cheque		
(i)	We paid creditor, B. Henry, by cheque		
(j)	Goods sold on credit to J. Mullings.		

3.5. Enter up the following transactions in the requisite accounts:

19-3

June	1	Bought goods on credit £72 from C. Blake
,,	3	Bought goods on credit £90 from C. Foster
,,	5	Returned goods to C. Blake £15
,,	19	Sold goods for cash £25
,,	21	Sold goods on credit £64 to E. Rose
,,	30	Bought goods on credit from A. Price £145.

3.6. You are to write up the following in the books:

19-4

July	1	Started business with £500 cash
,,	3	Bought goods for cash £85
,,	7	Bought goods on credit £116 from E. Morgan
,,	10	Sold goods for cash £42
,,	14	Returned goods to E. Morgan £28
,,	18	Bought goods on credit £98 from A. Moses
,,	21	Returned goods to A. Moses £19.
,,	24	Sold goods to A. Knight £55 on credit
,,	25	Paid E. Morgan's account by cash £88
,,	31	A. Knight paid us his account in cash £55.

3.7. You are to enter the following in the accounts needed:

19-6

Aug	1	Started business with £1,000 cash
,,	2	Paid £900 of the opening cash into the bank
,,	4	Bought goods on credit £78 from S. Holmes
,,	5	Bought a motor van by cheque £500
,,	7	Bought goods for cash £55
,,	10	Sold goods on credit £98 to D. Moore
,,	12	Returned goods to S. Holmes £18
,,	19	Sold goods for cash £28
,,	22	Bought fixtures on credit from Kingston Equipment Co £150
,,	24	D. Watson lent us £100 paying us the money by cheque
,,	29	We paid S. Holmes his account by cheque £60
,,	31	We paid Kingston Equipment Co by cheque £150.

3.8. Enter up the following transactions in the records of E. Sangster:

19-7

July 1 Started business with £10,000 in the bank
,, 2 T. Cooper lent us £400 in cash
,, 3 Bought goods on credit from F. Jones £840 and S. Charles £3,600
,, 4 Sold goods for cash £200
,, 6 Took £250 of the cash and paid it into the bank
,, 8 Sold goods on credit to C. Moody £180
,, 10 Sold goods on credit to J. Newman £220
,, 11 Bought goods on credit from F. Jones £370
,, 12 C. Moody returned goods to us £40
,, 14 Sold goods on credit to H. Morgan £190 and J. Peat £320
,, 15 We returned goods to F. Jones £140
,, 17 Bought motor van on credit from Manchester Motors £2,600
,, 18 Bought office furniture on credit from Faster Supplies Ltd £600
,, 19 We returned goods to S. Charles £110
,, 20 Bought goods for cash £220
,, 24 Goods sold for cash £70
,, 25 Paid money owing to F. Jones by cheque £1,070
,, 26 Goods returned to us by H. Morgan £30
,, 27 Returned some of office furniture costing £160 to Faster Supplies Ltd
,, 28 E. Sangster put a further £500 into the business in the form of cash
,, 29 Paid Manchester Motors £2,600 by cheque
,, 31 Bought office furniture for cash £100.

3.9A. Enter up the following transactions in the records:

19-5

May 1 Started business with £2,000 in the bank
,, 2 Bought goods on credit from C. Shaw £900
,, 3 Bought goods on credit from F. Hughes £250
,, 5 Sold goods for cash £180
,, 6 We returned goods to C. Shaw £40
,, 8 Bought goods on credit from F. Hughes £190
,, 10 Sold goods on credit to G. Wood £390
,, 12 Sold goods for cash £210
,, 18 Took £300 of the cash and paid it into the bank
,, 21 Bought machinery by cheque £550
,, 22 Sold goods on credit to L. Moore £220
,, 23 G. Wood returned goods to us £140
,, 25 L. Moore returned goods to us £10
,, 28 We returned goods to F. Hughes £30
,, 29 We paid Shaw by cheque £860
,, 31 Bought machinery on credit from D. Lee £270.

3.10A. You are to enter the following in the accounts needed:

June 1 Started business with £1,000 cash
,,   2 Paid £800 of the opening cash into a bank account for the firm
,,   3 Bought goods on credit from H. Grant £330
,,   4 Bought goods on credit from D. Clark £140
,,   8 Sold goods on credit to B. Miller £90
,,   8 Bought office furniture on credit from Barrett's Ltd £400
,,   10 Sold goods for cash £120
,,   13 Bought goods for credit from H. Grant £200
,,   14 Bought goods for cash £60
,,   15 Sold goods on credit to H. Sharples £180
,,   16 We returned goods £50 to H. Grant
,,   17 We returned some of the office furniture £30 to Barrett's Ltd
,,   18 Sold goods on credit to B. Miller £400
,,   21 Paid H. Grant's account by cheque £480
,,   23 B. Miller paid us the amount owing in cash £490
,,   24 Sharples returned to us £50 goods
,,   25 Goods sold for cash £150
,,   28 Bought goods for cash £370
,,   30 Bought motor van on credit from J. Kelly £600.

3.11A. The following transactions are to be entered up in the records of C. Williams:

19-6

Aug 1 Started business with £7,500 in cash
,,   2 Paid £6,800 of the opening cash into a bank account
,,   2 Bought goods on credit from E. Mills £880, D. Thomas £540, C. Owen £300
,,   3 Bought office equipment on credit from Hamilton & Co £188
,,   4 Sold goods for cash £120
,,   5 Sold goods on credit to Marshall Ltd £144, Green & Co £57, Coke Ltd £680
,,   6 Bought motor van paying by cheque £2,400
,,   7 Sold goods on credit to Marshall Ltd £76, H. White £150
,,   8 We returned goods to D. Thomas £40
,,   10 Bought office equipment, paying by cheque £70
,,   11 Goods returned to us by Coke Ltd £60, Green & Co £7
,,   13 We paid by cheque D. Thomas £500, C. Owen £300
,,   15 We paid by cheque Hamilton & Co £188
,,   18 Marshall paid us by cash £144
,,   21 D. Groves lent us £1,000 giving us the money by cheque
,,   22 Bought goods on credit from C. Owen £296
,,   23 Sold goods for cash £145
,,   25 Some office equipment £28 returned to Hamilton & Co. as it was faulty
,,   26 Goods returned to us by H. White £16
,,   27 Hamilton & Co paid us cash £28
,,   28 C. Williams put another £1,000 into the business bank account from his private monies outside the business.
,,   31 Repaid part of D. Grove's loan by cheque £300.

4

The Double Entry System for Expenses and Revenues. The Effect of Profit or Loss on Capital

Up to now this book has been concerned with the accounting need to record changes in assets and liabilities, but this is subject to one exception, the change in the capital caused by the profit earned in the business. By profit is meant the excess of revenues over expenses for a particular period. Revenues consist of the monetary value of goods and services that have been delivered to customers. Expenses consist of the monetary value of the assets used up in obtaining these revenues. Particularly in American accounting language the word 'income' is used instead of 'profit'.

It is possible to see the effect of profit upon capital by means of an example:

On 1 January the assets and liabilities of a firm are:

Assets: Motor van £500, Fixtures £200, Stock £700, Debtors £300, Cash at Bank £200.

Liabilities: Creditors £600.

The capital is therefore found by the formula Assets − Liabilities = Capital.

£500 + £200 + £700 + £300 + £200 − £600 = £1,300.

During January the whole of the £700 stock is sold for £1,100 cash. On the 31 January the assets and liabilities have become:

Assets: Motor van £500, Fixtures £200, Stock − , Debtors £300, Cash at Bank £1,300.

Liabilities: Creditors £600.

Assets − Liabilities = Capital
£500 + £200 + £300 + £1,300 − £600 = £1,700.

Profit therefore affects the capital thus:

Old Capital + Profit = New Capital
£1,300 + £400 = £1,700

On the other hand a loss would have reduced the capital so that it would become:

Old Capital – Loss = New Capital.

To alter the capital account it will therefore have to be possible to calculate profits and losses. They are, however, calculated only at intervals, usually annually but sometimes more often. This means that accounts will be needed to collect together the expenses and revenues pending the periodical calculation of profits. All the expenses could be charged to an omnibus 'Expenses Account', but obviously it is far more informative if full details of different expenses are shown in Profit and Loss Calculations. The same applies to revenues also. Therefore a separate account is opened for every type of expense and revenue. For instance there may be accounts as follows:

Rent Account	Postages Account
Wages Account	Stationery Account
Salaries Account	Insurance Account
Telephone Account	Motor Expenses Account
Rent Receivable Account	General Expenses Account

It is purely a matter of choice in a firm as to the title of each expense or revenue account. For example, an account for postage stamps could be called 'Postage Stamps Account', 'Postages Account', 'Communication Expenses Account' and so on. Also different firms amalgamate expenses, some having a 'Rent and Telephone Account', others a 'Rent, Telephone and Insurance Account', etc. Infrequent or small items of expense are usually put into a 'Sundry Expenses Account' or a 'General Expenses Account'.

Debit or Credit

It must now be decided as to which side of the records revenues and expenses are to be recorded. Assets involve expenditure by the firm and are shown as debit entries. Expenses also involve expenditure by the firm and are therefore also recorded on the debit side of the books. In fact assets may be seen to be expenditure of money for which something still remains, while expenses involve expenditure of money which has been used up in the running of the business and for which there is no benefit remaining at the date of the balance sheet.

Revenue is the opposite of expenses and therefore appears on the opposite side to expenses, that is revenue accounts appear on the credit side of the books. Revenue also increases profit, which in turn increases capital. Pending the periodical calculation of profit therefore, revenue is collected together in appropriately named accounts, and until it is transferred to the profit calculations it will therefore need to be shown as a credit.

An alternative explanation may also be used for expenses. Every expense results in a decrease in an asset or an increase in a liability, and because of the accounting equation this means that the capital is reduced by each expense. The decrease of capital needs a debit entry and therefore expense accounts contain debit entries for expenses.

Consider too that expenditure of money pays for expenses, which are used up in the short term, or assets, which are used up in the long term, both for the purpose of winning revenue. Both of these are shown on the debit side of the pages, while the revenue which has been won is shown in the credit side of the pages.

Effect of Transactions

A few illustrations will demonstrate the double entry required.

1. The rent of £20 is paid in cash.
Here the twofold effect is:
(a) The asset of cash is decreased. This means crediting the cash account to show the decrease of the asset.
(b) The total of the expenses of rent is increased. As expense entries are shown as debits, and the expense is rent, so the action required is the debiting of the rent account.
Summary: Credit the cash account with £20.
Debit the rent account with £20.

2. Motor expenses are paid by cheque £55.
The twofold effect is:
(a) The asset of money in the bank is decreased. This means crediting the bank account to show the decrease of the asset.
(b) The total of the motor expenses paid is increased. To increase an expenses account needs a debit, so the action required is to debit the motor expenses account.
Summary: Credit the bank account with £55
Debit the motor expenses account with £55.

3. £60 cash is received for commission earned by the firm.
(a) The asset of cash is increased. This needs a debit in the cash account to increase the asset.
(b) The revenue of commissions received is increased. Revenue is shown by a credit entry, therefore to increase the revenue account in question the Commissions Received Account is credited.
Summary: Debit the cash account
Credit the commissions received account

It is now possible to study the effects of some more transactions showing the results in the form of a table:

	Increase	Action	Decrease	Action
June 1 Paid for postage stamps by cash £5	Expense of postages	Debit postages account	Asset of cash	Credit cash account
,, 2 Paid for electricity by cheque £29	Expense of electricity	Debit electricity account	Asset of bank	Credit bank account
,, 3 Received rent in cash £38	Asset of cash	Debit cash account		
	Revenue of rent	Credit rent received account		
,, 4 Paid insurance by cheque £42	Expense of insurance	Debit insurance account	Asset of bank	Credit bank account

The above four examples can now be shown in account form:

Cash

	£		£
June 3 Rent received	38	June 1 Postages	5

Bank

		£
	June 2 Electricity	29
	,, 4 Insurance	42

Electricity

	£
June 2 Bank	29

Insurance

	£
June 4 Bank	42

Postages

	£
June 1 Cash	5

Rent Received

		£
	June 3 Cash	38

It is clear that from time to time the proprietor will want to take cash out of the business for his private use. In fact he will sometimes take goods. This will be dealt with later. However, whether the withdrawals are cash or goods they are known as 'Drawings'. Drawings in fact decrease the claim of the proprietor against the resources of the business, in other words they reduce the amount of capital. According to the way in which the accounting formula is represented by debits and credits the decrease of capital needs a debit entry in the capital account. However, the accounting custom has grown up of debiting a 'Drawings Account' as an interim measure.

An example will demonstrate the twofold effect of cash withdrawals from the business.

Example: 25 August. Proprietor takes £50 cash out of the business for his own use.

Effect	Action
1. Capital is decreased by £50	Debit the drawings account £50
2. Cash is decreased by £50	Credit the cash account £50

Cash

	£
Aug 25 Drawings	50

Drawings

	£
Aug 25 Cash	50

Exercises

MC13 Given the following, what is the amount of Capital? Assets: Premises £20,000, Stock £8,500, Cash £100. Liabilities: Creditors £3,000, Loan from A. Adams £4,000.
(A) £21,100
(B) £21,600
(C) £32,400
(D) None of the above.

MC14 Which of the following is correct?
(A) Profit does not alter Capital
(B) Profit reduces Capital
(C) Capital can only come from profit.
(D) Profit increases Capital

MC15 Which of the following are correct?

		Account to be debited	Account to be credited
(i)	Received commission by cheque	Bank	Commission Received
(ii)	Paid rates by cash	Rates	Cash
(iii)	Paid motor expenses by cheque	Motor Expenses	Bank
(iv)	Received refund of insurance by cheque	Insurance	Bank

(A) i and ii only
(B) i, ii and iii only
(C) ii, iii and iv only
(D) i, ii and iv only.

MC16 Of the following, which are incorrect?

		Account to be debited	Account to be credited
(i)	Sold Motor Van for Cash	Cash	Sales
(ii)	Bought stationery by cheque	Stationery	Bank
(iii)	Took cash out of business for private use	Cash	Drawings
(iv)	Paid General Expenses by cheque	General Expenses	Bank

(A) ii and iv only
(B) i and ii only
(C) i and iii only
(D) ii and iii only.

Exercises

4.1. You are to complete the following table, showing the accounts to be debited and those to be credited:

	Account to be debited	Account to be credited
(a) Paid rates by cheque		
(b) Paid wages by cash		
(c) Rent received by cheque		
(d) Received by cheque refund of insurance previously paid		
(e) Paid general expenses by cash		

4.2. Complete the following table:

	Account to be debited	Account to be credited
(a) Paid rent by cash		
(b) Paid for goods by cash		
(c) Received by cheque a refund of rates already paid		
(d) Paid general expenses by cheque		
(e) Received commissions in cash		
(f) Goods returned by us to T. Jones		
(g) Goods sold for cash		
(h) Bought office fixtures by cheque		
(i) Paid wages in cash		
(j) Took cash out of business for private use.		

4.3A. Complete the following table, showing the accounts to be debited and those to be credited:

		Account to be debited	Account to be credited
(a)	Paid insurance by cheque		
(b)	Paid motor expenses by cash		
(c)	Rent received in cash		
(d)	Paid rates by cheque		
(e)	Received refund of rates by cheque		
(f)	Paid for stationery expenses by cash		
(g)	Paid wages by cash		
(h)	Sold surplus stationery receiving proceeds by cheque		
(i)	Received sales commission by cheque		
(j)	Bought motor van by cheque.		

4.4A. The following table should be completed:

		Account to be debited	Account to be credited
(a)	Sold surplus stationery, receiving proceeds in cash		
(b)	Paid salaries by cheque		
(c)	Rent received for premises sub-let, by cheque		
(d)	Goods returned to us by B. Roberts		
(e)	Commission received by us previously in error, we now refund this by cheque		
(f)	Bought machinery by cheque		
(g)	Paid lighting expenses in cash		
(h)	Insurance rebate received by cheque		
(i)	Buildings bought by cheque		
(j)	Building repairs paid in cash.		

4.5. Enter the following transactions in the necessary accounts in double entry:

19-8

Jan	1	Started business with £200 in the bank
,,	2	U. Surer lent us £1,000 giving us the money by cheque
,,	3	Bought goods on credit £296 from T. Parkin
,,	5	Bought motor van by cheque £250
,,	6	Cash sales £105
,,	7	Paid motor expenses in cash £15
,,	8	Paid wages in cash £18
,,	10	Bought goods on credit from C. Moore £85
,,	12	Paid insurance by cheque £22
,,	25	Received commission in cash £15
,,	31	Paid electricity bill by cheque £17.

4.6. You are to enter the following transactions, completing double-entry in the books for the month of May 19-7:

19-7

May 1 Started business with £2,000 in the bank
,, 2 Purchased goods £175 on credit from M. Mills
,, 3 Bought fixtures and fittings £150 paying by cheque
,, 5 Sold goods for cash £275
,, 6 Bought goods on credit £114 from S. Waites
,, 10 Paid rent by cash £15
,, 12 Bought stationery £27, paying by cash
,, 18 Goods returned to M. Mills £23
,, 21 Let off part of the premises receiving rent by cheque £5
,, 23 Sold goods on credit to U. Henry for £77
,, 24 Bought a motor van paying by cheque £300
,, 30 Paid the month's wages by cash £117
,, 31 The proprietor took cash for himself £44.

4.7. Write up the following transactions in the books of L. Thompson:

19-8

March 1 Started business with cash £1,500
,, 2 Bought goods on credit from A. Hanson £296
,, 3 Paid rent by cash £28
,, 4 Paid £1,000 of the cash of the firm into a bank account
,, 5 Sold goods on credit to E. Linton £54
,, 7 Bought stationery £15 paying by cheque
,, 11 Cash sales £49
,, 14 Goods returned by us to A. Hanson £17
,, 17 Sold goods on credit to S. Morgan £29
,, 20 Paid for repairs to the building by cash £18
,, 22 E. Linton returned goods to us £14
,, 27 Paid Hanson by cheque £279
,, 28 Cash purchases £125
,, 29 Bought a motor van paying by cheque £395
,, 30 Paid motor expenses in cash £15
,, 31 Bought fixtures £120 on credit from A. Webster.

4.8A. Enter the following transactions in double entry:

July 1 Started business with £8,000 in the bank
,, 2 Bought stationery by cheque £30
,, 3 Bought goods on credit from I. Walsh £900
,, 4 Sold goods for cash £180
,, 5 Paid insurance by cash £40
,, 7 Bought machinery on credit from H. Morgan £500
,, 8 Paid for machinery expenses by cheque £50
,, 10 Sold goods on credit to D. Small £320
,, 11 Returned goods to I. Walsh £70
,, 14 Paid wages by cash £70
,, 17 Paid rent by cheque £100
,, 20 Received cheque £200 from D. Small
,, 21 Paid H. Morgan by cheque £500
,, 23 Bought stationery on credit from Express Ltd £80
,, 25 Sold goods on credit to N. Thomas £230
,, 28 Received rent £20 in cash for part of premises sub-let
,, 31 Paid Express Ltd by cheque £80.

4.9A. Write up the following transactions in the records of D. DaSilva:

Feb 1 Started business with £3,000 in the bank and £500 cash
,, 2 Bought goods on credit: T. Small £250; C. Todd £190; V. Ryan £180
,, 3 Bought goods for cash £230. Feb 4 Paid rent in cash £10
,, 5 Bought stationery paying by cheque £49
,, 6 Sold goods on credit: C. Crooks £140; R. Rogers £100; B. Grant £240
,, 7 Paid wages in cash £80
,, 10 We returned goods to C. Todd £60. Feb 11 Paid rent in cash £10
,, 13 R. Rogers returns goods to us £20
,, 15 Sold goods on credit to: J. Burns £90; J. Smart £130; N. Thorn £170
,, 16 Paid rates by cheque £130. Feb 18 Paid insurance in cash £40
,, 19 Paid rent by cheque £10
,, 20 Bought motor van on credit from C. White £600
,, 21 Paid motor expenses in cash £6. Feb 23 Paid wages in cash £90
,, 24 Received part of amount owing from B. Grant by cheque £200
,, 28 Received refund of rates £10 by cheque
,, 28 Paid by cheque: T. Small £250; C. Todd £130; C. White £600.

4.10A. You are to enter the following transactions, completing double-entry in the records of J. Collins for the month of June 19-5:

June 1 Started business with £10,000 in the bank and £300 cash
,, 1 Bought goods on credit from: J. Carby £400; F. McIntyre £1,188; C. Morrison £1,344
,, 2 Bought shop fittings by cheque £240
,, 3 Bought shop fittings on credit from M. Johnson Ltd £575
,, 5 Paid insurance by cash £88
,, 6 Bought motor van paying by cheque £3,200
,, 7 Sold goods for cash £140
,, 7 Sold goods on credit to: W. Graham & Co £450; F. Phillips Ltd £246; D. R. Edwards £80
,, 8 Bought office stationery £180 on credit from D. Ball & Co
,, 9 Paid rent by cheque £75. June 10 Paid rates by cheque £250
,, 11 We returned goods to F. McIntyre £168
,, 12 Paid D. Ball & Co £180 by cheque
,, 13 Sold goods on credit to K. P. Prince & Co £220; F. Phillips Ltd £154; Kay & Edwards Ltd £270
,, 14 Goods returned to us by W. Graham & Co £40
,, 15 Paid wages by cash £120
,, 16 Loan from D. Clayton by cheque £500
,, 17 W. Graham & Co paid us the amount owing by cheque £410
,, 18 Some of stationery was bought unwisely. We sell it for cash £15.
,, 20 We had overpaid insurance. A refund of £8 received by cheque
,, 21 Paid motor expenses by cash £55. June 23 Paid wages by cash £120
,, 25 Cheques received from K. P. Prince & Co £220; F. Phillips Ltd £100 (as part payment)
,, 26 Some of shop fittings were unsuitable and were returned to M. Johnson Ltd £25
,, 28 Paid F. McIntyre £1,188, rent £75
,, 30 J. Collins took drawings by cheque £200.

5

Balancing off Accounts

What you have been reading about so far is the recording of transactions in the books by means of debit and credit entries. Every so often we will have to look at each account to see what is revealed by the entries.

Probably the most obvious reason for this is to find out how much our customers owe us in respect of goods we have sold to them. In most firms the custom is that this should be done at the end of each month. Let us look at the account of one of our customers, D. Knight, at the end of a month.

D. Knight

19-6		£	19-6		£
Aug 1 Sales		158	Aug 28 Cash		158
,, 15 ,,		206			
,, 30 ,,		118			

You can see that Knight still owed £206 + £118 = £324 at the end of 31 August 19-6. Our firm will thus start its business for the next month on 1 September 19-6 with that amount owing to it. To show that our firm is carrying these outstanding items from one period to the next one, the 'balance' on each account is found. The 'balance' is the accounting term meaning the arithmetical difference between the two sides of an account.

To balance off an account:

(i) First add up the side of the account having the greatest total.
(ii) Second, insert the difference (the balance) on the other side of the account so as to make the totals of each side equal. When doing this, ensure that the two totals are written on a level with each other.
(iii) The balance has now been entered in the period which has finished, it now has to be entered on the other side of the books to ensure that double-entry of the item is carried out. This is done by making the second entry on the next line under the totals. Let us see Knight's account now 'balanced' off:

D. Knight

19-6		£	19-6		£
Aug 1 Sales		158	Aug 28 Cash		158
,, 15 ,,		206	,, 31 Balance carried down		324
,, 30 ,,		118			
		482			482
Sept 1 Balance brought down		324			

We can now look at another account prior to balancing:

H. Henry

19-6	£	19-6	£
Aug 5 Sales	300	Aug 24 Returns Inwards	50
,, 28 Sales	540	,, 29 Bank	250

This time, and we will always do this in future, for it will save us unnecessary writing, we will abbreviate 'carried down' to 'c/d' and 'brought down' to 'b/d'.

H. Henry

19-6		£	19-6		£
Aug 5 Sales		300	Aug 24 Returns Inwards		50
,, 28 Sales		540	,, 29 Bank		250
			,, 31 Balance	c/d	540
		840			840
Sept 1 Balance	b/d	540			

Notes:
1.   The date given to Balance c/d is the last day of the period which is finishing, and Balance b/d is given the opening date of the next period.
2.   As the total of the debit side originally exceeded the total of the credit side, the balance is said to be a debit balance. This being a personal account (for a person), the person concerned is said to be a debtor — the accounting term for anyone who owes money to the firm. The use of the term debtor for a person whose account has a debit balance can again thus be seen.

If accounts contain only one entry it is unnecessary to enter the total. A double line ruled under the entry will mean that the entry is its own total. For example:

B. Walters

19-6		£	19-6		£
Aug 18 Sales		51	Aug 31 Balance	c/d	51
Sept 1 Balance	b/d	51			

If an account contains only one entry on each side which are equal to one another, totals are again unnecessary. For example:

D. Hylton

19-6	£	19-6	£
Aug 6 Sales	214	Aug 12 Bank	214

Credit Balances

Exactly the same principles will apply when the balances are carried down to the credit side. We can look at two accounts of our suppliers which are to be balanced off.

E. Williams

19-6	£	19-6	£
Aug 21 Bank	100	Aug 2 Purchases	248
		,, 18 ,,	116

K. Patterson

19-6	£	19-6	£
Aug 14 Returns Outwards	20	Aug 8 Purchases	620
,, 28 Bank	600	,, 15 Purchases	200

When balanced these will appear as:

E. Williams

19-6		£	19-6		£
Aug 21 Bank		100	Aug 2 Purchases		248
,, 31 Balance	c/d	264	,, 18 ,,		116
		364			364
			Sept 1 Balance	b/d	264

K. Patterson

19-6		£	19-6		£
Aug 14 Returns Outwards		20	Aug 8 Purchases		620
,, 28 Bank		600	,, 15 Purchases		200
,, 31 Balance	c/d	200			
		820			820
			Sept 1 Balance	b/d	200

Before you read further attempt Exercises 5.1 and 5.2.

Computers and Book-keeping Machinery

Throughout the main part of this book the type of account used shows the left-hand side of the account as the debit side, and the right-hand side is shown as the credit side. However, when most computers or book-keeping equipment is used the style of the ledger account is different. It appears as three columns of figures, being one column for debit entries, another column for credit entries, and the last column for the balance. If you have a current account at a bank your bank statements will normally be shown using this method.

The accounts used in this chapter will now be redrafted to show the ledger accounts drawn up in this way.

D. Knight

	Debit	Credit	Balance (and whether debit or credit)
19-6	£	£	£
Aug 1 Sales	158		158 Dr
,, 15 ,,	206		364 Dr
,, 28 Cash		158	206 Dr
,, 30 Sales	118		324 Dr

H. Henry

	Debit	Credit	Balance
19-6	£	£	£
Aug 5 Sales	300		300 Dr
,, 24 Returns		50	250 Dr
,, 28 Sales	540		790 Dr
,, 29 Bank		250	540 Dr

B. Walters

	Debit	Credit	Balance
19-6	£	£	£
Aug 18 Sales	51		51 Dr

D. Hylton

	Debit	Credit	Balance
19-6	£	£	£
Aug 6 Sales	214		214 Dr
,, 12 Bank		214	0

E. Williams

	Debit	Credit	Balance
19-6	£	£	£
Aug 2 Purchases		248	248 Cr
,, 18 ,,		116	364 Cr
,, 21 Bank	100		264 Cr

K. Patterson

	Debit	Credit	Balance
19-6	£	£	£
Aug 8 Purchases		620	620 Cr
,, 14 Returns	20		600 Cr
,, 15 Purchases		200	800 Cr
,, 28 Bank	600		200 Cr

It will be noticed that the balance is calculated afresh after every entry. This can be done quite simply when using book-keeping machinery or a computer because it is the machine which automatically calculates the new balance. However, when manual methods are in use it is often too laborious to have to calculate a new balance after each entry, and it also means that the greater the number of calculations the greater the possible number of errors. For these reasons it is usual for students to use two-sided accounts. However, it is important to note that there is no difference in principle, the final balances are the same using either method.

Exercises

MC17 What is the balance on the following account on 31 May 19-5?

C. De Freitas

19-5		£	19-5		£
May	1 Sales	205	May 17 Cash		300
,,	14 Sales	360	,, 28 Returns		50
,,	30 Sales	180			

(A) A credit balance of £395
(B) A debit balance of £380
(C) A debit balance of £395
(D) There is a nil balance on the account.

MC18 What would have been the balance on the account of C. De Freitas in MC17 on 19 May 19-5?
(A) A debit balance of £265
(B) A credit balance of £95
(C) A credit balance of £445
(D) A credit balance of £265.

5.1. Enter the following items in the necessary debtors and creditors accounts only, do *not* write up other accounts. Then balance down each personal account at the end of the month. (Keep your answer, it will be used as a basis for question 5.3).

19-6

May	1	Sales on credit to H. Harvey £690, N. Morgan £153, J. Lindo £420
,,	4	Sales on credit to L. Masters £418, H. Harvey £66
,,	10	Returns inwards from H. Harvey £40, J. Lindo £20
,,	18	N. Morgan paid us by cheque £153
,,	20	J. Lindo paid us £400 by cheque
,,	24	H. Harvey paid us £300 by cash
,,	31	Sales on credit to L. Masters £203.

5.2. Enter the following in the personal accounts only. Do *not* write up the other accounts. Then balance down each personal account at the end of the month. (Keep your answer, it will be used as the basis of questions 5.4A).

19-8

June	1	Purchases on credit from J. Young £458, L. Williams £120, G. Norman £708
,,	3	Purchases on credit from L. Williams £77, T. Harris £880
,,	10	We returned goods to G. Norman £22, J. Young £55
,,	15	Purchases on credit from J. Young £80
,,	19	We paid T. Harris by cheque £880
,,	28	We paid J. Young by cash £250
,,	30	We returned goods to L. Williams £17.

5.3A. Redraft each of the accounts given in your answer to 5.1 in three column ledger style accounts.

5.4A. Redraft each of the accounts given in your answer to 5.2 in three column ledger style accounts.

5.5. Enter the following in the personal accounts only, do *not* write up the other accounts. Balance down each personal account at the end of the month. After completing this state which of the balances represent debtors and those which are creditors.

19-4

Sept	1	Sales on credit to D. Williams £458, J. Moore £235, G. Grant £98
,,	2	Purchases on credit A. White £77, H. Samuels £231, P. Owen £65
,,	8	Sales on credit to J. Moore £444, F. Franklin £249
,,	10	Purchases on credit from H. Samuels £12, O. Oliver £222
,,	12	Returns Inwards from G. Grant £9, J. Moore £26
,,	17	We returned goods to H. Samuels £24, O. Oliver £12
,,	20	We paid A. White by cheque £77
,,	24	D. Williams paid us by cheque £300
,,	26	We paid O. Oliver by cash £210
,,	28	D. Williams paid us by cash £100
,,	30	F. Franklin pays us by cheque £249.

5.4A. Enter the following in the necessary personal accounts. Do *not* write up the other accounts. Balance each personal account at the end of the month. (Keep your answer, it will be used as the basis of question 5.8A.)

19-4

Aug	1	Sales on credit to L. Sterling £445, L. Lindo £480, R. Spencer £221
,,	4	Goods returned to us by L. Sterling £15, R. Spencer £33
,,	8	Sales on credit to L. Lindo £66, R. Spencer £129, L. Banks £465
,,	9	We received a cheque for £430 from L. Sterling
,,	12	Sales on credit to R. Spencer £235, L. Banks £777
,,	19	Goods returned to us by L. Banks £21, R. Spencer £25
,,	22	We received cheques as follows: R. Spencer £300, L. Lindo £414
,,	31	Sales on credit to L. Lindo £887, L. Banks £442.

5.7A. Enter the following, personal accounts only. Bring down balances at end of the month. After completing this state which of the balances represent debtors and those which are creditors.

19-7

May	1	Credit sales B. Flynn £241, R. Kelly £29, J. Long £887, T. Fryer £124
,,	2	Credit purchases from S. Wood £148, T. DuQuesnay £27, R. Johnson £77, G. Henriques £108
,,	8	Credit sales to R. Kelly £74, J. Long £132
,,	9	Credit purchases from T. DuQuesnay £142, G. Henriques £44
,,	10	Goods returned to us by J. Long £17, T. Fryer £44
,,	12	Cash paid to us by T. Fryer £80
,,	15	We returned goods to S. Wood £8, G. Henriques £18
,,	19	We received cheques from J. Long £500, B. Flynn £241
,,	21	We sold goods on credit to B. Flynn £44, R. Kelly £280
,,	28	We paid by cheque the following: S. Wood £140; G. Henriques £50; R. Johnson £60
,,	31	We returned goods to G. Henriques £4.

5.8A. Redraft each of the accounts given in your answer to 5.6A in three column style accounts.

6

The Trial Balance

You have already seen that the method of book-keeping in use is that of the double entry method. This means:

1. For each debit entry there is a corresponding credit entry.
2. For every credit entry there is a corresponding debit entry.

All the items recorded in all the accounts on the debit side should equal in *total* all the items recorded on the credit side of the books. To see if the two totals are equal, or in accounting terminology to see if the two sides of the books 'balance', a Trial Balance may be drawn up periodically.

A form of a trial balance could be drawn up by listing all the accounts and adding together all the debit entries, at the same time adding together all the credit entries. Using the worked exercise on pages 25 and 26 such a trial balance would appear as follows, bearing in mind that it could not be drawn up until after all the entries had been made, and will therefore be dated as on 31 May 19 – 6.

Trial Balance as on 31 May 19 – 6

	Dr	Cr
	£	£
Purchases	309	
Sales		255
Returns outwards		15
Returns inwards	16	
D. Small	68	68
A. Lyon & Son		141
D. Hughes	60	60
M. Spencer	45	16
Cash	210	153
	708	708

However, this is not the normal method of drawing up a trial balance, but it is the easiest to understand in the first instance. Usually, a trial balance is a list of balances only, arranged as to whether they are debit balances or credit balances. If the above trial balance had been drawn up using the conventional balances method it would have appeared as follows:

Trial Balance as on 31 May 19 – 6

	Dr	Cr
	£	£
Purchases	309	
Sales		255
Returns outwards		15
Returns inwards	16	
A. Lyon and Son		141
M. Spencer	29	
Cash	57	
	411	411

Here the two sides also 'balance'. The sums of £68 in D. Small's account, £60 in D. Hughes' account, £16 in M. Spencer's account and £153 in the cash account have however been cancelled out from each side of these accounts by virtue of taking only the balances instead of totals. As equal amounts have been cancelled from each side, £297 in all, the new totals should still equal one another, as in fact they do at £411.

This latter form of trial balance is the easiest to extract when there are more than a few transactions during the period, also the balances are either used later when the profits are being calculated, or else appear in a balance sheet, so that it is not just for ascertaining whether or not errors have been made that trial balances are extracted.

Trial Balances and Errors

It may at first sight appear that the balancing of a trial balance proves that the books are correct. This however is quite wrong. It means that certain types of errors have not been made, but there are several types of errors that will not affect the balancing of a trial balance. Examples of the errors which would be revealed, provided there are no compensating errors which cancel them out, are errors in additions, using one figure for the debit entry and another figure for the credit entry, entering only one aspect of a transaction and so on. We shall consider these in greater detail in later chapters.

Exercises

MC19 Which of the following BEST describes a Trial Balance?
(A) Shows the financial position of a business
(B) It is a special account
(C) Shows all the entries in the books.
(D) It is a list of balances on the books

MC20 It is true that the trial balance totals should agree?
(A) No, there are sometimes good reasons why they differ
(B) Yes, except where the trial balance is extracted at the year end
(C) Yes, always
(D) No, because it is not a balance sheet.

6.1. You are to enter up the necessary amounts for the month of May from the following details, and then balance off the accounts and extract a trial balance as at 31 May 19-6:

19-6

May	1	Started firm with capital in cash of £250
,,	2	Bought goods on credit from the following persons: D. Ellis £54; C. Mendez 87; K. Gibson £25; D. Booth £76; L. Lowe £64
,,	4	Sold goods on credit to: C. Bailey £43; B. Hughes £62; H. Spencer £176
,,	6	Paid rent by cash £12
,,	9	Bailey paid us his account by cheque £43
,,	10	H. Spencer paid us £150 by cheque
,,	12	We paid the following by cheque: K. Gibson £25; D. Ellis £54
,,	15	Paid carriage by cash £23
,,	18	Bought goods on credit from C. Mendez £43; D. Booth £110
,,	21	Sold goods on credit to B. Hughes £67
,,	31	Paid rent by cheque £18.

6.2. Enter up the books from the following details for the month of March, and extract a trial balance as at 31 March 19-6:

19-6

March	1	Started business with £800 in the bank
,,	2	Bought goods on credit from the following persons: K. Henriques £76; M. Hyatt £27; T. Braham £56
,,	5	Cash sales £87
,,	6	Paid wages in cash £14
,,	7	Sold goods on credit to: H. Elliott £35; L. Lane £42; J. Carlton £72
,,	9	Bought goods for cash £46
,,	10	Bought goods on credit from: M. Hyatt £57; T. Braham £98
,,	12	Paid wages in cash £14
,,	13	Sold goods on credit to: L. Lane £32; J. Carlton £23
,,	15	Bought shop fixtures on credit from Betta Ltd £50
,,	17	Paid M. Hyatt by cheque £84
,,	18	We returned goods to T. Braham £20
,,	21	Paid Betta Ltd a cheque for £50
,,	24	J. Carlton paid us his account by cheque £95
,,	27	We returned goods to K. Henriques £24
,,	30	J. King lent us £60 by cash
,,	31	Bought a motor van paying by cheque £400.

6.3. The following transactions are to be entered up in the books for June, and accounts balanced off and a trial balance extracted as at 30 June 19-8:

19-8

June	1	Started business with £600 in the bank and £50 cash in hand
,,	2	Bought £500 goods on credit from C. Jones
,,	3	Credit sales: H. Henry £66; N. Neita £25; P. Potter £43
,,	4	Goods bought for cash £23
,,	5	Bought motor van paying by cheque £256
,,	7	Paid motor expenses by cheque £12
,,	9	Credit sales: B. Barnes £24; K. Lyn £26; M. Moore £65
,,	11	Goods bought on credit: C. Jones £240, N. Moss £62; O. Hughes £46
,,	13	Goods returned by us to C. Jones £25
,,	15	Paid motor expenses by cash £5
,,	19	Goods returned to us by N. Neita £11
,,	20	Cash taken for own use (drawings) £10
,,	21	We paid the following by cheque: N. Moss £62; O. Hughes £46
,,	23	H. Henry paid us in cash £66
,,	25	P. Potter paid us by cheque £43
,,	26	Cash sales £34
,,	27	Cash taken for own use £24
,,	28	Goods returned by us to C. Jones £42
,,	29	Paid for postage stamps by cash £4
,,	30	Credit sales: N. Neita £43; M. Edgar £67; K. Lyn £45.

6.4A. Record the following transactions of D. Chatsworth for the month of May 19-6, balance off all the accounts, and then extract a trial balance as on 31 May 19-6:

19-6

May	1	D. Chatsworth started business with £8,000 cash
,,	2	Put £7,500 of the cash into a bank account
,,	2	Bought goods on credit from: Burton Brothers £180; Lyew & Co £560; P. McDonald £380; K. Black Ltd £410
,,	3	Bought office fixtures by cheque £185
,,	4	Bought goods for cash £190
,,	5	Cash sales £110
,,	6	Goods sold on credit: J. Gayle & Son £190; P. Gentles £340; T. Sutherland £110; T. Brown Ltd £300
,,	7	Paid rent by cheque £100
,,	8	Paid wages by cash £70
,,	10	Bought goods on credit from: Lyew & Co £340; C. Rose £160
,,	11	Goods returned to us by J. Gayle & Son £60
,,	13	Goods sold on credit to: N. Mattis £44; J. Gayle & Son £300
,,	14	Bought office fixtures on credit from Tru-kits Ltd £178
,,	15	Bought office stationery for cash £90
,,	16	Paid cheques to the following: Tru-kits Ltd £178; Burton Brothers £180
,,	17	Paid wages by cash £90
,,	18	D. Chatsworth takes £100 drawings in cash
,,	20	We returned goods to P. McDonald £60; K. Black Ltd £44
,,	22	Bought office stationery £220 on credit from E.P. & Co
,,	24	Received cheques from N. Mattis £44; T. Brown Ltd £180
,,	26	Cash sales £140
,,	29	D. Chatsworth took cash drawings £150
,,	31	Paid sundry expenses by cash £5.

6.5A. Record the following details for the month of November 19-3 and extract a trial balance as at 30 November:

Nov 1 Started with £5,000 in the bank
,,   3 Bought goods on credit from: T. Henriques £160; J. Smith £230; W. Rogers £400; P. Boone £310
,,   5 Cash sales £240
,,   6 Paid rent by cheque £20
,,   7 Paid rates by cheque £190
,, 11 Sold goods on credit to: L. Matthews £48; K. Allen £32; R. Hall £1,170
,, 17 Paid wages by cash £40
,, 18 We returned goods to: T. Henriques £14; P. Boone £20
,, 19 Bought goods on credit from: P. Boone £80; W. Rogers £270; D. Diaz £130
,, 20 Goods were returned to us by K. Alberga £2; L. Matthews £4
,, 21 Bought motor van on credit from U.Z. Motors £500
,, 23 We paid the following by cheque: T. Henriques £146; J. Smith £230; W. Rogers £300
,, 25 Bought another motor van, paying by cheque immediately £700
,, 26 Received a loan of £400 cash from A. Williams
,, 28 Received cheques from: L. Matthews £44; K. Allen £30
,, 30 Proprietor brings a further £300 into the business, by a payment into the business bank account.

6.6A. Record the following for the month of January, balance off all the accounts, and then extract a trial balance as at 31 January 19-4:

19-4
Jan 1 Started business with £3,500 cash
,,   2 Put £2,800 of the cash into a bank account
,,   3 Bought goods for cash £150
,,   4 Bought goods on credit from: L. Coke £360; M. Burton £490; T. Hill £110; C. Small £340
,,   5 Bought stationery on credit from: Swift Ltd £170
,,   6 Sold goods on credit to: S. Walters £90; T. Binns £150; C. Howard £190; P. Peart £160
,,   8 Paid rent by cheque £55
,, 10 Bought fixtures on credit from Matalon Ltd £480
,, 11 Paid salaries in cash £120
,, 14 Returned goods to M. Burton £40; T. Hill £60
,, 15 Bought motor van by cheque £700
,, 16 Received loan from J. Henry by cheque £600
,, 18 Goods returned to us by: S. Walters £20; C. Howard £40
,, 21 Cash sales £90
,, 24 Sold goods on credit to: T. Binns £100; P. Peart £340; J. Smart £115
,, 26 We paid the following by cheque: M. Burton £450; T. Hill £50
,, 29 Received cheques from: J. Smart £115; T. Binns £250
,, 30 Received a further loan from J. Henry by cash £200
,, 30 Received £500 cash from P. Peart.

7

Trading and Profit and Loss Accounts: An Introduction

Probably the main objective of the accounting function is the calculation of the profits earned by a business or the losses incurred by it. The earning of profit is after all usually the main reason why the business was set up in the first place, and the proprietor will want to know for various reasons how much profit has been made. First he will want to know how the actual profits compare with the profits he had hoped to make. He may also want to know his profits for such diverse reasons as: to assist him to plan ahead, to help him to obtain a loan from a bank or from a private individual, to show to a prospective partner or to a person to whom he hopes to sell the business, or maybe he will need to know his profits for income tax purposes.

Chapter 4 was concerned with the grouping of revenue and expenses prior to bringing them together to compute profit. In the case of a trader, meaning by this someone who is mainly concerned with buying and selling, the profits are calculated by drawing up a special account called a Trading and Profit and Loss Account. For a manufacturer it is also useful to prepare Manufacturing Accounts as well, but this will be dealt with in a later chapter.

Undoubtedly one of the most important uses of the trading and profit and loss account is comparing the results obtained with the results expected. Many businesses attach a great deal of importance to their gross profit percentage. This is the amount of Profit made, before deducting expenses, for every £100 of sales. In order that this may easily be deduced from the profit calculations, the account in which profit is computed is split into two sections − one in which the Gross Profit is found, and the next section in which the Net Profit is calculated.

Gross Profit (calculated in the Trading Account)	This is the excess of sales over the cost of goods sold in the period.
Net Profit (calculated in the Profit and Loss Account)	What remains after all other costs used up in the period have been deducted from the gross profit.

The gross profit, found by the use of the Trading Account, is the excess of sales over the cost of goods sold. The net profit, found when the Profit and Loss Account is prepared, consists of the gross profit plus any revenue other than that from sales, such as discounts received or commissions earned, less the total costs used up during the period. Where the cost of goods sold is greater than the sales the result would be a Gross Loss, but this is a relatively rare occurrence. Where the costs used up exceed the gross profit plus other revenue then the result is said to be a Net Loss. By taking the figure of sales less the cost of goods sold, it can be seen that the accounting custom is to calculate a trader's profits only when the goods have been disposed of and not before.

As was seen in Chapter 4, profit increases the capital of the proprietor, profit in this context meaning the net profit. The fact that an interim figure of profit, known as the gross profit is calculated, is due to the two figures of profit being more useful for purposes of comparison with both these profits of previous periods, than by just comparing net profits only. Were it not for this accounting custom it would not be necessary to calculate gross profit at all.

The trial balance of B. Swift, Exhibit 7.1, drawn up as on 31 December 19-5 after the completion of his first year in business can now be looked at.

Exhibit 7.1

B. Swift

Trial Balance as on 31 December 19-5

	Dr	Cr
	£	£
Sales		3,850
Purchases	2,900	
Rent	240	
Lighting expenses	150	
General expenses	60	
Fixtures and fittings	500	
Debtors	680	
Creditors		910
Bank	1,510	
Cash	20	
Drawings	700	
Capital		2,000
	6,760	6,760

The first task is to draw up the trading account using the above information. Immediately there is a problem. Sales less the cost of goods sold is the definition of gross profit, but purchases will only equal cost of goods sold if in fact all the goods purchased had been sold leaving no stock of goods on 31 December 19-5. It would be normal to find that a trader always keeps a stock of goods for resale, as the stock of goods is constantly being replenished. However, there is no record in the books of the value of the stock of unsold goods, and the only way that Swift can find this out is by stock-taking on 31 December 19-5 after the business of that day. By stocktaking is meant that he would make a list of all the unsold goods and then find out their value. The value he would normally place on them would be the cost price of the goods. Assume that this was £300. Then the cost of purchases less the cost of unsold goods would equal the cost of goods sold, ignoring losses by theft or wastage. This figure would then be deducted from the figure of sales to find the gross profit.

Swift could perform this calculation arithmetically:

Sales – Cost of goods sold   = Gross Profit
   (Purchases – unsold stock)
£3,850 – (£2,900 – £300)   = £1,250

This however is not performing the task by using double entry accounts. In double entry the balance of the sales account is transferred to the trading account by debiting the sales account (thus closing it) and crediting the trading account. The balance of the purchases account would then be transferred by crediting the purchases account (thus closing it) and debiting the trading account. Now the accounts connected with stock movements have been closed, and accounts are being drawn up to a point in time, in this case 31 December 19-5. At this point of time Swift has an asset, namely stock (of unsold goods), for which no account exists. This must be rectified by opening a stock account and debiting the amount of the asset to it. Now as already stated, the closing stock needs to be brought into the calculation of the gross profit, and the calculation of the gross profit is effected in the trading account. Therefore the credit for the closing stock should be in the trading account thus completing the double entry.

It is now usual for the trading and profit and loss accounts to be shown under one combined heading, the trading account being the top section and the profit and loss account being the lower section of this combined account.

B. Swift

Trading and Profit and Loss Account for the year ended 31 December 19-5

	£		£
Purchases	2,900	Sales	3,850
Gross profit c/d	1,250	Closing stock	300
	4,150		4,150
		Gross profit b/d	1,250

The balance shown on the trading account is shown as gross profit rather than being described as a balance. When found the gross profit is carried down to the profit and loss section of the account.

The accounts so far used appear as follows:

Sales

19-5	£	19-5	£
Dec 31 Trading	3,850	Dec 31 Balance b/d	3,850

Purchases

19-5	£	19-5	£
Dec 31 Balance b/d	2,900	Dec 31 Trading	2,900

Stock

19-5	£
Dec 31 Trading	300

The entry of the Closing Stock on the credit side of the trading and profit and loss account is in effect a deduction from the purchases on the debit side. In present-day accounting it is usual to find the closing stock actually shown as a deduction from the purchases on the debit side, and the figure then disclosed being described as 'cost of goods sold'. This is illustrated in Exhibit 7.2.

The profit and loss account can now be drawn up. Any revenue accounts, other than sales which have already been dealt with, would be transferred to the credit of the profit and loss account. Typical examples are commissions received and rent received. In the case of B. Swift there are no such revenue accounts.

The costs used up in the year, in other words the expenses of the year, are transferred to the debit of the profit and loss account. It may also be thought, quite rightly so, that as the fixtures and fittings have been used during the year with the subsequent deterioration of the asset, that something should be charged for this use. The methods for doing this are left until Chapter 19.

The revised trading account with the addition of the profit and loss account will now appear as follows:

Exhibit 7.2

B. Swift

Trading and Profit and Loss Account for the year ended 31 December 19-5

	£		£
Purchases	2,900	Sales	3,850
Less Closing stock	300		
Cost of goods sold	2,600		
Gross Profit c/d	1,250		
	3,850		3,850
Rent	240	Gross profit b/d	1,250
Lighting expenses	150		
General expenses	60		
Net profit	800		
	1,250		1,250

The expense accounts closed off will now appear as:

Rent

19-5	£	19-5	£
Dec 31 Balance b/d	240	Dec 31 Profit and Loss	240

Lighting Expenses

19-5	£	19-5	£
Dec 31 Balance b/d	150	Dec 31 Profit and Loss	150

General Expenses

19-5	£	19-5	£
Dec 31 Balance b/d	60	Dec 31 Profit and Loss	60

Net profit increases the capital of the proprietor. The credit entry for the net profit is therefore in the capital account. The trading and profit and loss accounts, and indeed all the revenue and expense accounts can thus be seen to be devices whereby the capital account is saved from being concerned with unnecessary detail. Every sale of a good at a profit increases the capital of the proprietor as does each item of revenue such as rent received. On the other hand each sale of a good at a loss, or each item of expense decreases the capital of the proprietor. Instead of altering the capital afresh after each transaction the respective items of profit and loss and of revenue and expense are collected together using suitably described accounts. Then the whole of the details are brought together in one set of accounts, the trading and profit and loss account and the increase to the capital, i.e. the net profit is determined. Alternatively, the decrease in the capital as represented by the Net Loss is ascertained.

The fact that a separate drawings account has been in use can now also be seen to have been in keeping with the policy of avoiding unnecessary detail in the capital account. There will thus be one figure for drawings which will be the total of the drawings for the whole of the period, and will be transferred to the debit of the capital account..

The capital account, showing these transfers, and the drawings account now closed is as follows:

Capital

19-5		£	19-5		£
Dec 31 Drawings		700	Jan 1 Cash		2,000
,, 31 Balance c/d		2,100	Dec 31 Net Profit from		
			Profit and Loss		800
		2,800			2,800
			19-6		
			Jan 1 Balance b/d		2,100

Drawings

19-5		£	19-5		£
Dec 31 Balance b/d		700	Dec 31 Capital		700

It should be noticed that not all the items in the trial balance have been used in the Trading and Profit and Loss Account. The remaining balances are assets or liabilities or capital, they are not expenses or sales. These will be used up later when a balance sheet is drawn up, for as has been shown in Chapter 1, assets, liabilities and capital are shown in balance sheets.

In Exhibit 7.3, although it is not necessary to redraft the trial balance after the trading and profit and loss accounts have been prepared, it will be useful to do so in order to establish which balances still remain in the books. The first thing to notice is that the stock account, not originally in the trial balance, is in the redrafted trial balance, as the item was not created as a balance in the books until the trading account was prepared. These balances will be used by us when we start to look at the balance sheets.

Exhibit 7.3

B. Swift
Trial Balance as on 31 December 19-5
(after Trading and Profit and Loss Accounts completed)

	Dr	Cr
	£	£
Fixtures and fittings	500	
Debtors	680	
Creditors		910
Stock	300	
Bank	1,510	
Cash	20	
Capital		2,100
	3,010	3,010

The Next Step

Before attempting any of the questions at the end of this chapter the reader should turn to Appendix I, which is shown at the end of Chapter 45. Part of the way through the Appendix on page 447, at the chapter which starts off 'This is probably the first examination you will have taken in book-keeping and Accounting', there is a line of asterisks down the side of the page. Start to read that part of the Appendix and finish at the point where the asterisks finish, which is at the end of the sentence on page 448 'Always therefore put in the headings properly, don't wait until your examination to start this correct practice.'

The reason for this instruction should be obvious to the reader after going through that part of the Appendix. If effort is needed to bring work to the required standard, it is more likely that the effort will be made if the reader can understand why the author should make such a request.

Exercises

MC21 Gross Profit is:
(A) Excess of sales over cost of goods sold
(B) Sales less Purchases
(C) Cost of Goods Sold + Opening Stock
(D) Net Profit less expenses of the period.

MC22 Net Profit is calculated in the
(A) Trading Account
(B) Profit and Loss Account
(C) Trial Balance
(D) Balance Sheet.

MC23 To find the value of closing stock at the end of a period we
(A) Do this by stocktaking
(B) Look in the stock account
(C) Deduct opening stock from cost of goods sold
(D) Deduct cost of goods sold from sales.

MC24 The credit entry for Net Profit is on the credit side of
(A) The Trading Account
(B) The Profit and Loss Account
(C) The Drawings Account
(D) The Capital Account.

7.1. From the following trial balance of B. Webb, extracted after one year's trading, prepare a trading and profit and loss account for the year ended 31 December 19-6. A balance sheet is not required.

Trial Balance as at 31 December 19-6

	Dr	Cr
	£	£
Sales		18,462
Purchases	14,629	
Salaries	2,150	
Motor expenses	520	
Rent	670	
Insurance	111	
General expenses	105	
Premises	1,500	
Motor vehicles	1,200	
Debtors	1,950	
Creditors		1,538
Cash at bank	1,654	
Cash in hand	40	
Drawings	895	
Capital		5,424
	25,424	25,424

Stock at 31 December 19-6 was £2,548.
(Keep your answer − it will be used later in question 8.1)

7.2. From the following trial balance of C. Worth after his first year's trading, you are required to draw up a trading and profit and loss account for the year ended 30 June 19-4. A balance sheet is not required.

Trial Balance as at 30 June 19-4

	Dr	Cr
	£	£
Sales		28,794
Purchases	23,803	
Rent	854	
Lighting and Heating expenses	422	
Salaries and wages	3,164	
Insurance	105	
Buildings	50,000	
Fixtures	1,000	
Debtors	3,166	
Sundry expenses	506	
Creditors		1,206
Cash at bank	3,847	
Drawings	2,400	
Motor vans	5,500	
Motor running expenses	1,133	
Capital		65,900
	95,900	95,900

Stock at 30 June 19-4 was £4,166.

(Keep your answer, it will be used later in question 8.2)

7.3A. From the following trial balance of F. Chaplin drawn up on conclusion of his first year in business, draw up a trading and profit and loss account for the year ended 31 December 19-8. A balance sheet is not required.

Trial Balance as at 31 December 19-8

	Dr	Cr
	£	£
General expenses	210	
Rent	400	
Motor expenses	735	
Salaries	3,560	
Insurance	392	
Purchases	18,385	
Sales		26,815
Motor vehicle	2,800	
Creditors		5,160
Debtors	4,090	
Premises	20,000	
Cash at bank	1,375	
Cash in hand	25	
Capital		24,347
Drawings	4,350	
	56,322	56,322

Stock at 31 December 19-8 was £4,960.
(Keep your answer, it will be used later in question 8.3A.)

7.4A. Extract a trading and profit and loss account for the year ended 30 June 19-4 for F. Kidd. The trial balance as at 30 June 19-4 after his first year of trading, was as follows:

	Dr	Cr
	£	£
Rent	1,560	
Insurance	305	
Lighting and Heating expenses	516	
Motor expenses	1,960	
Salaries and wages	4,850	
Sales		35,600
Purchases	30,970	
Sundry expenses	806	
Motor vans	3,500	
Creditors		3,250
Debtors	6,810	
Fixtures	3,960	
Buildings	28,000	
Cash at bank	1,134	
Drawings	6,278	
Capital		51,799
	90,649	90,649

Stock at 30 June 19-4 was £9,960.
(Keep your answer, it will be used later in question 8.4A.)

8

Balance Sheets

After the trading and profit and loss accounts have been completed, a statement is drawn up in which the remaining balances in the books are arranged according to whether they are asset balances or liability or capital balances. This statement is called a balance sheet, and it may be recalled that Chapter 1 contained examples. The assets are shown on the left-hand side and the liabilities on the right-hand side.

It is very important to know that the balance sheet is not part of the double-entry system. This contrasts with the Trading and Profit and Loss Account which is part of double-entry. The use of the word 'account' indicates that it is part of double-entry.

It was seen in the last chapter that when sales, purchases and the various expenses were taken into the profit calculations an entry was actually made in each account showing that the item had been transferred to the Trading Account or the Profit and Loss Account. The balance sheet however is not part of double-entry, it is simply a list of the balances remaining after the Trading and Profit and Loss Accounts have been prepared. Therefore items are *not* transferred from accounts to the balance sheet, and accordingly entries are *not* made in the various accounts when a balance sheet is drawn up.

In Exhibit 8.1 the trial balance is shown again of B. Swift as on 31 December 19-5 *after* the Trading and Profit and Loss Account had been prepared.

Exhibit 8.1

B. Swift
Trial Balance as at 31 December 19-5
(after Trading and Profit and Loss Accounts completed)

	Dr	Cr
	£	£
Fixtures and fittings	500	
Debtors	680	
Creditors		910
Stock	300	
Bank	1,510	
Cash	20	
Capital		2,100
	3,010	3,010

A balance sheet, Exhibit 8.2, can now be drawn up as at 31 December 19-5. At this point we will not worry whether or not the balance sheet is set out in good style.

Exhibit 8.2

B. Swift
Balance Sheet as at 31 December 19-5

Assets	£	Capital and liabilities	£
Fixtures and fittings	500	Capital	2,100
Stock	300	Creditors	910
Debtors	680		
Bank	1,510		
Cash	20		
	3,010		3,010

Remember, all of the balances per Exhibit 8.1 still remain in the accounts, *no* entries were made in the accounts for the purpose of drawing up the balance sheet. As has been stated already, this is in direct contrast to the trading and profit and loss accounts. The word 'account' means in fact that it is part of the double entry system, so that anything which is not an account is outside the double entry system.

Balance Sheet Layout

You would not expect to go into a first-class store and see the goods for sale all mixed up and not laid out properly. You would expect that the goods would be so displayed so that you could easily find them. Similarly in balance sheets we do not want all the items shown in any order. We would really want them displayed so that desirable information could easily be seen.

For people such as bank managers, accountants and investors who look at a lot of different balance sheets, we would want to keep to a set pattern so as to enable comparison of balance sheets to be made easier. What you are about to look at is a suggested method for displaying items in balance sheets.

Let us look at the assets side first. We are going to show the assets under two headings, Fixed Assets and Current Assets.

Assets are called Fixed Assets when they are of long life, are to be used in the business and were *not* bought with the main purpose of resale. Examples are buildings, machinery, motor vehicles and fixtures and fittings.

On the other hand, assets are called Current Assets when they represent cash or are primarily for conversion into cash or have a short life. An example of a short-lived asset is that of the stock of oil held to power the boilers in a factory, as this will be used up in the near future. Other examples of current assets are cash itself, stocks of goods, debtors and bank balances.

There is a choice of two methods of listing the assets under their respective headings. The first, being the most preferable since it helps standardize the form of sole traders' accounts with those of limited companies, is that the assets are listed starting with the most permanent asset, or to put it another way, the most difficult to turn into cash, progressing to the asset which is least permanent or easiest to turn into cash. The fixed assets will thus appear under that heading followed by the current assets under their heading. The other method, used by banks but fast falling into disuse in most other kinds of organizations, is the complete opposite. In this method it is the least permanent asset that appears first and the most permanent asset which appears last.

Using the first method an illustration may now be seen of the order in which assets are displayed:

Fixed Assets

Land and buildings
Fixtures and fittings
Machinery
Motor vehicles

Current Assets

Stock
Debtors
Bank
Cash

The order with which most students would disagree is that stock has appeared before debtors. On first sight stock would appear to be more easily realizable than debtors. In fact, however, debtors could normally be more quickly turned into cash by factorizing them, i.e. selling the rights to the amounts owing to a finance company for an agreed amount. On the other hand, to dispose of all the stock of a business is often a long and difficult task. Another advantage is that the method follows the order in which full realization of the asset takes place. First, before any sale takes place there must be a stock of goods, which when sold on credit turns into debtors, and when payment is made by the debtors it turns into cash.

The order of the other side of the balance sheet is preferably that of starting with capital, progressing via Long-Term Liabilities such as loans not requiring repayment within the near future, and finishing with Current Liabilities, being liabilities such as debts for goods which will have to be discharged in the near future. This then would be the order in which the claims against the assets would be met. The other method of listing the liabilities is the complete opposite of this, starting with current liabilities and finishing at the bottom with capital. This method conflicts with company accounts and is best avoided if the benefits of standardization are to be attained.

Exhibit 8.3 shows Exhibit 8.2 drawn up in better style. Also read the notes following the exhibit.

Exhibit 8.3

B. Swift
Balance Sheet as at 31 December 19-5

Fixed Assets	£	£	*Capital*	£	£
Furniture and fittings		500	Cash introduced	2,000	
			Add Net profit		
Current Assets			for the year	800	
Stock	300				
Debtors	680			2,800	
Bank	1,510		Less Drawings	700	
Cash	20				2,100
		2,510	*Current Liabilities*		
			Creditors		910
		3,010			3,010

Notes to Exhibit 8.3

1. A total for capital and for each class of assets and liabilities should be shown, e.g. the £2,510 total of current assets. For this purpose the individual figures of current assets are inset and the resultant total extended into the end column.

2. It is not necessary to write the word 'account' after each item.

3. The proprietor will obviously be most interested in his capital. To have merely shown the balance of £2,100 would invariably invite his request to show how the final balance of the capital account had been arrived at. To overcome this, accounting custom always shows the full details of the capital account. Compare this with the other items above where only the closing balance is shown.

4. Compare the date on the balance sheet with that on the trading and profit and loss account. You can see from these that the essential natures of these two statements are revealed. A trading and profit and loss account is a period statement, because it covers a specifed period of time, in this case the whole of 19-5. On the other hand a balance sheet is a position statement; it is drawn up at a particular point in time, in this case at the precise end of 19-5.

Exercises

MC25 Which is the BEST definition of a balance sheet?
(A) An account proving the books balance
(B) A record of closing entries
(C) A listing of balances
(D) A statement of assets.

MC26 The descending order in which current assets should be shown in the balance sheet are:
(A) Stock, Debtors, Bank, Cash
(B) Cash, Book, Debtors, Stock
(C) Debtors, Stock, Bank, Cash
(D) Stock, Debtors, Cash, Bank.

MC27 Which is the BEST description of Fixed Assets?
(A) Are bought to be used in the business
(B) Are items which will not wear our quickly
(C) Are expensive items bought for the business
(D) Are of long-life and are not bought specifically for resale.

8.1. Complete question 7.1 by drawing up a balance sheet as at 31 December 19-6.

8.2. Complete question 7.2 by drawing up a balance sheet as at 30 June 19-4.

8.3A. Complete question 7.3A by drawing up a balance sheet as at 31 December 19-8.

8.4A. Complete question 7.4A by drawing up a balance sheet as at 30 June 19-4.

9

Trading and Profit and Loss Accounts and Balance Sheets: Further Considerations

1. Returns Inwards and Returns Outwards

In Chapter 3 the idea of different accounts for different movements of stock was introduced. There were accordingly sales, purchases, returns inwards and returns outwards accounts. In our first look at the preparation of a Trading Account in Chapter 7, returns inwards and returns outwards were omitted. This was done deliberately so that the first sight of Trading and Profit and Loss Accounts would not be a difficult one.

However, a large number of firms will return goods to their suppliers (returns outwards), and will have goods returned to them by their customers (returns inwards). When the gross profit is calculated these returns will have to come into the calculations. Suppose that in Exhibit 7.1, the trial balance of B. Swift, the balances showing stock movements had instead been as follows:

Trial Balance as at 31 December 19-5

	Dr	Cr
	£	£
Sales		4,000
Purchases	3,120	
Returns inwards	150	
Returns outwards		220

Looking at Exhibit 7.1 it can be seen that originally the example used was of Sales £3,850 and Purchases £2,900. If it had been as now shown instead, the Trading Account can be shown as it would have been for the year, and what gross profit would have been.

Comparing the two instances, they do in fact amount to the same things as far as gross profit is concerned. Sales were £3,850 in the original example. In the new example returns inwards should be deducted to get the correct figure for goods sold to customers and *kept* by them, i.e. £4,000 – £150 = £3,850. Purchases were £2,900; in the new example returns outwards should be deducted to get the correct figure of purchases *kept* by Swift. The gross profit will remain at £1,250 as per Exhibit 7.1.

The trading account will appear as in Exhibit 9.1.

Exhibit 9.1
Trading and Profit and Loss Account for the year ended 31 December 19-5

	£	£		£	£
Purchases	3,120		Sales	4,000	
Less Returns outwards	220	2,900	*Less* Returns inwards	150	3,850
Less Closing stock		300			
Cost of goods sold		2,600			
Gross profit c/d		1,250			
		3,850			3,850

The term used for Sales less Returns Inwards is often called 'Turnover'. In the illustration in Exhibit 9.1 it is £3,850.

2. Carriage

Carriage (cost of transport of goods) into a firm is called Carriage Inwards. Carriage of goods out of a firm to its customers is called Carriage Outwards.

When goods are bought the cost of carriage inwards may either be included as part of the price, or else the firm may have to pay separately for it. Suppose the firm was buying exactly the same goods. One supplier might sell them for £100, and he would deliver the goods and not send you a bill for carriage. Another supplier might sell the goods for £95, but you would have to pay £5 to a haulage firm for carriage inwards, i.e. a total cost of £100.

To keep cost of buying goods being shown on the same basis, carriage inwards is always added to the purchases in the Trading Account.

Carriage outwards to customers is not part of our firm's expenses in buying goods, and is always entered in the profit and loss account.

Suppose that in the illustration shown in this chapter, the goods had been bought for the same total figure of £3,120, but in fact £2,920 was the figure for purchases and £200 for carriage inwards. The trial balance and trading account appear as Exhibit 9.2.

Exhibit 9.2

Trial Balance as at 31 December 19-5

	Dr	Cr
	£	£
Sales		4,000
Purchases	2,920	
Returns inwards	150	
Returns outwards		220
Carriage inwards	200	

Trading and Profit and Loss Account for the year ended 31 December 19-5

	£	£		£	£
Purchases	2,920		Sales	4,000	
Less Returns outwards	220	2,700	*Less* Returns inwards	150	3,850
Carriage inwards		200			
		2,900			
Less Closing stock		300			
Cost of goods sold		2,600			
Gross profit c/d		1,250			
		3,850			3,850
			Gross profit b/d		1,250

It can be seen that Exhibits 7.1, 9.1 and 9.2 have been concerned with the same overall amount of goods bought and sold by the firm, at the same overall prices. Therefore, as shown, in each case the same gross profit of £1,250 is shown.

Before you proceed further you are to attempt Exercises 9.1 and 9.2A.

B. Swift's Second Year

At the end of his second year of trading, on 31 December 19-6, B. Swift extracts another trial balance.

Exhibit 9.3

B. Swift
Trial Balance as at 31 December 19-6

	Dr	Cr
	£	£
Sales		6,700
Purchases	4,260	
Lighting and Heating expenses	190	
Rent	240	
Wages: shop assistant	520	
General expenses	70	
Carriage outwards	110	
Buildings	2,000	
Fixtures and fittings	750	
Debtors	1,200	
Creditors		900
Bank	120	
Cash	40	
Loan from J. Marsh		1,000
Drawings	900	
Capital		2,100
Stock (at 31 December 19-5)	300	
	10,700	10,700

The stock shown in the trial balance is that brought forward from the previous year on 31 December 19-5; it is therefore the opening stock of 19-6. The closing stock at 31 December 19-6 can only be found by stocktaking. Assume it amounts at cost to be £550.

First of all calculate the cost of goods sold, showing the calculation in a normal arithmetical fashion.

	£
Stock of goods at start of year	300
Add purchases	4,260
Total goods available for sale	4,560
Less what remains at the end of the year:	
i.e. stock of goods at close	550
Therefore cost of goods that have been sold	4,010

Now look at a digram to illustrate this in Exhibit 9.4.

Exhibit 9.4

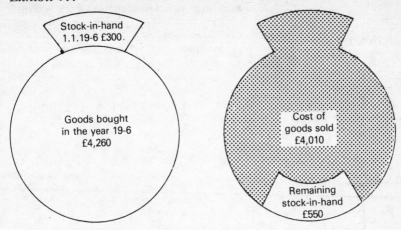

The sales were £6,700, so Sales £6,700 − Cost of Goods Sold £4,010 − Gross Profit £2,690.

Now the trading and profit and loss accounts can be drawn up using double-entry. See Exhibit 9.5.

Exhibit 9.5

B. Swift
Trading and Profit and Loss Account for the year ended 31 December 19-6

	£		£
Opening stock	300	Sales	6,700
Add Purchases	4,260		
	4,560		
Less Closing stock	550		
Cost of goods sold	4,010		
Gross profit c/d	2,690		
	6,700		6,700
Wages	520	Gross profit b/d	2,690
Lighting and Heating expenses	190		
Rent	240		
General expenses	70		
Carriage outwards	110		
Net profit	1,560		
	2,690		2,690

The balances now remaining in the books, including the new balance on the stock account, are now drawn up in the form of a balance sheet. See Exhibit 9.6.

Exhibit 9.6

B. Swift
Balance Sheet as at 31 December 19-6

Fixed Assets	£	£	Capital	£	£
Buildings		2,000	Balance 1 Jan 19-6	2,100	
Fixtures and fittings		750	Add Net Profit for year	1,560	
		——		——	
		2,750		3,660	
			Less Drawings	900	
Current Assets				——	2,760
Stock	550		Long-term liability		
Debtors	1,200		Loan from J. Marsh		1,000
Bank	120		Current Liabilities		
Cash	40		Creditors		900
	——	1,910			
		——			——
		4,660			4,660

Stock Account

It is perhaps helpful if the stock account covering both years can now be seen:

Stock

19-5		£	19-6		£
Dec 31	Trading A/c	300	Jan 1	Trading A/c	300
19-6					
Dec 31	Trading A/c	550			

Final Accounts

The term 'Final Accounts' is often used to mean collectively the trading and profit and loss accounts and the balance sheet. The term can be misleading as the balance sheet is not an account.

Other Expenses in the Trading Account

The costs of putting goods into a saleable condition should be charged in the Trading Account. In the case of a trader these are relatively few. An instance could be a trader who sells clocks packed in boxes. If he bought the clocks from one source, and the boxes from another source, both of these items would be charged in the Trading Account as Purchases. In addition, if a man's wages are paid to pack the clocks, then such wages would be charged in the Trading Account. The wages of shop assistants who sold the clocks would be charged in the Profit and Loss Account. The wages of the man packing the clocks would be the only wages in this instance concerned with 'putting the goods into a saleable condition'.

Exercises

MC28 Carriage Inwards is charged to the Trading Account because:
(A) It is an expense connected with buying goods
(B) It should not go in the Balance Sheet
(C) It is not part of motor expenses
(D) Carriage outwards goes in the Profit and Loss Account.

MC29 Given figures showing: Sales £8,200; Opening Stock £1,300; Closing Stock £900; Purchases £6,400; Carriage Inwards £200, the cost of goods sold figure is
(A) £6,800
(B) £6,200
(C) £7,000
(D) Another figure.

MC30 The costs of putting goods into a saleable condition should be charged to:
(A) Trading Account
(B) Profit and Loss Account
(C) Balance Sheet
(D) None of these.

9.1. From the following details draw up the Trading Account of T. Clarke for the year ended 31 December 19-3, which was his first year in business:

	£
Carriage inwards	670
Returns outwards	495
Returns inwards	890
Sales	38,742
Purchases	33,333
Stocks of goods: 31 December 19-3	7,489

9.2A. The following details for the year ended 31 March 19-8 are available. Draw up the Trading Account of K. Taylor for that year.

	£
Stocks: 31 March 19-8	18,504
Returns inwards	1,372
Returns outwards	2,896
Purchases	53,397
Carriage inwards	1,122
Sales	54,600

9.3. From the following trial balance of R. Graham draw up a trading and profit and loss account for the year ended 30 September 19-6, and a balance sheet as at that date.

	Dr	Cr
	£	£
Stock 1 October 19-5	2,368	
Carriage outwards	200	
Carriage inwards	310	
Returns inwards	205	
Returns outwards		322
Purchases	11,874	
Sales		18,600
Salaries and wages	3,862	
Rent	304	
Insurance	78	
Motor expenses	664	
Office expenses	216	
Lighting and Heating expenses	166	
General expenses	314	
Premises	5,000	
Motor vehicles	1,800	
Fixtures and fittings	350	
Debtors	3,896	
Creditors		1,731
Cash at bank	482	
Drawings	1,200	
Capital		12,636
	33,289	33,289

Stock at 30 September 19-6 was £2,946.

9.4. The following trial balance was extracted from the books of B. Jackson on 30 April 19-7. From it, and the notes, prepare his trading and profit and loss account for the year ended 30 April 19-7, and a balance sheet as at that date.

	Dr	Cr
	£	£
Sales		18,600
Purchases	11,556	
Stock 1 May 19-6	3,776	
Carriage outwards	326	
Carriage inwards	234	
Returns inwards	440	
Returns outwards		355
Salaries and wages	2,447	
Motor expenses	664	
Rent	576	
Sundry expenses	1,202	
Motor vehicles	2,400	
Fixtures and fittings	600	
Debtors	4,577	
Creditors		3,045
Cash at bank	3,876	
Cash in hand	120	
Drawings	2,050	
Capital		12,844
	34,844	34,844

Stock at 30 April 19-7 was £4,998.

9.5A. The following is the trial balance of J. Smailes as at 31 March 19-6. Draw up a set of final accounts for the year ended 31 March 19-6.

	Dr	Cr
	£	£
Stock 1 April 19-5	18,160	
Sales		92,340
Purchases	69,185	
Carriage inwards	420	
Carriage outwards	1,570	
Returns outwards		640
Wages and salaries	10,240	
Rent and Rates	3,015	
Communication expenses	624	
Commissions payable	216	
Insurance	405	
Sundry expenses	318	
Buildings	20,000	
Debtors	14,320	
Creditors		8,160
Fixtures	2,850	
Cash at bank	2,970	
Cash in hand	115	
Loan from K. Ball		10,000
Drawings	7,620	
Capital		40,888
	152,028	152,028

Stock at 31 March 19-6 was £22,390.

9.6A. L. Stokes drew up the following trial balance as at 30 September 19-8. You are to draft trading and profit and loss accounts for the year to 30 September 19-8 and a balance sheet as at that date.

	Dr £	Cr £
Loan from P. Owens		5,000
Capital		25,955
Drawings	8,420	
Cash at bank	3,115	
Cash in hand	295	
Debtors	12,300	
Creditors		9,370
Stock 30 September 19-7	23,910	
Motor van	4,100	
Office equipment	6,250	
Sales		130,900
Purchases	92,100	
Returns inwards	550	
Carriage inwards	215	
Returns outwards		307
Carriage outwards	309	
Motor expenses	1,630	
Rent	2,970	
Telephone charges	405	
Wages and salaries	12,810	
Insurance	492	
Office expenses	1,377	
Sundry expenses	284	
	171,532	171,532

Stock at 30 September 19-8 was £27,475.

10

Accounting Concepts and Statements of Standard Accounting Practice

The book so far has, in the main, been concerned with the recording of transactions in the books. Much of the rest of the book is about the classifying, summarizing and interpreting of the records that have been made. Before this second stage is reached it would be beneficial for the reader to examine the concepts of accounting, and the Statements of Standard Accounting Practice (from now on this will be abbreviated as SSAP).

The work that you have done in this subject so far has been based on various assumptions. These assumptions have deliberately not been discussed in much detail, they are much easier to understand after basic double entry has been dealt with. These assumptions are known as the 'concepts' of accounting.

The Trading and Profit and Loss Account and Balance Sheets shown in the previous chapter were drawn up so as to be of benefit to the owner of the business. Of course, as is shown later in the book, businesses are often owned by more than just one person and these accounting statements are for the benefit of them all. Now in the case of a sole trader he may well also use copies of the Final Accounts for the purpose of showing them as evidence when he wants to obtain a loan from a bank or from some other person. He may well also show a copy to someone who is interested in buying his business from him, or if he wants to have extended credit for a large amount from a supplier, as proof of his financial stability. In the case of partners and shareholders for businesses owned by more than one person the final accounts will be used for similar purposes.

Now of course if it had always been the custom to draft different kinds of final accounts for different purposes, so that one type was given to a banker, another type to someone wishing to buy the business, etc., then Accounting would be different than it is today. However, as yet it is deemed appropriate to give copies of the same set of final accounts to all the various parties, so that the banker, the prospective buyer of the business, the owner and the other people involved see the same Trading and Profit and Loss Account and Balance Sheet. This is not really an ideal situation as the interests of each party are different and really demand different kinds of information from that possessed by the others. For instance the bank manager would really like to know how much the assets would fetch if the firm ceased trading, so that he could judge in that case what the possibility would be of the bank obtaining repayment of its loan. Other parties would also like to see the information expressed in terms of values which were relevant to them. Yet in fact normally only one sort of final accounts is available for these different parties.

This means that Trading and Profit and Loss Accounts are multi-purpose documents, and to be of any use the various parties have to agree to the way in which they are drawn up. Assume that you are in a class of students and that you are faced with the problem of valuing your assets, which consists of 10 text-books. The first value you decide to assess is that of how much you could sell them for. Your own assessment is £30, but the other members of the class may give figures ranging from (say) £15 to £50. Suppose that you now decide to put a value on their use to you. You may well think that the use of these books will enable you to pass your examinations and so you will get a good job. Another person may well have completely the opposite idea concerning the use of the books to him. The use values placed on the book by individuals will therefore tend to vary widely. Finally you decide to value them by reference to cost. You take out of your pocket the bills for the books which show that you paid a total of £60 for the books. Assuming that the rest of the class do not think that you have altered the bills in any way, then they also can all agree that the value expressed as cost is £60. As this is the only value that you can all agree to then each of you decides to use the idea of showing the value of his asset of books at the cost price.

The use of a measure which gains consensus of opinion, rather than to use one's own measure which might conflict with other people's, is said to be objective. Thus the use of cost for asset valuation is an attempt to be objective. On the other hand the use of your own measure irrespective of whether people agree with it or not is said to be subjective. The desire to provide the same set of accounts for many different parties, and thus to provide a measure that gains their consensus of opinion, means that objectivity is sought for in financial accounting. If you are able to understand this desire for objectivity, then many of the apparent contradictions can be understood because it is often at the heart of the financial accounting methods in use at the present time.

Financial Accounting seeks objectivity, and of course it must have rules which lay down the way in which the activities of the business are recorded. These rules are known as concepts.

Basic Concepts

1. The Cost Concept

The need for this has already been described. It means that assets are normally shown at cost price, and that this is the basis for assessing the future usage of the asset.

2. The Money Measurement Concept

Accounting is only concerned with those facts that can be measured in monetary terms with a fair degree of objectivity. This means that Accounting can never show the whole of the information needed to give you a full picture of the state of the business or how well it is being conducted. Accounting does not record that the firm has a good, or a bad, management team. It does not show that the poor morale prevalent among the staff is about to lead to a serious strike, or that various managers will not co-operate with one another. Nor would it reveal that a rival product is about to take over a larger part of the market occupied at present by the firm's own goods.

This means quite simply that just looking at a set of accounting figures does not tell you all that you would like to know about a business. Some people imagine that Accounting gives you a full picture, but from what has been said they are quite obviously deluding themselves. Others would maintain that really Accounting ought to put monetary values on these other factors as yet ignored in Accounting. Those who object to this state that this would mean a considerable loss of objectivity. Imagine trying to place a value of the future services to be given to the firm by one of its managers. Different people would tend to give different figures, and so, at present, as the final accounts are of a multi-purpose nature, which figures would be acceptable to the many parties who use the accounts? As the answer is that no one set of acceptable figures could be agreed in this case by all parties, then in Accounting as it stands the task is just not undertaken at all. It would seem likely that, eventually the vital factor of placing a value on labour and management, usually known as 'Human Asset' accounting, will play a full part in the construction of balance sheets.

3. The Going Concern Concept

Unless the opposite is known accounting always assumes that the business will continue to operate for an indefinitely long period of time. Only if the business was going to be sold would it be necessary to show how much the assets would fetch. In the accounting records normally this is assumed to be of no interest to the firm. This is obviously connected with the cost concept, as if firms were not assumed to be going concerns the cost concept could not really be used, e.g. if firms were always to be treated as though they were going to be sold immediately after the accounting records were drafted, then the saleable value of the assets would be more relevant than cost.

4. The Business Entity Concept

The transactions recorded in a firm's books are the transactions that affect the firm. The only attempt to show how the transactions affect the owners of a business is limited to showing how their capital in the firm is affected. For instance, a proprietor puts £1,000 more cash into the firm as capital. The books will then show that the firm has £1,000 more cash and that his capital has increased by £1,000. They do not show that he has £1,000 less cash in his private resources. The accounting records are therefore limited to the firm and do not extend to the personal resources of the proprietors.

5. The Realization Concept

In accounting, profit is normally regarded as being earned at the time when the goods or services are passed to the customer and he incurs liability for them, i.e. this is the point at which the profit is treated as being realized. Note that it is not when the order is received, nor the contract signed, neither is it dependent on waiting until the customer pays for the goods or services. It can mean that profit is brought into account in one period, and it is found to have been incorrectly taken as such when the goods are returned in a later period because of some deficiency. Also the services can turn out to be subject to an allowance being given in a later period owing to poor performance. If the allowances or returns can be reasonably estimated an adjustment may be made to the calculated profit in the period when they passed to the customer.

6. The Dual Aspect Concept

This states that there are two aspects of Accounting, one represented by the assets of the business and the other by the claims against them. The concept states that these two aspects are always equal to each other. In other words:

Assets = Liabilities + Capital.

Double entry is the name given to the method of recording the transactions so that the dual aspect concept is upheld.

7. The Accruals Concept

The fact that net profit is said to be the difference between revenues and expenses rather than between cash receipts and expenditures is known as the Accruals Concept. A great deal of attention is therefore paid to this which, when the mechanics needed to bring about the Accruals Concept are being performed, is known as 'matching' expenses against revenues.

This concept is particularly misunderstood by people not well versed in Accounting. To many of them, actual payment of an item in a period is taken as being matched against the revenue of the period when the net profit is calculated. The fact that expenses consist of the assets used up in a particular period in obtaining the revenues of that period, and that cash paid in a period and expenses of a period are usually different as you will see later, comes as a surprise to a great number of them.

Further Over-riding Concepts

The concepts of Accounting already discussed have become accepted in the business world, their assimilation having taken place over many years. These concepts, however, are capable of being interpreted in many ways. What has therefore grown up in Accounting are generally accepted approaches to the application of the earlier concepts. The main ones in these further concepts may be said to be: 1. Materiality, 2. Prudence, 3. Consistency.

1. Materiality

Accounting does not serve a useful purpose if the effort of recording a transaction in a certain way is not worthwhile. Thus, if a box of paperclips was bought it would be used up over a period of time, and this cost is used up every time someone uses a paper-clip. It is possible to record this as an expense every time it happens, but obviously the price of a box of paper-clips is so little that it is not worth recording it in this fashion. The box of paper-clips is not a material item, and therefore would be charged as an expense in the period it was bought, irrespective of the fact that it could last for more than one accounting period. In other words do not waste your time in the elaborate recording of trivial items.

Similarly, the purchase of a cheap metal ashtray would also be charged as an expense in the period it was bought because it is not a material item, even though it may in fact last for twenty years. A motor lorry would however be deemed to be a material item, and so, as will be seen in chapter on depreciation, an attempt is made to charge each period with the cost consumed in each period of its use.

Firms fix all sorts of arbitrary rules to determine what is material and what is not. There is no law that lays down what these should be, the decision as to what is material and what is not is dependent upon judgment. A firm may well decide that all items under £100 should be treated as expenses in the period which they were bought even though they may well be in use in the firm for the following ten years. Another firm, especially a large one, may fix the limit of £1,000. Different limits may be set for different types of items.

It can be seen that the size and the type of firm will affect the decisions as to which items are material. With individuals, an amount of £1,000 may well be more than you, as a student, possess. For a multi-millionaire as to what is a material item and what is not will almost certainly not be comparable. Just as individuals vary then so do firms. Some firms have a great deal of machinery and may well treat all items of machinery costing less than £1,000 as not being material, whereas another firm which makes about the same amount of profits, but has very little machinery, may well treat a £600 machine as being a material item as they have fixed their limit at £250.

2. Prudence

Very often an accountant has to make a choice as to which figure he will take for a given item. The prudence concept means that normally he will take the figure which will understate rather than overstate the profit. Alternatively, this could be expressed as choosing the figure which will cause the capital of the firm to be shown at a lower amount rather than at a higher one. This could also be said to be to make sure that all losses are recorded in the books, but that profits should not be anticipated by recording them prematurely.

It was probably this concept that led to accountants being portrayed as being rather miserable by nature; they were used to favouring looking on the black side of things and ignoring the bright side. However, the concept has seen considerable changes in the last few decades, and there has been a shift along the scale away from the gloomy view and more towards the desire to paint a brighter picture when it is warranted.

The use of the term 'prudence' for this concept started in the 1970's. Prior to that it had always been known as 'conservatism', and this latter term will still be found in literature concerning Accounting.

3. Consistency

The concepts already listed are so broad that in fact there are many different ways in which items may be recorded in the accounts. Each firm should, within these limits, select the methods which give the most equitable picture of the activities of the business. However, this cannot be done if one method is used in one year and another method in the next year and so on. Constantly changing the methods would lead to a distortion of the profits calculated from the accounting records. Therefore the concept of consistency comes into play. This concept is that when a firm has once fixed a method of the accounting treatment of an item it will enter all similar items that follow in exactly the same way.

However, it does not bind the firm to following the method until the firm closes down. A firm can change the method used, but such a change is not affected without the deepest consideration. When such a change occurs and the profits calculated in that year are affected by a material amount, then either in the profit and loss account itself or in one of the reports accompanying it, the effect of the change should be stated.

The Assumption of the Stability of Currency₁

One does not have to be very old to remember that a few years ago many goods could be bought with less money than today. If one listens to one's parents or grandparents then many stories will be heard of how little this item or the other could be bought for x years ago. The currencies of the countries of the world are not stable in terms of what each unit of currency can buy over the years.

Accounting, however, uses the cost concept, this stating that the asset is normally shown at its cost price. This means that accounting statements will be distorted because assets will be brought at different points in time at the price then ruling, and the figures totalled up to show the value of the assets in cost terms. As an instance, suppose that you had bought a building 20 years ago for £20,000. You now decide to buy an identical additional building, but the price has now risen to £40,000. You buy it, and the buildings account now shows buildings at a figure of £60,000. One building is measured cost-wise in terms of the currency of 20 years ago, whilst the other is taken at today's currency value. The figure of a total of £60,000 is historically correct, but, other than that, the total figure cannot be said to be particularly valid for any other use.

This means that to make a correct assessment of accounting statements one must bear in mind the distorting effects of changing price levels upon the accounting entries as recorded. There are techniques of adjusting accounts so as to try and eliminate these distortions, but these are outside the scope of this volume. This will be dealt with in volume two.

Statements of Standard Accounting Practice (SSAP's)

Despite the use of the concepts there will still be differences of opinion between accountants when profits are being calculated. In the late 1960's a number of cases led to a general outcry against the lack of uniformity in Accounting. One concerned the takeover of AEI (Associated Electrical Industries) by GEC (General Electric Company). AEI had resisted the takeover, and had produced a profit forecast, in the tenth month of their financial year, that profit before tax for the year would be £10 million. After the takeover, the accounts for AEI for that year showed a loss of £4½ million. Of this difference of £14½ million, £5 million was said to be matters of fact, whilst the remaining £9½ million was attributed to adjustments which remain matters substantially of judgement arising from variations in accounting policies.

To reduce the possibility of such large variations in reported profits, the accountancy bodies have responded by issuing SSAP's, these are Statements of Standard Accounting Practice. 23 SSAP's had been issued to the date of writing this impression of the book. Accountants and auditors are expected to comply with the SSAP's, if they are now complied with then the audit report should give the reasons why the SSAP has been ignored.

The advent of the SSAP's does not mean that the two identical businesses already described will show exactly the same profits year by year. They have, however, considerably reduced the possibilities of very large variations in such profit reporting.

In this volume of the book the SSAP's will only be mentioned when it is essential. Volume two will examine the SSAP's in greater detail.

11

The Division of the Ledger

While the firm is very small indeed, all the double-entry accounts could be kept in one book, which we would call the ledger. As the firm grows it would be found impossible just to use one book, as the larger number of pages needed for a lot of transactions would mean that the book would be too big to handle (but see effect of computers − later in this chapter).

This problem could be solved in several ways. One method would be to have more than one ledger, but the accounts contained in each ledger would be chosen simply by chance. There would be no set method for deciding which account should go into which ledger. This would not be very efficient, as it would be difficult to remember which accounts were in each ledger.

Another method would be to divide the ledger up into different books and each book would be for a specific purpose or function. The functions could be:

(a) One book just for customers' personal accounts. We could call this the Sales Ledger.
(b) Another book just for suppliers' personal accounts. We could call this the Purchases Ledger or Bought Ledger.
(c) A book concerned with the receiving and paying out of money both by cash and cheque. This would be a Cash Book.
(d) The remaining accounts would be contained in a Ledger which we could call a General Ledger, an alternative name being a Nominal Ledger.

These ledgers all contain accounts and are part of double entry.

If more than one person becomes involved in book-keeping, the fact that the ledger has been divided into different books would make their job easier. The book-keeping to be done could be split between the people concerned, each book-keeper having charge of one or more books.

The General Ledger would be used quite a lot, because it would contain the sales account, purchases accounts, returns inwards and returns outwards accounts, as well as all the other accounts for assets, expenses, income, etc.

When the General Ledger becomes overloaded, we could deal with this problem by taking a lot of the detailed work out of it. Most entries in it would have been credit sales, credit purchases and returns inwards and returns outwards. We can therefore start four new books, for credit transactions only. One book will be for credit sales (the Sales Journal), one for credit purchases (the Purchases Journal) and one each for Returns Inwards (Returns Inwards Journal) and Returns Outwards (Returns Outwards Journal).

When a credit sale is made it will be entered in the customer's personal account in the Sales Ledger exactly the same as before. However, instead of entering the sale in the sales account in the General Ledger, we would enter it in the Sales Journal. At regular intervals, usually once a month, the total of the Sales Journal would be transferred to the credit of the Sales Account in the General Ledger.

What this means is that even if there were 1,000 credit sales in the month, only one entry, the total of the Sales Journal, would need entering in the General Ledger. This saves the General Ledger from being overloaded with detail.

Similarly credit purchases are entered in the suppliers' account and listed in a Purchases Journal. The total is then entered, at regular intervals, in the debit side of the Purchases Account.

Returns Inwards are entered in the customer's personal accounts, and are listed in the Returns Inwards Journal. The total is then transferred to the debit of the Returns Inwards Account.

Returns Outwards are entered in the suppliers' personal accounts, and are listed in the Returns Outwards Journal. The total is then transferred to the credit of the Returns Outwards Account.

This can be summarized:

Sales Ledger	
Purchases Ledger	All contain accounts and are therefore part of
Cash Book	the double-entry system
General Ledger	

Sales Journal	
Purchases Journal	Mere listing devices to save the accounts in the
Returns Inwards Journal	General Ledger from unnecessary detail.
Returns Outwards Journal	

These will be described in full detail in the following chapters.

Computers and Accounting

In chapter 25 the effect of computers on accounting is examined. At this point it might be thought that the author had never heard of computers, as the text has been discussing 'books' of various sorts, and it is well-known that computers do not use bound books.

In fact the term 'book' or 'journal' is simply a convenient way of describing what is in effect a 'collection point' for a particular type of information. The principles of accounting can therefore be more easily discussed if the author keeps to standard terms. The principles remain exactly the same no matter whether manual, computerised or other mechanical methods are in use.

Classifications of Accounts

Some people describe all accounts either as Personal Accounts or as Impersonal Accounts. Personal accounts are those of debtors and creditors. Impersonal accounts are then divided up further into Real accounts and Nominal accounts. Real accounts refer to accounts in which property is recorded, such as building, machinery, or stock. Nominal accounts are those which are concerned with revenue and expenses.

The Accountant As A Communicator

Quite often the impression is given that all that the accountant does is to produce figures, arranged in various ways. Naturally, such forms of computation do take up quite a lot of the accountant's time, but what then takes up the rest of his time is exactly how he communicates these figures to other people.

First of all, he can obviously arrange the figures in such a way as to present the information in as meaningful a way as possible. Suppose for instance that the figures he has produced are to be given to several people all of whom are very knowledgeable about accounting. He could, in such an instance, present the figures in a normal accounting way, knowing full well that the recipients of the information will understand it.

On the other hand, the accounting figures may well be needed by people who have absolutely no knowledge at all of accounting. In such a case a normal accounting statement would be no use to them at all, they would not understand it. In this case he might set out the figures in a completely different way to try to make it easy for them to grasp. For instance, instead of preparing a normal Trading and Profit and Loss Account he might show it as follows:

		£
In the year ended 31 December 19-6 you sold goods for		50,000

Now how much had those goods cost you to buy?

At the start of the year you had stock costing	6,000
+ You bought some more goods in the year costing	28,000

So altogether you had goods available to sell of	34,000
− At the end of the year you had stock of goods unsold of	3,000

So the goods you had sold in the year had cost you	31,000	
Let us deduct this from what you had sold the goods for		31,000

This means that you had made a profit on buying and selling goods, before any other expenses had been paid, amounting to   19,000
(We call this sort of profit the Gross Profit)

But you suffered other expenses such as wages, rent, lighting and so on, and during the year the amount of those expenses, not including anything taken for yourself, amounted to   9,000

So, for this year your sales value exceeded all the costs involved in running the business, so that the sales could be made, by   £10,000
(We call this sort of profit the Net Profit)

If an accountant cannot arrange the figures to make them meaningful to the recipient then he is failing in his task. His job is not just to produce figures for himself to look at, his job is to communicate these results to other people.

Very often the accountant will have to talk to people to explain the figures, or send a letter or write a report concerning them. He will also have to talk or write to people to find out exactly what sort of accounting information is needed by them or explain to them what sort of information he could provide. This means that if accounting examinations consist simply of computational type questions then they will not test the ability of the candidate to communicate in any other way than by writing down accounting figures. In recent years more attention has been paid by examining boards to these aspects of an accountant's work.

Exercises

MC31 Suppliers' personal accounts are found in
(A) Nominal Ledger
(B) General Ledger
(C) Purchases Ledger
(D) Sales Ledger.

MC32 The Sales Journal is BEST described as
(A) Part of the double entry system
(B) Containing customers' accounts
(C) Containing real accounts
(D) A list of credit sales.

MC33 Of the following which are Personal Accounts?
(i) Buildings
(ii) Wages
(iii) Debtors
(iv) Creditors.
(A) i and iv only
(B) ii and iii only
(C) iii and iv only
(D) ii and iv only.

12

The Banking System

Banks operate two main types of account, a current account and a deposit or savings account.

(a) Current Accounts

These are the accounts used for the regular banking and withdrawal of money. With this type of account a cheque book will be given by the bank to the customer for him to make payments to people to whom he owes money. He will also be given a paying-in book for him to pay money into the account.

(b) Deposit Accounts

This kind of account is one which will be concerned normally with putting money into the bank and not withdrawing it for some time. The usual object of having a deposit account is that interest is given on the balance held in the account, whilst interest is not usually given on balances in current accounts.

The remainder of this chapter will be concerned with current accounts.

Cheques

When the bank has agreed to let you open a current account it will ask you for a specimen signature. This enables them to ensure that your cheques are in fact signed by you, and have not been forged. You will then be issued with a cheque book.

We can then use the cheques to make payments out of the account. Normally we must ensure that we have banked more in the account than the amount paid out. If we wish to pay out more money than we have banked, we will have to see the bank manager. We will then discuss the reasons for this with him, and if he agrees he will give his permission for us to 'overdraw' our account. This is known as a 'bank overdraft'.

The person filling in the cheque and using it for payment, is known as the *drawer*.

The person to whom the cheque is paid is known as the *payee*.

We can now look at Exhibit 12.1, which is a blank cheque form before it is filled in.

Exhibit 12.1

On the face of the cheque are various sets of numbers. These are:

914234   Every cheque printed for the Cheshire Bank will be given a different number, so that individual items can be traced.

09-07-99   Each branch of each bank in the United Kingdom has a different number given to it. Thus this branch has a 'code' number 09-07-99.

058899   Each account with the bank is given a different number. This particular number is kept only for the account of J. Woodstock at the Stockport branch.

When we fill in the cheque we copy the details on the counterfoil which we then detach and keep for our records.

We can now look at the completion of a cheque. Let us assume that we are paying seventy-two pounds and eighty-five pence to K. Marsh on 22 May 19-5. Exhibit 12.2 shows the completed cheque.

Exhibit 12.2

May 22 19-5	**Cheshire Bank Ltd.** May 22 19 _5_ 09-07-99
PAYEE_____	Stockport Branch
K. Marsh	324 Low Road, Stockport, Cheshire SK6 8AP
	PAY K. Marsh _____ OR ORDER
	Seventy two Pounds 85p — £72 === 85p
	J WOODSTOCK
£72 = 85p	⑨14234⑨ 09⑨07⑨99⑨: 058899⑨ J.-Woodstock
914234	

In Exhibit 12.2:

The drawer is: J. Woodstock

The payee is: K. Marsh

The two parallel lines across the face of the cheque are drawn as a safeguard. If we had not done this the cheque would have been an 'uncrossed cheque'. If someone had stolen a signed uncrossed cheque he could have gone to the Stockport branch of the Cheshire Bank and obtained cash in exchange for the cheque. When the cheque is crossed it means it *must* be paid into a bank account, Post Office Giro bank or Savings Bank.

Cheques can be further safeguarded by using specific crossings, i.e. writing a form of instruction within the crossing on the cheques as shown in Exhibit 12.3.

Exhibit 12.3

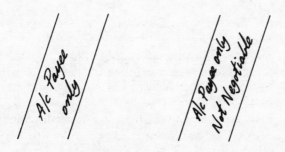

These are specific instructions to the banks about the use of the cheque. The use of 'Account Payee only' means the cheques should be paid only into the account of the payee named. If cheques are lost or stolen the drawer must advise his bank immediately and confirm by letter. These cheques will be 'stopped', i.e. payment will not be made on these cheques, provided you act swiftly. The safest crossing is that of 'A/c Payee only, Not Negotiable'. If the cheque is lost or stolen it will be of no use to the thief or finder. This is because it is impossible for this cheque to be paid into any bank account other than that of the named payee.

Paying-in Slips

When we want to pay money into our current accounts, either cash or cheques, or both, we use a paying-in slip. One of these is shown as Exhibit 12.4.

J. Woodstock has banked the following items:

Four	£5 notes
Three	£1 coins
One	50p coin
Other silver	30p
Bronze coins	12p

Cheques received from:		Code numbers:
E. Kane & Son	£184.15	02-58-76
J. Gale	£ 65.44	05-77-85

Exhibit 12.4

Face of paying in-slip

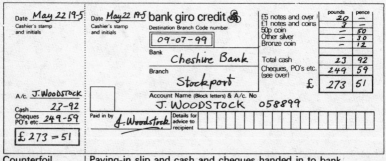

Reverse side of paying-in slip

Details of Cheques, PO's etc					
for cheques please specify **Drawers Name** and	**Bank Code Number** as shown in top right corner				
E. KANE & SON	02-58-76	184	15	184	15
J. GALE	05-77-85	65	44	65	44
In view of the risk of loss in course of clearing, customers are advised to keep an independent record of the drawers of cheques.	Total carried over £	249	59	249	59

Reverse of counterfoil

Cheque Clearings

We will now look at how cheques paid from one person's bank account pass into another person's bank account.

Let us look at the progress of the cheque in Exhibit 12.2. We will assume that the Post Office is being very efficient and delivering all letters the following day after being posted.

19-5
May 22   Woodstock, in Stockport, sends the cheque to K. Marsh, who lives in Leeds. Woodstock enters the payment in his cash book.

May 23   Cheque received by Marsh. He banks it the same day in his bank account at Barclays Bank in Leeds. Marsh shows the cheque in his cash book as being received and banked on 23 May.

May 24   Barclays in London receive it. They exchange it with the Head Office of the Cheshire Bank in London.
The Cheshire bank send the cheque to their Stockport branch.

May 25   The Stockport branch of the Cheshire bank examine the cheque. If there is nothing wrong with it, the cheque can now be debited by the bank to J. Woodstock's account.

In Chapter 22 we will be examining bank reconciliation statements. What we have looked at −

19-5
May 22   This is the day on which Woodstock has made the entry in his cash book.

May 25   This is the day when the bank makes an entry in Woodstock's account in respect of the cheque.

− will become an important part of your understanding such statements.

Exercises

MC34 When Lee makes out a cheque for £50 and sends it to Young, then Lee is known as
(A) The payee
(B) The banker
(C) The drawer
(D) The creditor.

MC35 If you want to make sure that your money will be safe if cheques sent are lost in the post, you should
(A) Not use the Postal Service in future
(B) Always pay by cash
(C) Always take the money in person
(D) Cross your cheques "Account Payee only, Not Negotiable'.

MC36 When banking money in to your current bank account you should always use
(A) A cheque book
(B) A paying-in slip
(C) A cash book
(D) A general ledger.

13

Two Column Cash Books

The cash book is merely the cash account and the bank account brought together in one book. Previously we would have shown these two accounts on two separate pages of the ledger. Now it is more convenient to place the account columns together so that the recording of all money received and of all money paid out on a particular date can be found on the same page. The cash book is ruled so that the debit column of the cash account is placed alongside the debit column of the bank account, and the credit columns of the cash and the bank accounts are also placed alongside each other.

We can now look at a cash account and a bank account in Exhibit 13.1 as they would have been if they had been kept separately, and then in Exhibit 13.2 as they would be shown if the transactions had instead been kept in a cash book.

The bank column contains details of the payments made by cheques and of the money received and paid into the bank account. The bank which is handling the firm's money will of course have a copy of the account in its own books. The bank will periodically send a copy of the account in the bank's books to the firm, this copy usually being known as the Bank Statement. When the firm receives the bank statement it will check it against the bank column in its own cash book to ensure that there are no discrepancies.

Exhibit 13.1

Cash

19-5		£	19-5		£
Aug	1 Balance b/d	33	Aug	8 Rent	20
,,	5 G. Bernard	25	,,	12 M. Prince	19
,,	15 B. Hussey	37	,,	28 Wages	25
,,	30 H. Howe	18	,,	31 Balance c/d	49
		113			113
Sept	1 Balance b/d	49			

Bank

19-5		£	19-5		£
Aug	1 Balance b/d	949	Aug	7 Rates	105
,,	3 I. Powell Ltd	295	,,	12 D. Squire Ltd	95
,,	16 G. Potter	408	,,	26 N. Foster	268
,,	30 B. Smith	20	,,	31 Balance c/d	1,204
		1,672			1,672
Sept	1 Balance b/d	1,204			

Exhibit 13.2

Cash Book

19-5		Cash £	Bank £	19-5		Cash £	Bank £
Aug	1 Balances b/d	33	949	Aug	7 Rates		105
,,	3 I. Powell Ltd		295	,,	8 Rent	20	
,,	5 G. Bernard	25		,,	12 M. Prince	19	
,,	15 B. Hussey	37		,,	,, D. Squire Ltd		95
,,	16 G. Potter		408	,,	26 N. Foster		268
,,	30 B. Smith		20	,,	28 Wages	25	
,,	,, H. Howe	18		,,	31 Balance c/d	49	1,204
		113	1,672			113	1,672
Sept	1 Balances b/d	49	1,204				

Cash Paid into the Bank

In Exhibit 13.2, the payments into the bank have consisted of cheques received by the firm which have been banked immediately. There is, however, the case to be considered of cash being paid into the bank.

Now let us look at the position when a customer pays his account in cash, and later a part of this cash is paid into the bank. The receipt of the cash is debited to the cash column on the date received, the credit entry being in the customer's personal account. The cash banked has the following effect needing action as shown:

Effect	Action
1. Asset of cash is decreased	Credit the asset account, i.e. the cash account which is represented by the cash column in the cash book.
2. Asset of bank is increased	Debit the asset account, i.e. the bank account which is represented by the bank column in the cash book.

A cash receipt of £100 from J. Davies on 1 August 19-5, later followed by the banking on 3 August of £80 of this amount would appear in the cash book as follows:

19-5	Cash £	Bank £	19-5	Cash £	Bank £
Aug 1 J. Davies	100		Aug 3 Bank	80	
,, 3 Cash		80			

The details column shows entries against each item stating the name of the account in which the completion of double entry had taken place. Against the cash payment of £80 appears the word 'bank', meaning that the debit £80 is to be found in the bank column, and the opposite applies.

Where the whole of the cash received is banked immediately the receipt can be treated in exactly the same manner as a cheque received, i.e. it can be entered directly in the bank column.

Sometimes, when the firm requires cash for future payments and it has not got a sufficient amount of cash in hand for the purpose, it may withdraw cash from the bank. This is done by making out a cheque to pay itself a certain amount of cash. The proprietor, or an authorized person, visits the bank where he is given cash in exchange for the cheque. This is sometimes known as 'cashing' a cheque for business use.

The twofold effect and the action required may be summarized:

Effect	Action
1. Asset of bank is decreased.	Credit the asset account, i.e. the bank column in the cash book.
2. Asset of cash is increased.	Debit the asset account, i.e. the cash column in the cash book.

A withdrawal of £75 cash on 1 June 19-5 from the bank would appear in the cash book thus:

19-5	Cash £	Bank £	19-5	Cash £	Bank £
June 1 Bank	75		June 1 Cash		75

Where an item does not need entering in another book as double entry has already taken place within the cash book, then this item is known as a 'contra' being the Latin word for against. Thus cash paid into the bank and cash withdrawn from the bank are both contra items. As there is a debit item and a credit item for the same amount double entry has already been completed, so that no account exists elsewhere for contra items in the cash book.

The Use of Folio Columns

As you have already seen, the details column in an account contains the name of the other account in which double entry has been completed. Anyone looking through the books for any purpose would therefore be helped to find where the other half of the double entry was situated. However, with the growth in the number of books in use the mere mention of the name of the other account would not be sufficient to give quick reference to the other account. An extra aid is therefore needed and this is brought about by the use of a 'folio' column. In each account and in each book in use an extra column is added, this always being shown on the immediate left of the money columns. In this column the name of the other book, in abbreviated form, and the number of the page in the other book where double entry is completed is stated against each and every entry in the books.

Thus an entry of receipt of cash from C. Koote whose account was on page 45 of the sales ledger, and the cash recorded on page 37 of the cash book, would use the folio column thus:

In the cash book.   In the folio column alongside the entry of the amount would appear SL 45.

In the sales ledger.   In the folio column alongside the entry of the amount would appear CB 37.

By this means full cross reference would be given. Each of the contra items, being shown on the same page of the cash book, would use the letter 'C' in the folio column.

The folio column is only filled in when double entry for the item has been completed. The act of using one book as a means for entering the items to the other account so as to complete double entry is known as 'posting' the items. Where the folio column has not been filled it will be seen at a glance that double entry has not been completed, thus the error made when only one-half of the double-entry is completed is made less often and can often be detected easily.

A Worked Example

The following transactions are written up in the form of a cash book. The folio columns are also filled in as though double entry had been completed to the other ledgers.

19-5   £

			£
Sept	1	Balances brought forward from last month:	
		Cash	20
		Bank	940
,,	2	Received cheque from M. Black	115
,,	4	Cash sales	82
,,	6	Paid rent by cash	35
,,	7	Banked £50 of the cash held by the firm	50
,,	15	Cash sales paid direct into the bank	40
,,	23	Paid cheque to M. Brown	277
,,	29	Withdrew cash from bank	120
,,	30	Paid wages in cash	118

Cash Book

	Folio	Cash	Bank		Folio	Cash	Bank
19-5		£	£	19-5		£	£
Sept 1 Balances	b/d	20	940	Sept 6 Rent	GL65	35	
,, 2 M. Black	SL98		115	,, 7 Bank	C	50	
,, 4 Sales	GL87	82		,, 23 M. Brown	PL23		277
,, 7 Cash	C		50	,, 29 Cash	C		120
,, 15 Sales	GL87		40	,, 30 Wages	GL39	118	
,, 29 Bank	C	120		,, 30 Balances	c/d	19	748
		222	1,145			222	1,145
Oct 1 Balances	b/d	19	748				

Exercises

MC37 A debit balance of £100 in a cash account shows that:
(A) There was £100 cash in hand
(B) Cash has been overspent by £100
(C) £100 was the total of cash paid out
(D) The total of cash received was less than £100.

MC38 £50 cash taken from the cash till and banked is entered:
(A) Debit cash column £50: Credit bank column £50
(B) Debit bank column £50: Credit cash column £50
(C) Debit cash column £50: Credit cash column £50
(D) Debit bank column £50: Credit bank column £50.

MC39 A credit balance of £200 on the cash columns of the cash book would mean
(A) We have spent £200 more cash than we have received
(B) We have £200 cash in hand
(C) The book-keeper has made a mistake
(D) Someone has stolen £200 cash.

13.1. Write up a two-column cash book from the following details, and balance off as at the end of the month:

19-5

May 1 Started business with capital in cash £100
,, 2 Paid rent by cash £10
,, 3 F. Lake lent us £500, paying by cheque
,, 4 We paid B. McKenzie by cheque £65
,, 5 Cash sales £98
,, 7 N. Miller paid us by cheque £62
,, 9 We paid B. Burton in cash £22
,, 11 Cash sales paid direct into the bank £53
,, 15 G. Moores paid us in cash £65
,, 16 We took £50 out of the cash till and paid it into the bank account
,, 19 We repaid F. Lake £100 by cheque
,, 22 Cash sales paid direct into the bank £66
,, 26 Paid motor expenses by cheque £12
,, 30 Withdrew £100 cash from the bank for business use
,, 31 Paid wages in cash £97.

13.2. Write up a two-column cash book from the following details, and balance off as at the end of the month:

19-6

Mar 1 Balances brought down from last month:
     Cash in hand £56: Cash in bank £2,356
,, 2 Paid rates by cheque £156
,, 3 Paid for postage stamps in cash £5
,, 5 Cash sales £74
,, 7 Cash paid into bank £60
,, 8 We paid T. Lee by cheque £75: We paid C. Brooks in cash £2
,, 12 J. Moores pays us £150, £50 being in cash and £100 by cheque
,, 17 Cash drawings by proprietor £20
,, 20 P. Jones pays us by cheque £79
,, 22 Withdrew £200 from the bank for business use
,, 24 Bought a new motor van for £195 cash
,, 28 Paid rent by cheque £40
,, 31 Cash sales paid direct into the bank £105.

13.3A. A two-column cash book is to be written up from the following, carrying the balances down to the following month:

19-4

Jan 1 Started business with £4,000 in the bank
,, 2 Paid for fixtures by cheque £660
,, 4 Cash sales £225: Paid rent by cash £140
,, 6 T. Thomas paid us by cheque £188
,, 8 Cash sales paid direct into the bank £308
,, 10 J. King paid us in cash £300
,, 12 Paid wages in cash £275
,, 14 J. Walters lent us £500 paying by cheque
,, 15 Withdrew £200 from the bank for business use
,, 20 Bought stationery paying by cash £60
,, 22 We paid J. French by cheque £166
,, 28 Cash Drawings £100
,, 30 J. Scott paid us by cheque £277
,, 31 Cash Sales £66.

13.4A. Write up a two-column cash book from the following:

19-6

Nov 1 Balance brought forward from last month: Cash £105; Bank £2,164
,, 2 Cash Sales £605
,, 3 Took £500 out of the cash till and paid it into the bank
,, 4 J. Matthews paid us by cheque £217
,, 5 We paid for postage stamps in cash £60
,, 6 Bought office equipment by cheque £189
,, 7 We paid J. Lucas by cheque £50
,, 9 Received rates refund by cheque £72
,, 11 Withdrew £250 from the bank for business use
,, 12 Paid wages in cash £239
,, 14 Paid motor expenses by cheque £57
,, 16 L. Levy lent us £200 in cash
,, 20 R. Norman paid us by cheque £112
,, 28 We paid general expenses in cash £22
,, 30 Paid insurance by cheque £74.

14

Cash Discounts and the Three Column Cash Book

Cash Discounts

To encourage customers to pay their accounts promptly a firm may offer to accept a lesser sum in full settlement providing payment is made within a specified period of time. The amount of the reduction of the sum to be paid is known as a cash discount. The term 'cash discount' thus refers to the allowance given for speedy payment, it is still called cash discount, even if the account is paid by cheque.

The rate of cash discount is usually quoted as a percentage, and full details of the percentage allowed and the period within which payment is to be made are quoted on all sales documents by the selling company. A typical period during which discount may be allowed is one month from the date of the original transaction.

A firm will meet with cash discounts in two different ways. First, it may allow cash discounts to firms to whom it sells goods, and second it may receive cash discounts from firms from whom it buys goods. To be able to distinguish easily between the two, the first kind are known as Discounts Allowed, the second kind are known as Discounts Received.

We can now see the effect of discounts by looking at two examples.

Example 1

W. Clarke owed us £100. He pays on 2 September 19-5 by cash within the time limit laid down, and the firm allows him 5 per cent cash discount. Thus he will pay £100 − £5 = £95 in full settlement of his account.

Effect	Action
1. Of cash: Cash is increased by £95.	Debit cash account, i.e. enter £95 in debit column of cash book.
Asset of debtors is decreased by £95.	Credit W. Clarke £95.

Effect	Action
2. Of discounts:	
Asset of debtors is decreased by £5. (After the cash was paid the balance still appeared of £5. As the account is deemed to be settled this asset must now be cancelled.)	Credit W. Clarke £5.
Expenses of discounts allowed increased by £5.	Debit discounts allowed account £5.

Example 2

The firm owed W. Small £400. It pays him on 3 September 19-5 by cheque within the time limit laid down by him and he allows 2½ per cent cash discount. Thus the firm will pay £400 − £10 = £390 in full settlement of the account.

Effect	Action
1. Of cheque:	
Asset of bank is reduced by £390.	Credit bank, i.e. enter in credit bank column, £390.
Liability of creditors is reduced by £390.	Debit W. Small's account £390.
2. Of discounts:	
Liability of creditors is reduced by £10. (After the cheque was paid the balance of £10 remained. As the account is deemed to be settled the liability must now be cancelled.)	Debit W. Small's account £10.
Revenue of discounts received increased by £10.	Credit discounts received account £10.

The accounts in the firm's books would appear:

Cash Book (Page 32)

			Cash	Bank				Cash	Bank
19-5			£	£	19-5			£	£
Sept 2	W. Clarke	SL12	95		Sept 3	W. Small	PL75		390

Discounts Received (General Ledger page 18)

				19-5			£
				Sept 2	W. Small	PL75	10

Discounts Allowed (General Ledger page 17)

19-5		£
Sept 2 W. Clarke SL12		5

W. Clarke (Sales Ledger page 12)

19-5		£	19-5		£
Sept 1 Balance b/d		100	Sept 2 Cash	CB32	95
		___	,, 2 Discount	GL17	5
		100			100

W. Small (Purchases Ledger page 75)

19-5		£	19-5	£
Sept 3 Bank	CB32	390	Sept 1 Balance b/d	400
,, 3 Discount	GL18	10		
		400		400

It is the accounting custom merely to enter the word 'Discount' in the personal account, not stating whether it is a discount received or a discount allowed. This is obviously to save time as the full description against each discount would be unnecessary. After all, the sales ledger accounts will only contain discounts allowed, and the purchases ledger accounts will only contain discounts received.

The discounts allowed account and the discounts received account are contained in the general ledger along with all the other revenue and expense accounts. It has already been stated that every effort should be made to avoid constant reference to the general ledger. In the case of discounts this is achieved quite simply by adding an extra column on each side of the cash book in which the amounts of discounts are entered. Discounts received are entered in the discounts column on the credit side of the cash book, and discounts allowed in the discounts column on the debit side of the cash book.

The cash book, if completed for the two examples so far dealt with, would appear:

Cash Book

	Discount	Cash	Bank		Discount	Cash	Bank
19-5	£	£	£	19-5	£	£	£
Sept 2 W. Clarke SL12	5	95		Sept 3 W. Small PL75	10		390

There is no alteration to the method of showing discounts in the personal accounts.

The discounts columns in the cash book are not however part of the double entry system. They are merely lists of discounts. Half of the double entry has already been made in the personal accounts.

What is now required is the entry in the discounts accounts. The way that is done in this case is by transferring the total of the discounts received column to the credit of a discounts received account, and the total of the discounts allowed account is transferred to the debit of a discounts allowed account.

This at first sight appears to be incorrect. How can a debit total be transferred to the debit of an account? Here one must look at the entries for discounts in the personal accounts. Discounts allowed have been entered on the credit sides of the individual personal accounts. The entry of the total in the expense account of discount allowed must therefore be on the debit side to preserve double entry balancing. The opposite sides apply to discounts received.

The following is a worked example of a three-column cash book for the whole of a month, showing the ultimate transfer of the totals of the discount columns to the discount accounts.

19-5		£
May 1	Balances brought down from April:	
	Cash Balance	29
	Bank Balance	654
	Debtors accounts:	
	B. King	120
	N. Campbell	280
	D. Shand	40
	Creditors accounts:	
	U. Barrow	60
	A. Allen	440
	R. Long	100
,, 2	B. King pays us by cheque, having deducted 2½ per cent cash discount £3	117
,, 8	We pay R. Long his account by cheque, deducting 5 per cent cash discount £5	95
,, 11	We withdrew £100 cash from the bank for business use	100
,, 16	N. Campbell pays us his account by cheque, deducting 2½ per cent discount £7	273
,, 25	We paid wages in cash	92
,, 28	D. Shand pays us in cash after having deducted 2½ per cent cash discount	38
,, 29	We pay U. Barrow by cheque less 5 per cent cash discount £3	57
,, 30	We pay A. Allen by cheque less 2½ per cent cash discount £11	429

Cash Book — Page 64

	Folio	Discount	Cash	Bank		Folio	Discount	Cash	Bank
19-5		£	£	£	19-5		£	£	£
May 1					May 8				
Balances	b/d		29	654	R. Long	PL58	5		95
May 2					May 11				
B. King	SL13	3		117	Cash	C			100
May 11					May 25				
Bank	C		100		Wages	GL77		92	
May 16					May 29				
N. Campbell	SL84	7		273	U. Barrow	PL15	3		57
May 28					May 30				
D. Shand	SL91	2	38		A. Allen	PL98	11		429
					May 31				
					Balances	c/d		75	363
		12	167	1,044			19	167	1,044
Jun 1 Balances	b/d		75	363					

Sales Ledger

B. King — Page 13

19-5		£	19-5			£
May 1	Balance b/d	120	May 2	Bank	CB 64	117
			,, 2	Discount	CB 64	3
		120				120

N. Campbell — Page 84

19-5		£	19-5			£
May 1	Balance b/d	280	May 16	Bank	CB 64	273
			,, 16	Discount	CB 64	7
		280				280

D. Shand — Page 91

19-5		£	19-5			£
May 1	Balance b/d	40	May 28	Cash	CB 64	38
			,, 28	Discount	CB 64	2
		40				40

Purchases Ledger

U. Barrow — Page 15

19-5			£			£
May 29	Bank	CB 64	57	May 1	Balance b/d	60
,, 29	Discount	CB 64	3			
			60			60

R. Long — Page 58

19-5			£	19-5		£
May 8	Bank	CB 64	95	May 1	Balance b/d	100
,, 8	Discount	CB 64	5			
			100			100

A. Allen — Page 98

19-5			£	19-5		£
May 30	Bank	CB 64	429	May 1	Balance b/d	440
,, 30	Discount	CB 64	11			
			440			440

General Ledger
Wages

19-5			£
May 25 Cash	CB 64	92	

Discounts Received

			19-5		£
			May 31 Total for the month	CB 64	19

Discounts Allowed

19-5			£
May 31 Total for the month	CB 64	12	

As you can check, the discounts received entered in all of the purchases ledger accounts are £3 + £5 + £11 = £19 on the debit side; the total entered in the discounts received account on the credit side amounts also to £19. Thus double-entry principles are upheld. A check on the discounts allowed will reveal a debit of £12 in the discounts allowed account and a total of £3 + £7 + £2 = £12 on the credit side of the accounts in the sales ledger.

Bank Overdrafts

A firm may borrow money from a bank by means of a bank overdraft. This means that the firm is allowed to pay more out of the bank account, by paying out cheques, for a total amount greater than that which it has placed in the account.

Up to this point the bank balances have all represented money at the bank, thus they have all been assets, i.e. debit balances. When the account is overdrawn the firm owes money to the bank, the account is a liability and the balance becomes a credit one.

Taking the cash book last illustrated, suppose that the amount payable to A. Allen was £1,429 instead of £429. Thus the amount placed in the account, £1,044, is exceeded by the amount withdrawn. The Cash book would appear as follows:

Cash Book

	Discount	Cash	Bank		Discount	Cash	Bank
19-5	£	£	£	19-5	£	£	£
May 1 Balances b/d		29	654	May 8 R. Long	5		95
,, 2 B. King	3		117	,, 11 Cash			100
,, 11 Bank		100		,, 25 Wages		92	
,, 16 N. Campbell	7		273	,, 29 U. Barrow	3		57
,, 28 D. Shand	2	38		,, 30 A. Allen	11		1,429
,, 31 Balance c/d			637	,, 31 Balance c/d		75	
	12	167	1,681		19	167	1,681
Jun 1 Balance b/d		75		Jun 1 Balance b/d			637

On a balance sheet a bank overdraft will be shown as an item included under the heading Current Liabilities.

Exercises

MC40 A cash discount is BEST described as a reduction in the sum to be paid
(A) If payment is made within a previously agreed period
(B) If payment is made by cash, not cheque
(C) If payment is made either by cash or cheque
(D) If purchases are made for cash, not on credit.

MC41 Discounts Received are
(A) Deducted when we receive cash
(B) Given by us when we sell goods on credit
(C) Deducted by us when we pay our accounts
(D) None of these.

MC42 The total of the Discounts Allowed column in the Cash Book is posted to
(A) the debit of the Discounts Allowed Account
(B) the debit of the Discounts Received Account
(C) the credit of the Discounts Allowed Account
(D) the credit of the Discounts Received Account.

MC43 An invoice shows a total of £240 less 2½ per cent cash discount. If paid in time the cheque paid would be for
(A) £228
(B) £220
(C) £216
(D) £234.

14.1. Enter up a three column cash book from the details following. Balance off at the end of the month, and show the relevant discount accounts as they would appear in the general ledger.

19-7
May 1 Started business with £6,000 in the bank
,, 1 Bought fixtures paying by cheque £950
,, 2 Bought goods paying by cheque £1,240
,, 3 Cash Sales £407
,, 4 Paid rent in cash £200
,, 5 N. Morgan paid us his account of £220 by a cheque for £210, we allowed him £10 discount
,, 7 Paid S. Thompson & Co £80 owing to them by means of a cheque £76, they allowed us £4 discount
,, 9 We received a cheque for £380 from S. Cooper, discount having been allowed £20
,, 12 Paid rates by cheque £410
,, 14 L. Curtis pays us a cheque for £115
,, 16 Paid M. Monroe his account of £120 by cash £114, having deducted £6 cash discount
,, 20 P. Exeter pays us a cheque for £78, having deducted £2 cash discount
,, 31 Cash Sales paid direct into the bank £88.

14.2. A three column cash book is to be written up from the following details, balanced off and the relevant discount accounts in the general ledger shown.

19-5

Mar 1   Balances brought forward: Cash £230; Bank £4,756

,,   2   The following paid their accounts by cheque, in each case deducting 5 per cent cash discounts; Accounts: R. Burton £140; E. Taylor £220; R. Harris £300

,,   4   Paid rent by cheque £120

,,   6   J. Cotton lent us £1,000 paying by cheque

,,   8   We paid the following accounts by cheque in each case deducting a 2½ per cent cash discount; N. Black £360; P. Towers £480; C. Rowse £800.

,, 10 Paid motor expenses in cash £44

,, 12 H. Hankins pays his account of £77 by cheque £74, deducting £3 cash discount

,, 15 Paid wages in cash £160

,, 18 The following paid their accounts by cheque, in each case deducting 5 per cent cash discount: Accounts: C. Winston £260; R. Wilson & Son £340; H. Winter £460

,, 21 Cash withdrawn from the bank £350 for business use

,, 24 Cash Drawings £120

,, 25 Paid T. Briers his account of £140, by cash £133, having deducted £7 cash discount

,, 29 Bought fixtures paying by cheque £650

,, 31 Received commission by cheque £88.

14.3. From the following details write up a three-column cash book, balance off at the end of the month, and show the relevant discount accounts as they would appear in the general ledger:

19-3

Mar 1   Balances brought forward:

             Cash in hand £211

             Cash at bank £3,984

,,   2   We paid each of the following accounts by cheque, in each case we deducted a 5 per cent discount: T. Adams £80; C. Bibby £260; D. Clarke £440

,,   4   C. Potts pays us a cheque for £98

,,   6   Cash Sales paid direct into the bank £49

,,   7   Paid insurance by cash £65

,,   9   The following persons pay us their accounts by cheque, in each case they deducted a discount of 2½ per cent: R. Smiley £160; J. Turner £640; R. Pimlott £520

,, 12 Paid motor expenses by cash £100

,, 18 Cash Sales £98

,, 21 Paid salaries by cheque £120

,, 23 Paid rent by cash £60

,, 28 Received a cheque for £500 being a loan from R. Godfrey

,, 31 Paid for stationery by cheque £27.

14.4A. Enter the following in a three column cash book. Balance off the cash book at the end of the month and show the discount accounts in the general ledger.

19-8
June 1 Balances brought forward: Cash £97; Bank £2,186.
,,   2 The following paid us by cheque in each case deducting a 5 per cent cash discount: R. Harris £1,000; C. White £280; P. Peers £180; O. Hardy £600
,,   3 Cash Sales paid direct into the bank £134
,,   5 Paid rent by cash £88
,,   6 We paid the following accounts by cheque, in each case deducting 2½ per cent cash discount J. Charlton £400; H. Sobers £640; D. Shallcross £200
,,   8 Withdrew cash from the bank for business use £250
,, 10 Cash Sales £206
,, 12 D. Deeds paid us their account of £89 by cheque less £2 cash discount
,, 14 Paid wages by cash £250
,, 16 We paid the following accounts by cheque: L. Lucas £117 less cash discount £6; D. Fisher £206 less cash discount £8
,, 20 Bought fixtures by cheque £8,000
,, 24 Bought motor lorry paying by cheque £7,166
,, 29 Received £169 cheque from D. Steel
,, 30 Cash Sales £116
,, 30 Bought stationery paying by cash £60.

14.5A. You are to write up a three column cash book for M. Pinero from the details which follow. Then balance off at the end of the month and show the discount accounts in the general ledger.

19-6
May 1 Balances brought forward:
            Cash in hand £58
            Bank overdraft £1,470
,,   2 M. Pinero pays further Capital into the bank £1,000
,,   3 Bought office fixtures by cheque £780
,,   4 Cash Sales £220
,,   5 Banked cash £200
,,   6 We paid the following by cheque, in each case deducting 2½ per cent cash discount: B. Barnes £80; T. Horton £240; T. Jacklin £400
,,   8 Cash Sales £500
,, 12 Paid motor expenses in cash £77
,, 15 Cash withdrawn from the bank £400
,, 16 Cash Drawings £120
,, 18 The following firms paid us their accounts by cheque, in each case deducting a 5 per cent discount: L. Graham £80; B. Crenshaw £140; H. Green £220
,, 20 Salaries paid in cash £210
,, 22 T. Weiskopf paid us his account in cash £204
,, 26 Paid insurance by cheque £150
,, 28 We banked all the cash in our possession except for £20 in the cash till
,, 31 Bought motor van, paying by cheque £4,920.

15

The Sales Journal

You have read in Chapter 11 that the recording of transactions has been divided up into the various functions of the business. Mention has been made on page 89 of the fact that, in order to keep the general ledger free from unnecessary detail, separate journals are kept for credit transactions concerning sales and purchases. The Sales Journal can now be examined in detail.

There will be many businesses, such as a lot of retail shops, where all the sales will be cash sales. On the other hand, in many businesses a considerable proportion of sales will be made on credit rather than for immediate cash. In fact, the sales of some businesses will consist entirely of credit sales. For each credit sale the selling firm will send a document to the buyer showing full details of the goods sold and the prices of the goods. This document is known as an Invoice, and to the seller it is known as a Sales Invoice. The seller will keep one or more copies of each sales invoice for his own use. Exhibit 15.1 is an example of an invoice.

Exhibit 15.1

Your Purchase Order 10/A/980		J. Blake 7 Over Warehouse Leicester LE1 2AP 1 September 19-5
INVOICE No. 16554		
To: D. Prendergast 45 Charles Street Manchester M1 5ZN		
	Per unit	Total
	£	£
21 cases McBrand Pears	20	420
5 cartons Kay's Flour	4	20
6 cases Joy's Vinegar	20	120
		560
Terms: 1¼% cash discount if paid within one month		

You must not think that all invoices will look exactly like the one chosen as Exhibit 15.1. Each business will have its own design. All invoices will be numbered, and they will contain the names and addresses both of the supplier and of the customer. In this case the supplier is J. Blake and the customer is D. Prendergast.

As soon as the sales invoices for the goods being sent have been made out, whether they are typed, hand-written, or produced by a computer, they are then despatched to the customer. The firm will keep copies of all these sales invoices. These copies will have been automatically produced at the same time as the original, usually by using some form of carbon paper or special copying paper.

It is from the copy sales invoices that the seller enters up his sales journal. This book is merely a list, in date order, of each sales invoice, showing the date, the name of the the firm to whom the goods have been sold, the number of the invoice for reference purposes, and the net amount of the invoice. There is no need to show in the sales journal a description of the goods sold, as this information can be found by referring to the copy of the sales invoice which will have been filed after recording it in the sales journal. The practice of copying all the details of the goods sold in the sales journal finished many years ago.

We can now look at Exhibit 15.2, which is a sales journal, starting with the record of the sales invoice already shown in Exhibit 15.1.

Exhibit 15.2

	Sales Journal		
	Invoice No.	Folio	Page 26
19-5			£
Sept 1 D. Prendergast	16554	SL 12	560
,, 8 T. Cockburn	16555	SL 39	1,640
,, 28 C. Carter	16556	SL 125	220
,, 30 D. Stevens & Co	16557	SL 249	1,100
Transferred to Sales Account		GL 44	3,520

The entry of these credit sales in the customers' accounts in the sales ledger keeps to the same principles of personal accounts as described in earlier chapters. Apart from the fact that the customers' accounts are now contained in a separate book known as the sales ledger, and that the reference numbers in the folio columns will be different, each individual personal account is the same as previous. The act of using the sales journal entries as the basis for entering up the customers' accounts is known as 'posting' the sales journal.

Sales Ledger

D. Prendergast   Page 12

19-5			£
Sept 1 Sales	SJ 26		560

T. Cockburn   Page 39

19-5			£
Sept 8 Sales	SJ 26		1,640

C. Carter   Page 125

19-5			£
Sept 28 Sales	SJ 26		220

D. Stevens & Co   Page 249

19-5			£
Sept 30 Sales	SJ 26		1,100

You can see that the customers' personal accounts have been debited with a total of £3,520 for these sales. However, as yet no credit entry has been made for these items. The sales journal is simply a list, it is not an account and is therefore not a part of the double-entry system. We must complete double-entry however, and this is done by taking the total of the sales journal for the period and entering it on the credit side of the sales account in the general ledger.

General Ledger

Sales   Page 44

	19-5		£
	Sept 30 Credit Sales for		
	the month SJ 26		3,520

If you now compare this with entries that would have been made when all the accounts were kept in one ledger, the overall picture should become clearer. The eventual answer is the same, personal accounts would have been debited with credit sales amounting in total to £3,520 and the sales account would have been credited with sales amounting in total to £3,520. The differences are now that first the personal accounts are contained in a separate sales ledger, and second, the individual items of credit sales have been listed in the sales journal, merely the total being credited to the sales account. The different books in use also mean a change in the reference numbers in the folio columns.

Alternative names for the Sales Journal are Sales Book and Sales Day Book.

Before you proceed further you are to attempt question 15.1.

Trade Discounts

Suppose you are the proprietor of a business. You are selling to three different kinds of customers:

(a) Traders who buy a lot of goods from you.
(b) Traders who buy only a few items from you.
(c) Direct to the general public.

The traders themselves have to sell the goods to the general public in their own areas. They have to make a profit to help finance their businesses, so they will want to pay you less than retail price.

The traders (a) who buy in large quantities will not want to pay as much as traders (b) who buy in small quantities. You want to attract such large customers, and so you are happy to sell to traders (a) at a lower price.

All of this means that your selling prices are at three levels: (a) to traders buying large quantities, (b) to traders buying small quantities, and (c) to the general public.

To save your staff from dealing with three different price lists, (a), (b) and (c), all goods are shown at the same price. However, a reduction (discount), called a *trade discount,* is given to traders (a) and (b).

Example

You are selling a make of food mixing machine. The basic price is £200. Traders (a) are given 25 per cent trade discount, traders (b) 20 per cent, the general public get no trade discount. The prices paid by each type of customer would be:

	Trader (a) £	Trader (b) £	General Public (c) £
Basic Price	200	200	200
Less Trade discount	(25%) 50	(20%) 40	nil
Price to be paid by customer	150	160	200

Exhibit 15.3 is an invoice for goods sold to D. Prendergast. It is for the same items as were shown in Exhibit 15.1, but this time the seller is R. Grant and he uses trade discounts to get to the price paid by his customers.

Exhibit 15.3

	Your Purchase Order 11/A/G80		R. Grant Higher Side Preston PR1 2NL 2 September 19-5

INVOICE No. 30756

To: D. Prendergast
45 Charles Street
Manchester M1 5ZN

	Per unit	Total
	£	£
21 cases McBrand Pears	25	525
5 cartons Kays' Flour	5	25
6 cases Joys' Vinegar	25	150
		700
Less 20% Trade discount		140
		560

By comparing Exhibits 15.1 and 15.3 you can see that the prices paid by D. Prendergast were the same. It is simply the method of calculating the price that is different.

As Trade Discount is simply a way of calculating sales prices, no entry for trade discount should be made in the double entry records nor in the Sales Journal. The record of this item in R. Grant's Sales Journal and Prendergast's personal account will appear:

Sales Journal

		Invoice No.	Folio	Page 87
19-5				£
Sept 2 D. Prendergast		30756	SL 32	560

Sales Ledger (page 32)

D. Prendergast

19-5		£
Sept 2 Sales	SJ87	560

This is in complete contrast to *Cash Discounts* which are shown in the double-entry accounts.

There are in fact several other reasons for using Trade Discounts to the one described in this chapter. However, the calculation of the Trade Discount and its display on the invoice will remain the same as that described in this book.

Exercises

MC44 Sales Invoices are first entered in
(A) The Cash Book
(B) The Purchases Journal
(C) The Sales Account
(D) The Sales Journal.

MC45 The total of the Sales Journal is entered on
(A) The credit side of the Sales Account in the General Ledger
(B) The credit side of the General Account in the Sales Ledger
(C) The debit side of the Sales Account in the General Ledger
(D) The debit side of the Sales Day Book.

MC46 Given a purchases invoice showing 5 items of £80, each less trade discount of 25 per cent and cash discount of 5 per cent, if paid within the credit period, your cheque would be made out for
(A) £285
(B) £280
(C) £260
(D) None of these.

MC47 An alternative name for a Sales Journal is
(A) Sales Invoice
(B) Sales Day Book
(C) Daily Sales
(D) Sales Ledger.

15.1. You are to enter up the sales journal from the following details. Post the items to the relevant accounts in the sales ledger and then show the transfer to the sales account in the general ledger.

19-6

Mar	1	Credit sales to J. Gordon	£187
,,	3	Credit sales to G. Abrahams	£166
,,	6	Credit sales to V. White	£12
,,	10	Credit sales to J. Gordon	£55
,,	17	Credit sales to F. Williams	£289
,,	19	Credit sales to U. Richards	£66
,,	27	Credit sales to V. Wood	£28
,,	31	Credit sales to L. Simes	£78

15.2A. Enter up the sales journal from the following, then post the items to the relevant accounts in the sales ledger. Then show the transfer to the sales account in the general ledger.

19-8

May	1	Credit sales to J. Johnson	£305
,,	3	Credit sales to T. Royes	£164
,,	5	Credit sales to B. Howe	£45
,,	7	Credit sales to M. Lee	£100
,,	16	Credit sales to J. Jakes	£308
,,	23	Credit sales to A. Vinden	£212
,,	30	Credit sales to J. Samuels	£1,296

15.3. F. Benjamin of 10 Lower Street, Plymouth, is selling the following items, the recommended retail prices as shown: white tape £10 per roll, green baize at £4 per metre, blue cotton at £6 per sheet, black silk at £20 per dress length. He makes the following sales:

19-7

May 1   To F. Gray, 3 Keswick Road, Portsmouth: 3 rolls white tape, 5 sheets blue cotton, 1 dress length black silk. Less 25 per cent trade discount.

,, 4   To A. Gray, 1. Shilton Road, Preston: 6 rolls white tape, 30 metres green baize. Less 33⅓ per cent trade discount.

,, 8   To E. Hines, 1 High Road, Malton: 1 dress length black silk. No trade discount.

,, 20   To M. Allen, 1 Knott Road, Southport: 10 rolls white tape, 6 sheets blue cotton, 3 dress lengths black silk, 11 metres green baize. Less 25 per cent trade discount.

,, 31   To B. Cooper, 1 Tops Lane, St. Andrews: 12 rolls white tape, 14 sheets blue cotton, 9 metres green baise. Less 33⅓ per cent trade discount.

You are to (*a*) draw up a sales invoice for each of the above sales, (*b*) enter them up in the Sales Journal, post to the personal accounts, (*c*) transfer the total to the Sales Account in the General Ledger.

15.4A. J. Fisher, White House, Bolton, is selling the following items, the retail prices as shown: plastic tubing at £1 per metre, polythene sheeting at £2 per length, vinyl padding at £5 per box, foam rubber at £3 per sheet. He makes the following sales:

19-5

June 1   To A. Portsmouth, 5 Rockley Road, Worthing: 22 metres plastic tubing, 6 sheets foam rubber, 4 boxes vinyl padding. Less 25 per cent trade discount.

,, 5   To B. Butler, 1 Wembley Road, Colwyn Bay: 50 lengths polythene sheeting, 8 boxes vinyl padding, 20 sheets foam rubber. Less 20 per cent trade discount.

,, 11   To A. Gate, 1 Bristol Road, Hastings: 4 metres plastic tubing, 33 lengths of polythene sheeting, 30 sheets foam rubber. Less 25 per cent trade discount.

,, 21   To L. Mackeson, 5 Maine Road, Bath: 29 metres plastic tubing. No trade discount is given.

,, 30   To M. Alison, Daley Road, Box Hill: 32 metres plastic tubing, 24 lengths polythene sheeting, 20 boxes vinyl padding. Less 33⅓ per cent trade discount.

Required:
(*a*) Draw up a sales invoice for each of the above sales, (*b*) then enter up in the Sales Journal and post to the personal accounts, (*c*) transfer the total to the Sales Account in the general ledger.

16

The Purchases Journal

When a firm buys goods on credit it will receive an invoice from the seller for those goods. In the last chapter, Exhibit 15.1, J. Blake sold goods to D. Prendergast and sent an invoice with those goods.

To the seller, J. Blake, that invoice is a sales invoice. To the buyer, D. Prendergast, that same invoice is regarded as a purchases invoice. This often confuses students. What we have to do to identify whether or not an invoice is a sales invoice or a purchases invoice is to think about it from the point of view as to which firm's books we are entering up. If the firm is the buyer of the goods then the invoice is a purchases invoice.

The net amount of the invoice, i.e. after deduction of trade discount, is listed in the purchases journal and the items are then posted to the credit of the personal accounts in the purchases ledger. The invoice is then filed away for future reference. At the end of the period the total of the purchases journal is transferred to the debit of the purchases account in the general ledger. An example of a purchase journal and the posting of the entries to the purchases ledger and the total to the purchases account is now shown:

Purchases Journal

	Invoice No.	Folio	Page 49
19-5			£
Sept 2 R. Simpson	9/101	PL 16	670
,, 8 B. Hamilton	9/102	PL 29	1,380
,, 19 C. Brown	9/103	PL 55	120
,, 30 K. Gabriel	9/104	PL 89	510
Transferred to Purchases Account		GL63	2,680

Purchases Ledger
R. Simpson

				£
19-5				
Sept	2	Purchases	P J 49	670

B. Hamilton
Page 29

				£
19-5				
Sept	8	Purchases	P J 49	1,380

C. Brown
Page 55

				£
19-5				
Sept	19	Purchases	P J 49	120

K. Gabriel
Page 89

				£
19-5				
Sept	30	Purchases	P J 49	510

General Ledger
Purchases
Page 63

19-5		£
Sept 30 Credit purchases for the month	P J 49	2,680

The Purchases Journal is often known also as the Purchases Book or as the Purchases Day Book.

Exercises

MC48 Entered in the Purchases Journal are
(A) Payments to Suppliers
(B) Trade Discounts
(C) Purchases Invoices
(D) Discounts Received.

MC49 The total of the Purchases Journal is transferred to the
(A) Credit side of the Purchases Account
(B) Debit side of the Purchases Day Book
(C) Credit side of the Purchases Book
(D) Debit side of the Purchases Account.

16.1. B. Mann has the following purchases for the month of May 19-4:

19-4

May 1   From K. King: 4 radios at £30 each, 3 music centres at £160 each. Less 25 per cent trade discount.

,,   3   From A. Bell: 2 washing machines at £200 each, 5 vacuum cleaners at £60 each, 2 dish dryers at £150 each. Less 20 per cent trade discount.

,, 15   From J. Kelly: 1 music centre at £300 each, 2 washing machines at £250 each. Less 25 per cent trade discount.

,, 20   From B. Powell: 6 radios at £70 each, less $33\frac{1}{3}$ per cent trade discount.

,, 30   From B. Lewis: 4 dish dryers at £200 each, less 20 per cent trade discount.

Required:

(a) Enter up the Purchases Journal for the month.

(b) Post the transactions to the suppliers' accounts.

(c) Transfer the total to the Purchases Account.

16.2A. A. Rowland has the following purchases for the month of June 19-9:

19-9

June 2   From C. Lee: 2 sets golf clubs at £250 each. 5 footballs at £20 each. Less 25 per cent trade discount.

,, 11   From M. Elliott: 6 cricket bats at £20 each, 6 ice skates at £30 each, 4 rugby balls at £25 each. Less 25 per cent trade discount.

,, 18   From B. Wood: 6 sets golf trophies at £100 each, 4 sets golf clubs at £300. Less $33\frac{1}{3}$ per cent trade discount.

,, 25   From B. Parkinson: 5 cricket bats at £40 each. Less 25 per cent trade discount.

,, 30   From N. Francis: 8 goal posts at £70 each. Less 25 per cent trade discount.

Required:

(a) Enter up the Purchases Journal for the month.

(b) Post the items to the suppliers' accounts.

(c) Transfer the total to the Purchases Account.

16.3. C. Phillips, a sole trader, has the following purchases and sales for March 19-5:

19-5

Mar 1   Bought from Smith Stores: silk £40, cotton £80, all less 25 per cent trade discount

,, 8   Sold to A. Grantley: linen goods £28, woollen items £44. No trade discount

,, 15   Sold to A. Henry: silk £36, linen £144, cotton goods £120. All less 20 per cent trade discount

,, 23   Bought from C. Kelly: cotton £88, linen £52. All less 25 per cent trade discount

,, 24   Sold to D. Sangster: linen goods £42, cotton £48. Less 10 per cent trade discount

,, 31   Bought from J. Hamilton: linen goods £270 less $33\frac{1}{3}$ per cent trade discount.

Required:

(a) Prepare the Purchases and Sales Journals of C. Phillips from the above.

(b) Post the items to the personal accounts.

(c) Post the totals of the journals to the Sales and Purchases Accounts.

16.4A. A. Henriques has the following purchases and sales for May 19-6:

19-6

May 1 Sold to M. Marshall: brass goods £24, bronze items £36. Less 25 per cent trade discount

  ,,   7 Sold to R. Richards: tin goods £70, lead items £230. Less 33⅓ per cent trade discount

  ,,   9 Bought from C. Clarke: tin goods £400 less 40 per cent trade discount

  ,, 16 Bought from A. Charles: copper goods £320 less 50 per cent trade discount

  ,, 23 Sold to T. Young: tin goods £50, brass items £70, lead figures £80. All less 20 per cent trade discount

  ,, 31 Bought from M. Nelson: brass figures £100 less 50 per cent trade discount.

Required:

(a) Write up Sales and Purchases Journals.

(b) Post the items to the personal accounts.

(c) Post the totals of the journals to the Sales and Purchases Accounts.

17

The Returns Journals

The Returns Inwards Journal

Sometimes we will agree to customers returning goods to us. It may be that they had been sent goods of the wrong colour, the wrong type etc., or simply that the customer had found that he had bought more than he needed. At other times goods will have been supplied and there will be something wrong with them. The customer may agree to keep the goods if an allowance is given so as to reduce their price.

In each of these cases a document known as a 'credit note' will be sent to the customer, showing the amount of the allowance given by us in respect of the returns or of the faulty goods. The term 'credit note' takes its name from the fact that the customer's account will be credited with the amount of the allowance, so as to show the reduction in the amount owing by him.

Exhibit 17.1

		R. Grant, Higher Side, Preston PR1 2NL 8 September 19-5
To: D. Prendergast 45 Charles Street, Manchester M1 5ZN		
CREDIT NOTE No. 9/37		
	Per Unit	Total
	£ 25	£ 50
2 cases McBrand Pears *Less* 20% Trade Discount		10 — 40 =

Very often credit notes are printed in red so that they are easily distinguishable from invoices.

Imagine that the firm of D. Prendergast to whom goods were sold on 1 September 19-5 as per Exhibit 15.3 returned some of the goods on 8 September 19-5. The credit note might appear as shown in Exhibit 17.1.

The credit notes are listed in a Returns Inwards Journal which is then used to post the items to the credit of the personal accounts in the sales ledger. To complete the double entry the total of the returns inwards book for the period is transferred to the debit of the Returns Inwards Account in the general ledger.

An example of a returns inwards book showing the items posted to the sales ledger and the general ledger is now shown:

Returns Inwards Journal

	Note No.	Folio	Page 10
19-5			£
Sept 8 D. Prendergast	9/37	SL 12	40
,, 17 A. Brewster	9/38	SL 58	120
,, 19 C. Vickers	9/39	SL 99	290
,, 29 M. Nelson	9/40	SL 112	160
Transferred to Returns Inwards Account		GL 114	610

Sales Ledger
D. Prendergast
Page 12

		£
19-5		
Sept 8 Returns		
Inwards	RI 10	40

A. Brewster
Page 58

		£
19-5		
Sept 17 Returns		
Inwards	RI 10	120

C. Vickers
Page 99

		£
19-5		
Sept 19 Returns		
Inwards	RI 10	290

M. Nelson
Page 112

		£
19-5		
Sept 29 Returns		
Inwards	RI 10	160

19-5			£
Sept 30 Returns for the month	RI 10		610

Alternative names in use for the returns inwards journal are Returns Inwards Book or Sales Returns Book, the latter name arising from the fact that it is the sales which are returned at a later date.

The Returns Outwards Journal

The exact opposite to returns inwards is when goods are returned to a supplier. A document called a 'debit note' is sent to the supplier stating the amount of allowance to which the firm returning the goods is entitled. The debit note could also cover allowances due because the goods bought were deficient in some way. The term 'debit note' stems from the fact that as the liability to the supplier is accordingly reduced his personal account must be debited to record this. The debit note is the evidence that this has been done.

The debit notes are listed in a Returns Outwards Journal and the items then posted to the debit of the personal accounts in the purchases ledger. To complete double-entry the total of the returns outwards journal for the period is transferred to the credit of the Returns Outwards Account in the general ledger. An example of a returns outwards journal followed by the subsequent postings to the purchases ledger and the general ledger is now shown:

Returns Outwards Journal

	Note No.	Folio	Page 7
19-5			£
Sept 11 B. Hamilton	9/34	PL 29	180
,, 16 B. Rose	9/35	PL 46	100
,, 28 C. Blake	9/36	PL 55	30
,, 30 S. Saunders	9/37	PL 87	360
Transferred to Returns Outwards Account		GL 116	670

Purchases Ledger
B. Hamilton   Page 29

19-5			£
Sept 11 Returns Outwards	RO 7		180

128

19-5			£
Sept 16 Returns			
Outwards	RO 7		100

C. Blake   Page 55

19-5			£
Sept 28 Returns			
Outwards	RO 7		30

S. Saunders   Page 87

19-5			£
Sept 30 Returns			
Outwards	RO 7		360

General Ledger
Returns Outwards   Page 116

	19-5			£
	Sept 30 Returns for			
	the month	RO 7		670

Alternative names in use for the returns outwards journal are Returns Outwards Book or Purchases Returns Book, the latter name arising from the fact that it consists of the purchases which are returned to the supplier at a later date.

Internal Check

When sales invoices are being made out they should be scrutinized very carefully. A system is usually set up so that each stage of the preparation of the invoice is checked by someone other than the person whose job it is to send out the invoice. If this was not done then it would be possible for someone inside a firm to send out an invoice, as an instance, at a price less than the true price. Any difference could then be split between that person and the outside firm. If an invoice should have been sent to Ivor Twister & Co for £2,000, but the invoice clerk made it out deliberately for £200, then, if there was no cross-check, the difference of £1,800 could be split between the invoice clerk and Ivor Twister & Co.

Similarly outside firms could send invoices for goods which were never received by the firm. This might be in collaboration with an employee within the firm, but there are firms sending false invoices which rely on the firms receiving them being inefficient and paying for items never received. There have been firms sending invoices for such items as advertisements which have never been published. The cashier of the firm receiving the invoice, if the firm is an inefficient one, might possibly think that someone in the firm had authorized the advertisements and would pay the bill.

Besides these there are of course genuine errors, and these should also be detected. A system is therefore set up whereby the invoices have to be subject to scrutiny, at each stage, by someone other than the person who sends out the invoices or is responsible for paying them. Incoming invoices will be stamped with a rubber stamp, with spaces for each stage of the check. For instance, one person will have authority to certify that the goods were properly ordered, another that the goods were delivered in good order, another that the prices are correct, that the calculations are correct, and so on. Naturally in a small firm, simply because the office staff might be quite small, this cross-check may be in the hands of only one person other than the person who will pay it. A similar sort of check will be made in respect of sales invoices being sent out.

Statements

At the end of each month a statement should be sent to each debtor who owes money on the last day of the month. The statement is really a copy of the account for the last month, showing the amount owing at the start of the month, then the totals of each of the sales invoices sent to him in that month, the credit notes sent to him in the month for the goods returned, the cash and cheques received from the debtor, and finally the amount owing at the end of the month.

The debtor will use this to see if the account in his accounting records agree with his account in our records. Put simply, if in our books he is shown as owing £798 then, depending on items in transit between us, his books should show us as a creditor for £798. The statement also acts as a reminder to the debtor that he owes us money and will show the date by which he should make payment.

Credit Control

Any organisation which sells goods on credit should ensure that a tight control is kept on the amount owing from individual debtors. Failure to do so could mean that the amount of debtors increases past the point which the organisation can afford to finance, also there is a much higher possibility of bad debts occurring if close control is not kept.

For each debtor a credit limit should be set. This will depend partly on the past record of dealings with the debtor, whether or not the relationship has been a good one with the debtor always paying his account on time or not. The size of the debtor firm and the nature of its financial backing will also help determine what would be a safe credit limit to set. For instance, you might set a credit limit of only £250 for a fairly new and untried customer, but this could be as much as (say) £20,000 for a large well-known international firm with large financial resources. In the business world most business men are optimistic by nature, and they usually feel that they can manage to pay off debts much easier than is the case. Therefore it is a wise policy to err on the side of caution. On the other hand this should be tempered down by the fact that if you are too cautious you will probably not do much business, so a sensible middle course is the answer.

Therefore the debtor should know the length of the term of credit, i.e. how many days or weeks or months he has in which to pay the bill. He should also know that you will not supply goods to him if the amount that he owes you exceeds a stated amount.

Factoring

One of the problems that face many businesses is the time taken by debtors to pay their accounts. Few businesses have so much cash available to them that they do not mind how long the debtor takes to pay. It is a rather surprising fact that a lot of businesses which become bankrupt do so, not because the business is not making profits, but instead because the business has run out of cash funds. Once that happens, the confidence factor in business evaporates, and the business then finds that very few people will supply it with goods, and it also cannot pay its employees. Closure of the firm then happens fairly quickly in many cases.

In the case of debtors, the cash problem may be alleviated by using the services of a financial intermediary called a 'factor':

Factoring is a financial service designed to improve the cash flow of healthy, growing companies, enabling them to make better use of management time and the money tied up in trade credit to customers.

In essence, factors provide their clients with three closely integrated services covering sales accounting and collection, credit management which can include protection against bad debts, and the availability of finance against sales invoices.

Factors assume total responsibility for these functions, including assessing the creditworthiness of customers, the maintenance of a sales ledger, the dispatch of statements and the collection of money owed.

Factors provide clients with a predictable cash flow by paying them against sales factored either as each individual invoice is settled or on an agreed future date which represents the average time taken by the clients' customers to pay.

In addition, a factor will, if required, make payments against its clients' sales invoices: up to 80 per cent being available immediately with the balance paid when the customers pay the factor or after an agreed period.

In the case of non-recourse factoring, the factor gives 100 per cent protection against bad debts on all approved sales.

The benefits of factoring include savings in administration costs and management time, the elimination of bad debts, a guaranteed cash flow and the availability of funds which would otherwise be financing debtors. Factoring, therefore, provides a logical way for companies to develop, with their cash position always under control and the availability of finance linked to actual sales performance.

Exercises

MC50 Credit notes issued by us will be entered in our
(A) Sales Account
(B) Returns Inwards Account
(C) Returns Inwards Journal
(D) Returns Outwards Journal

MC51 The total of the Returns Outwards Journal is transferred to
(A) The credit side of the Returns Outwards Account
(B) The debit side of the Returns Outwards Account
(C) The credit side of the Returns Outwards Book
(D) The debit side of the Purchases Returns Book.

MC52 We originally sold 25 items at £12 each, less 33⅓ per cent trade discount. Our customer now returns 4 of them to us. What is the amount of the credit note to be issued?
(A) £48
(B) £36
(C) £30
(D) £32.

17.1. You are to enter up the purchases journal and the returns outwards journal from the following details, then to post the items to the relevant accounts in the purchases ledger and to show the transfers to the general ledger at the end of the month.

19-7

May 1 Credit purchase from H. Lloyd £119
,,   4 Credit purchases from the following: D. Scott £98; A. Simpson £114; A. Williams £25; S. Wood £56
,,   7 Goods returned by us to the following: H. Lloyd £16; D. Scott £14
,, 10 Credit purchase from A. Simpson £59
,, 18 Credit purchases from the following: M. White £89; J. Wong £67; H. Miller £196; H. Lewis £119
,, 25 Goods returned by us to the following: J. Wong £5; A. Simpson £11
,, 31 Credit purchases from: A. Williams £56; C. Cooper £98.

17.2A. Enter up the sales journal and the returns inwards journal from the following details. Then post to the customer's accounts and show the transfers to the general ledger.

19-4

June 1 Credit sales to: A. Simes £188; P. Tulloch £60; J. Flynn £77; B. Lopez £88
,,   6 Credit sales to: M. Howells £114; S. Thompson £118; J. Flynn £66
,, 10 Goods returned to us by: A. Simes £12; B. Lopez £17
,, 20 Credit sales to M. Barrow £970
,, 24 Goods returned to us by S. Thompson £5
,, 30 Credit sales to M. Parkin £91.

17.3. You are to enter up the sales, purchases and the returns inwards and returns outwards journals from the following details, then to post the items to the relevant accounts in the sales and purchase ledgers. The total of the journals are then to be transferred to the accounts in the general ledger.

19-6

May	1	Credit sales: T. Thompson £56; L. Rodriguez £148; K. Barton £145
,,	3	Credit purchases: P. Potter £144; H. Harris £25; B. Spencer £76
,,	7	Credit sales: K. Kelly £89; N. Mendes £78; N. Lee £257
,,	9	Credit purchases: B. Perkins £24; H. Harris £58; H. Miles £123
,,	11	Goods returned by us to: P. Potter £12; B. Spencer £22
,,	14	Goods returned to us by: T. Thompson £5; K. Barton £11; K. Kelly £14
,,	17	Credit purchases: H. Harris £54; B. Perkins £65; L. Nixon £75
,,	20	Goods returned by us to B. Spencer £14
,,	24	Credit sales: K. Mohammed £57; K. Kelly £65; O. Green £112
,,	28	Goods returned to us by N. Mendes £24
,,	31	Credit sales: N. Lee £55.

17.4. Enter up sales, purchases, returns inwards and returns outwards books, post the items to the relevant accounts in the personal accounts in the sales and purchases ledger, and show the transfers to the general ledger.

19-7

Apl	1	Credit sales to: L. Nelson £105
,,	2	Credit purchases from F. Duncan £800
,,	4	Credit sales to: H. Francis £306; W. Russell £208
,,	15	Credit purchases from: C. Wellington £125; J. Nunez £305; J. Hastings £201; K. Grant £550
,,	16	Returns Inwards from L. Nelson £12; W. Russell £44
,,	18	Credit sales to: W. Russell £905; D. Cummings £289; A. Bruce £400
,,	21	Credit purchases from: J. Nunez £609; T. Palmer £106; J. De Silva £300
,,	24	Returns outwards to: C. Wellington £15; J. Hastings £19; K. Grant £60
,,	30	Returns inwards from D. Cummings £66.

17.5A. You are to enter the following items in the books, post to personal accounts, and show transfers to the general ledger:

19-5

July	1	Credit purchases from: K. Hill £380; M. Norman £500; N. Senior £106
,,	3	Credit sales to: E. Rigby £510; E. Phillips £246; F. Thompson £356
,,	5	Credit purchases from: R. Morton £200; J. Cook £180; D. Edwards £410; C. Davies £66
,,	8	Credit sales to: A. Green £307; H. George £250; J. Ferguson £185
,,	12	Returns outwards to: M. Norman £30; N. Senior £16
,,	14	Returns inwards from: E. Phillips £18; F. Thompson £22
,,	20	Credit sales to: E. Phillips £188; F. Powell £310; E. Lee £420
,,	24	Credit purchases from: C. Ferguson £550; K. Ennevor £900
,,	31	Returns inwards from E. Phillips £27; E. Rigby £30
,,	31	Returns outwards to: J. Cook £13; C. Davies £11.

18

Value Added Tax

Value Added Tax, which will be shown hereafter in its abbreviated form as VAT, is charged in the United Kingdom on both the supply of goods and of services by persons and firms who are taxable. Some goods and services are not liable to VAT. Examples of this are food and postal charges. The rates at which VAT is levied have changed from time to time. Some goods have also attracted a different rate of VAT from the normal rate. Instances of this in the past have been motor-cars and electrical goods which have varied from the rates levied on most other goods. In this book the examples shown will all be at a VAT rate of 10 per cent. This does not mean that this is the rate applicable at the time when you are reading this book. It is, however, an easy figure to work out in an examination room, and most examining bodies have set questions assuming that the VAT rate was 10 per cent.

The Government department which deals with VAT in the United Kingdom is the Customs and Excise department.

Taxable Firms

Imagine that firm A takes raw materials that it has grown and processes them and then wants to sell them. If VAT did not exist it would sell them for £100, but VAT of 10 per cent must be added, so it sells them to firm B for £100 + VAT £10 = £110. Firm A must now pay the figure of £10 VAT to the tax authorities. Firm B having bought for £110 alters the product slightly and then resells to firm C for £140 + 10 per cent VAT £14 = £154. Firm B now give the tax authorities a cheque for the amount added less the amount it had paid to firm A for VAT £10, so that the cheque payable to the tax authorities by firm B is £4. Firm C is a retailer who then sells the goods for £200 to which he must add VAT 10 per cent £20 = £220 selling price to the customer. Firm C then remits £20 − £14 = £6 to the tax authorities.

It can be seen that the full amount of VAT tax has fallen on the ultimate customer who bought the goods from the retail shop, and that he suffered a tax of £20. The machinery of collection was however geared to the value added at each stage of the progress of the goods from manufacture to retailing, i.e. Firm A handed over £10, Firm B £4 and Firm C £6, making £20 in all.

Exempted Firms

If a firm is exempted then this means that it does not have to add the VAT tax on to the price at which it sells its products or services. On the other hand it will not get a refund of the amount it has paid itself on the goods and services which it has bought and on which it has paid VAT tax. Thus such a firm may buy goods for £100 + VAT tax £10 = £110. When it sells them it may sell at £130, there being no need to add VAT tax at all. It will not however get a refund of the £10 VAT tax it had itself paid on those goods.

Instances of firms being exempted are insurance companies, which do not charge VAT on the amount of insurance premiums payable by its customers, and banks, which do not add VAT on to their bank charges. Small firms with a turnover of less than a certain amount (the limit is changed upwards from time to time and so is not given here) do not have to register for VAT if they don't want to, and they would not therefore charge VAT on their goods and services. On the other hand many of these small firms could register if they wished, but they would then have to keep full VAT records in addition to charging out VAT. It is simply an attempt by the U.K. Government to avoid crippling very small businesses with unnecessary record-keeping that gives most small businesses this right to opt out of charging VAT.

Zero Rated Firms

These do not add VAT tax to the final selling price of their products or services. They do however obtain a refund of all VAT tax paid by them on goods and services. This means that if one of the firms buys goods for £200 + VAT tax £20 = £220, and later sells them for £300 it will not have to add VAT on to the selling price of £300. It will however be able to claim a refund of the £20 VAT tax paid when the goods were purchased. It is this latter element that distinguishes it from an exempted firm. A zero rated firm is therefore in a better position than an exempted firm. Illustrations of these firms are food, publishing and the new construction of buildings.

Partly Exempt Traders

Some traders will find that they are selling some goods which are exempt and some which are zero rated and others which are standard rated. These traders will have to apportion their turnover accordingly, and follow the rules already described for each separate part of their turnover.

Accounting for VAT

It can be seen that, except for firms that are exempted from VAT, firms do not suffer VAT as one expense. They either get a refund of whatever VAT they have paid, in the case of zero-rated business, or else additionally collect VAT from their customers and merely therefore act as tax collectors in the case of taxable firms. Only the exempted firms actually suffer VAT as they pay it and are not allowed a refund and cannot specifically pass it on to their customers. The following discussion will therefore be split between those two sorts of firms who do not suffer VAT expense, compared with the exempted firms who do suffer VAT.

Firms Which Can Recover VAT Paid

1. Taxable Firms

Value Added Tax and Sales Invoices   A taxable firm will have to add VAT to the value of the Sales invoices. It must be pointed out that this is based on the amount of the invoice *after* any trade discount has been deducted.

Exhibit 18.1 is an invoice drawn up from the following details:

On 2 March 19-2, W. Frank & Co, Hayburn Road, Stockport, sold the following goods to R. Bainbridge Ltd, 267 Star Road, Colchester: Bainbridge's order No was A/4/559, for the following items:

      200 Rolls T56 Black Tape at £6 per 10 rolls
      600 Sheets R64 Polythene at £10 per 100 sheets
      7,000 Blank Perspex B49 Markers at £20 per 1,000

All of these goods are subject to VAT at the rate of 10 per cent.

A trade discount of 25 per cent is given by Frank & Co. The sales invoice is numbered 8851.

Exhibit 18.1

W. Frank & Co, Hayburn Road, Stockport SK2 5DB	
INVOICE No. 8851 Date: 2 March 19-2	
To: R. Bainbridge Ltd Your order no. A/4/559 267 Star Road Colchester CO1 1BT	
	£
200 Rolls T56 Black Tape @ £6 per 10 rolls	120
600 Sheets R64 Polythene @ £10 per 100 sheets	60
7,000 Blank Perspex B49 Markers @ £20 per 1,000	140
	320
Less Trade Discount 25%	80
	240
Add VAT 10%	24
	264

Where a cash discount is offered for speedy payment, VAT is calculated on an amount represented by the value of the invoice less such a discount. Even if the cash discount is lost because of late payments, the VAT will not change.

The Sales Book will normally have an extra column for the VAT content of the Sales Invoices. This is needed to facilitate accounting for VAT. The entry of several sales invoices in the Sales Book and in the ledger accounts can now be examined:

W. Frank & Co sold the following goods during the month of March 19-2:

	Total of Invoice, after trade discount deducted but before VAT added	VAT 10%
19-2	£	£
March 2 R. Bainbridge Ltd (see Exhibit 18.1)	240	24
,, 10 S. Lange & Son	300	30
,, 17 K. Bishop	160	16
,, 31 R. Andrews & Associates	100	10

	Sales Book				Page 58
		Invoice No.	Folio	Net	VAT
19-2				£	£
March 2	R. Bainbridge Ltd	8851	SL 77	240	24
,, 10	S. Lange & Son	8852	SL 119	300	30
,, 17	K. Bishop	8853	SL 185	160	16
,, 31	R. Andrews & Associates	8854	SL 221	100	10

Transferred to General Ledger   GL 76 800 GL 90 80

The Sales Book having been written up, the first task is then to enter the invoices in the individual customer's accounts in the Sales Ledger. The customer's accounts are simply charged with the full amounts of the invoices including VAT. For instance, K. Bishop will owe £176 which he will have to pay to W. Frank & Co. He does not remit the VAT £16 to the Customs and Excise, instead he is going to pay the £16 to W. Frank & Co. who will thereafter ensure that the £16 is included in the total cheque payable to the Customs and Excise.

Sales Ledger

R. Bainbridge Ltd   Page 77

19-2			£
March 2 Sales	SB 58		264

S. Lang & Son   Page 119

19-2			£
March 10 Sales	SB 58		330

K. Bishop   Page 185

19-2			£
March 17 Sales	SB 58		176

R. Andrews & Associates   Page 221

19-2			£
March 31 Sales	SB 58		110

In total therefore the personal accounts have been debited with £880, this being the total of the amounts which the customers will have to pay. The actual sales of the firm are not £880, the amount which is actually sales is £800, the other £80 being simply the VAT that W. Frank & Co are collecting on behalf of the Government. The credit transfer to the Sales Account in the General Ledger is restricted to the Sales content, i.e. £800. The other £80, being VAT, is transferred to a VAT account.

General Ledger

Sales   Page 76

	19-2		£
	March 31 Credit Sales for the		
	month	SB 58	800

Value Added Tax   Page 90

	19-2		£
	March 31 Sales Book: VAT		
	content	SB 58	80

Value Added Tax and Purchases In the case of a taxable firm, the firm will have to add VAT to its sales invoices, but it will also be able to claim a refund of the VAT which it pays on its purchases. What will happen is that the total of the amount of VAT paid on Purchases will be deducted from the total of the VAT collected by the additions to the Sales Invoices. Normally the VAT on Sales will be greater than that on Purchases, and therefore periodically the net difference will be paid to the Customs and Excise. It can happen sometimes that more VAT has been suffered on Purchases than has been charged on Sales, and in this case it would be the Customs and Excise which would refund the difference to the firm. These payments or receipts via the Customs and Excise will be either monthly or quarterly depending on the arrangement which the particular firm has made.

The recording of Purchases in the Purchases Book and Purchases Ledger is similar to that of Sales, naturally with items being shown in a reverse fashion. These can now be illustrated by continuing the month of March 19-2 in the books of the firm already considered, W. Frank & Co, this time for Purchases.

W. Frank & Co made the following purchases during the month of March 19-2:

	Total of Invoice, after trade discount deducted but before VAT added	VAT 10%
19-2	£	£
March 1 E. Lyal Ltd (see Exhibit 18.2)	180	18
,, 11 P. Portsmouth & Co	120	12
,, 24 J. Davidson	40	4
,, 29 B. Cofie & Son Ltd	70	7

Before looking at the recording of these in the Purchases Records, compare the first entry for E. Lyal Ltd with Exhibit 18.2, to ensure that the correct amounts have been shown.

Exhibit 18.2

E. Lyal Ltd
College Avenue
St Albans
Hertfordshire ST2 4JA

INVOICE No. K453/A

Date: 1/3/19-2
Your order No. BB/667

To: W. Frank & Co   Terms: Strictly net 30 days
Hayburn Road
Stockport

	£
50 metres of BYC plastic 1 metre wide × £3 per metre	150
1,200 metal tags 500 mm × 10p each	120
	270
Less Trade Discount at 33⅓%	90
	180
Add VAT 10%	18
	198

It can be seen that the purchases invoice from E. Lyal Ltd differs slightly in its layout to that of W. Frank & Co per Exhibit 18.3. This is to illustrate that in fact each firm designs its own invoices, and there will be wide variations. The basic information shown will be similar, but they may have such information displayed in quite different ways.

Purchases Book			Page 38
Folio		*Net*	*VAT*
		£	£
19-2			
March 1 E. Lyal Ltd	PL 15	180	18
,, 11 P. Portsmouth & Co	PL 70	120	12
,, 24 J. Davidson	PL 114	40	4
,, 29 B. Cofie & Son Ltd	PL 166	70	7
Transferred to General Ledger		GL 54 410	GL 90 41

These are entered in the Purchases Ledger. Once again there is no need for the VAT to be shown as separate amounts in the accounts of the suppliers.

Purchases Ledger

E. Lyal Ltd   Page 15

			£
19-2			
March 1 Purchases	PB 38	198

P. Portsmouth & Co.   Page 70

			£
19-2			
March 11 Purchases	PB 38	132

J. Davidson   Page 114

			£
19-2			
March 24 Purchases	PB 38	44

B. Cofie & Son Ltd   Page 166

		£	
19-2			
March 29 Purchases	PB 38	77

The personal accounts have accordingly been credited with a total of £451, this being the total of the amounts which Frank & Co will have to pay to them. The actual purchases are not however, £451; the correct amount is £410 and the other £41 is the VAT which the various firms are collecting for the Customs & Excise, and which amount is reclaimable from the Customs and Excise by Frank & Co. The debit transfer to the Purchases Account is therefore restricted to the figure of £410, for this is the true amount that the goods are costing the firm. The other £41 is transferred to the debit of the VAT account. It will be noticed that in this account there is already a credit of £80 in respect of VAT on Sales for the month.

General Ledger

Purchases

19-2		£
March 31	Credit Purchases for the month	410

Value Added Tax

19-2		£	19-2		£
March 31	Purchase Book: VAT content PB 38	41	March 31	Sales Book: VAT content SB 58	80
,, 31	Balance c/d	39			
		80			80
			April 1	Balance b/d	39

Assuming that a Trading and Profit and Loss Account was being drawn up for the month, the Trading Account would be debited with £410 as a transfer from the Purchases Account, whilst the £800 in the Sales Account would be transferred to the credit side of the Trading Account. The Value Added Tax would simply appear as a creditor of £39 in the Balance Sheet as at 31 March 19-2.

2. Zero Rated Firms

It has been already stated that these firms do not have to add VAT on to their sales invoices, as their rate of VAT is zero or nil. On the other hand any VAT that they pay on Purchases can be reclaimed from the Customs and Excise. Such firms, which include publishers, are therefore in a rather fortunate position. There will accordingly be no need at all to enter VAT in the Sales Book as VAT simply does not apply to Sales in such a firm. The Purchases Book and the Purchases Ledger will appear exactly as has been seen in the case of W. Frank & Co. The VAT account will only have debits in it, representing the VAT on Purchases. This balance will be shown on the Balance Sheet as a debtor until it is settled by the Customs and Excise.

Firms Which Cannot Recover VAT Paid

These firms do not have to add VAT on to the value of their Sales Invoices. On the other hand they do not get a refund of VAT paid on Purchases. All that happens in this type of firm is that there is no Value Added Tax Account, the VAT paid is simply included as part of the cost of goods. If therefore a firm receives an invoice from a supplier for Purchases of £80, with VAT added of £8, then £88 will have to be paid for these goods and the firm will not receive a refund from the Customs and Excise. In the Purchases Book the item of

Purchases will be shown as £88, and the supplier's account will be credited with £88. As VAT is not added to Sales Invoices then there cannot be any entries for VAT in the Sales Book.

Perhaps a comparison of two firms with identical Purchases from the same supplier, one a zero rated firm, and one a firm which cannot recover VAT paid, would not come amiss here. On the assumption that for each firm the only item of Purchases for the month was that of goods £120 plus VAT £12 from D. Oswald Ltd, the entries for the month of May 19-4 would be as follows:

(a) Firm which cannot recover VAT:

Purchases Book

	£
19-4	
May 16 D. Oswald Ltd.	132

Purchases Ledger
D. Oswald Ltd

		£
	19-4	
	May 16 D. Oswald Ltd.	132

General Ledger
Purchases

19-4	£	19-4	£
May 31 Credit Purchases for the month	132	May 31 Transfer to Trading Account	132

Trading Account for the month ended 31 May 19-4 (extract)

	£
Purchases	132

(b) Firm which can recover VAT (e.g. zero rated firm):

Purchases Book

	Net	VAT
	£	£
19-4		
May 16 D. Oswald Ltd	120	12

Purchases Ledger
D. Oswald Ltd

		£
	19-4	
	May 16 Purchases	132

General Ledger
Purchases

19-4		£	19-4˙		£
May 31 Credit Purchases for			May 31 Transfer to		
the month		120	Trading Account		120

Value Added Tax

19-4		£
May 31 Purchases Book		12

Trading Account for the month ended 31 May 19-4 (extract)

	£
Purchases	120

Balance Sheet as at 31 May 19-4 (extract)

	£
Debtor	12

VAT included in Gross Amount

You will often know only the gross amount of an item, this figure will in fact be made up of the net amount plus VAT. To find the amount of VAT which has been added to the net amount, a formula capable of being used with any rate of VAT can be used. It is:

$$\frac{\% \text{ rate of VAT}}{100 + \% \text{ Rate of VAT}} \times \text{Gross Amount} = \text{VAT in £}$$

Suppose that the gross amount of sales was £1,650 and the rate of VAT was 10%. Find the amount of VAT and the net amount before VAT was added.
Using the
formula: –
$$\frac{10}{100 + 10} \times £1,650 = \frac{10}{110} \times £1,650 = £150.$$

Therefore the net amount was £1,500, which with VAT £150 added, becomes £1,650 gross.

VAT on Items Other Than Sales and Purchases

Value Added Tax is not just paid on purchases, it is also payable on many items of expense and on the purchase of fixed assets. In fact it would not be possible for this to be otherwise, as an item which is a Purchase for one firm would be a Fixed Asset in another. For instance, if a firm which dealt in shop fittings buys a display counter as a fixed asset. The firm which sells goods on which VAT is added does not concern itself whether or not the firm buying it is doing so for resale, or whether it is for use. The VAT will therefore be added to all of its Sales Invoices. The treatment of VAT in the accounts of the firm buying the item will depend on whether or not that firm can reclaim VAT paid or not. The general rule is that if the VAT can be reclaimed then the item should be shown net, i.e. VAT should be excluded from the expense or fixed asset account. When VAT cannot be reclaimed then VAT should be included in the expense or fixed asset account as part of the cost of the item. For example, two businesses buying similar items, would treat the following items as shown:

	Firm which can reclaim VAT	*Firm which cannot reclaim VAT*
Buys Machinery £200 + VAT £20	Debit Machinery £200 Debit VAT Account £20	Debit Machinery £220
Buys Stationery £150 + VAT £15	Debit Stationery £150 Debit VAT Account £15	Debit Stationery £165

VAT Owing

VAT owing by or to the firm can be included with debtors or creditors, as the case may be. There is no need to show the amount(s) owing as separate items.

Exercises

18.1. On 1 May 19-7, D. Wilson Ltd, 1 Hawk Green Road, Stockport, sold the following goods on credit to G. Christie & Son, The Golf Shop, Hole-in-One Lane, Marple, Cheshire:

Order No. A/496
3 sets of 'Boy Michael' golf clubs at £270 per set.
150 Watson golf balls at £8 per 10 balls.
4 Faldo golf bags at £30 per bag.
Trade discount is given at the rate of 33⅓%.
All goods are subject to VAT at 10%.
(i) Prepare the Sales Invoice to be sent to G. Christie & Son. The invoice number will be 10586.
(ii) Show the entries in the Personal Ledgers of D. Wilson Ltd and G. Christie & Son.

18.2. The following sales have been made by S. Thompson Ltd during the month of June 19-5. All the figures are shown net after deducting trade discount, but before adding VAT at the rate of 10 per cent.

19-5
August 1 to M. Sinclair & Co	£150
,, 8 to M. Brown & Associates	£260
,, 19 to A. Axton Ltd	£80
,, 31 to T. Christie	£30

You are required to enter up the Sales Book, Sales Ledger and General Ledger in respect of the above items for the month.

18.3. The following sales and purchases were made by R. Colman Ltd during the month of May 19-6.

			Net	VAT added
19-6			£	£
May	1	Sold goods on credit to B. Davies & Co	150	15
,,	4	Sold goods on credit to C. Grant Ltd	220	22
,,	10	Bought goods on credit from:		
		G. Cooper & Son	400	40
		J. Wayne Ltd	190	19
,,	14	Bought goods on credit from B. Lugosi	50	5
,,	16	Sold goods on credit to C. Grant Ltd	140	14
,,	23	Bought goods on credit from S. Hayward	60	6
,,	31	Sold goods on credit to B. Karloff	80	8

Enter up the Sales and Purchases Books, Sales and Purchases Ledgers and the General Ledger for the month of May 19-6. Carry the balance down on the VAT account.

18.4A. On 1 March 19-6, C. Black, Curzon Road, Stockport, sold the following goods on credit to J. Booth, 89 Andrew Lane, Stockport. Order No. 1697.

20,000 Coils Sealing Tape @ £4.46 per 1,000 coils
40,000 Sheets Bank A5 @ £4.50 per 1,000 sheets
24,000 Sheets Bank A4 @ £4.20 per 1,000 sheets

All goods are subject to VAT at 10%.
(a) Prepare the Sales Invoice to be sent to J. Booth.
(b) Show the entries in the Personal Ledgers of J. Booth, and C. Black.

18.5A. The credit sales and purchases for the month of December 19-3 in respect of C. Dennis & Son Ltd were:

			Net, after trade discount	VAT 10%
19-3			£	£
December	1	Sales to M. Morris	140	14
,,	4	Sales to G. Ford Ltd	290	29
,,	5	Purchases from P. Hillman & Son	70	7
,,	8	Purchases from J. Lancia	110	11
,,	14	Sales to R. Volvo Ltd	180	18
,,	18	Purchases from T. Leyland & Co	160	16
,,	28	Sales to G. Ford Ltd	100	10
,,	30	Purchases from J. Lancia	90	9

Write up all of the relevant books and ledger accounts for the month.

19

Depreciation of Fixed Assets: Nature and Calculations

Fixed Assets have already been stated to be those assets of material value that are of long-life, are held to be used in the business, and are not primarily for resale or for conversion into cash.

Usually, with the exception of land, fixed assets have a limited number of years of useful life. Motor vans, machines, buildings and fixtures, for instance, do not last for ever. Even land itself may have all or part of its usefulness exhausted after a few years. Some types of land used for quarries, mines, or land of another sort of wasting nature would be examples. When a fixed asset is bought, then later put out of use by the firm, that part of the cost that is not recovered on disposal is called depreciation.

It is obvious that the only time that depreciation can be calculated accurately is when the fixed asset is disposed of, and the difference between the cost to its owner and the amount received on disposal is then ascertained. If a motor van was bought for £1,000 and sold five years later for £20, then the amount of depreciation is £1,000 − £20 = £980.

Depreciation is thus the part of the cost of the fixed asset consumed during its period of use by the firm. Therefore, it has been a cost for services consumed in the same way as costs for such items as wages, rent, lighting etc. Depreciation is, therefore, an expense and will need charging to the profit and loss account before ascertaining net profit or loss. Provision for depreciation suffered will therefore have to be made in the books in order that the net profits may be profits remaining after charging all the expenses of the period.

In fact SSAP 12 defines depreciation as 'the measure of the wearing out, consumption or other loss of *value* of a fixed asset whether arising from use, effluxion of time or obsolescence through technology and market changes.' This definition refers to loss of *value* rather than cost. This has been done deliberately so that it also covers depreciation in any form of inflation accounting system, such systems will be considered in volume 2 of this book.

Causes of Depreciation

These may be divided into the main classes of physical deterioration, economic factors, the time factor, and depletion.

Physical deterioration is caused mainly from wear and tear when the asset is in use, but also from erosion, rust, rot, and decay from being exposed to wind, rain, sun and other elements of nature.

Economic factors may be said to be those that cause the asset to be put out of use even though it is in good physical condition. These are largely obsolescence and inadequacy.

Obsolescence means the process of becoming obsolete or out of date. An example of this were the steam locomotives, some of them in good physical condition, which were rendered obsolete by the introduction of diesel and electric locomotives. The steam locomotives were put out of use by British Rail when they still had many more miles of potential use, because the newer locomotives were more efficient and economical to run.

Inadequacy refers to the termination of the use of an asset because of the growth and changes in the size of a firm. For instance, a small ferryboat that is operated by a firm at a seaside resort is entirely inadequate when the resort becomes more popular. It is found that it would be more efficient and economical to operate a larger ferry-boat, and so the smaller boat is put out of use by the firm.

Both obsolescence and inadequacy do not necessarily mean that the asset is scrapped. It is merely put out of use by the firm. Another firm will often buy it. For example, many of the aeroplanes put out of use by large airlines are bought by smaller firms.

The time factor is obviously associated with all the causes mentioned already. However, there are fixed assets to which the time factor is connected in another way. These are assets with a fixed period of legal life such as leases, patents and copyrights. For instance a lease can be entered into for any period, while a patent's legal life is sixteen years, but there are certain grounds on which this can be extended. Provision for the consumption of these assets is called amortisation rather than depreciation.

Other assets are of a wasting character, perhaps due to the extraction of raw materials from them. These materials are then either used by the firm to make something else, or are sold in their raw state to other firms. Natural resources such as mines, quarries and oil wells come under this heading. To provide for the consumption of an asset of a wasting character is called provision for depletion.

Land and Buildings

Prior to SSAP 12, which applied to periods starting on or after 1st January 1978, freehold and long leasehold properties were very rarely subject to a charge for depreciation. It was contended that, as property values tended to rise instead of fall, it was inappropriate to charge depreciation.

However, SSAP 12, requires that depreciation be written off over the property's useful life, with the exception that freehold *land* will not *normally* require a provision for depreciation. This is because land does not *normally* depreciate. Buildings do however eventually fall into disrepair or become obsolete, and must be subject to a charge for depreciation each year. When a revaluation of property takes place the depreciation charge must be on the revalued figure.

An exception to all this are 'Investment Properties'. These are properties owned not for use, but simply for investment. In this case investment properties will be shown in the balance sheet at their open market value.

Appreciation

At this stage of the chapter the reader may well begin to ask himself about the assets that increase (appreciate) in value. The answer to this is that normal accounting procedure would be to ignore any such appreciation, as to bring appreciation into account would be to contravene both the cost concept and the prudence concept as discussed in Chapter 10. Nevertheless, in certain circumstances appreciation is taken into account in partnership and limited company accounts, but this is left until partnerships and limited companies are considered.

Provisions for Depreciation as Allocation of Cost

Depreciation in total over the life of an asset can be calculated quite simply as cost less amount receivable when the asset is put out of use by the firm. If the item is bought and sold within the one accounting period then the depreciation for that period is charged as a revenue expense in arriving at that period's Net Profit. The difficulties start when the asset is used for more than one accounting period, and an attempt has to be made to charge each period with the depreciation for that period.

Even though depreciation provisions are now regarded as allocating cost to each accounting period (except for accounting for inflation), it does not follow that there is any 'true' method of performing even this task. All that can be said is that the cost should be allocated over the life of the asset in such a way as to charge it as equitably as possible to the periods in which the asset is used. The difficulties involved are considerable and some of them are now listed.
1. Apart from a few assets, such as a lease, how accurately can a firm assess an assets useful life? Even a lease may be put out of use if the premises leased have become inadequate.
2. How does one measure use? A car owned by a firm for two years may have been driven one year by a very careful driver and another year by a reckless driver. The standard of driving will affect the motor car and also the amount of cash receivable on its disposal. How should such a firm apportion the car's depreciation costs?

3. There are other expenses besides depreciation such as repairs and maintenance of the fixed asset. As both of these affect the rate and amount of depreciation should they not also affect the depreciation provision calculations?

4. How can a firm possibly know the amount receivable in x years time when the asset is put out of use?

These are only some of the difficulties. Therefore, the methods of calculating provisions for depreciation are mainly accounting customs.

The Main Methods of Calculating Provisions for Depreciation

The two main methods in use are the Straight Line Method and the Reducing Balance Method. In fact it has now become regarded that though other methods may be more applicable in certain cases, the straight line method is the one that is generally most suitable.

1. Straight Line Method

This allows an equal amount to be charged as depreciation for each year of expected use of the asset.

The basic formula is:

$$\frac{\text{Cost} - \text{Estimated Residual Value}}{\text{Number of years of expected use}} = \text{Depreciation provision per annum.}$$

The reason for this method being called the straight line method is that if the charge for depreciation was plotted annually on a graph and the points joined together, then the graph would reveal a straight line.

For example, a machine costs £10,000, it has an expected life of four years, and has an estimated residual value of £256. The depreciation provision per annum will be

$$\frac{£10,000 - £256}{4} = £2,436.$$

In practice, the residual value is often ignored where it would be a relatively small amount.

2. Reducing Balancing Method

To calculate the depreciation provision annually, a fixed percentage is applied to the balance of costs not yet allocated as an expense at the end of the previous accounting period. The balance of unallocated costs will therefore decrease each year, and as a fixed percentage is being used the depreciation provision will therefore be less with each passing year. Theoretically, the balance of unallocated costs at the end of the expected life should equal the estimated residual value.

The basic formula used to find the requisite percentage to apply with this method is:

$$r = 1 - \sqrt[n]{\frac{s}{c}}$$

where n = the number of years
   s = the net residual value (this must be a significant amount or the answers will be absurd, since the depreciation rate would amount to nearly one)
   c = the cost of the asset
   r = the rate of depreciation to be applied.

Using, as an example, the figures used for the machine for which depreciation provisions were calculated on the straight line method, the calculations would appear as:

$$r = 1 - \sqrt[4]{\frac{£256}{£10,000}} = 1 - \frac{4}{10} = 0.6 \text{ or } 60 \text{ per cent}$$

The depreciation calculation applied to each of the four years of use would be:

	£
Cost	10,000
Year 1. Depreciation provision 60 per cent of £10,000	6,000
Cost not yet apportioned, end of year 1.	4,000
Year 2. Depreciation provision 60 per cent of £4,000	2,400
Cost not yet apportioned, end of year 2.	1,600
Year 3. Depreciation provision 60 per cent of £1,600	960
Cost not yet apportioned, end of year 3.	640
Year 4. Depreciation provision 60 per cent of £640	384
Cost not yet apportioned, end of year 4.	256

In this case the percentage to be applied worked out conveniently to a round figure. However, the answer will often come out to several places of decimals. In this case it would be usual to take the nearest whole figure as a percentage to be applied.

The percentage to be applied, assuming a significant amount for residual value, is usually between two to three times greater for the reducing balance method than for the straight line method.

The advocates of this method usually argue that it helps to even out the total charged as expenses for the use of the asset each year. They state that provisions for depreciation are not the only costs charged, there are the running costs in addition and that the repairs and maintenance element of running costs usually increase with age. Therefore, to equate total usage costs for each year of use the depreciation provisions should fall as the repairs and maintenance element increases. However, as can be seen from the figures of the example already given, the repairs and maintenance element would have to be comparatively large to bring about an equal total charge for each year of use.

To summarise, the people who favour this method say that:

In the early years		*In the later years*
A higher charge for depreciation		A lower charge for depreciation
+	will tend to be fairly	+
A lower charge for repairs and upkeep	equal to	A higher charge for repairs and upkeep

Exhibit 19.1 gives a comparison of the calculations using the two methods, if the same cost is given for the two methods.

Exhibit 19.1

A firm has just bought a machine for £8,000. It will be kept in use for 4 years, when it will be disposed of for an estimated amount of £500. They ask for a comparison of the amounts charged as depreciation using both methods.

For the straight line method a figure of (£8,000 − £500) ÷ 4 = £7,500 ÷ 4 = £1,875 per annum is to be used. For the reducing balance method a percentage figure of 50 per cent will be used.

	Method 1 Straight Line		Method 2 Reducing Balance
	£		£
Cost	8,000		8,000
Depreciation: Year 1	1,875	(50% of £8,000)	4,000
	6,125		4,000
Depreciation: Year 2	1,875	(50% of £4,000)	2,000
	4,250		2,000
Depreciation: Year 3	1,875	(50% of £2,000)	1,000
	2,375		1,000
Depreciation: Year 4	1,875	(50% of £1,000)	500
Disposal value	500		500

This illustrates the fact that using the reducing balance method has a much higher charge for depreciation in the early years, and lower charges in the later years.

Another name for the Reducing Balance Method is the 'Diminishing Balance Method'.

Depreciation Provisions and Assets Bought or Sold

There are two main methods of calculating depreciation provisions for assets bought or sold during an accounting period.

1. To ignore the dates during the year that the assets were bought or sold, merely calculating a full period's depreciation on the assets in use at the end of the period. Thus, assets sold during the accounting period will have had no provision for depreciation made for that last period irrespective of how many months they were in use. Conversely, assets bought during the period will have a full period of depreciation provision calculated even though they may not have been owned throughout the whole of the period.

2. Provision for depreciation made on the basis of one month's ownership, one month's provision for depreciation. Fractions of months are usually ignored. This is obviously a more scientific method than that already described.

For examination purposes, where the date on which assets are bought and sold are shown then method No. 2 is the method expected by the examiner. If no such dates are given then obviously method No. 1 will have to be used.

Other Methods of Calculating Depreciation

There are many more methods of calculating depreciation but they are outside the scope of this volume. These will be fully considered in volume two.

Exercises

MC53 Depreciation is
(A) The amount spent to buy a fixed asset
(B) The salvage value of a fixed asset
(C) The part of the cost of the fixed asset consumed during its period of use by the firm
(D) The amount of money spent in replacing assets.

MC54 A firm bought a machine for £3,200. It is to be depreciated at a rate of 25 per cent using the Reducing Balance Method. What would be the remaining book value after 2 years?
(A) £1,600
(B) £2,400
(C) £1,800
(D) Some other figure.

MC55 A firm bought a machine for £16,000. It is expected to be used for 5 years then sold for £1,000. What is the annual amount of depreciation if the straight line method is used?
(A) £3,200
(B) £3,100
(C) £3,750
(D) £3,000.

19.1. D. Sankey, a manufacturer, purchases a lathe for the sum of £4,000. It has an estimated life of 5 years and a scrap value of £500.

Sankey is not certain whether he should use the 'Straight Line' or 'the Reducing Balance' basis for the purpose of calculating depreciation on the machine.

You are required to calculate the depreciation on the lathe using both methods, showing clearly the balance remaining in the lathe account at the end of each of the five years for each method. (Assume that 40 per cent per annum is to be used for the Reducing Balance Method.)

(Calculations to the nearest £.)

19.2. A machine costs £12,500. It will be kept for 4 years, and then sold for an estimated figure of £5,120. Show the calculations of the figures for depreciation for each of the four years using (*a*) the straight-line method, (*b*) the reducing balance method, for this method using a depreciation rate of 20 per cent.

19.3. A motor vehicle costs £6,400. It will be kept for 5 years, and then sold for scrap £200. Calculate the depreciation for each year using (*a*) the reducing balance method, using a depreciation rate of 50 per cent, (*b*) the straight line method.

19.4A. A machine costs £5,120. It will be kept for 5 years, and then sold at an estimated figure of £1,215. Show the calculations of the figures for depreciation each year using (*a*) the straight line method, (*b*) the reducing balance method using a depreciation rate of 25 per cent.

19.5A. A bulldozer costs £12,150. It will be kept in use for 5 years. At the end of that time agreement has already been made that it will be sold for £1,600. Show your calculation of the amount of depreciation each year if (*a*) the reducing method at a rate of 33⅓ per cent was used, (*b*) the straight line method was used.

19.6A. A tractor is bought for £6,000. It will be used for 3 years, and then sold back to the supplier for £3,072. Show the depreciation calculations for each year using (*a*) the reducing balance method with a rate of 20 per cent, (*b*) the straight line method.

19.7. A company, which makes up its accounts annually to 31 December, provides for depreciation of its machinery at the rate of 10 per cent per annum on the diminishing balance system.

On 31 December 19-6, the machinery consisted of three items purchased as under:

	£
On 1 January 19-4 Machine A	Cost 3,000
On 1 April 19-5 Machine B	Cost 2,000
On 1 July 19-6 Machine C	Cost 1,000

Required: Your calculations showing the depreciation provision for the year 19-6.

20

Double Entry Records for Depreciation

Looking back quite a few years, the charge for depreciation always used to be shown in the fixed asset accounts themselves. This method is now falling into disuse but as a fair number of small firms still use it this will be illustrated and called the 'old method'.

The method now normally used is where the fixed assets accounts are always kept for showing the assets at cost price. The depreciation is shown accumulating in a separate 'provision for depreciation' account.

An illustration can now be looked at, using the same information, but showing the records using both methods.

In a business with financial years ended 31 December a machine is bought for £2,000 on 1 January 19-5. It is to be depreciated at the rate of 20 per cent using the reducing balance method. The records for the first three years are now shown:

1. The Old Method

Here the double-entry for each year's depreciation charge is:

Debit the depreciation account
Credit the asset account

and then, this is transferred to the profit and loss account, by the following:

Debit the profit and loss account
Credit the depreciation account

Machinery

19-5	£	19-5	£
Jan 1 Cash	2,000	Dec 31 Depreciation	400
		,, ,, Balance c/d	1,600
	2,000		2,000
19-6		19-6	
Jan 1 Balance b/d	1,600	Dec 31 Depreciation	320
		,, ,, Balance c/d	1,280
	1,600		1,600
19-7		19-7	
Jan 1 Balance b/d	1,280	Dec 31 Depreciation	256
		,, ,, Balance c/d	1,024
	1,280		1,280
19-8			
Jan 1 Balance b/d	1,024		

Depreciation

19-5	£	19-5	£
Dec 31 Machinery	400	Dec 31 Profit and Loss	400
19-6		19-6	
Dec 31 Machinery	320	Dec 31 Profit and Loss	320
19-7		19-7	
Dec 31 Machinery	256	Dec 31 Profit and Loss	256

Profit and Loss Account for the year ended 31 December

19-5 Depreciation	400
19-6 Depreciation	320
19-7 Depreciation	256

Usually shown on the balance sheet as follows:

Balance Sheets

	£	£
As at 31 December 19-5		
Machinery at cost	2,000	
Less Depreciation for the year	400	
		1,600
As at 31 December 19-6		
Machinery as at 1 January 19-6	1,600	
Less Depreciation for the year	320	
		1,280
As at 31 December 19-7		
Machinery as at 1 January 19-7	1,280	
Less Depreciation for the year	256	
		1,024

2. The Modern Method

Here, no entry is made in the asset account for depreciation. Instead, the depreciation is shown accumulating in a separate account.

The double entry is:

Debit the profit and loss account
Credit the provision for depreciation account

Machinery

19-5	£
Jan 1 Cash	2,000

Provision for Depreciation – Machinery

19-5	£	19-5	£
Dec 31 Balance c/d	400	Dec 31 Profit and Loss	400
19-6		19-6	
Dec 31 Balance c/d	720	Jan 1 Balance b/d	400
		Dec 31 Profit and Loss	320
	720		720
19-7		19-7	
Dec 31 Balance c/d	976	Jan 1 Balance b/d	720
		Dec 31 Profit and Loss	256
	976		976
		19-8	
		Jan 1 Balance b/d	976

Profit and Loss Account for the year ended 31 December

19-5 Depreciation	400
19-6 Depreciation	320
19-7 Depreciation	256

Now the balance on the Machinery Account is shown on the balance sheet at the end of each year less the balance on the Provision for Depreciation Account.

Balance Sheets

	£	£
As at 31 December 19-5		
Machinery at cost	2,000	
Less Depreciation to date	400	
		1,600
As at 31 December 19-6		
Machinery at cost	2,000	
Less Depreciation to date	720	
		1,280
As at 31 December 19-7		
Machinery at cost	2,000	
Less Depreciation to date	976	
		1,024

The modern method is much more revealing as far as the balance sheet is concerned. By comparing the depreciation to date with the cost of the asset, a good indication as to the relative age of the asset can be obtained. In the second and third balance sheets using the old method no such indication is available. For instance an item in a balance sheet as follows:

Motor Car as at 1 January 19-5	500	
Less Depreciation for the year	100	
		400

might turn out to be using the new method as either of the following:

Motor Car at cost	6,000	
Less Depreciation to date	5,600	
		400
Motor Car at cost	600	
Less Depreciation to date	200	
		400

The modern method is therefore more revealing and is far preferable from the viewpoint of more meaningful accounting reports.

The Sale of An Asset

When we charge depreciation on a fixed asset we are having to make guesses. We cannot be absolutely certain how long we will keep the asset in use, nor can we be certain at the date of purchase how much the asset will be sold for when we dispose of it. To get our guesses absolutely correct would be quite rare. This means that when we dispose of an asset, the cash received for it is usually different from our original guess.

This can be shown by looking back at the illustration already shown in this chapter. At the end of 19-7 the value of the machinery on the balance sheet is shown as £1,024. Using both the old and new methods of depreciation in the recording accounts, we can now see the entries needed if (a) the machinery was sold on 2 January 19-8 for £1,070 and then (b) if instead it have been sold for £950.

1. Old Method

(a) Asset sold at a profit
Book-keeping entries needed –
    For cheque received: Dr Bank
                              Cr Machinery Account
    For profit on sale: Dr Machinery Account
                              Cr Profit and Loss Account

Machinery

19-8	£	19-8	£
Jan 1 Balance b/d	1,024	Jan 2 Bank	1,070
Dec 31 Profit and Loss	46		
	1,070		1,070

Cash Book (bank columns)

19-8	£
Jan 2 Bank	1,070

Profit and Loss Account for the year ended 31 December 19-8

	£
Profit on sale of machinery	46

(b) Asset sold at a loss
Book-keeping entries needed –
    For cheque received: Dr Bank
                              Cr Machinery Account
    For loss on sale: Dr Profit and Loss Account
                              Cr Machinery Account

Machinery

19-8		£	19-8		£
Jan 1 Balance b/d		1,024	Jan 2 Bank		950
			Dec 31 Profit and Loss		74
		1,024			1,024

Cash Book (bank columns)

19-8		£
Jan 2 Bank		950

Profit and Loss Account for the year ended 31 December 19-8

	£
Loss on sale of machinery	74

2. Modern Method

For most examinations at the first stage, other than for professional bodies, if the reader can understand the book-keeping entries needed using the old method then that is sufficient. For the sake of those students who will need to know how to enter the items using the modern method, the description is now given.

(A) Transfer the cost price of the asset sold to an Assets Disposal Account (in this case a Machinery Disposals Account).

Dr Machinery Disposals Account
Cr Machinery Account

(B) Transfer the depreciation already charged to the Assets Disposal Account.

Dr Provision for Depreciation – Machinery
Cr Machinery Disposals Account

(C) For remittance received on disposal.

Dr Cash Book
Cr Machinery Disposals Account

(D) Transfer balance (difference) on Machinery Disposals Account to the Profit and Loss Account.

If the difference is on the debit side of the disposal account, it is a profit on sale.

Debit Machinery Disposals Account
Credit Profit and Loss Account

If the difference is on the credit side of the disposal account, it is a loss on sale.

Debit Profit and Loss Account
Cr Machinery Disposals Account

(a) Asset sold at a profit

Machinery

19-5		£	19-8			£
Jan 1 Cash		2,000	Jan 2 Machinery Disposals	(A)		2,000

Provision for Depreciation: Machinery

19-8		£	19-8		£
Jan 2 Machinery Disposals	(B)	976	Jan 1 Balance b/d		976

Machinery Disposals

19-8		£	19-8			£
Jan 2 Machinery	(A)	2,000	Jan 2 Cash	(C)		1,070
Dec 31 Profit and Loss	(D)	46	Jan 2 Provision for Depreciation	(B)		976
		2,046				2,046

Profit and Loss Account for the year ended 31 December 19-8

			£
Profit on sale of machinery	(D)		46

(b) Asset sold at a loss

Machinery

19-5		£	19-8			£
Jan 1 Cash		2,000	Jan 2 Machinery Disposals	(A)		2,000

Provision for Depreciation: Machinery

19-8		£	19-8		£
Jan 2 Machinery Disposals	(B)	976	Jan 1 Balance b/d		976

Machinery Disposals

19-8		£	19-8			£
Jan 2 Machinery	(A)	2,000	Jan 2 Cash	(C)		950
			Jan 2 Provision for Depreciation	(B)		976
			Dec 31 Profit and Loss	(D)		74
		2,000				2,000

Profit and Loss Account for the year ended 31 December 19-8

		£
Loss on sale of machinery	(D)	74

Modern Method: Further Examples

So far the examples shown have been deliberately kept simple. Only one item of an asset has been shown in each case. Exhibits 20.1 and 20.2 give examples of more complicated cases.

Exhibit 20.1

A machine is bought on 1 January 19-5 for £1,000 and another one on 1 October 19-6 for £1,200. The first machine is sold on 30 June 19-7 for £720. The firm's financial year ends on 31 December. The machinery is to be depreciated at ten per cent, using the straight line method and based on assets in existence at the end of each year ignoring items sold during the year.

Machinery

	£		£
19-5			
Jan 1 Cash	1,000		
19-6		19-6	
Oct 1 Cash	1,200	Dec 31 Balance c/d	2,200
	2,200		2,200
19-7		19-7	
Jan 1 Balance b/d	2,200	Jun 30 Disposals	1,000
		Dec 31 Balance c/d	1,200
	2,200		2,200
19-8			
Jan 1 Balance b/d	1,200		

Provision for Depreciation – Machinery

	£		£
		19-5	
		Dec 31 Profit and Loss	100
19-6		19-6	
Dec 31 Balance c/d	320	Dec 31 Profit and Loss	220
	320		320

19-7	£	19-7	£
Jun 30 Disposals		Jan 1 Balance b/d	320
(2 years × 10 per cent		Dec 31 Profit and Loss	120
× £1,000)	200		
Dec 31 Balance c/d	240		
	440		440
		19-8	
		Jan 1 Balance b/d	240

Disposals of Machinery

19-7		19-7	
Jun 30 Machinery	1,000	Jun 30 Cash	720
		Jun 30 Provision for	
		Depreciation	200
		Dec 31 Profit and Loss	80
	1,000		1,000

Profit and Loss Account for the year ended 31 December

19-5 Provision for	
Depreciation	100
19-6 Provision for	
Depreciation	220
19-7 Provision for	
Depreciation	120
Loss on machinery sold	80

Balance Sheet (Extracts) as at 31 December

	£	£
19-5 Machinery		
at cost	1,000	
Less		
Depreciation		
to date	100	900
19-6 Machinery		
at cost	2,200	
Less		
Depreciation		
to date	320	1,880
19-7 Machinery		
at cost	1,200	
Less		
Depreciation		
to date	240	960

Another example can now be given. This is somewhat more complicated owing first to a greater number of items, and secondly because the depreciation provisions are calculated on a proportionate basis, i.e. one month's depreciation for every one month's ownership.

Exhibit 20.2

A business with its financial year end being 31 December buys two motor vans, No. 1 for £800 and No. 2 for £500, both on 1 January 19-1. It also buys another motor van, No. 3, on 1 July 19-3 for £900 and another, No. 4, on 1 October 19-3 for £720. The first two motor vans are sold, No. 1 for £229 on 30 September 19-4, and the other No. 2, was sold for scrap £5 on 30 June 19-5.

Depreciation is on the straight line basis, 20 per cent per annum, ignoring scrap value in this particular case when calculating depreciation per annum. Show the extracts from the assets account, provision for depreciation account, disposal account, profit and loss account for the years ended 31 December 19-1, 19-2, 19-3, 19-4, and 19-5, and the balance sheets as at those dates.

Motor Vans

		£			£
19-1					
Jan	1 Cash	1,300			
19-3					
July	1 Cash	900	19-3		
Oct	1 Cash	720	Dec 31 Balance c/d		2,920
		2,920			2,920
19-4			19-4		
Jan	1 Balance b/d	2,920	Sept 30 Disposals		800
			Dec 31 Balance c/d		2,120
		2,920			2,920
19-5			19-5		
Jan	1 Balance b/d	2,120	June 30 Disposals		500
			Dec 31 Balance c/d		1,620
		2,120			2,120
19-6					
Jan	1 Balance b/d	1,620			

Provision for Depreciation – Motor Vans

	£		£
		19-1	
		Dec 31 Profit and Loss	260
19-2		19-2	
Dec 31 Balance c/d	520	Dec 31 Profit and Loss	260
	520		520
19-3		19-3	
		Jan 1 Balance b/d	520
Dec 31 Balance c/d	906	Dec 31 Profit and Loss	386
	906		906
19-4		19-4	
Sept 30 Disposals	600	Jan 1 Balance b/d	906
Dec 31 Balance c/d	850	Dec 31 Profit and Loss	544
	1,450		1,450
19-5		19-5	
June 30 Disposals	450	Jan 1 Balance b/d	850
Dec 31 Balance c/d	774	Dec 31 Profit and Loss	374
	1,224		1,224
		19-6	
		Jan 1 Balance b/d	774

Workings – Depreciation Provisions

		£	£
19-1	20% of £1,300		260
19-2	20% of £1,300		260
19-3	20% of £1,300 × 12 months	260	
	20% of £900 × 6 months	90	
	20% of £720 × 3 months	36	
			386
19-4	20% of £2,120 × 12 months	424	
	20% of £800 × 9 months	120	
			544
19-5	20% of £1,620 × 12 months	324	
	20% of £500 × 6 months	50	
			374

Workings – Transfers of Depreciation Provisions to Disposal Accounts

Van 1 Bought Jan 1 19-1 Cost £800
      Sold Sept 30 19-4
      Period of ownership 3¾ years
      Depreciation provisions 3¾ × 20% × £800 = £600
Van 2 Bought Jan 1 19-1 Cost £500
      Sold June 30 19-5
      Period of ownership 4½ years
      Depreciation provisions 4½ × 20% × £500 = £450

Disposals of Motor Vans

19-4	£	19-4	£
Sept 30 Motor Van	800	Sept 30 Provision for	
Dec 31 Profit and Loss	29	Depreciation	600
		,, ,, Cash	229
	829		829
19-5		19-5	
June 30 Motor Van	500	June 30 Provision for	
		Depreciation	450
		,, ,, Cash	5
		Dec 31 Profit and Loss	45
	500		500

Profit and Loss Account for the year ended 31 December (extracts)

	£		
19-1 Provision for			
Depreciation	260		
19-2 Provision for			
Depreciation	260		
19-3 Provision for			
Depreciation	386		
19-4 Provision for		19-4 Profit on motor van sold	29
Depreciation	544		
19-5 Provision for			
Depreciation	374		
Loss on motor van sold	45		

Balance Sheets (Extracts) as at 31 December

	£	£
19-1 Motor Vans at cost	1,300	
Less Depreciation to date	260	
		1,040
19-2 Motor Vans at cost	1,300	
Less Depreciation to date	520	
		780
19-3 Motor Vans at cost	2,920	
Less Depreciation to date	906	
		2,014
19-4 Motor Vans at cost	2,120	
Less Depreciation to date	850	
		1,270
19-5 Motor Vans at cost	1,620	
Less Depreciation to date	774	
		846

Depreciation Provisions and the Replacement of Assets

The purpose of making provision for depreciation is to ensure that the cost of an asset is charged as an expense in an equitable fashion over its useful life in the firm. Parts of the cost are allocated to different years until the whole of the asset's cost has been expensed. This does not mean that depreciation provisions of the type described already provide funds with which to replace the asset when it is put out of use. Such provisions might affect the owner's actions so that funds were available to pay for the replacement of the asset, but this is not necessarily true in all cases.

Imagine a case when a machine is bought for £1,000 and it is expected to last for 5 years, at the end of which time it will be put out of use and will not fetch any money from its being scrapped. If the machine has provisions for depreciation calculated on the straight line basis then £200 per year will be charged as an expense for 5 years. This means that the recorded net profit will be decreased £200 for each of the 5 years because of the depreciation provisions. Now the owner may well, as a consequence, because his profits are £200 less also reduce his drawings by £200 per annum. If the action of charging £200 each year for depreciation also does reduce his annual drawings by £200, then that amount will increase his bank balance (or reduce his bank overdraft), so that at the end of 5 years he may have the cash available to buy a new machine for £1,000 to replace the one that has been put out of use. In fact this is not necessarily true at all, the owner may still take the same amount of drawings for each of the 5 years whether or not a provision for depreciation is charged. In this case nothing has been deliberately held back to provide the cash with which to buy the replacement machine.

There is nothing by law that say that if your recorded profits are £x then the drawings must not exceed £y. For instance a man may make £5,000 profit for his first year in business whilst his drawings were £1,000 in that year, whilst in the second year his profit might be £2,000 and his drawings are £4,000. In the long run an owner may go out of business if his drawings are too high, but in the short term his drawings may well bear no relationship to profits whatsoever. This means that the amounts charged for depreciation provisions thus affecting the profits recorded may not affect the drawings at all in the short term.

Exercises

MC56 At the balance sheet date the balance on the Provision for Depreciation Account is
(A) transferred to Depreciation Account
(B) transferred to Profit and Loss Account
(C) simply deducted from the asset in the Balance Sheet
(D) transferred to the Asset Account.

MC57 In the trial balance the balance on the Provision for Depreciation Account is

(A) shown as a credit item

(B) not shown, as it is part of depreciation

(C) shown as a debit item

(D) sometimes shown as a credit, sometimes as a debit.

MC58 If a provision for depreciation account is in use then the entries for the year's depreciation would be

(A) credit Provision for Depreciation account, debit Profit and Loss Account

(B) debit Asset Account, credit Profit and Loss Account

(C) credit Asset Account, debit Provision for Depreciation Account

(D) credit Profit and Loss Account, debit Provision for Depreciation Account.

20.1. A company starts in business on 1 January 19-1. You are to write up the motor vans account and the provision for depreciation account for the year ended 31 December 19-1 from the information given below. Depreciation is at the rate of 20 per cent per annum, using the basis of 1 month's ownership needs one month's depreciation.

19-1 Bought two motor vans for £1,200 each on 1 January

Bought one motor van for £1,400 on 1 July

20.2. A company starts in business on 1 January 19-3, the financial year end being 31 December. You are to show:

(a) The machinery account

(b) The provision for depreciation account

(c) The balance sheet extracts

for each of the years 19-3, 19-4, 19-5, 19-6.

The machinery bought was:

19-3 1 January   1 machine costing £800

19-4 1 July   2 machines costing £500 each

      1 October   1 machine costing £600

19-6 1 April   1 machine costing £200

Depreciation is at the rate of 10 per cent per annum, using the straight line method, machines being depreciated for each proportion of a year.

20.3. A company maintains its fixed assets at cost. Depreciation provision accounts, one for each type of asset, are in use. Machinery is to be depreciated at the rate of 12½ per cent per annum, and fixtures at the rate of 10 per cent per annum, using the reducing balance method. Depreciation is to be calculated on assets in existence at the end of each year, giving a full year's depreciation even thought the asset was bought part of the way through the year.

The following transactions in assets have taken place:

19-5 1 January   Bought machinery £640, Fixtures £100

      1 July   Bought fixtures £200

19-6 1 October   Bought machinery £720

      1 December   Bought fixtures £50

The financial year end of the business is 31 December.

You are to show:

(a) The machinery account

(b) The fixtures account

(c) The two separate provision for depreciation accounts

(d) The fixed assets section of the balance sheet at the end of each year, for the years ended 31 December 19-5 and 19-6.

20.4. A company depreciates its plant at the rate of 20 per cent per annum, straight line method, for each month for ownership. From the following details draw up the Plant Account and the provision for depreciation account for each of the years 19-4, 19-5, 19-6, and 19-7.

19-4 Bought plant costing £900 on 1 January
      Bought plant costing £600 on 1 October
19-6 Bought plant costing £550 on 1 July
19-7 Sold plant which had been bought on 1 January 19-4 for £900 for the sum of £275 on 30 September 19-7.

You are also required to draw up the plant disposal account and the extracts from the balance sheet as at the end of each year.

20.5. A company maintains its fixed assets at cost. Depreciation provision accounts for each asset are kept.

At 31 December 19-8 the position was as follows:

	Total cost to date	Total depreciation to date
Machinery	52,590	25,670
Office Furniture	2,860	1,490

The following additions were made during the financial year ended 31 December 19-9:

Machinery £2,480, office furniture £320

Some old machines bought in 19-5 for £2,800 were sold for £800 during the year

The rates of depreciation are:

Machinery 10 per cent, office furniture 5 per cent,

using the straight line basis, calculated on the assets in existence at the end of each financial year irrespective of date of purchase.

You are required to show the asset and depreciation accounts for the year ended 31 December 19-9 and the balance sheet entries at that date.

20.6. The vehicles and plant register of Hexagon Transport Ltd shows the following vehicles in service at 30 September 19-3:

Registration No.	HT 1	HT 2	HT 3	HT 4	HT 5
Purchased during the year ended 30 September	19-9	19-0	19-1	19-2	19-3
Original cost	£800	£860	£840	£950	£980

Up to 30 September 19-3, the company had depreciated its motor vehicles by 20 per cent per annum on the diminishing balance system, but as from 1 October 19-3, it is decided to adopt the straight line method of depreciation, and to write all the vehicles down to an estimated residual value of £20 each over an estimated life of five years. The company wishes to adjust the accrued depreciation provisions on the existing vehicles in line with this policy.

During the year ended 30 September 19-4, the company has purchased vehicle HT 6 for £960 and sold HT 2 for £60.

A whole year's depreciation is provided for every vehicle on hand at the end of any accounting period.

You are required to:

(a) reconstruct the entries for each vehicle in the register, as it appeared on 30 September 19-3

(b) calculate the necessary adjustments to be made in respect of the depreciation provisions on 1 October 19-3.

(c) complete the entries in the register for the year to 30 September 19-4, showing clearly how you calculate any adjustment necessary in respect of the sale of HT 2.

Calculations should be made to the nearest £1.

(*Institute of Cost and Management Accountants*)

20.7A. On 1 January, 19-5 John Smith purchased 6 machines for £1,500 each. His accounting year ends on 31 December. Depreciation at the rate of 10 per cent per annum on cost has been charged against income each year and credited to a provision for depreciation account.

On 1 January, 19-6 one machine was sold for £1,250 and on 1 January 19-7 a second machine was sold for £1,150. An improved model which cost £2,800 was purchased on 1 July, 19-6. Depreciation was charged on this new machine at the same rate as that on earlier purchases.

Required:

(a) the machinery account and the provision for depreciation account for 19-5, 19-6 and 19-7; and

(b) the entry for machines in the balance sheet at 31 December, 19-7.

(*Institute of Bankers*)

20.8A. The balance sheet of T. Ltd, as at 31 December, 19-7, contains the following item:

Motor vehicles	£	£
Balance, 1 January, 19-7, at cost		297,000
Add: Purchases during 19-7, at cost		17,000
		314,000
Less: Sales during 19-7 (cost price)	11,000	
Depreciation as at 31 December, 19-7	71,000	
		82,000
		232,000

Depreciation is charged at 20 per cent per annum on cost over five years. A full year's depreciation is charged in the year of acquisition but none in the year of disposal.

During 19-8 the following motor vehicle transactions took place:

Purchases

		£
March 31	Lorry	6,500
April 30	Lorry	8,400
Aug 31	Saloon	1,650
Dec 31	Lorry	4,200

Sales

	Purchased	Cost	Proceeds
		£	£
April 30	Lorry 31.1.-6	3,500	450
June 30	Saloon 30.6.-4	950	75
Sept 30	Lorry 31.12.-1	4,000	250
Nov 30	Lorry 1.1.-7	3,500	800

Required:

Write up the motor vehicles, motor vehicles depreciation provision and motor vehicles disposal accounts for 19-8 in the company's ledger. Also show the relevant entries in the company's profit and loss account and balance sheet at the end of 19-8.

(*Chartered Institute of Secretaries and Administrators*)

20.9A. Hall Ltd, which makes up its accounts to June 30 in each year, has a fleet of motor lorries. Annual depreciation on motor lorries is calculated at a rate of 25 per cent on the reducing balances, with a full year's charge being made in the year in which a lorry is purchased, but no charge in the year of sale.

An extract from the company's Balance Sheet as on 30 June, 19-6, showed the following:

	£
Motor lorries at cost	164,900
Less provision for depreciation	93,382
	71,518

During the year ended 30 June 19-7 purchases and sales of motor lorries were:

Purchases

		£
19-6		
July 30	H 11	8,500
Oct 14	H 12	7,000
19-7		
Feb 25	H 13	9,000
June 24	H 14	5,900

Sales

		Purchased	Cost	Proceeds
			£	£
19-6				
July 30	H 1	14 May, 19-2	1,592	300
Oct 1	H 4	10 July, 19-3	2,560	850
19-7				
Mar 1	H 6	9 Mar, 19-5	8,000	4,600
June 25	H 7	21 Sept, 19-5	3,648	2,700

You are required to write up the following accounts in the company's books for the year ended 30 June 19-7:

(*a*) Motor Lorries Account;

(*b*) Motor Lorries Depreciation Provision Account; and

(*c*) Motor Lorries Disposal Account.

20.10A. Distance Ltd owned three lorries at 1 April 19-6, viz:

A	Purchased 21 May 19-2	Cost £3,120
B	,, 20 June 19-4	,, £1,960
C	,, 1 January 19-6	,, £4,880

Depreciation is taken at 20 per cent of cost per annum, ignoring fractions of a year. No depreciation to be written off in year of sale.

During the year to 31 March 19-7, the following transactions occurred:

(a) 1 June 19-6   B was involved in an accident and considered a write-off by the Insurance Company, who paid £1,050 compensation.

(b) 7 June 19-6   D was purchased for £3,280.

(c) 21 August 19-6   A was sold for £700.

(d) 30 October 19-6   E was purchased for £3,900.

(e) 6 March 19-7   E was not considered suitable for carrying the type of goods required and was exchanged for F. The value of F was considered to be £3,760.

You are required to show the accounts to record these transactions, including the depreciation charge for the year to 31 March, 19-7, in Distance Ltd's books.

20.11A. The net profits of Abel, Baker and Co for 19-5, 19-6 and 19-7 were £2,960, £3,155 and £3,187 respectively. It has now been found that the wrong method was used for depreciation of machinery and fixtures and fittings when calculating these profit figures.

All the assets in question were acquired on 1 January 19-5 for £12,800 (machinery) and £2,560 (fixtures and fittings).

The method used was the straight line (or equal instalment) method, assuming for the machinery a working life of 8 years and scrap value £1,000, and for the fixtures and fittings a working life of 12 years and scrap value £400. The method which should have been used was the reducing balance method (machinery 25 per cent per annum, fixtures and fittings 12½ per cent per annum).

You are asked to re-calculate the net profits for 19-5, 19-6 and 19-7.

(*Oxford Local Examination, 'O' Level*)

21

Bad Debts, Provisions for Doubtful Debts, Provisions for Discounts on Debtors

With many businesses a large proportion, if not all, of the sales are on a credit basis. The business is therefore taking the risk that some of the customers may never pay for the goods sold to them on credit. This is a normal business risk, and therefore bad debts as they are called are a normal business expense, and must be charged as such when calculating the profit or loss for the period.

When a debt is found to be bad, the asset as shown by the debtor's account is worthless, and must accordingly be eliminated as an asset account. This is done by crediting the debtor's account to cancel the asset and increasing the expenses account of bad debts by debiting it there. Sometimes the debtor will have paid part of the debt, leaving the remainder to be written off as a bad debt. The total of the bad debts account is later transferred to the profit and loss account.

An example of debts being written off as bad can now be shown:

Exhibit 21.1

C. Bloom

19-5		£	19-5		£
Jan 8	Sales	50	Dec 31	Bad Debts	50

R. Shaw

19-5		£	19-5		£
Feb 16	Sales	240	Aug 17	Cash	200
			Dec 31	Bad Debts	40
		240			240

Bad Debts

19-5		£	19-5		£
Dec 31 C. Bloom		50	Dec 31 Profit and Loss		90
,, ,, R. Shaw		40			
		90			90

Profit and Loss Account for the year ended 31 December 19-5

	£
Bad Debts	90

Provision for Bad Debts

The ideal situation from the accounting point of view of measuring net income, i.e. calculating net profit, is for the expenses of the period to be matched against the revenue of that period which the expenses have helped to create. Where an expense such as bad debt is matched in the same period with the revenue from the sale, then all is in order for the purposes of net profit calculation. However, it is very often the case that it is not until a period later than that in which the sale took place is it realized that the debt is a bad debt.

Therefore, to try to bring into the period in which the sale was made a charge for the bad debts resulting from such sales, the accountant brings in the concept of an estimated expense. Such an item of expense for an expense that had taken place, but which cannot be calculated with substantial accuracy is known as a Provision. The item of estimated expense for bad debts is therefore known as a Provision for Bad Debts.

Thus, in addition to writing off debts that are irrecoverable i.e. bad, it is necessary as a matter of business prudence, to charge the Profit and Loss Account with the amount of the provision for any debt the recovery of which is in doubt.

The estimate is arrived at on the basis of experience, a knowledge of the customers and of the state of the country's economy at that point in time with its likely effect on customers' debt paying capacity. Sometimes the schedules of debtors are scrutinized and a list of the doubtful debts made. Other firms work on an overall percentage basis to cover possible doubtful debts. Sometimes a provision is based on specified debtors. Another method is that of preparing an ageing schedule and taking different percentages for debts owing for different lengths of time. This is somewhat more scientific than the overall percentage basis, as in most trades and industries the longer a debt is owed the more chance there is of it turning out to be a bad debt. The schedule might appear as in Exhibit 21.2.

Exhibit 21.2

Ageing Schedule for Doubtful Debts

Period debt owing	Amount	Estimated percentage doubtful	Provision for bad debts
	£		£
Less than one month	5,000	1	50
1 month to 2 months	3,000	3	90
2 months to 3 months	800	4	32
3 months to 1 year	200	5	10
Over 1 year	160	20	32
	9,160		214

There are in fact two different methods of recording the provisions for doubtful debts. An adjustment may be made in the Bad Debts Account, or alternatively a completely separate account can be opened catering for the bad debts provision only. The net amount shown as bad debt expenses will be the same using the two methods, also the balance sheet will look exactly the same whichever method is used. The two methods are best illustrated in Exhibit 21.3.

It should be pointed out that, in practice, the more likely method will be that shown in Method A where the adjustment is shown in the Bad Debts Account. Examiners have however very often tended to choose a style having a completely separate account for the provision, this is shown as Method B. Either way is perfectly correct, and if the reader finds that he/she has difficulty with one method, but finds the other method simpler to follow, then obviously the simpler method will be the choice for that person.

(It should be noted that provisions for bad debts are frequently called provisions for doubtful debts).

Exhibit 21.3

A business starts on 1 January 19-2 and its financial year end is 31 December annually. A table of the debtors, the bad debts written off and the estimated doubtful debts at the end of each year is now given.

Year to 31 December	Debtors at end of year (after bad debts written off)	Bad Debts written off during year	Debts thought at end of year to be doubtful to collect
	£	£	£
19-2	6,000	423	120
19-3	7,000	510	140
19-4	8,000	604	155
19-5	6,400	610	130

Method A – using a Bad Debts Account only with adjustments being used for provisions for bad debts.

Profit and Loss Account for the year ended 31 December (extracts)

	£		£
19-2 Bad Debts	543		
19-3 Bad Debts	530		
19-4 Bad Debts	619		
19-5 Bad Debts	585		

Bad Debts

19-2		£	19-2		£
Dec 31 Sundries		423			
,, ,, Provision c/d		120	Dec 31 Profit and Loss		543
		543			543
19-3			19-3		
Dec 31 Sundries		510	Jan 1 Provision b/d		120
,, ,, Provision c/d		140	Dec 31 Profit and Loss		530
		650			650
19-4			19-4		
Dec 31 Sundries		604	Jan 1 Provision b/d		140
,, ,, Provision c/d		155	Dec 31 Profit and Loss		619
		759			759
19-5			19-5		
Dec 31 Sundries		610	Jan 1 Provision b/d		155
,, ,, Provision c/d		130	Dec 31 Profit and Loss		585
		740			740
			19-6		
			Jan 1 Provision for Doubtful debts b/d		130

Balance Sheets as at 31 December (extracts)

	£	£
19-2 Debtors	6,000	
Less Provision for Bad Debts	120	
		5,880
19-3 Debtors	7,000	
Less Provision for Bad Debts	140	
		6,860
19-4 Debtors	8,000	
Less Provision for Bad Debts	155	
		7,845
19-5 Debtors	6,400	
Less Provision for Bad Debts	130	
		6,270

Method B – using a separate Bad Debts Account and a provision for Bad Debts Account.

The Bad Debts Account is charged with the debts found to be bad during the accounting period, while the provision for Bad Debts Account shows the provision as at the end of each period. Once the provision account is created it stays open until the end of the next accounting period, and all that it then requires is the amount needed to increase it or reduce it to the newly estimated figure. In the balance sheet at the end of each period the provision for bad debts is shown as a deduction from debtors, so that the net amount is the expected amount of collectable debts.

Profit and Loss Accounts for the year ended 31 December (extracts)

	£		£
19-2 Bad Debts	423		
Provision for Bad Debts	120		
19-3 Bad Debts	510		
Increase in provision for Bad Debts	20		
19-4 Bad Debts	604		
Increase in provision for Bad Debts	15		
19-5 Bad Debts	610	19-5 Reduction in provision for Bad Debts	25

Provision for Bad Debts

	£		£
		19-2	
		Dec 31 Profit and Loss	120
19-3		19-3	
Dec 31 Balance c/d	140	Dec 31 Profit and·Loss	20
	140		140
19-4		19-4	
Dec 31 Balance c/d	155	Jan 1 Balance b/d	140
		Dec 31 Profit and Loss	15
	155		155
19-5	£	19-5	£
Dec 31 Profit and Loss	25	Jan 1 Balance b/d	155
,, ,, Balance c/d	130		
	155		155
		19-6	
		Jan 1 Balance b/d	130

Bad Debts

	£		£
19-2		19-2	
Dec 31 Sundries	423	Dec 31 Profit and Loss	423
19-3		19-3	
Dec 31 Sundries	510	Dec 31 Profit and Loss	510
19-4		19-4	
Dec 31 Sundries	604	Dec 31 Profit and Loss	604
19-5		19-5	
Dec 31 Sundries	610	Dec 31 Profit and Loss	610

The balance sheet for Method B will be exactly the same as the balance sheet in Method A.

Comparing the amounts charged as expense to the Profit and loss Account it can be seen that:

	Method A	Method B
19-2	543	423 + 120 = total 543
19-3	530	510 + 20 = total 530
19-4	619	604 + 15 = total 619
19-5	585	610 − 25 = net 585

At first sight it might appear that the provisions were far short of reality. For instance at the end of the first year the provision was £120 yet bad debts in the second year amounted to £510. This, however, is not a fair comparison if the amount of debtors at each year end equalled in amount approximately three months of sales, this being the average time in which debtors pay their accounts. In this case the provision is related to three months of sales, while the bad debts written off are those relating to twelve months of sales.

Bad Debts Recovered

It is not uncommon for a debt written off in previous years to be recovered in later years. When this occurs, the bookkeeping procedures are as follows:

First, re-instate the debt by making the following entries:

Dr Debtors Account

Cr Bad Debts Recovered Account.

The reason for re-instating the debt in the ledger account of the debtor is to have a detailed history of his/her account as a guide for granting credit in future. By the time a debt is written off as bad, it will be recorded in the debtor's ledger account. It is prudent therefore that when such debt is recovered, it also must be reflected in the debtor's ledger acount.

When cash/cheque is subsequently received from the debtor in settlement of the account or part thereof,

Dr Cash/Bank

Cr Debtor's Account

with the amount received.

At the end of the financial year, the credit balance in the Bad Debts Recovered Account will be transferred to either Bad Debts Account or direct to the credit side of the profit and loss account. The effect is the same since the bad debts account will in itself be transferred to the profit and loss account at the end of the financial year.

Provisions for Discounts on Debtors

Some firms create provisions for Discounts to be allowed on the debtors outstanding at the balance sheet date. This, they maintain, is quite legitimate, as the amount of debtors less any doubtful debt provision is not the best estimate of collectable debts, owing to cash discounts which will be given to debtors if they pay within a given time. The cost of discounts, it is argued, should be charged in the period when the sales were made.

To do this the procedure is similar to the doubtful debts provision. It must be borne in mind that the estimate of discounts to be allowed should be based on the net figure of debtors less bad debts provision, as it is obvious that discounts are not allowed on bad debts!

Example

Year ended 31 December	Debtors	Provision for Bad Debts	Provision for discounts allowed
	£	£	%
19-3	4,000	200	2
19-4	5,000	350	2
19-5	4,750	250	2

Profit and Loss Account for the year ended 31 December (extracts)

	£		£
19-3 Provision for discounts on debtors (2 per cent of £3,800)	76		
19-4 Increase in Provision for discounts on debtors (to 2 per cent of £4,650)	17		
		19-5 Reduction in provision for discounts on debtors (to 2 per cent of £4,500)	3

Provision for Discounts on Debtors

		£			£
				Dec 31 Profit and Loss	76
19-4			19-4		
Dec 31 Balance c/d		93	Dec 31 Profit and Loss		17
		93			93
19-5			19-5		
Dec 31 Profit and Loss		3	Jan 1 Balance b/d		93
,, ,, Balance c/d		90			
		93			93
			19-6		
			Jan 1 balance b/d		90

Balance Sheets as at 31 December (extracts)

	£	£	£
19-3 Debtors		4,000	
Less Provision for Bad Debts	200		
,, Provision for discounts on debtors	76		
		276	3,724
19-4 Debtors		5,000	
Less Provision for Bad Debts	350		
,, Provision for discounts on debtors	93		
		443	4,557
19-5 Debtors		4,750	
Less Provision for Bad Debts	250		
,, Provision for discounts on debtors	90		
		340	4,410

Discounts on Creditors

It is also the practice of some firms to take into account the fact that the amount of creditors at the balance sheet date does not represent the amount which will be paid. This is because where advantage is taken of cash discount arrangements, a smaller sum will be payable to discharge the debts.

This is anticipating income, and therefore contravenes the accounting convention of conservatism. However, it is perhaps felt that if a firm creates a provision for discounts on debtors, it should also take into account discounts on creditors.

Example

Year ended 31 December	Creditors	Discounts receivable
	£	%
19-4	5,000	2
19-5	5,600	2
19-6	4,800	2

Profit and Loss Account for the year ended 31 December (extracts)

	£		£
		19-4 Discounts on creditors	100
		19-5 Discounts on creditors	12
19-6 Reduction in discounts on creditors	16		

Allowance for Discounts on Creditors

	£		£
19-4 Dec 31 Profit and Loss	100		
19-5 Dec 31 Profit and Loss	12	19-5 Dec 31 Balance c/d	112
	112		112
19-6 Jan 1 Balance b/d	112	19-6 Dec 31 Profit and Loss	16
		,, ,, Balance c/d	96
	112		112
19-7 Jan 1 Balance b/d	96		

Balance Sheets as at 31 December (extracts)

	£	£
19-4 Creditors	5,000	
Less Allowance for discounts	100	
		4,900
19-5 Creditors	5,600	
Less Allowance for discounts	112	
		5,488
19-6 Creditors	4,800	
Less Allowance for discounts	96	
		4,704

Exercises

MC59 When the final accounts are prepared the Bad Debts Account is closed by a transfer to the
(A) Balance Sheet
(B) Profit and Loss Account
(C) Trading Account
(D) Provision for Bad Debts Account.

MC60 A Provision for Bad Debts is created
(A) When debtors become bankrupt
(B) When debtors cease to be in business
(C) To provide for possible bad debts
(D) To write off bad debts.

21.1. In a new business during the year ended 31 December 19-4 the following debts are found to be bad, and are written off on the dates shown:

30 April	H. Gordon	£110
31 August	D. Bellamy Ltd	£64
31 October	J. Alderton	£12

On 31 December 19-4 the schedule of remaining debtors, amounting in total to £6,850, is examined, and it is decided to make a provision, for doubtful debts of £220.

You are required to show:
(i) The bad debts account, with the provision to be a part of it.
(ii) The charge to the Profit and Loss Account.
(iii) The relevant extracts from the Balance Sheet as at 31 December 19-4.
(*also see question 21.5*)

21.2. A business started trading on 1 January 19-6. During the two years ended 31 December 19-6 and 19-7 the following debts were written off to bad debts account on the dates stated:

31 August 19-6	W. Best	£85
30 September 19-6	S. Avon	£140
28 February 19-7	L. J. Friend	£180
31 August 19-7	N. Kelly	£60
30 November 19-7	A. Oliver	£250

On 31 December 19-6 there had been a total of debtors remaining of £40,500. It was decided to make a provision for doubtful debts of £550.

On 31 December 19-7 there had been a total of debtors remaining of £47,300. It was decided to make a provision for doubtful debts of £600.

You are required to show:
(i) The Bad Debts Account for each of the two years, with the provisions included in this account.
(ii) The charges to the Profit and Loss Account for each of the two years.
(iii) The relevant extracts from the balance sheets as at 31 December 19-6 and 19-7.

(*also see question 21.5*)

21.3. A business had always made a provision for bad debts at the rate of 5 per cent of debtors. On 1 January 19-3 the provision for this, brought forward from the previous year, was £260.

During the year to 31 December 19-3 the bad debts written off amounted to £540.

On 31 December 19-3 the remaining debtors totalled £6,200 and the usual provision for bad debts is to be made.

You are to show:
(i) The Bad Debts Account for the year ended 31 December 19-3.
(ii) Extract from the Profit and Loss Account for the year.
(iii) The relevant extract from the balance sheet as at 31 December 19-3.

21.4A. A business, which started trading on 1 January 19-5, adjusted its bad debt provisions at the end of each year on a percentage basis, but each year the percentage rate is adjusted in accordance with the current 'economic climate'. The following details are available for the three years ended 31 December 19-5, 19-6 and 19-7.

Bad Debts written off year to 31 December	Debtors at 31 December	Per cent provision for Bad Debts
	£	£	
19-5	656	22,000	5
19-6	1,805	40,000	7
19-7	3,847	60,000	6

Using the method shown as Method A in Chapter 21, you are required to show the following:
(i) Bad Debts Accounts for each of the three years, showing provisions carried forward.
(ii) Balance Sheet extracts as at 31 December 19-5, 19-6 and 19-7.

(*also see question 21.5*)

21.5. For students sitting examinations where separate Provision for Bad Debt account questions are asked, attempt questions 21.1, 21.2 and 21.4 using Method B as stated in Chapter 21.

21.6A. A firm makes a provision for bad debts of 5 per cent on debtors, also a provision of 2½ per cent for discount on debtors.

On 1 January 19-7 the balances brought forward on the relevant accounts were provision for bad debts £672 and provision for discounts on debtors £631.

You are required to:
(a) Enter the balances in the appropriate accounts, using a separate Provision for Bad Debts Account
(b) During 19-7 the firm incurred bad debts £2,960 and allowed discounts £6,578. On 31 December 19-7 debtors amounted to £25,600. Show the entries in the appropriate accounts for the year 19-7, assuming that the firm's accounting year ends on 31 December 19-7, also balance sheet extracts at 31 December 19-7.

21.7A. E. Chivers commenced business on 1 January 19-7 and makes his accounts to 31 December every year. For the year ended 31 December 19-7, bad debts written off amounted to £1,200. It was also found necessary to create a provision for doubtful debts of £2,000.

In 19-8, debts amounting to £1,600 proved bad and were written off. Mrs. P. Iles whose debt of £350 was written off as bad in 1977 settled her account in full on 30 November 19-8. As at 31 December 19-8 total debts outstanding were £56,000. It was decided to bring the provision up to 5% of this figure on that date.

In 19-9, £2,350 debts were written off during the year, and another recovery of £150 was made in respect of debts written off in 1977. As at 31 December 19-9, total debts outstanding were £42,000. The provision for doubtful debts is to be maintained at 5% of this figure.

You are required to show for the years 19-7, 19-8 and 19-9, the
(a) Bad Debts Account.
(b) Bad Debts Recovered Account.
(c) Provision for Bad Debts Account.
(d) Extract from the Profit and Loss Accounts.

22

Other Adjustments for Final Accounts: Accruals, Prepayments etc.

The trading and profit and loss accounts looked at so far have taken the sales for a period and all the expenses for that period have been deducted, the result being a net profit (or a net loss).

Up to this part of the book it has always been assumed that the expenses belonged exactly to the period of the trading and profit and loss account. If the trading and profit and loss account for the year ended 31 December 19-5 was being drawn up, then the rent paid as shown in the trial balance was exactly for 19-5. There was no rent owing at the beginning of 19-5 nor any owing at the end of 19-5, nor had any rent been paid in advance.

However, where on the other hand the costs used up and the amount paid are not equal to one another, then an adjustment will be required in respect of the overpayment or underpayment of the costs used up during the period.

In all of the following examples the trading and profit and loss accounts being drawn up are for the year ended 31 December 19-5.

Accrued Expenses

Consider the case of rent being charged at the rate of £1,000 per year. It is payable at the end of each quarter of the year for the three months' tenancy that has just expired. It can be assumed that the tenancy commenced on 1 January 19-5. The rent was paid for 19-5 on 31 March, 2 July and 4 October and on 5 January 19-6.

During the year ended 31 December 19-5 the rent account will appear:

Rent

19-5		£
Mar 31 Cash		250
Jul 2 ,,		250
Oct 4 ,,		250

The rent paid 5 January 19-6 will appear in the books of the year 19-6 as part of the double-entry.

The costs used up during 19-5 are obviously £1,000, as that is the year's rent, and this is the amount needed to be transferred to the profit and loss account. But if £1,000 was put on the credit side of the rent account (the debit being in the profit and loss account) the account would not balance. There would be £1,000 on the credit side of the account and only £750 on the debit side. To make the account balance the £250 rent owing for 19-5, but paid in 19-6, must be carried down to 19-6 as a credit balance because it is a liability on 31 December 19-5. Instead of Rent Owing it could be called Rent Accrued or just simply as an accrual. The completed account can now be shown.

Rent

19-5	£	19-5	£
Mar 31 Cash	250	Dec 31 Profit and Loss A/c	1,000
Jul 2 ,,	250		
Oct 4 ,,	250		
Dec 31 Owing c/d	250		
	1,000		1,000
		19-6	
		Jan 1 Owing b/d	250

Expenses Prepaid

Insurance premiums have been paid as follows:

Feb 28 19-5 £210 for period of three months to 31 March 19-5.
Aug 31 19-5 £420 for period of six months to 30 September 19-5.
Nov 18 £420 for period of six months to 31 March 19-6.

The insurance account will be shown in the books:

Insurance

19-5	£
Feb 28 Cash	210
Aug 31 ,,	420
Nov 18 ,,	420

Now the last payment of £420 is not just for 19-5, it can be split as to £210 for the three months to 31 December 19-5 and £210 for the three months ended 31 March 19-6. For a period of 12 months the cost of insurance is £840 and this is therefore the figure needing to be transferred to the profit and loss account. The amount needed to balance the account will therefore be £210 and at 31 December 19-5 this is a benefit paid for but not used up; it is an asset and needs carrying forward as such to 19-6, i.e. as a debit balance.

The account can now be completed.

Insurance

19-5	£	19-5	£
Feb 28 Cash	210	Dec 31 Profit and Loss A/c	840
Aug 31 ,,	420	,, ,, Prepaid c/d	210
Nov 18 ,,	420		
	1,050		1,050
19-6			
Jan 1 Prepaid b/d	210		

Prepayment will also happen when items other than purchases are bought for use in the business, and they are not fully used up in the period.

For instance, packing materials are normally not entirely used up during the period in which they are bought, there being a stock of packing materials in hand at the end of the period. This stock is therefore a form of prepayment and needs carrying down to the following period in which it will be used.

This can be seen in the following example:

Year ended 31 December 19-5
Packing materials bought in the year £2,200
Stock of packing materials in hand as at 31 December 19-5 £400

Looking at the example, it can be seen that in 19-5 the packing materials used up will have been £2,200 − £400 = £1,800 and there will still be a stock of £400 packing materials at 31 December 19-5 to be carried forward to 19-6. The £400 stock of packing materials will accordingly be carried forward as an asset balance (debit balance) to 19-6.

Packing Materials

19-5	£	19-5	£
Dec 31 Cash	2,200	Dec 31 Profit and Loss A/c	1,800
		,, ,, Stock c/d	400
	2,200		2,200
19-6			
Jan 1 Stock b/d	400		

The stock of packing materials is not added to the stock of unsold goods in hand in the balance sheet, but is added to the other prepayments of expenses.

Outstanding Revenue other than Sales

Sales revenue outstanding is already shown in the books as debit balances on the customers' personal accounts, i.e. debtors. It is the other kinds of revenue such as rent receivable, commissions receivable, etc. which need to be considered. Such revenue to be brought into the profit and loss account is that which has been earned during the period. Should all the revenue earned actually be received during the period, then revenue received and revenue earned will be the same amount and no adjustment would be needed in the revenue account. Where the revenue has been earned, but the full amount has not been received, the revenue due to the business must be brought into the accounts; the amount receivable is after all the revenue used when calculating profit.

Example

The warehouse is larger than is needed. Part of it is rented to another firm for £800 per annum. For the year ended 31 December 19-5 the following cheques were received.

19-5
Apr 4 For three months to 31 March 19-5   £200
Jul   6 For three months to 30 June 19-5   £200
Oct 9 For three months to 30 September 19-5   £200

The £200 for the three months to 31 December 19-5 was received 7 January 19-6.

The account for 19-5 appeared:

Rent Receivable

		£
19-5		
Apr 4	Bank	200
Jul 6	Bank	200
Oct 9	Bank	200

Any rent paid by the firm would be charged as a debit to the profit and loss account. Any rent received, being the opposite, is accordingly eventually transferred to the credit of the profit and loss account. The amount to be transferred for 19-5 is that earned for the twelve months. i.e. £800. The rent received account is completed by carrying down the balance owing as a debit balance to 19-6. The £200 owing is, after all, an asset on 31 December 19-5.

The Rent Receivable Account can now be completed:

Rent Receivable

19-5		£	19-5		£
Dec 31 Profit and Loss		800	Apr 4 Bank		200
			Jul 6 Bank		200
			Oct 9 Bank		200
			Dec 31 Accrued c/d		200
		800			800
19-6					
Jan 1 Accrued b/d		200			

Expenses and Revenue Account Balances and the Balance Sheet

In all the cases listed dealing with adjustments in the final accounts, there will still be a balance on each account after the preparation of the trading and profit and loss accounts. All such balances remaining should appear in the balance sheet. The only question left is to where and how they shall be shown.

The amounts owing for expenses are usually added together and shown as one figure. These could be called Expense Creditors, Expenses Owing, or Accrued Expenses. The item would appear under current liabilities as they are expenses which have to be discharged in the near future.

The items prepaid are also added together and called Prepayments, Prepaid Expenses, or Payments in Advance. Often they are added to the debtors in the balance sheet, otherwise they are shown next under the debtors.

Amounts owing for rents receivable or other revenue owing are usually added to debtors.

The balance sheet in respect of the accounts so far seen in this chapter would appear:

Balance Sheets as at 31 December 19-5

Current Assets	£	Current Liabilities	£
Stock		Trade creditors	
Debtors	200	Accrued Expenses	250
Prepayments	610		
Bank			
Cash			

Goods for Own Use

A trader will often take items out of his business stocks for his own use, without paying for them. There is certainly nothing wrong about this, but an entry should be made to record the event. This is effected by:

> Credit Purchases Account
> Debit Drawings Account

Adjustments may also be needed for other private items. For instance, if a trader's private insurance had been incorrectly charged to the Insurance Account, then the correction would be:

> Credit Insurance Account
> Debit Drawings Account

Final Accounts for Non-Traders

If the final accounts are for someone who is not trading in goods as such, for instance accountants, insurance agents, lawyers and the like, there will be no need for a Trading Account. All of the revenue and expense items will be shown in a Profit and Loss Account, disclosing a net profit (or net loss). Balance Sheets for such providers of services (i.e. not goods) will be the same as for traders.

Vertical Form of Accounts

Throughout this book to this point the two-sided presentation of Trading and Profit and Loss Accounts and Balance Sheets is used. For many reasons this is easier to use from a teaching point of view. However, in practice you would not necessarily have to show the final accounts drawn up in that fashion. It would be completely up to the owner(s) of a business to decide on the method of presentation. What really matters is whether or not the presentation still results in the correct answer being shown.

Final accounts are more normally shown in a vertical fashion. This is also referred to as narrative style, or columnar presentation. When this is done the chance is usually taken of displaying 'working capital' as a separate figure. 'Working Capital' is the term for the excess of the current assets over the current liabilities of a business.

The translation of a Trading and Profit and Loss Account from a horizontal format to a vertical format can be shown by means of a diagram Exhibit 22.2

Exhibit 22.2

Horizontal form:

A. Client
Trading and Profit and Account for the year ended 31 December 19-5

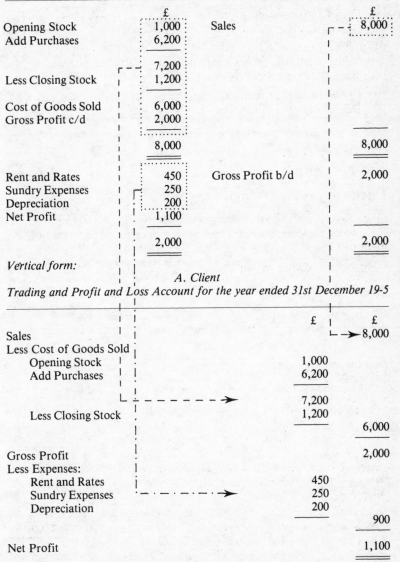

	£		£
Opening Stock	1,000	Sales	8,000
Add Purchases	6,200		
	7,200		
Less Closing Stock	1,200		
Cost of Goods Sold	6,000		
Gross Profit c/d	2,000		
	8,000		8,000
Rent and Rates	450	Gross Profit b/d	2,000
Sundry Expenses	250		
Depreciation	200		
Net Profit	1,100		
	2,000		2,000

Vertical form:

A. Client
Trading and Profit and Loss Account for the year ended 31st December 19-5

	£	£
Sales		8,000
Less Cost of Goods Sold		
Opening Stock	1,000	
Add Purchases	6,200	
	7,200	
Less Closing Stock	1,200	
		6,000
Gross Profit		2,000
Less Expenses:		
Rent and Rates	450	
Sundry Expenses	250	
Depreciation	200	
		900
Net Profit		1,100

If there had been any revenue such as commissions or rent received, then this would have followed the figure of gross profit as an addition.

Exhibit 22.3 shows the translation of a balance sheet from the horizontal form to a vertical form.

Exhibit 22.3

Horizontal form:

A. Client
Balance Sheet as at 31 December 19-5

	£	£			£
Fixed Assets:				**Capital:**	
Fixtures at cost	2,600			Balance as at 1.1.19-5	5,000
Less Depreciation				Add Net Profit	1,300
to date	200				
		2,400			6,300
				Less Drawings	1,100
Current Assets					
Stock	1,200				5,200
Debtors	2,900				
Cash at Bank	700	4,800		**Current Liabilities**	
				Trade Creditors	1,850
				Accrued Expenses	150	2,000
		7,200			7,200

Vertical form:

A. Client
Balance Sheet as at 31 December 19-5

	£	£	£
Fixed Assets			
Fixtures at cost		2,600	
Less Depreciation to date		200	2,400
Current Assets			
Stock		1,200	
Debtors		2,900	
Cash at Bank		700	
		4,800	
Less Current Liabilities			
Trade Creditors	1,850		
Accrued Expenses	150	2,000	
Working Capital			2,800
			5,200
Financed by:			
Capital			
Balance as at 1.1.19-5			5,000
Add Net Profit			1,300
			6,300
Less Drawings			1,100
			5,200

You should note that there is not just one way of presenting final accounts in a vertical fashion, but the ones shown are in a good style.

From this point most of the final accounts are shown in vertical style, as it accords with normal practice in business and would be looked on with favour by examiners. However, on occasion, because of display reasons in fitting a lot of information on a page the horizontal style will be used.

Distinctions Between Various Kinds of Capital

The capital account represents the claim of the proprietor against the assets of the business at a point in time. The word 'Capital' is, however, often used in a specific sense. The main meanings are listed below:

1. Capital invested. This means the actual amount of money, or money's worth, brought into the business by the proprietor from his outside interests. The amount of capital invested is not disturbed by the amount of profits made by the business or losses incurred.

2. Capital employed. Candidates at an early stage in their studies are often asked to define this term. In fact, for those who progress to a more advanced stage, it will be seen in Volume 2 that it could have several meanings as the term is often used quite loosely. At an elementary level it is taken to mean the effective amount of money that is being used in the business. Thus, if all the assets were added together and the liabilities of the business deducted the answer would be that the difference is the amount of money employed in the business. You will by now realize that this is the same as the closing balance of the capital account. It is also sometimes called Net Assets.

3. Working capital is a term for the excess of the current assets over the current liabilities of a business.

Exercises

MC61 Working Capital is a term meaning
(A) The amount of capital invested by the proprietor
(B) The excess of the current assets over the current liabilities
(C) The capital less drawings
(D) The total of Fixed Assets + Current Assets.

MC62 A credit balance brought down on a Rent Account means
(A) We owe that rent at that date
(B) We have paid that rent in advance at that date
(C) We have paid too much rent
(D) We have paid too little in rent.

MC63 A debit balance brought down on a Packing Materials Account means
(A) We owe for packing materials
(B) We are owed for packing materials
(C) We have lost money on packing materials
(D) We have a stock of packing materials unused.

MC64 If we take goods for own use we should
(A) Debit Drawings Account: Credit Purchases Account
(B) Debit Purchases Account: Credit Drawings Account
(C) Debit Drawings Account: Credit Stock Account
(D) Debit Sales Account: Credit Stock Account.

22.1. The financial year of H. Saunders ended on 31 December 19-6. Show the ledger accounts for the following items including the balance transferred to the necessary part of the final accounts, also the balances carried down to 19-7:

(a) Motor Expenses: Paid in 19-6 £744; Owing at 31 December 19-6 £28.
(b) Insurance: Paid in 19-6 £420; Prepaid as at 31 December 19-6 £35.
(c) Stationery: Paid during 19-6 £1,800; Owing as at 31 December 19-5 £250; Owing as at 31 December 19-6 £490.
(d) Rent: Paid during 19-6 £950; Prepaid as at 31 December 19-5 £220; Prepaid as at 31 December 19-6 £290.
(e) Saunders sub-lets part of the premises. Receives £550 during the year ended 31 December 19-6. Tenant owed Saunders £180 on 31 December 19-5 and £210 on 31 December 19-6.

22.2A. J. Owen's year ended on 30 June 19-4. Write up the ledger accounts, showing the transfers to the final accounts and the balances carried down to the next year for the following:

(a) Stationery: Paid for the year to 30 June 19-4 £855; Stocks of stationery at 30 June 19-3 £290; at 30 June 19-4 £345.
(b) General expenses: Paid for the year to 30 June 19-4 £590; Owing at 30 June 19-3 £64; Owing at 30 June 19-4 £90.
(c) Rent and Rates (combined account): Paid in the year to 30 June 19-4 £3,890; Rent owing at 30 June 19-3 £160; Rent paid in advance at 30 June 19-4 £250; Rates owing 30 June 19-3 £205; Rates owing 30 June 19-4 £360.
(d) Motor Expenses: paid in the year to 30 June 19-4 £4,750; Owing as at 30 June 19-3 £180; Owing as at 30 June 19-4 £375.
(e) Owen earns commission from the sales of one item. Received for the year to 30 June 19-4 £850; Owing at 30 June 19-3 £80; Owing at 30 June 19-4 £145.

22.3. On 1 January 19-8 the following balances, among others, stood in the books of M. Baldock, a sole trader:
(a) Rates, £104 (Dr);
(b) Packing Materials, £629 (Dr).
During the year ended 31 December 19-8 the information related to these two accounts is as follows:
(i) Rates of £1500 were paid to cover the period 1 April 19-8 to 31 March 19-9;
(ii) £5,283 was paid for packing materials bought;
(iii) £357 was owing on 31 December 19-8 in respect of packing materials bought on credit;
(iv) Old materials amounting to £172 were sold as scrap for cash;
(v) Closing stock was valued at £598.
You are required to write up the two accounts showing the appropriate amounts transferred to the Profit and Loss Account at 31 December 19-8, the end of the financial year of the trader.
Note: No separate accounts are opened for creditors for packing materials bought on credit.

22.4A. On 1 January 19-6 the following balances, among others, stood in the books of T. Thomas:

(a) Lighting and Heating, (Dr) £277.

(b) Insurance, (Dr) £307.

During the year ended 31 December 19-6 the information related to these two accounts is as follows:

(i) Fire Insurance, £960, covering the year ended 30 April 19-7 was paid.

(ii) General Insurance, £630, covering the year ended 31 August 19-7 was paid.

(iii) An insurance rebate of £55 was received on 30 June 19-6.

(iv) Electricity bills of £874 were paid.

(v) An electricity bill of £83 for December 19-6 was unpaid as on 31 December 19-6.

(vi) Oil bills of £1,260 were paid.

(vii) Stock of oil as on 31 December was £92.

22.5. On 1 January 19-6 B. Allison started business as a wholesale confectioner. The following were among the balances extracted from his books at 31 December 19-6.

From the following information you are required to prepare the Trading and Profit and Loss Accounts for the Year ended 31 December 19-6 using vertical style accounts:

	£
Purchases	11,377
Sales	13,475
Returns Inwards	242
Returns Outwards	268
Carriage on Purchases	47
Motor Van Expenses	155
Wages of Driver	652
Office Expenses	104
Bad Debts	79
Insurances	26
Electricity	30
Interest on Loan	21
Discounts Allowed	337
Discounts Received	210
Rent and Rates	365
Rent of Premises Sublet	104

You are given the following additional information:

(i) Stock in hand at 31 December 19-6 was valued at £898.

(ii) A motor van which costs £660 is to be depreciated by 15% on cost.

(iii) Provide £105 for Bad and Doubtful Debts.

(iv) A half year's interest £21 was due on the loan.

(v) A demand notice for rates for the half year ending 31 March 19-7, £56 had been received but no payment made.

(vi) Insurance £6 was prepaid.

(vii) £12 was owing in respect of repairs to the motor van.

22.6A. From the following Trial Balance of J. Oliphant, store owner, prepare a Trading Account and Profit and Loss Account using the vertical style, taking into consideration the adjustments shown below:

Trial Balance as at 31 December 19-7

	Dr £	Cr £
Sales		80,000
Purchases	70,000	
Sales Returns	1,000	
Purchases Returns		1,240
Opening Stock at 1 January 19-7	20,000	
Provision for Bad Debt		160
Wages and salaries	7,200	
Telephone	200	
Store fittings at cost	8,000	
Van at cost	6,000	
Debtors and creditors	1,960	1,400
Bad Debts	40	
Capital		35,800
Bank balance	600	
Drawings	3,600	
	118,600	118,600

Adjustments:
(i) Closing stock at 31 December 19-7 £24,000.
(ii) Accrued wages £450.
(iii) Telephone prepaid £20.
(iv) The Provision for Bad Debts to be increased to 10 per cent of Debtors.
(v) Depreciate store fittings at 10 per cent per annum, and van at 20 per cent per annum, on cost.
A Balance Sheet is not required.

22.7. The following Trial Balance was extracted from the books of A. Scholes at the close of business on 28 February 19-7.

	Dr £	Cr £
Purchases and sales	11,280	19,740
Cash at bank	1,140	
Cash in hand	210	
Capital Account 1 March 19-6		9,900
Drawings	2,850	
Office furniture	1,440	
Rent	1,020	
Wages and salaries	2,580	
Discounts	690	360
Debtors and creditors	4,920	2,490
Stock 1 March 19-6	2,970	
Provision for Bad and Doubtful Debts 1 March 19-6		270
Delivery van	2,400	
Van running costs	450	
Bad Debts written off	810	
	32,760	32,760

Notes:
(a) Stock 28 February 19-7 £3,510.
(b) Wages and salaries accrued at 28 February 19-7 £90.
(c) Rent prepaid at 28 February 19-7 £140.
(d) Van running costs owing at 28 February 19-7 £60.
(e) Increase the provision for Bad and Doubtful Debts by £60.
(f) Provide the depreciation as follows: Office furniture £180. Delivery van
£480.

Required:
Draw up the Trading and Profit and Loss Accounts for the year ending 28
February 19-7 together with a Balance Sheet as on 28 February 19-7, using
vertical formats throughout.

22.8. T. Morgan, a sole trade, extracted the following Trial Balance from his
books at the close of business on 31 March 19-9:

	Dr £	Cr £
Purchases and sales	22,860	41,970
Stock 1 April 19-8	5,160	
Capital 1 April 19-8		7,200
Bank overdraft		4,350
Cash	90	
Discounts	1,440	930
Returns inwards	810	
Returns outwards		570
Carriage outwards	2,160	
Rent and insurance	1,740	
Provision for Bad and Doubtful Debts		660
Fixtures and fittings	1,200	
Delivery van	2,100	
Debtors and creditors	11,910	6,060
Drawings	2,880	
Wages and salaries	8,940	
General office expenses	450	
	61,740	61,740

Notes:
(a) Stock 31 March 19-9 £4,290.
(b) Wages and salaries accrued at 31 March 19-9 £210, Office expenses owing
£20.
(c) Rent prepaid 31 March 19-9 £180.
(d) Increase the provision for Bad and Doubtful Debts by £150 to £810.
(e) Provide for depreciation as follows: Fixtures and fittings £120, Delivery
van £300.

Required:
Prepare the Trading and Profit and Loss Accounts for the year ended 31
March 19-9 together with a Balance Sheet as at that date, using vertical
formats.

22.9A. A. Jakes is a retail trader. From the following information prepare a Trading and Profit and Loss Account for the year ended 31 December 19-4 and a Balance Sheet on that date.

Trial Balance – 31 December 19-4

	£	£
Capital 1 January 19-4		32,000
Land and buildings at cost	30,000	
Motor vehicles (at cost)	6,000	
Drawings	7,050	
Stock	4,500	
Bank overdraft		480
Sales		71,300
Purchases	55,500	
Motor expenses	1,550	
Sundry expenses	530	
Wages	7,800	
Debtors	4,100	
Creditors		6,050
Telephone and Insurance	800	
Provision for depreciation:		
Motor vehicles		3,000
Land and Buildings		5,000
	117,830	117,830

The following items should be taken into consideration:
(a) Stock at 31 December 19-4 £9,100.
(b) A provision for doubtful debts of 5 per cent on the debtors at 31 December 19-4 is to be created.
(c) Depreciation is to be provided on motor vehicles at 20 per cent on cost, and buildings at £1,000 per annum.
(d) Insurance prepaid at 31 December 19-4 £60.
(e) Motor expenses bill for December £130 is owing at 31 December 19-4.
(f) Sundry expenses includes £75 for a private telephone bill of A. Jakes.
(g) A cheque for £1,250 was paid to a creditor on 31 December 19-4 but had not been entered in the books at the time of extracting the trial balance.
(h) Wages owing £350.

22.10A. The following trial balance was extracted from the books of Rodney, a trader, at 31 December 19-7:

	£	£
Capital		20,271
Drawings	2,148	
Debtors and creditors	7,689	5,462
Sales		81,742
Purchases	62,101	
Rent and rates	880	
Lighting and heating	246	
Salaries and wages	8,268	
Bad debts	247	
Provision for doubtful debts at 31 December 19-6		326
Stock-in-trade, 31 December 19-6	9,274	
Insurances	172	
General expenses	933	
Bank balance	1,582	
Motor vans at cost	8,000	
Provision for depreciation of motor vans at 31 December 19-6		3,600
Proceeds of sale on van		250
Motor expenses	861	
Freehold premises at cost	15,000	
Rent received		750
Provision for depreciation: buildings		5,000
	117,401	117,401

The following matters are to be taken into account:
1. Stock-in-trade 31 December 19-7, £9,884.
2. Rates paid in advance 31 December 19-7, £40.
3. Rent receivable, due at 31 December 19-7, £250.
4. Lighting and heating due at 31 December 19-7, £85.
5. Provision for doubtful debts to be increased to £388.
6. Included in the amount for insurances, £172, is an item for £82 for motor insurances and this amount should be transferred to motor expenses.
7. Depreciation has been and is to be charged on vans at the annual rate of 20 per cent of cost.
8. Depreciate buildings £500.
9. On 1 January 19-7 a van which had been purchased for £1,000 on 1 January 19-4 was sold for £250. The only record of the matter is the credit of £250 to proceeds of sale of van account.

Required:
A trading and profit and loss account for 19-7 and a balance sheet at 31 December 19-7 using vertical style accounts.

23

A Fully Worked Exercise

When learning to keep a set of books, and to draw up a Trading and Profit and Loss Account and Balance Sheet after the period is over, students learn the whole thing in parts. They learn to enter up a Cash Book, how to enter up the Sales Book and the Purchases Book, how to enter up the Sales Ledger, and so on. They are often very puzzled about various parts of the whole exercise when the complete task has to be undertaken, rather than simply one part of it. Some authors undertake this task by showing the complete records for a period. However, another problem then crops up for many students, and that is that they still do not understand how one period's accounts link up with those for the next period. In this chapter, therefore, the full sets of records for two consecutive periods are examined, so that the full recording of a period, and its link with the next period, can both be seen properly.

Naturally enough, in a real business the number of transactions for a month may be exceedingly large. In this simulation of a business in this book, for reasons of space, the items will be kept to as low a number as possible. Details of the business are as follows:

G. Cheadle started in business on 1 January 19-5 by putting £20,000 into a bank account for the business.

19-5
Jan 2 He paid £160 cheque for rent for the two months January and February
,, 2 Bought warehouse fixtures paying by cheque immediately for £2,400
,, 3 Withdrew £300 cash from the bank for business use
,, 4 Paid wages in cash for three weeks of January £240
,, 5 Bought £1,400 goods paying for them immediately by cheque
,, 6 Bought goods on credit from: T. Price £600; F. Ratcliffe Ltd. £2,400; C. Norton & Co. £1,100
,, 8 Motor van bought by cheque £4,800
,, 11 Paid for motor expenses by cash £30

,, 12 Sold goods on credit to: K. Kitchen Ltd. £640; E. Griffiths £1,400
,, 13 Cash Sales £280
,, 15 Paid for light and heat by cheque for the first two weeks of January £160
,, 16 Paid Insurance by cheque £240 for the 12 months to 31 December 19-5
,, 19 Bought goods on credit from: P. Goddard £3,200
,, 21 Sold goods on credit to: K. Kitchen Ltd. £6,800; N. Fryer £240
,, 24 Cheadle withdrew £500 by cheque for his personal use
,, 26 Received cheques from: E. Griffiths £1,365 (after deducting £35 cash discount); K. Kitchen on account £1,000
,, 27 Returned goods to: C. Norton & Co. £240; F. Ratcliffe £200
,, 29 Paid by cheque, after deducting 5 per cent cash discount, the accounts of T. Price and P. Goddard
,, 30 Goods returned to us by: K. Kitchen Ltd. £80; N. Fryer £40
,, 31 Cheadle withdrew £40 cash for his personal use.

Cash Book — Page 1

			Discount	Cash	Bank				Discount	Cash	Bank
19-5			£	£	£	19-5			£	£	£
Jan 1	Capital	GL 1			20,000	Jan 2	Rent	GL 9			160
,, 3	Bank	C		300		,, 2	Warehouse				
,, 13	Sales	GL 5		280			fixtures	GL 7			2,400
,, 26	E. Griffiths	SL 2	35		1,365	,, 3	Cash				300
,, 26	K. Kitchen					,, 4	Wages	GL 10		240	
	Ltd.	SL 1			1,000	,, 5	Purchases	GL 3			1,400
						,, 8	Motor van	GL 8			4,800
						,, 11	Motor expenses	GL 11		30	
						,, 15	Light & Heat	GL 12			160
						,, 16	Insurance	GL 13			240
						,, 24	Drawings	GL 2			500
						,, 29	T. Price	PL 1	30		570
						,, 29	P. Goddard	PL 4	160		3,040
						,, 31	Drawings	GL 2		40	
						,, 31	Balance c/d			270	8,795
			35	580	22,365				190	580	22,365
Feb 1	Balance b/d			270	8,795						

Sales Book — Page 1

19-5		Folio	£
Jan 12	K. Kitchen Ltd.	SL 1	640
,, 12	E. Griffiths	SL 2	1,400
,, 21	K. Kitchen Ltd.	SL 1	6,800
,, 21	N. Fryer	SL 3	240
	Transferred to Sales Account	GL 5	9,080

Returns Inwards Book

19-5		Folio	£
Jan 30 K. Kitchen Ltd.		SL 1	80
,, 30 N. Fryer		SL 3	40
Transferred to Returns Inwards Account GL 6			120

Sales Ledger
K. Kitchen Ltd.

19-5			£	19-5			£
Jan 12 Sales	SB 1		640	Jan 26 Cash	CB 1		1,000
,, 21 Sales	SB 1		6,800	,, 30 Returns Inwards	RI 1		80
				,, 31 Balance	c/d		6,360
			7,440				7,440
Feb 1 Balance	b/d		6,360				

Sales Ledger
E. Griffiths

19-5			£				£
Jan 12 Sales	SB 1		1,400	Jan 26 Cash	CB 1		1,365
				,, 26 Discount	CB 1		35
			1,400				1,400

N. Fryer

19-5			£	19-5			£
Jan 21 Sales	SB 1		240	Jan 30 Returns Inwards	RI 1		40
				,, 31 Balance	c/d		200
			240				240
Feb 1 Balance	b/d		200				

Purchases Book

19-5		Folio	£
Jan 6 T. Price		PL 1	600
,, 6 F. Ratcliffe Ltd.		PL 2	2,400
,, 6 C. Norton & Co.		PL 3	1,100
,, 19 P. Goddard		PL 4	3,200
Transferred to Purchases Account		GL 3	7,300

Returns Outwards Book

19-5		Folio	£
Jan 27 C. Norton & Co.		PL 3	240
,, 27 F. Ratcliffe Ltd.		PL 2	200
Transferred to Returns Outwards Account		GL 4	440

Purchases Ledger Page 1
T. Price

19-5			£	19-5			£
Jan 29 Bank	CB 1		570	Jan 6 Purchases	PB 1		600
,, 29 Discount	CB 1		30				
			600				600

F. Ratcliffe Ltd. Page 2

19-5			£	19-5			£
Jan 30 Returns				Jan 6 Purchases	PB 1		2,400
Outwards	RO 1		200				
,, 31 Balance	c/d		2,200				
			2,400				2,400
				Feb 1 Balance	b/d		2,200

C. Norton & Co. Page 3

19-5			£	19-5			£
Jan 30 Returns				Jan 6 Purchases	PB 1		1,100
Outwards	RO 1		240				
,, 31 Balance	c/d		860				
			1,100				1,100
				Feb 1 Balance	b/d		860

P. Goddard Page 4

19-5			£	19-5			£
Jan 29 Bank	CB 1		3,040	Jan 3 Purchases	PB 1		3,200
,, 29 Discount	CB 1		160				
			3,200				3,200

General Ledger
(before making adjustments and drawing up Trading and
Profit and Loss Accounts and Balance Sheet)

				Capital			Page 1

			19-5			£
			Jan	1 Bank	CB 1	20,000

				Drawings			Page 2

19-5			£	
Jan	24 Bank	CB 1	500	
,,	31 Cash	CB 1	40	

				Purchases			Page 3

19-5			£	
Jan	5 Bank	CB 1	1,400	
,,	31 Credit Purchases for the month	PB 1	7,300	

				Returns outwards			Page 4

		19-5			£
		Jan	31 Returns for the month	RO 1	440

				Sales			Page 5

		19-5			£
		Jan	13 Cash	CB 1	280
		,,	31 Credit Sales for the month	SB 1	9,080

				Returns inwards			Page 6

19-5			£	
Jan	31 Returns for the month	RI 1	120	

				Warehouse fixtures			Page 7

19-5			£	
Jan	2 Bank	CB 1	2,400	

				Motor Van			Page 8

19-5			£	
Jan	8 Bank	CB 1	4,800	

Rent   Page 9

19-5			£
Jan	2 Bank	CB 1	160

Wages   Page 10

19-5			£
Jan	4 Bank	CB 1	240

Motor expenses   Page 11

19-5			£
Jan	11 Cash	CB 1	30

Light and Heat   Page 12

19-5			£
Jan	15 Bank	CB 1	160

Insurance   Page 13

19-5			£
Jan	16 Bank	CB 1	240

Discounts allowed   Page 14

19-5			£
Jan	31 Total for the month	CB 1	35

Discounts received   Page 15

		19-5			£
		Jan	31 Total for the month	CB 1	190

Now that all of the accounts have been entered up, the next step is to draw up a Trial Balance as on 31 January 19-5.

G. Cheadle
Trial Balance as on 31 January 19-5

		£	£
Capital	GL 1		20,000
Drawings	GL 2	540	
Purchases	GL 3	8,700	
Returns outwards	GL 4		440
Sales	GL 5		9,360
Returns inwards	GL 6	120	
Warehouse fixtures	GL 7	2,400	
Motor Van	GL 8	4,800	
Rent	GL 9	160	
Wages	GL 10	240	
Motor expenses	GL 11	30	
Light and heat	GL 12	160	
Insurance	GL 13	240	
Discounts allowed	GL 14	35	
Discounts received	GL 15		190
Bank	CB 1	8,795	
Cash	CB 1	270	
Debtors	per Sales Ledger	6,560	
Creditors	per Purchases Ledger		3,060
		33,050	33,050

Now that the Trial Balance has been seen to 'balance', the next step is to draw up a Trading and Profit and Loss Account for the month ended 31 January 19-5, followed by a Balance Sheet as at 31 January 19-5. Adjustments are needed for the following items (a) to (e) which were ascertained by G. Cheadle at the end of the working day of 31 January 19-5. He had:

(a) Valued his stock of goods at cost to be £2,360.
(b) Estimated that depreciation provisions should be at the rate of 10 per cent per annum for warehouse fixtures, and 20 per cent per annum for the motor van. In both cases the straight line method is to be used and salvage value is to be ignored. A full month's depreciation is to be given for January.
(c) He owed £180 for light and heating.
(d) He owed £60 for wages, and £80 for motor expenses.
(e) Noticed that the fire insurance was prepaid 11 months and rent is prepaid 1 month.

Of course, in real life, in a business as small as this it is unlikely that final accounts would be drawn up each month. However, it is much more simple to see the basic principles if a relatively few items are dealt with.

G. Cheadle
Trading and Profit and Loss Account for the month ended 31 January 19-5

	£	£	£
Sales		9,360	
Less Returns Inwards		120	
			9,240
Less Cost of Goods Sold			
Purchases	8,700		
Less Returns Outwards	440		
		8,260	
Less Closing Stock		2,360	
			5,900
Gross Profit			3,340
Add Discounts Received			190
			3,530
Less Expenses			
Wages		300	
Rent		80	
Light and Heat		340	
Insurance		20	
Motor Expenses		110	
Discounts Allowed		35	
Depreciation			
Warehouse Fixtures		20	
Motor Van		80	
			985
Net Profit			2,545

G. Cheadle
Balance Sheet as at 31 January 19-5

	£	£	£
Fixed Assets			
Warehouse Fixtures at cost		2,400	
Less Depreciation to date		20	
			2,380
Motor Van at Cost		4,800	
Less Depreciation to date		80	
			4,720
			7,100
Current Assets			
Stock		2,360	
Debtors		6,560	
Prepaid Expenses		300	
Bank		8,795	
Cash		270	
		18,285	
Less Current Liabilities			
Trade Creditors	3,060		
Expenses Accrued	320		
		3,380	
Working Capital			14,905
			22,005
Financed by:			
Capital			
Cash Introduced			20,000
Add Net Profit for the month			2,545
			22,545
Less Drawings			540
			22,005

In drawing up the Trading and Profit and Loss Account various transfers will have been made from the accounts in the General Ledger, such as the transfer from the Sales Account. It must be remembered that the Trading and Profit and Loss Accounts are part of the double entry system.

All of the accounts in the General Ledger will now be shown after being completely written up for the month. These should be compared with the accounts as they appeared before being written up, so that the adjustments can be seen clearly. In a real firm each account would be shown once only, as it appears after being written up. For teaching purposes only the General Ledger is shown twice, once before the Trading and Profit and Loss Account has been drawn up, and once afterwards.

General Ledger
(after being fully written up)

Capital

19-5			£	19-5			£
Jan	31 Drawings	GL 2	540	Jan	1 Bank	CB 1	20,000
,,	31 Balance	c/d	22,005	,,	31 Net Profit for the month		2,545
			22,545				22,545
				Feb	1 Balance	b/d	22,005

Drawings

19-5			£	19-5			£
Jan	24 Bank	CB 1	500	Jan	31 Capital	GL 1	540
,,	31 Cash	CB 1	40				
			540				540

Purchases

19-5			£	19-5		£
Jan	5 Bank	CB 1	1,400	Jan	31 Trading A/c	8,700
,,	31 Credit Purchases for the month	PB 1	7,300			
			8,700			8,700

Returns outwards

19-5		£	19-5			£
Jan	31 Trading A/c	440	Jan	31 Returns for the month	RO 1	440

Sales

19-5		£	19-5			£
Jan	31 Trading A/c	9,360	Jan	13 Cash	CB 1	280
			,,	31 Credit Sales for the month	SB 1	9,080
		9,360				9,360

Returns Inwards   Page 6

19-5			£	19-5		£
Jan 31 Returns for the month	RI 1		120	Jan 31 Trading A/c		120

Warehouse fixtures   Page 7

19-5			£	
Jan 2 Bank	CB 1		2,400	(see note at end re balance)

Motor van   Page 8

19-5			£
Jan 8	CB 1		4,800

Rent   Page 9

19-5			£	19-6		£
Jan 2 Bank	CB 1		160	Jan 31 Profit & Loss A/c		80
				Jan 31 Prepaid c/d		80
			160			160
Feb 1 Prepaid b/d			80			

Wages   Page 10

19-5			£	19-5		£
Jan 4 Bank	CB 1		240	Jan 31 Profit & Loss A/c		300
,, 31 Accrued c/d			60			
			300			300
				Feb 1 Accrued b/d		60

Motor Expenses   Page 11

19-5			£	19-5		£
Jan 11 Cash	CB 1		30	Jan 31 Profit & Loss A/c		110
,, 31 Accrued c/d.			80			
			110			110
				Feb 1 Accrued b/d		80

Lighting

19-5			£	19-5			£
Jan 15 Bank	CB 1		160	Jan 31 Profit & Loss A/c			340
,, 31 Accrued c/d			180				
			340				340
				Feb 1 Accrued b/d			180

Insurance

19-5			£	19-5			£
Jan 16 Bank	CB 1		240	Jan 31 Profit & Loss A/c			20
				,, 31 Prepaid c/d			220
			240				240
Feb 1 Prepaid b/d			220				

Discounts allowed

19-5			£	19-5			£
Jan 31 Total for the				Jan 31 Profit & Loss A/c			35
month	CB 1		35				

Discounts received

19-5			£	19-5			£
Jan 31 Profit & Loss A/c			190	Jan 31 Total for the			
				month	CB 1		190

Provision for depreciation: Motor van

				19-5			£
				Jan 31 Profit & Loss A/c			80

Provision for depreciation: Warehouse fixtures

				19-5			£
				Jan 31 Profit & Loss A/c			20

Stock

19-5		£
Jan 31 Trading A/c		2,360

N.B. As the accounts on pages 7, 8, 16, 17 and 18 of the General
Ledger contain one entry only, there is no point in carrying each
item down as a balance. Each item is its own balance.

The following transactions for the month of February can now be listed and entered.

19-5

Feb 1 Bought warehouse fixtures paying in cash £480

,, 3 Paid for lighting and heating by cheque £180

,, 5 Bought goods on credit: C. Norton & Co. £800; C. Stoddard Ltd. £4,000; F. Ratcliffe Ltd. £4,600

,, 7 Paid cheque for a total of £210 motor expenses by cheque, including £80 owing from last month

,, 10 Cash Sales £1,260

,, 12 Sold goods on credit to: K. Kitchen Ltd. £5,600; R. Antrobus & Co. £660; N. Fryer £1,700

,, 15 Paid wages owing for January, and those for the whole of February, a total by cash of £430

,, 16 Cash Drawings £500

,, 17 Returns received from: K. Kitchen Ltd. £160; R. Antrobus & Co. £60

,, 18 Received cheque from: K. Kitchen Ltd. of £4,000 on account

,, 20 We returned goods to: C. Stoddard Ltd. £400; F. Ratcliffe Ltd. £180

,, 24 Received cheque from R. Antrobus & Co. to settle account, after deducting 2½ per cent discount

,, 25 Paid cheque of £3,420 to settle Stoddard's account. A cash discount of 5 per cent had been deducted.

,, 25 Cash Sales paid direct into the bank £1,358

,, 26 Bought goods on credit from F. Ratcliffe Ltd. £190

,, 28 Paid rent for the months of March and April by cheque £160

,, 28 Paid motor expenses by cash £45

Cash Book   Page 2

		Discount	Cash	Bank				Discount	Cash	Bank
		£	£	£				£	£	£
19-5					19-5					
Feb 1	Balances		270	8,795	Feb 1	Warehouse				
,, 10	Sales	GL 5	1,260			fixtures	GL 7		480	
,, 18	K. Kitchen									
	Ltd.	SL 1		4,000	,, 3	Lighting &				
,, 24	R. Antrobus &					Heating	GL 12			180
	Co.	SL 4	15	585	,, 7	Motor expenses	GL 11			210
,, 25	Sales	GL 5		1,358	,, 15	Wages	GL 10		430	
					,, 16	Drawings	GL 2		500	
					,, 25	C. Stoddard				
3,420						Ltd.	PL 5	180		3,420
					,, 28	Rent	GL 9			160
					,, 28	Motor expenses	GL 11		45	
					,, 28	Balances c/d			75	10,768
			—						—	
		15	1,530	14,738				180	1,530	14,738
Mar 1	Balances b/d		75	10,768						

Sales Book   Page 2

19-5		Folio	£
Feb 12	K. Kitchen Ltd.	SL 1	5,600
,, 12	R. Antrobus & Co.	SL 4	660
,, 12	N. Fryer	SL 3	1,700
	Transferred to Sales Account	GL 5	7,960

Returns Inwards Book   Page 2

19-5		Folio	£
Feb 17	K. Kitchen Ltd.	SL 1	160
,, 17	R. Antrobus & Co.	SL 4	60
	Transferred to Returns Inwards Account	GL 6	220

Sales Ledger   Page 1
K. Kitchen Ltd.

19-5			£	19-5			£
Feb 1	Balance b/d		6,360	Feb 17	Returns Inwards	RI 2	160
,, 12	Sales	SB 2	5,600	,, 18	Bank	CB 2	4,000
				,, 28	Balance c/d		7,800
			11,960				11,960
Mar 1	Balance b/d		7,800				

N. Fryer   Page 3

19-5			£	19-5		£
Feb 1	Balance b/d		200	Feb 28 Balance c/d		1,900
,, 12	Sales	SB 2	1,700			
			1,900			1,900
Mar 1	Balance b/d		1,900			

R. Antrobus & Co.   Page 4

19-5			£	19-5			£
Feb 12	Sales	SB 2	660	Feb 17	Returns inwards	RI 2	60
				,, 24	Bank	CB 2	585
				,, 24	Discount	CB 2	15
			660				660

Purchases Book

19-5		Folio	£
Feb 5 C. Norton & Co.		PL 3	800
,, 5 C. Stoddard Ltd.		PL 5	4,000
,, 5 F. Ratcliffe Ltd.		PL 2	4,600
,, 26 F. Ratcliffe Ltd.		PL 2	190
Transferred to Purchases Account		GL 3	9,590

Returns Outwards Book

19-5		Folio	£
Feb 20 C. Stoddard Ltd.		PL 5	400
,, 20 F. Ratcliffe Ltd.		PL 2	180
Transferred to Returns Outwards Account	GL 4		580

Purchases Ledger

F. Ratcliffe Ltd.

19-5			£	19-5			£
Feb 20 Returns				Feb 1 Balance b/d			2,200
outwards	RO 2		180	,, 5 Purchases	PB 2		4,600
,, 28 Balance c/d			6,810	,, 26 Purchases	PB 2		190
			6,990				6,990
				Mar 1 Balance b/d			6,810

C. Norton & Co.

19-5		£	19-5			£
Feb 28 Balance c/d		1,660	Feb 1 Balance b/d			860
			,, 5 Purchases	PB 2		800
		1,660				1,660
			Mar 1 Balance b/d			1,660

C. Stoddard Ltd.

19-5			£	19-5			£
Feb 20 Returns				Feb 5 Purchases	PB 2		4,000
outwards	RO 2		400				
,, 25 Bank	CB 2		3,420				
,, 25 Discount	CB 2		180				
			4,000				4,000

General Ledger

(before making adjustments and drawing up Trading
and Profit and Loss Accounts and Balance Sheet)

			Capital			Page 1
				19-5		£
				Feb	1 Balance b/d	22,005

			Drawings		Page 2
19-5			£		
Feb	16 Cash	CB 2	500		

			Purchases		Page 3
19-5			£		
Feb	28 Credit purchases				
	for the month	PB 2	9,590		

		Returns outwards			Page 4
		19 - 5			£
		Feb	28 Returns for the		
			month	RO 2	580

		Sales			Page 5
		19 - 5			£
		Feb	10 Cash	CB 2	1,260
		,,	25 Bank	CB 2	1,358
		,,	28 Credit sales for		
			the month	SB 2	7,960

			Returns inwards		Page 6
19-5			£		
Feb	28 Returns for the				
	month	RI 2	220		

			Warehouse fixtures		Page 7
19-5			£		
Jan	2 Bank	CB 1	2,400		
Feb	1 Cash	CB 2	480		

Motor Van   Page 8

19-5			£
Jan 8 Bank	CB 1		4,800

Rent   Page 9

19-5			£
Feb 1 Prepaid b/d			80
,, 28 Bank	CB 2		160

Wages   Page 10

19-5			£	19-5		£
Feb 15 Cash	CB 2		430	Feb 1 Accrued b/d		60

Motor expenses   Page 11

19-5			£	19-5		£
Feb 7 Bank	CB 2		210	Feb 1 Accrued b/d		80
,, 28 Cash	CB 2		45			

Lighting and Heating   Page 12

19-5			£	19-5		£
Feb 3 Bank	CB 2		180	Feb 1 Accrued b/d		180

Insurance   Page 13

19-5		£	19-5	£
Feb 1 Prepaid b/d		220		

Discounts allowed   Page 14

19-5			£
Feb 28 Total for the month	CB 2		15

Discounts received   Page 15

			19-5		£
			Feb 28 Total for the month	CB 2	180

Provision for depreciation: Motor van   Page 16

		19-5	£
		Jan 31 Profit & Loss A/c	80

Provision for depreciation: Warehouse fixtures Page 17

		£
19-5		
Jan 31 Profit & Loss A/c		20

Stock Page 18

	£
19-5	
Jan 31 Trading A/c	2,360

The Trial Balance as on 28 February 19-5 can now be drawn up.

G. Cheadle
Trial Balance as on 28 February 19-5

		£	£
Capital	GL 1		22,005
Drawings	GL 2	500	
Purchases	GL 3	9,590	
Returns outwards	GL 4		580
Sales	GL 5		10,578
Returns inwards	GL 6	220	
Warehouse fixtures	GL 7	2,880	
Motor van	GL 8	4,800	
Rent	GL 9	240	
Wages	GL 10	370	
Motor expenses	GL 11	175	
Light & Heat	GL 12	–	
Insurance	GL 13	220	
Discounts allowed	GL 14	15	
Discounts received	GL 15		180
Provision for depreciation, motor van	GL 16		80
Provision for depreciation, warehouse fittings	GL 17		20
Stock	GL 18	2,360	
Cash	CB 2	75	
Bank	CB 2	10,768	
Debtors – per Sales Ledger		9,700	
Creditors – per Purchases Ledger			8,470
		41,913	41,913

The Trading and Profit and Loss Account for the month ended 28 February 19-5 is now drawn up. Adjustments are needed for the following items (*a*) to (*d*) which were ascertained by G. Cheadle at the end of the working day of 28 February 19-5. He had:

(*a*) Valued his stock of goods at cost to be £4,830
(*b*) He owed £270 for light and heating.
(*c*) He owed £40 for motor expenses.
(*d*) Noticed that insurance and rent had been prepaid.

G. Cheadle

Trading and Profit and Loss Account for the month ended 28 February 19-5

	£	£	£
Sales		10,578	
Less Returns Inwards		220	
			10,358
Less Cost of Goods Sold			
Opening Stock		2,360	
Add Purchases	9,590		
Less Returns Outwards	580		
		9,010	
		11,370	
Less Closing Stock		4,830	
			6,540
Gross Profit			3,818
Add Discounts Received			180
			3,998
Less Expenses			
Wages		370	
Rent		80	
Light and Heat		270	
Insurance		20	
Motor Expenses		215	
Discounts Allowed		15	
Depreciation:			
Warehouse Fixtures		24	
Motor Van		80	
			1,074
Net Profit			2,924

General Ledger

(after all adjustments made to 28 February 19-5)

Capital — Page 1

19-5		£	19-5		£
Feb 28 Drawings	GL 2	500	Feb 1 Balance b/d		22,005
,, 28 Balance c/d		24,429	,, 28 Net Profit for		
			the month		2,924
		24,929			24,929
			Mar 1 Balance b/d		24,429

Drawings — Page 2

19-5		£	19-5		£
Feb 16 Cash	CB 2	500	Feb 28 Capital	GL 1	500

G. Cheadle
Balance Sheet as at 28 February 19-5

	£	£	£
Fixed Assets			
Warehouse Fixtures at cost		2,880	
Less Depreciation to date		44	
			2,836
Motor Van at cost		4,800	
Less Depreciation to date		160	
			4,640
			7,476
Current Assets			
Stock		4,830	
Debtors		9,700	
Prepaid Expenses		360	
Bank		10,768	
Cash		75	
		25,733	
Less Current Liabilities			
Trade Creditors	8,470		
Expenses Accrued	310		
		8,780	
Working Capital			16,953
			24,429
Financed by:			
Capital			
Balance as at 1.2.19-5			22,005
Add Net Profit for the month			2,924
			24,929
Less Drawings			500
			24,429

General Ledger *(continued)*

Purchases Page 3

19-5		£	19-5		£
Feb 28	Credit Purchases for the month PB 2	9,590	Feb 28	Trading A/c	9,590

General Ledger
(after all adjustments made to 28 February 19-5)

Returns outwards
Page 4

19-5			£	19-5			£
Feb 28 Trading A/c			580	Feb 28 Returns for the month		RO 2	580

Sales
Page 5

19-5			£	19-5			£
Feb 28 Trading A/c			10,578	Feb 10 Cash		CB 2	1,260
				,, 25 Bank		CB 2	1,358
				,, 28 Credit Sales for the month		SB 2	7,960
			10,578				10,578

Returns inwards
Page 6

19-5			£	19-5		£
Feb 28 Returns for the month		RI 2	220	Feb 28 Trading A/c		220

Warehouse fixtures
Page 7

19-5			£	19-5		£
Jan 2 Bank		CB 1	2,400	Feb 28 Balance c/d		2,880
Feb 1 Cash		CB 2	480			
			2,880			2,880
Mar 1 Balance b/d			2,880			

Motor van
Page 8

19-5			£
Jan 8 Bank		CB 1	4,800

Rent
Page 9

19-5			£	19-5		£
Feb 1 Prepaid b/d			80	Feb 28 Profit & Loss A/c		80
,, 28 Bank		CB 2	160	,, 28 Prepaid c/d		160
			240			240
Mar 1 Prepaid b/d			160			

General Ledger
(after all adjustments made to 28 February 19-5)

Wages   Page 10

19-5			£	19-5		£
Feb 15 Cash		CB 2	430	Feb 1 Accrued b/d		60
				,, 28 Profit & Loss A/c		370
			430			430

Motor expenses   Page 11

19-5			£	19-5		£
Feb 7 Bank		CB 2	210	Feb 1 Accrued b/d		80
,, 28 Cash		CB 2	45	,, 28 Profit & Loss A/c		215
,, 28 Accrued c/d			40			
			295			295
				Mar 1 Accrued b/d		40

Light and Heat   Page 12

19-5			£	19-5		£
Feb 3 Bank		CB 2	180	Feb 1 Accrued b/d		180
,, 28 Accrued c/d			270	,, 28 Profit & Loss A/c		270
			450			450
				Mar 1 Accrued b/d		270

Insurance   Page 13

19-5		£	19-5		£
Feb 1 Prepaid b/d		220	Feb 28 Profit & Loss A/c		20
			,, 28 Prepaid c/d		200
		220			220
Mar 1 Prepaid b/d		200			

Discounts allowed   Page 14

19-5			£	19-5	£
Feb 28 Total for the month		CB 2	15	Feb 28 Profit & Loss A/c	15

General Ledger
(after all adjustments made to 28 February 19-5)

Discounts received   Page 15

19-5		£	19-5		£
Feb 28	Profit & Loss A/c	180	Feb 28	Total for the month	180

Provision for depreciation: Motor van   Page 16

19-5		£	19-5		£
Feb 28	Balance c/d	160	Jan 31	Profit & Loss A/c	80
			Feb 28	Profit & Loss A/c	80
		160			160
			Mar 1	Balance b/d	160

Provision for depreciation: Warehouses fixtures   Page 17

19-5		£	19-5		£
Feb 28	Balance c/d	44	Jan 31	Profit & Loss A/c	20
			Feb 28	Profit & Loss A/c	24
		44			44
			Mar 1	Balance b/d	44

Stock   Page 18

19-5		£	19-5		£
Jan 31	Trading A/c	2,360	Feb 28	Trading A/c	2,360
Feb 28	Trading A/c	4,830			

24

Capital and Revenue Expenditure

When fixed assets are bought, or when a firm spends money to add to the value of an existing fixed asset, such expenditure is called 'Capital Expenditure'. This should include the costs of acquiring the fixed assets and bringing them into the firm; this would include legal costs on buying buildings, carriage inwards on machinery bought and so on.

When there is expenditure which is not concerned with adding to the value of fixed assets, but represents the costs of running the business on a day-to-day basis, then this expenditure is known as 'Revenue Expenditure'.

This means that buying a motor van, which will be used in the business for the next few years, is Capital Expenditure. Paying for the petrol to run the motor van, such petrol to be used within a relatively short time, is Revenue Expenditure. Buying a machine is Capital Expenditure. Repairing the machine when it breaks down is not adding to the original value of the machine, and is therefore Revenue Expenditure. If, on the other hand, £900 was spent on the machine, £300 of which was to repair the machine and the other £600 was to make improvements to the machine in some way – for instance, to fit an extra attachment to it – then £300 would be Revenue Expenditure, whilst the £600 would be Capital Expenditure, as it represents an improvement.

It can be seen that Revenue Expenditure is that chargeable to the Trading or Profit and Loss Account, whilst Capital Expenditure will result in increased figures for Fixed Assets in the balance sheet.

The importance of ensuring that Capital Expenditure is not charged as Revenue Expenditure, and vice-versa, cannot be stressed often enough. Two cases can now be looked at where the different forms of expenditure have got mixed up.

Revenue Expenditure Overstated
Exhibit 24.1

The following trial balance of F. Rankin has been extracted as on 31 December 19-8. In fact, two of the figures shown in it are incorrect.

Included in purchases is £1,500 for the purchase of building materials which were for an addition to the premises. In error they have been charged to purchases, i.e. they have been charged as revenue expenditure instead of as capital expenditure. First will be shown the Trading and Profit and Loss Account for the year, and the Balance Sheet as at the year ended (a) as they were drawn up incorrectly, and (b) drawn up correctly, showing the £1,500 buildings materials as adding to the value of Premises.

Trial Balance as at 31 December 19-8

	Dr £	Cr £
General expenses	490	
Motor expenses	1,247	
Salaries	3,560	
Purchases	14,305	
Sales		26,815
Stock 1 January 19-8	4,080	
Motor vehicle	2,800	
Creditors		5,160
Debtors	4,090	
Premises	20,000	
Cash at bank	1,400	
Capital		24,347
Drawings	4,350	
	56,322	56,322

Stock at 31 December 19-8 was £4,960.

F. Rankin
Trading and Profit and Loss Account for the year ended 31 December 19-8

	(a) Incorrect £	£	(b) Corrected £	£
Sales		26,815		26,815
Less Cost of Goods Sold				
Opening Stock	4,080		4,080	
Add Purchases	14,305		12,805*	
	18,385		16,885	
Less Closing Stock	4,960	13,425	4,960	11,925
Gross Profit		13,390		14,890*
Less Expenses				
Salaries	3,560		3,560	
Motor Expenses	1,247		1,247	
General Expenses	490	5,297	490	5,297
Net Profit		8,093		9,593*

Balance Sheet as at 31 December 19-8

	(a) Incorrect		(b) Corrected	
	£	£	£	£
Fixed Assets				
Premises		20,000		21,500*
Motor Vehicle		2,800		2,800
		22,800		24,300
Current Assets				
Stock	4,960		4,960	
Debtors	4,090		4,090	
Bank	1,400		1,400	
	10,450		10,450	
Less Current Liabilities				
Creditors	5,160		5,160	
Working Capital		5,290		5,290
		28,090		29,590
Financed by:				
Capital				
Balance as at 1.1.19-8		24,347		24,347
Add Net Profit		8,093		9,593*
		32,440		33,940
Less Drawings		4,350		4,350
		28,090		29,590

The items showing amendments are indicated by asterisks(*).

It can now be seen that, in this particular case, the overstatement of revenue expenditure has resulted in (i) gross profit was understated £1,500, (ii) net profit was understated £1,500, (iii) a fixed asset, Premises, was understated by £1,500.

Capital Expenditure Overstated
Exhibit 24.2

What happens when capital expenditure is overstated? Take the trial balance of F. Rankin, as in Exhibit 24.1, but assume that a different error has been made. Suppose, instead of the error already shown, that one was made which resulted in an overstatement of capital expenditure. Assume that a replacement engine costing £420 has been fitted in the motor vehicle. Instead of charging the cost to Motor Expenses, it had instead been added in to the value of Motor Vehicle to give a total of £2,800. The final accounts can now be looked at (a) before correction, and (b) after correction.

F. Rankin

Trading and Profit and Loss Account for the year ended 31 December 19-8

	(a) Incorrect		(b) Corrected	
	£	£	£	£
Sales		26,815		26,815
Less Cost of Goods Sold				
Opening Stock	4,080		4,080	
Add Purchases	14,305		14,305	
	18,385		18,385	
Less Closing Stock	4,960	13,425	4,960	13,425
Gross Profit		13,390		13,390
Less Expenses				
Salaries	3,560		3,560	
Motor Expenses	1,247		1,667*	
General Expenses	490	5,297	490	5,717
Net Profit		8,093		7,673*

Balance Sheet as at 31 December 19-8

	(a) Incorrect		(b) Corrected	
	£	£	£	£
Fixed Assets				
Premises		20,000		20,000
Motor Vehicle		2,800		2,380*
		22,800		22,380
Current Assets				
Stock	4,960		4,960	
Debtors	4,090		4,090	
Bank	1,400		1,400	
	10,450		10,450	
Less Current Liabilities				
Creditors	5,160		5,160	
Working Capital		5,290		5,290
		28,090		27,670
Financed by:				
Capital				
Balance as at 1.1.19-8		24,347		24,347
Add Net Profit		8,093		7,673*
		32,440		32,020
Less Drawings		4,350		4,350
		28,090		27,670

The items showing amendment are indicated by asterisks (*).

It can now be seen in this particular case, that overstatement of capital expenditure resulted in (i) overstatement of net profit, (ii) overstatement of value of fixed asset.

Apportioning Expenditure

Sometimes one item of expenditure will need splitting between capital and revenue expenditure. A builder was engaged to tackle some work on your premises, the total bill being for £3,000. If one-third of this was for repair work and two-thirds for improvements, then £1,000 should be charged in the profit and loss account as revenue expenditure, and £2,000 added to the value of premises and shown as such in the balance sheet.

Capital and Revenue Receipts

As seen, 'Capital' items are long term and have an enduring influence on the profit-making capacity of the business. 'Revenue' items are short term and have only a temporary influence on the profit making capacity of the business. The expenditure side of these items has been considered. There will also be a receipts side. 'Capital Receipts' will therefore consist of the sale of 'Capital' items, e.g. the sale of a vehicle used in the business, the sale of premises. 'Revenue Receipts' will be those receipts which cover revenue items received, such as Rent Receivable or Commissions Receivable.

Exercises

MC65 Capital Expenditure is
(A) The extra capital paid in by the proprietor
(B) The costs of running the business on a day-to-day basis
(C) Money spent on buying fixed assets or adding value to them
(D) Money spent on selling fixed assets.

MC66 In the business of C. Sangster, who owns a clothing store, which of the following are Capital Expenditure?
(i) Shop fixtures bought
(ii) Wages of assistants
(iii) New motor van bought
(iv) Petrol for motor van
(A) i and iii
(B) i and ii
(C) ii and iii
(D) ii and iv.

MC67 If £500 was shown added to Purchases instead of being added to a fixed asset
(A) Net Profit only would be understated
(B) Net Profit only would be overstated
(C) It would not affect net profit
(D) Both Gross and Net Profits would be understated.

24.1. For the business of J. Charles, wholesale chemist, classify the following between 'Capital' and 'Revenue' expenditure:

(a) Purchase of an extra motor van.
(b) Cost of rebuilding warehouse wall which had fallen down.
(c) Building extension to the warehouse.
(d) Painting extension to warehouse when it is first built.
(e) Repainting extension to warehouse three years later than that done in (d).
(f) Carriage costs on bricks for new warehouse extension.
(g) Carriage costs on purchases.
(h) Carriage costs on sales.
(i) Legal costs of collecting debts.
(j) Legal charges on acquiring new premises for office.
(k) Fire insurance premium.
(l) Costs of erecting new machine.

24.2A. For the business of H. Ward, a food merchant, classify the following between 'Capital' and 'Revenue' expenditure:

(a) Repairs to meat slicer.
(b) New tyre for van.
(c) Additional shop counter.
(d) Renewing signwriting on shop.
(e) Fitting partitions in shop.
(f) Roof repairs.
(g) Installing thief detection equipment.
(h) Wages of shop assistant.
(i) Carriage on returns outwards.
(j) New cash register.
(k) Repairs to office safe.
(l) Installing extra toilet.

24.3. Explain clearly the different between capital expenditure and revenue expenditure. State which of the following you would classify as capital expenditure, giving your reasons:

(i) Cost of building extension to factory.
(ii) Purchase of extra filing cabinets for sales office.
(iii) Cost of repairs to accounting machine.
(iv) Cost of installing reconditioned engine in delivery van.
(v) Legal fees paid in connection with factory extension.

24.4A. The data which follows was extracted from the books of account of H. Kirk, an engineer, on 31 March 19-6, his financial year end.

		£
(a)	Purchase of extra milling machine (includes £300 for repair of an old machine)	2,900
(b)	Rent	750
(c)	Electrical expenses (includes new wiring £600, part of premises improvement)	3,280
(d)	Carriage inwards (includes £150 carriage on new cement mixer)	1,260
(e)	Purchase of extra drilling machine	4,100

You are required to allocate each or part of the items above to either 'Capital' or 'Revenue' expenditure.

24.5. (*a*) What is meant by (i) Capital Expenditure, and (ii) Revenue Expenditure?

(*b*) Some of the following items should be treated as Capital and some as Revenue. For each of them state which classification applies:

(i) The purchase of machinery for use in the business,

(ii) Carriage paid to bring the machinery in (i) above to the works,

(iii) Complete re-decoration of the premises at a cost of £1,500,

(iv) A quarterly account for heating,

(v) The purchase of a soft drinks vending machine for the canteen with a stock of soft drinks,

(vi) Wages paid by a building contractor to his own workmen for the erection of an office in the builder's stockyard.

(Joint Matriculation Board 'O' level)

24.6A. (*a*) Distinguish between "revenue" expenditure and "capital" expenditure.

(*b*) Indicate which of the following would be revenue items and which would be capital items in a wholesale bakery.

(i) Purchase of new motor van

(ii) Purchase of replacement engine for existing motor van

(iii) Cost of altering interior of new van to increase carrying capacity

(iv) Cost of motor taxation licence for new van

(v) Cost of motor taxation licence for existing van

(vi) Cost of painting firm's name on new van

(vii) Repair and maintenance of existing van.

(Associated Examining Board 'O' level)

25

Modern Methods of Processing Data

So far this book has been dealing mainly with the principles of double entry, and the book-keeping records have been in the form of the basic conventional system. However, it must not be thought that all the book-keeping methods in use are necessarily the same as the one described in this book. What is important is that the main ends which the financial book-keeping records purport to serve remain the same, but it is the means by which the actual records are effected that can be altered. Just because a mechanized or streamlined system is used does not mean that the answers will change. The question 'What is the total of debtors?' should receive the same answer whether the firm uses bound books, loose-leaf ledgers, keyboard accounting machines, punched card equipment, or a computer. The final accounts should remain the same whatever system is in use. The change takes place in the means by which the information or data is gathered together and processed so as to give the answers, and the speed with which this is accomplished.

It would, however, be a mistake to think that a more advanced system would only give, more quickly, exactly the same answers as before and nothing else. The system should be designed so that besides the essential answers which must be given by any book-keeping system further desirable information is obtainable as a by-product. Any such information must stand up to the criticism of whether or not it is worth obtaining. If the cost of obtaining it is greater than the benefits which flow to the firm from having it, then clearly it is not worthwhile information. The system should therefore be designed so as to give worthwhile information and exclude information which fails to stand up to the test.

You may well ask why it is that so far you have been studying mainly the basic conventional double entry book-keeping system. Has it not all been a waste of time? The answer to that must be that all of the more modern methods have developed from the conventional system. The basic information obtainable from any other book-keeping method remains the same. This consists of the changes in assets and liabilities, and convenient collection points are established to aggregate expenses and revenue so that the changes in the capital can be calculated. Thus the double entry system is capable of being used by any type of firm. When a person first learns book-keeping, he does not know exactly which systems will be in use at firms that he will be in contact with during his working life. In five years time from now, a small firm using manual methods may use a computer, and the reverse could even be possible. A firm using one type of computer could be using one of a completely different type. By understanding the ends towards which the double entry system is aimed, the student will therefore appreciate the ends towards which the other methods are aimed.

There is also another very simple answer. Book-keeping, like other mathematical subjects, needs a certain amount of practice if one is to be fluent in its use. The cost of equipping each student with accounting machinery on which the exercises are to be done would be prohibitive. It would also obviously preclude exercises being done at any other but fixed places where machinery was situated.

Probably one of the best ways to introduce modern methods is to trace their development from the conventional double entry system. The firm at which you are employed, or will be employed, would then be at some stage along this span of development. You should then be able to relate the firms book-keeping methods to what used to be done, and also to what may be done in your firm in the future.

It must always be borne in mind that, barring the legal needs which accounts fulfil, the costs of running the system should not exceed the benefits. To take an exaggerated example, a very small store could hardly be expected to use an expensive computer, as the costs of running it would far exceed any benefits which the firm might receive. Before advocating a more advanced system of book-keeping this test should always be applied.

The Development of Modern Methods

1. Bound Books

Up to the advent of the typewriter in 1866, bound volumes were universally used for book-keeping records. The accounts took the basic double entry form described in this book, but there was much manual copying of items that have now been eliminated from the present basic system. As carbon paper had not been invented, the sales invoices, debit and credit notes were copied into the sales and returns books before they were dispatched to customers and suppliers. Now, of course, copy sales invoices and debit and credit notes obtained by the use of carbon paper obviate any need for a copy to be made in the books. It is rather interesting to note that the purchases invoices were also usually copied into the purchases book, even though reference could easily be made to the purchases invoice received by the firm.

2. Loose-Leaf Ledgers and Carbon Paper

The typewriter and the consequent development of carbon paper led to the transition away from bound books to loose-leaf ledgers.

Typewriters could obviously be used more easily with loose sheets of paper, and with the use of carbon paper could give several copies of such things as invoices and debit and credit notes. Typed ledger accounts were also neater than hand-written records.

At first, the loose-leaf ledgers were kept in covers which could be opened and closed by operating a key. The loose sheets therefore had to be extracted and placed into the typewriter, then removed from the typewriter and replaced in the covers. Soon it was seen that continually extracting them and replacing them in the covers was a waste of time. The loose leaves, especially if they were somewhat sturdier and in the form of cards, could easily be kept in trays.

Experiments then began as to how one operation could produce several different records. This was done by designing special stationery with interleaved carbon or with a carbon backing on the sheets. This stationery was in the form of sets. For instance, one typing operation with a sales set might produce the following records:

Two sales invoices − one to be retained as a copy and the other sent to the customer.

An advice note for the customer.

Instructions to the warehouse to send the goods.

3. The Typewriter and the Adding Machine to the Accounting Machines

Adding machines were in existence in the latter part of the nineteenth century. In 1901, an accounting machine was constructed in the United States which was a combination of the adding machine and the typewriter. Other machines were developed, some primarily being based on the adding machine while others were developed from the typewriter.

These machines were used eventually in combination with multi-copy carbon stationery much more sophisticated than the sales set already described. Different coloured paper for forms so that it was easy to distinguish between various records came more into use. One operation produced not only several records but also automatically calculated the new balance on the account after the entry was made, and also totalled up the amount of each type of entry made for control purposes. These machines were used not only for financial accounting records but for costing records as well. Very often they are specially designed for use by particular firms.

4. Punched Card Accounting Machines

A class of accounting machine which worked in an entirely different way was also developed. This was the punched card machine developed in the United States by Dr Hollerith in 1884.

This method of accounting was based on information which was recorded by the means of holes being punched into cards. The whole system can be summarized into:

1. Punching holes into cards to represent the information that is being dealt with.
2. Sorting the cards out into a required order.
3. Getting the machines to tabulate the information in printed form in a way desired by the firm.

To do this the firm needed three basic kinds of machines:

1. A punch
2. A sorter
3. A tabulator

However, the most important part of the system was the actual punched cards. These were all the same size with one corner cut off so that in a pile of cards it was easy to see if one was facing the wrong way. The card consisted of a number of columns across with ten positions running down the card.

Since the advent of the electronic computer, the punched card accounting machine has fallen into disuse.

Computers

For accounting work computers follow on logically from punched cards. Computers were first used for business purposes around the year 1952.

The first computers were quite large machines. As a rough illustration of the comparison with today, a machine that would fill up the whole of the space in a room could today have its work performed quicker and more efficiently by a machine that would easily fit on to the top of your desk.

A computer has five basic component parts:

(i) An input unit.
(ii) A store or memory unit.
(iii) An arithmetic unit.
(iv) An output unit.
(v) A control unit.

When computers were first used the input was made by using punched cards or punched paper tape. The 1960's and 1970's saw considerable changes, both as regards the input to computers and the capabilities of them, so that such an input is now more or less obsolete.

What is now being seen is a whole new world of mini-computers. These were a 'spin-off' from the technology employed in outer space and in defence. Whereas at one time it would only be the larger firms which had computers, the world is now witnessing the introduction of computers into all but the very small organisations. The use of micro-circuits has meant a considerable reduction both in the size of computers and of their costs.

The world of computers is changing so rapidly that whatever was written now would be outdated to some extent by the time that the textbook was printed. As already stated, input into a computer used to be by way of punched card or punched paper tape. Some computers now can have data and control instructions fed into them by using a keyboard with a sort of typewriter layout. On top of the central processing unit of the computer will be a visual display unit, rather like a television. Instructions fed in, and a certain amount of computer output information can be viewed on the visual display unit.

With certain types of computers input can be put onto a disc, weighing under 2 ozs, and known as a 'floppy disk' or diskette. This small disc can hold a considerable amount of information. The floppy disks are then used as input instead of punched cards etc.

Computers should be seen as more than just machines which can handle book-keeping. They are tools of management, and a large number of problems can be solved by using them correctly. Some of these can be as automatic by-products of the book-keeping system. Stock control is an obvious choice, as this is done in so many firms.

Modern developments in statistical methods, allied with the computer's ability to handle vast quantities of data quickly and efficiently, have given a new dimension to accounting data. For many years, statistical theory has known *how* to analyse and present information as a basis for decision taking and control. But it is only with the advent of the computer that it has been possible to handle efficiently the mass of data that such theory demands. The drudgery and inaccuracy of data collection, once employing an army of clerks, has been all but eliminated. Never before has management had at its fingertips so much relevant information. Without doubt, the speed and accuracy of the modern digital computer has made statistical information cost effective.

This section can be concluded by saying that the developments now in hand are revolutionising the world of book-keeping and accounting. At the same time the reader should not think that the basis of accounting has changed, but simply that the recording function and the automatic reproduction of certain desirable information as a by-product of the accounting system is now capable of being performed by a computer, cheaply and easily, in all but the very smallest firms.

26

Bank Reconciliation Statements

Let us assume that we have just written up our cash book. We call at the bank on 30 June 19-5 and obtain from the bank manager a copy of our bank statement. On our return we tick off in our cash book and on the bank statement the items that are similar. A copy of our cash book (bank columns only) and of our bank statement are now shown as Exhibit 26.1.

Exhibit 26.1

Cash Book (bank columns only)

19-5		£	19-5		£
June 1 Balance b/f	✓	80	June 27 I. Gordon	✓	35
,, 28 D. Johnson	✓	100	,, 29 B. Tyrell		40
			,, 30 Balance c/d		105
		180			180
July 1 Balance b/d		105			

Bank Statement

19-5		Dr £	Cr £	Balance £
June 26 Balance b/fwd	✓			80 CR
,, 28 Banking	✓		100	180 CR
,, 30 I. Gordon	✓	35		145 CR

By comparing the cash book and the bank statement, it can be seen that the only item that was not in both of these was the cheque payment to B. Tyrell £40 in the cash book.

The reason this was in the cash book, but not on the bank statement, is simply one of timing. The cheque had been posted to B. Tyrell on 29 June, but there had not been time for it to be banked by Tyrell and pass through the banking system. Such a cheque is called an 'unpresented cheque' because it has not yet been presented at the drawer's bank.

To prove that, although they are different figures the balances are not different because of errors, a bank reconciliation statement is drawn up. This is as follows:

Bank Reconciliation Statement
as at 30 June 19-5

	£
Balance in Hand as per Cash Book	105
Add unpresented cheque: Tyrell	40
Balance in Hand as per Bank Statement	145

It would have been possible for the bank reconciliation statement to have started with the bank statement balance:

Bank Reconciliation Statement
as at 30 June 19-5

	£
Balance in Hand as per Bank Statement	145
Less unpresented cheque: Tyrell	40
Balance in Hand as per Cash Book	105

You should notice that the bank account is shown as a debit balance in the firm's cash book because to the firm it is an asset. In the bank's books the bank account is shown as a credit balance because this is a liability of the bank to the firm.

We can now look at a more complicated example in Exhibit 26.2. Similar items in both cash book and bank statement are shown ticked.

Exhibit 26.2

Cash Book

19-5		£	19-5		£
Dec 27 Total b/fwd		2,000	Dec 27 Total b/fwd		1,600
,, 29 J. Potter	✓	60	,, 28 J. Jacobs	✓	105
,, 31 M. Johnson (B)		220	,, 30 M. Chatwood (A)		15
			,, 31 Balance c/d		560
		2,280			2,280
19-6					
Jan 1 Balance b/d		560			

Bank Statement

		Dr	Cr	Balance
19-5		£	£	£
Dec 27 Balance b/fwd				400 CR
,, 29 Cheque	✓		60	460 CR
,, 30 J. Jacobs	✓	105		355 CR
,, ,, Credit transfers: L. Shaw (C)			70	425 CR
,, ,, Bank Charges (D)		20		405 CR

The balance brought forward in the bank statement £400 is the same figure as that in the cash book, i.e. totals b/fwd £2,000 – £1,600 = £400. However, items (A) and (B) are in the cash book only, and (C) and (D) are on the bank statement only. We can now examine these in detail:

(A) This is a cheque sent by us yesterday to Mr Chatwood. It has not yet passed through the banking system and been presented to our bank, and is therefore an 'unpresented cheque'.

(B) This is a cheque banked by us on our visit to the bank when we collected the copy of our bank statement. As we handed this banking over the counter at the same time as the bank clerk gave us our bank statement, naturally it has not yet been entered on the statement.

(C) A customer, L. Shaw has paid his account by instructing his bank to pay us direct through the banking system, instead of paying by cheque. Such a transaction is usually called a 'Bank Giro Transfer'. The term previously used was 'Credit Transfer'.

(D) The bank has charged us for the services given in keeping a bank account for us. It did not send us a bill: it simply takes the money from our account by debiting it and reducing the amount of our balance.

We can show these differences in the form of a table. This is followed by bank reconciliation statements drawn up both ways. This is for illustration only; we do not have to draw up a table or prepare two bank reconciliation statements. All we need in practice is one bank reconciliation statement, drawn up whichever way we prefer.

Items not in boths sets of books	Effect on Cash Book balance	Effect on Bank Statement	Adjustment required to one balance to reconcile it with the other	
			To Cash Book balance	To Bank Statement balance
1. Payment M. Chatwood £15	reduced by £15	none – not yet entered	add £15	deduct £15
2. Banking M. Johnson £220	increased by £220	none – not yet entered	deduct £220	add £220
3. Bank Commission £20	none – not yet entered	reduced by £20	deduct £20	add £20
4. Credit Transfers £70	none – not yet entered	increased by £70	add £70	deduct £70

Bank Reconciliation Statement as on 31 December 19-5

	£	£
Balance in hand as per Cash Book		560
Add unpresented cheque	15	
Credit transfers	70	
		85
		645
Less Bank commission	20	
Bank lodgement not yet entered on bank statement	220	
		240
Balance in hand as per bank statement		405

Bank Reconciliation Statement as on 31 December 19-5

	£	£
Balance in hand as per bank statement		405
Add Bank commission	20	
Bank lodgement not yet entered on bank statement	220	
		240
		645
Less Unpresented Cheques	15	
Traders Credit Transfers	70	
		85
Balance in Hand as per Cash Book		560

Standing Orders and Direct Debits

A firm can instruct its bank to make regular payments of fixed amounts at stated dates to certain persons or firms. These are standing orders. These payments would be automatically effected by the bank without the firm having to make out cheques or doing anything else once the instructions have been given to the bank. At a particular date such a payment might have been made by the bank, but the payment might not have been shown in the firm's cash book on that date. Such standing orders can only be altered by the paying firm.

There are also payments which have to be made, and where the authority to get the money is given to the firm to whom the money is to be paid, instead of giving one's bank the instructions to pay certain amounts. Instead of one's bank remembering to make the payment, the creditor can automatically charge one's bank account with the requisite amount. These are called 'direct debits'.

Writing up the Cash Book Before Attempting a Reconciliation

It will soon become obvious that in fact the best procedure is to complete entering up the cash book before attempting the reconciliation, this being done by finding out the items that are on the bank statement but not in the cash book and making entries for them in the cash book. By this means the number of adjustments needed in the reconciliation statement are reduced. However, in examinations the questions sometimes ask for the reconciliation to take place before completing the cash book entries.

If, in Exhibit 26.2, the cash book had been written up before the bank reconciliation statement had been drawn up, then the cash book and reconciliation statement would have appeared as follows in Exhibit 26.3.

Exhibit 26.3

Cash Book

19-5		£	19-5		£
Dec	27 Total b/fwd	2,000	Dec	27 Total b/fwd	1,600
,,	29 J. Potter	60	,,	28 J. Jacobs	105
,,	31 M. Johnson	220	,,	30 M. Chatwood	15
,,	31 Credit transfers		,,	31 Bank commission	20
	L. Shaw	70	,,	31 Balance c/d	610
		2,350			2,350
19-6					
Jan	1 Balance b/d	610			

Bank Reconciliation Statement as on 31 December 19-5

	£
Balance in hand as per cash book	610
Add unpresented cheque	15
	625
Less Bank lodgement not yet entered on bank statement	220
Balance in hand as per bank statement	405

Bank Overdrafts

The adjustments needed to reconcile the bank overdraft according to the firm's books with that shown in the bank's books are the complete opposite of that needed when the account is not overdrawn. It should be noticed that most banks show that an account has been overdrawn by putting the letters O/D after the amount of the balance; this is obviously the abbreviation for overdraft.

Exhibit 26.4 shows a cash book fully written up to date, and the bank reconciliation statement needed to reconcile the cash book and bank statement balances.

Exhibit 26.4

Cash Book

19-4		£	19-4		£
Dec	5 I. Howe	308	Dec	1 Balance b/f	709
,,	24 L. Mason	120	,,	9 P. Davies	140
,,	29 K. King	124	,,	27 J. Kelly	63
,,	31 G. Cumberbatch	106	,,	29 United Trust	77
,,	,, Balance c/f	380	,,	31 Bank Charges	49
		1,038			1,038

Bank Statement

19-4		Dr £	Cr £	Balance £
Dec	1 Balance b/f			709 O/D
,,	5 Cheque		308	401 O/D
,,	14 P. Davies	140		541 O/D
,,	24 Cheque		120	421 O/D
,,	29 K. King: Credit Transfer		124	297 O/D
,,	29 United Trust: Standing order	77		374 O/D
,,	31 Bank Charges	49		423 O/D

Bank Reconciliation Statement as on 31 December 19-4

	£
Overdraft as per cash book	380
Add Bank Lodgements not on bank statement	106
	486
Less Unpresented cheque	63
Overdraft per bank statement	423

Dishonoured cheques

When a cheque is received from a customer and paid into the bank, it is recorded on the debit side of the cash book. It is also shown on the bank statement as a banking by the bank. However, at a later date it may be found that the cheque has not gone through the account of the drawer, in other words his bank have failed to 'honour' the cheque, the cheque therefore is known as a 'dishonoured' cheque.

There are several possible reasons for this. Let us suppose that J. Hewitson gave us a cheque for £5,000 on May 20th 19-2. We bank it, but a few days later our bank return the cheque to us. Typical reasons are:

(a) Hewitson had put £5,000 in figures on the cheque, but had written it in words as five thousand five hundred pounds. You will have to give the cheque back to Hewitson for amendment.

(b) Normally cheques are considered 'stale' six months after the date on the cheque, in other words the banks will not 'honour' cheques over six months old. If Hewitson had put the year 19-1 on the cheque instead of 19-2, then the cheque would be returned to us by our bank.

(c) Hewitson simply did not have sufficient funds in his bank account. Suppose he had previously got only a £2,000 balance, and his bank would not allow him an overdraft. In such a base the cheque would be dishonoured. The bank would write on the cheque 'refer to drawer', and we would have to get in touch with Hewitson to see what he was going to do to put matters right.

In all of these cases the bank would automatically show the original banking as being cancelled by showing the cheque paid out of our bank account. As soon as this happens they will notify us, and we will then also show the cheque as being cancelled by a credit in the cash book. We will then debit that amount to his account.

When Hewitson originally paid his account our records would appear as:

J. Hewitson

19-2	£	19-2	£
May 1 Balance b/d	5,000	May 20 Bank	5,000

Bank Account

19-2	£
May 20 J. Hewitson	5,000

After our recording the dishonour, the records will appear as:

J. Hewitson

19-2	£	19-2	£
May 1 Balance b/d	5,000	May 20 Bank	5,000
May 25 Bank: cheque dishonoured	5,000		

Bank Account

19-2	£	19-2	£
May 20 J. Hewitson	5,000	May 25 J. Hewitson: cheque dishonoured	5,000

In other words Hewitson is once again shown as owing us £5,000.

Exercises

MC68 A cheque paid by you, but not yet passed through the banking system is

(A) A standing order

(B) A dishonoured cheque

(C) A credit transfer

(D) An unpresented cheque.

MC69 A Bank Reconciliation Statement is a statement
(A) Sent by the bank when the account is overdrawn
(B) Drawn up by us to verify our cash book balance with the bank statement balance
(C) Drawn up by the bank to verify the cash book
(D) Sent by the bank when we have made an error.

MC70 Which of the following are not true? A Bank Reconciliation Statement is
(i) Part of the double entry system
(ii) Not part of the double entry system
(iii) Sent by the firm to the bank
(iv) Posted to the ledger accounts
(A) i, iii and iv
(B) i and ii
(C) i, ii and iv
(D) ii, iii and iv.

26.1. From the following draw up a bank reconciliation statement from details as on 31 December 19-6:

	£
Cash at bank as per bank column of the Cash Book	678
Unpresented cheques	256
Cheques received and paid into the bank, but not yet entered on the bank statement	115
Credit transfers entered as banked on the bank statement but not entered in the Cash Book	56
Cash at bank as per bank statement	875

26.2A. Draw up a bank reconciliation statement, after writing the cash book up-to-date, ascertaining the balance on the bank statement, from the following as on 31 March 19-9:

	£
Cash at bank as per bank column of the cash book (Dr)	3,896
Bankings made but not yet entered on bank statement	606
Bank charges on bank statement but not yet in cash book	28
Unpresented cheques C. Clarke	117
Standing order to A.B.C. Ltd entered on bank statement, but not in cash book	55
Credit transfer from A. Wood entered on bank statement, but not yet in cash book	189

26.3. The following are extracts from the cash book and the bank statement of J. Roche.

You are required to:
(a) Write the cash book up-to-date, and state the new balance as on 31 December 19-5, and
(b) Draw up a bank reconciliation statement as on 31 December 19-5.

Cash Book

19-5	Dr.	£	19-5	Cr.	£
Dec	1 Balance b/f	1,740	Dec	8 A. Dailey	349
Dec	7 T. J. Masters	88	Dec	15 R. Mason	33
Dec	22 J. Ellis	73	Dec	28 G. Small	115
Dec	31 K. Wood	249	Dec	31 Balance c/d	1,831
Dec	31 M. Barrett	178			
		2,328			2,328

Bank Statement

19-5		Dr.	Cr.	Balance
		£	£	£
Dec	1 Balance b/f			1,740
Dec	7 Cheque		88	1,828
Dec	11 A. Dailey	349		1,479
Dec	20 R. Mason	33		1,446
Dec	22 Cheque		73	1,519
Dec	31 Credit transfer: J. Walters		54	1,573
Dec	31 Bank Charges	22		1,551

26.4A. The bank columns in the cash book for June 19-7 and the bank statement for that month for C. Grant are as follows:

Cash Book

19-7	Dr	£	19-7	Cr	£
Jun	1 Balance b/f	2,379	Jun	5 D. Blake	150
Jun	7 B. Green	158	Jun	12 J. Gray	433
Jun	16 A. Silver	93	Jun	16 B. Stephens	88
Jun	28 M. Brown	307	Jun	29 Orange Club	57
Jun	30 K. Black	624	Jun	30 Balance c/d	2,833
		3,561			3,561

Bank Statement

19-7		Dr	Cr	Balance
		£	£	£
Jun	1 Balance b/f			2,379
Jun	7 Cheque		158	2,537
Jun	8 D. Blackness	150		2,387
Jun	16 Cheque		93	2,480
Jun	17 J. Gray	433		2,047
Jun	18 B. Stephens	88		1,959
Jun	28 Cheque		307	2,266
Jun	29 U.D.T. standing order	44		2,222
Jun	30 Johnson: trader's credit		90	2,312
Jun	30 Bank Charges	70		2,242

You are required to:
(a) Write the cash book up-to-date to take the above into account, and then
(b) Draw up a bank reconciliation statement as on 30 June 19-7.

26.5. The following statement for May 19-9 was supplied to Jackson's Ltd. by their bankers.

		Debits £	Credits £	Balance £
May	1 Balance brought forward			760 (*Cr*)
,,	1 Credit		228	988
,,	1 Allan	64		924
,,	3 Cash	12		912
,,	5 Ashley	324		588
,,	5 Kelly	114		474
,,	8 Credit		472	946
,,	11 Bishop	162		784
,,	11 Sykes	136		648
,,	12 Cash	20		628
,,	16 Bank charges	50		578
,,	16 Bennett	58		520
,,	17 Taylor	82		438
,,	17 Shand	56		382
,,	23 Credit		254	636
,,	25 Credit		362	998
,,	25 Cash	20		978
,,	28 Hurst	38		940
,,	28 Kemp	106		834
,,	31 Balance carried forward			

The firm's cash book had been destroyed in a fire but a statement prepared from cheque counterfoils and the Paying-in Book showed the followed details.

		£			£
May	1 Balance b/d	?	May	2 Cash	12
,,	7 Receipts	472	,,	2 Ashley	324
,,	22 ,,	254	,,	2 Taylor	82
,,	23 ,,	362	,,	2 Kelly	114
,,	31 ,,	120	,,	3 Bishop	162
			,,	8 Kemp	106
			,,	11 Cash	20
			,,	12 Shand	56
			,,	18 Good	76
			,,	20 Hurst	38
			,,	24 Cash	20
			,,	26 Burns	54
			,,	27 Kirk	148

Amounts paid into Bank are not credited by the Bank until the following day.

You are required
(*a*) to ascertain the balance in the cash book at 1 May, and
(*b*) to prepare a list of unpresented cheques at 31 May.
(Joint Matriculation Board 'O' level)

26.6. Following is the cash book (bank columns) of E. Flynn for December 19-3.

19-3 Dr	£	19-3 Cr	£
Dec 6 J. Hall	155	Dec 1 Balance b/f	3,872
Dec 20 C. Walters	189	Dec 10 P. Wood	206
Dec 31 P. Miller	211	Dec 19 M. Roberts	315
Dec 31 Balance c/d	3,922	DEc 29 P. Phillips	84
	4,477		4,477

The bank statement for the month is:

19-3	Dr. £	Cr. £	Balance £
Dec 1 Balance			3,872 O/D
Dec 6 Cheque		155	3,717 O/D
Dec 13 P. Wood	206		3,923 O/D
Dec 20 Cheque		189	3,734 O/D
Dec 22 M. Roberts	315		4,049 O/D
Dec 30 Mercantile: standing order	200		4,249 O/D
Dec 31 K. Saunders: trader's credit		180	4,069 O/D
Dec 31 Bank charges	65		4,134 O/D

You are required to:
(a) Write the cash book up-to-date to take the necessary items into account, and
(b) Draw up a bank reconciliation statement as on 31 December 19-3.

26.7A. The bank statement for G. Greene for the month of March 19-6 is:

19-6	Dr. £	Cr. £	Balance £
Mar 1 Balance			5,197 O/D
Mar 8 L. Tulloch	122		5,319 O/D
Mar 16 Cheque		244	5,075 O/D
Mar 20 A. Bennett	208		5,283 O/D
Mar 21 Cheque		333	4,950 O/D
Mar 31 M. Turnbull: trader's credit		57	4,893 O/D
Mar 31 B.K.S.: standing order	49		4,942 O/D
Mar 31 Bank Charges	28		4,970 O/D

The cash book for March 19-6 is:

19-6 Dr.	£	19-6 Cr.	£
Mar 16 N. Marsh	244	Mar 1 Balance b/f	5,197
Mar 21 K. Alexander	333	Mar 6 L. Tulloch	122
Mar 31 U. Sinclair	160	Mar 30 A. Bennett	208
Mar 31 Balance c/d	5,280	Mar 30 J. Shaw	490
	6,017		6,017

You are to:
(a) Write the cash book up-to-date and
(b) Draw up a bank reconciliation statement as on 31 March 19-6.

26.8. The summary of the bank column in the cash book of D.V.T. Ltd. for the year ending 30th November 19-0 is as follows:

	£
Opening balance	1,654
Receipts	332,478
	334,132
Payments	316,735
Closing balance	£17,397

Your investigation of the accounting records for this period reveals the following information:

(i) Cheques paid to suppliers of £1,435 have not yet been presented at the bank, and cheques paid into the bank of £1,620 on 30th November 19-0 have not yet been credited to the company's account.

(ii) Standing orders entered in the bank statement have been omitted from the cash book in respect of lease payments on company car, 12 months at £96 per month, and annual insurance of £150.

(iii) Bank charges of £452 shown in the bank statement have not been entered in the cash book.

(iv) A cheque drawn for £127 has been entered in the cash book as £172, and a cash book page on the receipts side has been under-added by £200.

(v) A cheque for £238 has been debited to the company's bank account in error by the bank.

(vi) The bank statement shows a favourable balance as at 30th November 19-0 of £15,465.

Required:

Bank reconciliation statement as at 30th November 19-0 together with a corrected cash book position.

(Chartered Institute of Secretaries and Administrators)

26.9A. Ben Bailey had recently received his bank statement showing that he had £1,051 to the credit of his current account.

Unfortunately, he had not been keeping his own private record of his bank account, but at least he had details in his cheque book and paying-in book regarding his recent transactions. Items *not* included in the bank statement were:

(a) Cheque payable to A. Smith for £125.

(b) Cash and cheques paid into the bank of £459.

(c) A recently submitted standing order of £28 per annum for fire insurance due immediately.

(d) Cash withdrawn to be used in paying wages £157.

The following item appeared in the bank statement:

A monthly direct debit payable to a hire purchase company for £96 was incorrectly debited twice in the same month.

Required:

A statement showing much money would be standing to the credit of Ben Bailey's bank account once all the above have been passed through the banking system.

(Associated Examining Board 'O' level).

26.10A. On 15 May 19-8, Mr. Lakes received his monthly bank statement for the month ended 30 April 19-8. The bank statement contained the following details.

Mr. Lakes
Statement of Account with Baroyds Limited
(*Balance indicates account is overdrawn)

Date	Particulars	Payments	Receipts	Balance
		£	£	£
1 April	Balance			1,053.29
2 April	236127	210.70		842.59
3 April	Bank Giro Credit		192.35	1,034.94
6 April	236126	15.21		1,019.73
6 April	Charges	12.80		1,006.93
9 April	236129	43.82		963.11
10 April	427519	19.47		943.64
12 April	236128	111.70		831.94
17 April	Standing Order	32.52		799.42
20 April	Sundry Credit		249.50	1,048.92
23 April	236130	77.87		971.05
23 April	236132	59.09		911.96
25 April	Bank Giro Credit		21.47	933.43
27 April	Sundry Credit		304.20	1,237.63
30 April	236133	71.18		1,166.45

For the corresponding period, Mr. Lakes' own records contained the following bank account:

Date	Detail	£	Date	Detail	Cheque No.	£
1 April	Balance	827.38	5 April	Purchases	128	111.70
2 April	Sales	192.35	10 April	Electricity	129	43.82
18 April	Sales	249.50	16 April	Purchases	130	87.77
24 April	Sales	304.20	18 April	Rent	131	30.00
30 April	Sales	192.80	20 April	Purchases	132	59.09
			25 April	Purchases	133	71.18
			20 April	Wages	134	52.27
			30 April	Balance		1,310.40
		£1,766.23				£1,766.23

Required:

(a) Prepare a statement reconciling the balance at 30 April as given by the bank statement to the balance at 30 April as stated in the bank account.

(b) Explain briefly which items in your bank reconciliation statement would require further investigation.
(Association of Certified Accountants)

27

The Journal

Previously it has been shown that the work of recording transactions is divided up into its different functions, there being a separate book (or some other sort of collection point for data) for each major function. The books in which entries are made prior to their posting to the ledgers are known as subsidiary books or as books of prime entry. Thus the sales, purchases, returns inwards and returns outwards books are all books of prime entry. The cash book is also regarded as a book of prime entry, although many would regard it as a ledger, for as it has been seen it originated from the cash and bank accounts being detached from the ledger. However, it is the book in which cash and bank entries are first made and from this point of view it may be taken as a book of prime entry.

It is to the firm's advantage if all transactions which do not pass through a book of prime entry are entered in a book called The Journal. The journal is a form of diary for such transactions. It shows:

1. The date.
2. The name of the account(s) to be debited and the amount(s).
3. The name of the account(s) to be credited and the amount(s).
4. A description of the transaction (this is called a 'narrative').

One would also expect to find a reference number for the documents supporting the transaction.

The advantages to be gained from using a journal may be summarized:

1. It eliminates the need for a reliance on the memory of the book-keeper. Some transactions are of a complicated nature, and without the journal the entries may be difficult, if not impossible, to understand. One must also bear in mind that if the book-keeper left the firm the absence of a journal could leave many unexplained items in the books.
2. Errors, irregularities and fraud are more easily effected when entries are made direct into the ledgers without any explanations being given. The journal acts as an explanation of the entries and details the necessary supporting evidence.

3.   The risk of omitting the transaction altogether, or of making one entry only is reduced.

Despite these advantages there are many firms which do not have such a book.

Typical Uses of the Journal

Some of the main uses of the journal are listed below. It must not be thought that this list is exhaustive.

1.   The purchase and sale of fixed assets on credit.
2.   The correction of errors.
3.   Opening entries. These are the entries needed to open a new set of books.
4.   Other transfers.

The layout of the journal can now be shown:

The Journal

Date	Folio	Dr	Cr
The name of the account to be debited.			
The name of the account to be credited.			
The Narrative.			

To standardize matters the name of the account to be debited should always be shown first. It also helps with the reading of the journal if the name of the account to be credited is written not directly under the name of the account to be debited, but is inset to the right-hand side.

It must be remembered that the journal is not an integral part of the double entry book-keeping system. It is purely a form of diary, and entering an item in the journal is not the same as recording an item in an account. Once the journal entry is made the necessary entry in the double entry accounts can then be effected.

Examples of the uses of the journal are now given.

1. Purchase and Sale on Credit of Fixed Assets

(a) A machine is bought on credit from Toolmakers Co. for £550 on 1 July.

	Dr	Cr
	£	£
July 1 Machinery	550	
Toolmakers Co.		550
Purchase of milling machine on credit, Capital		
Purchases invoice No. 7/159		

(b) Sale of a Motor Vehicle for £300 on credit to A. Barnes on 2 July.

	Dr	Cr
	£	£
July 2 A. Barnes	300	
Motor vehicles		300
Sales of Motor vehicles per Capital		
Sales Invoice No. 7/43		

2. Correction of Errors

These are dealt with in detail in chapters 29 and 30.

3. Opening Entries

J. Brew, after being in business for some years without keeping proper records, now decides to keep a double entry set of books. On 1 July he establishes that his assets and liabilities are as follows:

Assets: Motor Van £840, Fixtures £700, Stock £390, Debtors – B. Young £95, D. Blake £45, Bank £80, Cash £20.
Liabilities: Creditors – M. Quinn £129, C. Walters £41.

The Assets therefore total £840 + £700 + £390 + £95 + £45 + £80 + £20 = £2,170; and the Liabilities total £129 + £41 = £170.

The Capital consists of: Assets – Liabilities, £2,170 – £170 = £2,000

To start the books off on 1 July showing the existing state of the assets and liabilities and capital, these amounts therefore need entering in the relevant asset, liability and capital accounts. The asset accounts will be opened with debit balances and the liability and capital accounts will be opened with credit balances. The journal therefore shows the accounts which are to be debited and those which are to be credited and this is shown in Exhibit 27.1.

Exhibit 27.1   **The Journal**   Page 5

	Fol	Dr	Cr
		£	£
July 1 Motor Van	GL 1	840	
Fixtures	GL 2	700	
Stock	GL 3	390	
Debtors – B. Young	SL 1	95	
D. Blake	SL 2	45	
Bank	CB 1	80	
Cash	CB 1	20	
Creditors – M. Quinn	PL 81		129
C. Walters	PL 2		41
Capital	GL 4		2,000
Assets and liabilities at this date entered			
to open the books.			
		2,170	2,170

Now that the journal has been written up, the accounts can be opened as follows:

General Ledger

Motor Van			Page 1
		£	
July 1 Balance	J 5	840	

Fixtures			Page 2
		£	
July 1 Balance	J 5	700	

Stock			Page 3
		£	
July 1 Balance	J 5	390	

Capital			Page 4
			£
July 1 Balance	J 5		2,000

Sales Ledger

B. Young			Page 1
		£	
July 1 Balance	J 5	95	

D. Blake			Page 2
		£	
July 1 Balance	J 5	45	

Purchases Ledger

M. Quinn			Page 1
			£
July 1 Balance	J 5		129

C. Walters			Page 2
			£
July 1 Balance	J 5		41

Cash Book

Cash Bank			Page 1
		£	£
July 1 Balances	J 5	20	80

Once these opening balances have been recorded in the books the day-to-day transactions can be entered in the normal manner. The need for opening entries will not occur very often. They will not be needed each year as the balances from last year will have been brought forward. At the elementary level of examinations in book-keeping, questions are often asked which entail opening a set of books and recording the day-by-day entries for the ensuing period.

4. Other Transfers

These can be of many kinds and it is impossible to construct a complete list. However, two examples can be shown.

(*a*) S. Bennett, a debtor, owed £200 on 1 July. He was unable to pay his account in cash, but offers a motor car in full settlement of the debt. The offer is accepted on 5 July.

The personal account is therefore discharged and needs crediting. On the other hand the firm now has an extra asset, a motor car, therefore the motor car account needs to be debited.

The Journal

	Dr	Cr
	£	£
July 5 Motor Car	200	
S. Bennett		200
Accepted motor car in full settlement of debt per letter dated 5/7/-5		

(*b*) G. Ames is a creditor. On 10 July his business is taken over by A. Iddon to whom the debt now is to be paid.

Here it is just the identity of one creditor being exchanged for another one. The action needed is to cancel the amount owing to G. Ames by debiting his account, and to show it owing to Iddon by opening an account for Iddon and crediting it.

The Journal

	Dr	Cr
	£	£
July 10 G. Ames	150	
A. Iddon		150
Transfer of indebtedness as per letter from Ames ref. A/1335		

Exercises

MC71 Which of the following should be entered in the Journal?

(i) Payment for cash purchases
(ii) Fixtures bought on credit
(iii) Credit sale of goods
(iv) Sale of surplus machinery.

(A) i and iv
(B) ii and iii
(C) iii and iv
(D) ii and iv.

MC72 The Journal is

(A) Part of the double-entry system
(B) A supplement to the Cash Book
(C) Not part of the double entry system
(D) Used when other journals have been mislaid.

27.1. You are to open the books of K. Mullings, a trader, via the journal to record the assets and liabilities, and are then to record the daily transactions for the month of May. A trial balance is to be extracted as on 31 May 19-6.

19-6

May 1 *Assets* — Premises £2,000; Motor Van £450; Fixtures £600; Stock £1,289. Debtors — N. Hardy £40; M. Nelson £180. Cash at bank £1,254; Cash in hand £45.

Liabilities — Creditors; B. Blake £60; V. Reagan £200.

May 1 Paid rent by cheque £15

,, 2 Goods bought on credit from B. Blake £20; C. Harris £56; H. Gordon £38; N. Lee £69

,, 3 Goods sold on credit to: K. O'Connor £56; M. Benjamin £78; L. Staines £98; N. Duffy £48; B. Green £118; M. Nelson £40

,, 4 Paid for motor expenses in cash £13

,, 7 Cash drawings by proprietor £20

,, 9 Goods sold on credit to: M. Benjamin £22; L. Pearson £67

,, 11 Goods returned to Mullings by: K. O'Connor £16; L. Staines £18

,, 14 Bought another motor van on credit from Better Motors Ltd £300

,, 16 The following paid Mullings their accounts by cheque less 5 per cent cash discount: N. Hardy; M. Nelson; K. O'Connor; L. Staines

,, 19 Goods returned by Mullings to N. Lee £9

,, 22 Goods bought on credit from: J. Johnson £89; T. Best £72

,, 24 The following accounts were settled by Mullings by cheque less 5 per cent cash discount: B. Blake; V. Reagan; N. Lee

,, 27 Salaries paid by cheque £56

,, 30 Paid rates by cheque £66

,, 31 Paid Better Motors Ltd a cheque for £300.

27.2. You are to show the journal entries necessary to record the following items:

(i) 19-5 May 1 Bought a motor vehicle on credit from Kingston Garage for £6,790

(ii) 19-5 May 3 A debt of £34 owing from H. Newman was written off as a bad debt

(iii) 19-5 May 8 Office furniture bought by us for £490 was returned to the supplier Unique Offices, as it was unsuitable. Full allowance will be given us

(iv) 19-5 May 12 We are owed £150 by W. Charles. He is declared bankrupt and we receive £39 in full settlement of the debt

(v) 19-5 May 14 We take £45 goods out of the business stock without paying for them

(vi) 19-5 May 28 Some time ago we paid an insurance bill thinking that it was all in respect of the business. We now discover that £76 of the amount paid was in fact insurance of our private house

(vii) 19-5 May 29 Bought machinery £980 on credit from Systems Accelerated.

27.3A. Show the journal entries necessary to record the following items:

19-7

Apr 1 Bought fixtures on credit from J. Harper £1,809

,, 4 We take £500 goods out of the business stock without paying for them

,, 9 £28 of the goods taken by us on 4 April is not returned back into stock by us. We do not take any money for the return of the goods

,, 12 K. Lamb owes us £500. He is unable to pay his debt. We agree to take some office equipment from him at the value and so cancel the debt

,, 18 Some of the fixtures bought from J. Harper, £65 worth, are found to be unsuitable and are returned to him for full allowance

,, 24 A debt owing to us by J. Brown of £68 is written off as a bad debt

,, 30 Office equipment bought on credit from Super Offices for £2,190.

28

The Analytical Petty Cash Book and the Imprest System

With the growth of the firm it has been seen that it became necessary to have several books instead of just one ledger. As the firm further increased in size these books also were further sub-divided.

These ideas can be extended to the cash book. It is obvious that in almost any firm there will be a great deal of small cash payments to be made. It would be an advantage if the records of these payments could be kept separate from the main cash book. Where a separate book is kept it is known as a Petty Cash Book.

The advantages of such an action can be summarized:

1. The task of handling and recording the small cash payments could be delegated by the cashier to a junior member of staff who would then be known as the petty cashier. Thus, the cashier, who is a relatively higher paid member of staff, would be saved from routine work easily performed by a junior and lower paid member of staff.

2. If small cash payments were entered into the main cash book these items would then need posting one by one to the ledgers. If travelling expenses were paid to staff on a daily basis this could involve over 250 postings to the Staff Travelling Expenses Account during the year. However, if a form of analytical petty cash book is kept it would only be the periodical totals that need posting to the general ledger. If this was done only 12 monthly entries would be needed in the staff travelling expenses account instead of over 250.

When the petty cashier makes a payment to someone, then that person will have to fill in a voucher showing exactly what the expense was. He may well have to attach bills obtained by him − e.g. bills for petrol − to the petty cash voucher. He would sign the voucher to certify that his expenses had been paid to him by the petty cashier.

The Imprest System

The basic idea of this system is that the cashier gives the petty cashier an adequate amount of cash to meet his needs for the ensuing period. At the end of the period the cashier ascertains the amount spent by the petty cashier, and gives him an amount equal to that spent. The Petty Cash in hand should then be equal to the original amount with which the period was started.

Exhibit 28.1 shows an example of this procedure:

Exhibit 28.1

	£
Period 1 The cashier gives the petty cashier	100
The petty cashier pays out in the period	78
Petty cash now in hand	22
The cashier now reimburses the petty cashier the amount spent	78
Petty cash in hand end of period 1	100
Period 2 The petty cashier pays out in the period	84
Petty cash now in hand	16
The cashier now reimburses the petty cashier the amount spent	84
Petty cash in hand end of period 2	100

Of course, it may sometimes be necessary to increase the fixed sum, often called the cash 'float', to be held at the start of each period. In the above case if it had been desired to increase the 'float' at the end of the second period to £120, then the cashier would have given the petty cashier an extra £20, i.e. £84 + £20 = £104.

Illustration of an Analytical Cash Book

An analytical Petty Cash Book is often used. One of these is shown as Exhibit 28.2.

The receipts column represents the debit side of the petty cash book. On giving £50 to the petty cashier on 1 September the credit entry is made in the cash book while the debit entry is made in the petty cash book. A similar entry is made on 30 September for the £44 reimbursement.

The entries on the credit side of the petty cash book are first of all made in the totals column, and then are extended into the relevant expense column. At the end of the period, in this case a month, the payments are totalled, it being made sure that the total of the totals column equals the sum of the other payments totals, in this case £44. The expense columns have been headed with the type of expense.

To complete double entry, the total of each expense column is debited to the relevant expense account in the general ledger, the folio number of the page in the general ledger then being shown under each column of the petty cash book.

The end column has been chosen as a ledger column. In this column items paid out of petty cash which need posting to a ledger other than the general ledger are shown. This would happen if a purchases ledger account was settled out of petty cash, or if a refund was made out of the petty cash to a customer who had overpaid his account.

The double-entry for all the items in Exhibit 28.2 appears as Exhibit 28.3

19-4

			£
Sept	1	The cashier gives £50 as float to the petty cashier	
		Payments out of petty cash during September:	
,,	2	Petrol	6
,,	3	J. Green – travelling expenses	3
,,	3	Postages	2
,,	4	D. Davies – travelling expenses	2
,,	7	Cleaning expenses	1
,,	9	Petrol	1
,,	12	K. Jones – travelling expenses	3
,,	14	Petrol	3
,,	15	L. Black – travelling expenses	5
,,	16	Cleaning expenses	1
,,	18	Petrol	2
,,	20	Postages	2
,,	22	Cleaning expenses	1
,,	24	G. Wood – travelling expenses	7
,,	27	Settlement of C. Brown's account in the Purchases Ledger	3
,,	29	Postages	2
,,	30	The cashier reimburses the petty cashier the amount spent in the month.	

Exhibit 28.2

Petty Cash Book (page 31)

Receipts	Folio	Date	Details	Voucher No.	Total	Motor Expenses	Staff Travelling Expenses	Postages	Cleaning	Ledger Folio	Ledger Accounts
£					£	£	£	£	£		£
50	CB 19	Sept 1	Cash								
		,, 2	Petrol	1	6	6					
		,, 3	J. Green	2	3		3				
		,, 3	Postages	3	2			2			
		,, 4	D. Davies	4	2		2				
		,, 7	Cleaning	5	1				1		
		,, 9	Petrol	6	1	1					
		,, 12	K. Jones	7	3		3				
		,, 14	Petrol	8	3	3					
		,, 15	L. Black	9	5		5				
		,, 16	Cleaning	10	1				1		
		,, 18	Petrol	11	2	2					
		,, 20	Postages	12	2			2			
		,, 22	Cleaning	13	1				1		
		,, 24	G. Wood	14	7		7				
		,, 27	C. Brown	15	3					PL 18	3
		,, 29	Postages	16	2			2			
					44	12	20	6	3		3
						GL 17	GL 29	GL 44	G 64		
44	CB 22	30	Cash								
		,, 30	Balance	c/d	50						
94					94						
50		Oct 1	Balance	b/d	50						

Exhibit 28.3

| | Cash Book (Bank Column only) | | Page 19 |

		19-4	£
		Sept 1 Petty Cash PCB 31	50
		,, 30 Petty Cash PCB 31	44

General Ledger
Motor Expenses   Page 17

19-4		£
Sept 30 Petty Cash PCB 31		12

Staff Travelling Expenses   Page 29

19-4		£
Sept 30 Petty Cash PCB 31		20

Postages   Page 44

19-4		£
Sept 30 Petty Cash PCB 31		6

Cleaning   Page 64

19-4		£
Sept 30 Petty Cash PCB 31		3

Purchases Ledger
C. Brown   Page 18

19-4		£	19-4		£
Sept 30 Petty Cash PCB 31		3	Sept 1 Balance b/d		3

In a firm with both a cash book and a petty cash book, the cash book is often known as a bank cash book. This means that *all* cash payments are entered in the petty cash book, and the bank cash book will contain *only* bank columns and discount columns. In this type of firm any cash sales will be paid direct into the bank.

In such a cash book, as in fact could happen in an ordinary cash book, an extra column could be added. In this would be shown the details of the cheques banked, just the total of the banking being shown in the total column.

Example 28.4 shows the receipts side of the Bank Cash Book. The totals of the bankings made on the three days were £192, £381 and £1,218. The details column shows what the bankings are made up of.

Exhibit 28.4

Bank Cash Book (Receipts side)

Date 19-6	Details	Discount £	Items £	Total banked £
May 14	G. Archer	5	95	
,, 14	P. Watts	3	57	
,, 14	C. King		40	192
,, 20	K. Dooley	6	114	
,, 20	Cash Sales		55	
,, 20	R. Jones		60	
,, 20	P. Mackie	8	152	381
,, 31	J. Young		19	
,, 31	T. Broome	50	950	
,, 31	Cash Sales		116	
,, 31	H. Tiller	7	133	1,218

Exercises

MC73 Given a desired cash float of £200, if £146 is spent in the period, how much will be reimbursed at the end of the period?
(A) £200
(B) £54
(C) £254
(D) £146.

MC74 When a petty cash book is kept there will be
(A) More entries made in the general ledger
(B) Fewer entries made in the general ledger
(C) The same number of entries in the general ledger
(D) No entries made at all in the general ledger for items paid by petty cash.

28.1. Enter the following transactions in a petty cash book, having analysis columns for motor expenses, postages and stationery, cleaning, sundry expenses, and a ledger column. This is to be kept on the imprest system, the amount spent to be reimbursed on the last day of the month. The opening petty cash float is £100.

19-6		£
May	1 Cleaning	3
,,	3 Speedy Garage – Petrol	2
,,	4 Postage stamps	5
,,	5 Envelopes	1
,,	6 Poison licence	1
,,	8 Unique Garage – Petrol	5
,,	9 Corner Garage – Petrol	6
,,	11 Postage stamps	5
,,	12 F. Lessor – Ledger account	9
,,	13 H. Norris – Ledger account	4
,,	15 Sweeping brush (cleaning)	2
,,	16 Bends Garage – petrol	7
,,	17 K. Kelly – Stationery	6
,,	19 Driving licences	1
,,	21 J. Green – Ledger account	7
,,	25 Cleaning	6
,,	27 Licence for guard dog	1
,,	28 Guard dog – Food	2
,,	31 Corner garage – Petrol	5

28.2. Enter the following transactions in a petty cash book, having analysis columns for hotel charges, postages and stationery, motor expenses, sundry expenses and ledger accounts.

19-1

Apr	1	Received cash float of £200
,,	3	Paid sundry expenses £2, Hotel charges £6
,,	4	Paid J. Jones' account £9
,,	5	F. Garner − Ledger account £4
,,	7	Petrol £2, Envelopes £3
,,	9	Sundry expenses £4, hotel expenses £7
,,	10	Postages £5
,,	11	Petrol £4, J. Jordan ledger account £2
,,	18	Stationery £3, Petrol £2, Hotel charges £7
,,	23	Sundry expenses £1, hotel charges £9
,,	25	Petrol £4, Postages £6, Ledger account Lucas £7
,,	26	Billheadings printed £3
,,	30	Received amount to bring petty cash balance up to £200.

28.3A. Rule up a petty cash book with analysis columns for office expenses, motor expenses, cleaning expenses, and casual labour. The cash float is £350 and the amount spent is reimbursed on 30 June.

19-7			£
June	1	H. Sangster − casual labour	13
,,	2	Letterheadings	22
,,	2	Unique Motors − motor repairs	30
,,	3	Cleaning Materials	6
,,	6	Envelopes	14
,,	8	Petrol	8
,,	11	J. Higgins − casual labour	15
,,	12	Mrs. Body − cleaner	7
,,	12	Paper clips	2
,,	14	Petrol	11
,,	16	Typewriter repairs	1
,,	19	Petrol	9
,,	21	Motor Taxation	50
,,	22	T. Sweet − casual labour	21
,,	23	Mrs. Body − cleaner	10
,,	24	P. Dennis − casual labour	19
,,	25	Copy paper	7
,,	26	Flat Cars − motor repairs	21
,,	29	Petrol	12
,,	30	J. Young − casual labour	16

28.4A. The following is a summary of the petty cash transactions of Jockfield Ltd. for May 19-2.

May 1 Received from Cashier £300 as petty cash float

		£
,,	2 Postages	18
,,	3 Travelling	12
,,	4 Cleaning	15
,,	7 Petrol for delivery van	22
,,	8 Travelling	25
,,	9 Stationery	17
,,	11 Cleaning	18
,,	14 Postage	5
,,	15 Travelling	8
,,	18 Stationery	9
,,	18 Cleaning	23
,,	20 Postage	13
,,	24 Delivery van 5,000 mile service	43
,,	26 Petrol	18
,,	27 Cleaning	21
,,	29 Postage	5
,,	30 Petrol	14

You are required to:
(a) Rule up a suitable petty cash book with analysis columns for expenditure on cleaning, motor expenses, postage, stationery, travelling;
(b) Enter the month's transactions;
(c) Enter the receipt of the amount necessary to restore the imprest and carry down the balance for the commencement of the following month;
(d) State how the double entry for the expenditure is completed.

(Association of Accounting Technicians)

29

Errors Not Affecting Trial Balance Agreement

In Chapter 6 it was seen that if someone followed these rules:

> Every debit entry needs a corresponding credit entry
> Every credit entry needs a corresponding debit entry

and entered up his books using these rules, then when he extracted the trial balance its totals would agree, i.e. it would 'balance'.

Suppose he correctly entered cash sales £70 to the debit of the cash book, but did not enter the £70 to the credit of the sales account. If this was the only error in the books, the trial balance totals would differ by £70. However, there are certain kinds of errors which would not affect the agreement of the trial balance totals, and we will now look at in this chapter.

These are:

1. Errors of omission — where a transaction is completely omitted from the books. If we sold £90 goods to J. Brewer, but did not enter it in either the sales or Brewer's personal account, the trial balance would still 'balance'.

2. Errors of commission — this type is where the correct amount is entered but in the wrong person's account, e.g. where a sale of £11 to C. Green is entered in the account of K. Green. It will be noted that the correct class of account was used, both the accounts concerned being personal accounts.

3. Errors of principle — where an item is entered in the wrong class of account, e.g. if a fixed asset such as a motor van is debited to an expenses account such as motor expenses account.

4. Compensating errors — where errors cancel out each other. If the sales account was added up to be £10 too much and the purchases account also added up to be £10 too much, then these two errors would cancel out in the trial balance. This is because totals both of the debit side of the trial balance and of the credit side will be £10 too much.

5. Errors of original entry — where the original figure is incorrect, yet double-entry is still observed using this incorrect figure. An instance of this could be where there were sales of £150 goods but an error is made in calculating the sales invoice. If it was calculated as £130, and £130 was credited as sales and £130 debited to the personal account of the customer, the trial balance would still 'balance'.

6. Complete reversal of entries — where the correct accounts are used but each item is shown on the wrong side of the account. Suppose we had paid a cheque to D. Williams for £200, the double-entry of which is Cr Bank £200, Dr D. Williams £200. In error it is entered as Cr D. Williams £200, Dr Bank £200. The trial balance totals will still agree.

Correction of Errors

When these errors are found they have to be corrected. The entries have to be made in the double entry accounts. In addition, an entry should be made in The Journal, to explain the correction. We can now look at one of these for each type of error.

1. Error of Omission

The sale of goods, £59 to E. George, has been completely omitted from the books. We must correct this by entering the sale in the books.

The Journal

	Dr	Cr
	£	£
E. George	59	
Sales account		59

Correction of omission of Sales Invoice No. . . . . . . from sales journal.

2. Error of Commission

A purchase of goods, £44 from C. Simons, was entered in error in C. Simpson's account. To correct this, it must be cancelled out of C. Simpson's account, and then entered where it should be in C. Simon's account. The double-entry will be:

C. Simpson

19-5		£	19-5		£
Sept 30 C. Simons: Error corrected		44	Sept 30 Purchases		44

C. Simons

	19-5		£
	Sept 30 Purchases:		
	Entered originally		
	in C. Simpson's A/c		44

The Journal entry will be:

The Journal

	Dr	Cr
	£	£
C. Simpson	44	
C. Simons		44
Purchase Invoice No. . . . . . entered in wrong		
personal account, now corrected		

3. Error of Principle

The purchase of a machine, £200, is debited to Purchases account instead of being debited to a Machinery account. We therefore cancel the item out of the Purchases account by crediting that account. It is then entered where it should be by debiting the Machinery account.

The Journal

	Dr	Cr
	£	£
Machinery account	200	
Purchases account		200
Correction of error purchase of fixed asset debited		
to purchases account.		

4. Compensating Error

The sales account is overcast by £200, as also is the wages account. The trial balance therefore still 'balances'. This assumes that these are the only two errors found in the books.

The Journal

	Dr	Cr
	£	£
Sales Account	200	
Wages Account		200
Correction of overcasts of £200 each in the sales		
account and the wages account which compensated		
for each other.		

5. *Error of Original Entry*

A sale of £98 to A. Smailes was entered in the books as £89. It needs another £9 of sales entering now.

The Journal

	Dr	Cr
	£	£
A. Smailes	9	
Sales Account		9
Correction of error whereby sales were understated by £9.		

6. *Complete Reversal of Entries*

A payment of cash of £16 to M. Dickson was entered on the receipts side of the cash book in error and credited to M. Dickson's account. This is somewhat more difficult to adjust. First must come the amount needed to cancel the error, then comes the actual entry itself. Because of this, the correcting entry is double the actual amount first recorded. We can now look at why this is so:

What we should have had:

Cash

			£
		M. Dickson	16

M. Dickson

	£		
Cash	16		

Was entered as:

Cash

	£		
M. Dickson	16		

M. Dickson

			£
		Cash	16

We can now see that we have to enter double the original amount to correct the error.

Cash

	£		£
M. Dickson	16	M. Dickson (error corrected)	32

M. Dickson

	£		£
Cash (error corrected)	32	M. Dickson	16

Overall, when corrected, the cash account showing £16 debit and £32 credit means a net credit of £16. Similarly, Dickson's account shows £32 debit and £16 credit, a net debit of £16. As the final (net) answer is the same as what should have been entered originally, the error is now corrected.

The Journal entry appears:

The Journal

	Dr	Cr
	£	£
M. Dickson	32	
Cash		32

Payment of cash £16 debited to cash and credited to
M. Dickson in error on . . . . Error now corrected.

Casting

You will often notice the use of the expression 'to cast', which means 'to add up'. Overcasting means incorrectly adding up a column of figures to give an answer which is greater than it should be. Undercasting means incorrectly adding up a column of figures to give an answer which is less than it should be.

Exercises

MC75 Which of the following do *not* affect trial balance agreement?
(i) Sales £105 to A. Henry entered in P. Henry's account.
(ii) Cheque payment of £134 for Motor Expenses entered only in Cash Book.
(iii) Purchases £440 from C. Browne entered in both accounts as £404.
(iv) Wages account added up incorrectly, being totalled £10 too much.
(A) i and iv
(B) i and iii
(C) ii and iii
(D) iii and iv.

MC76 Which of the following are *not* errors of principle?
(i)   Motor expenses entered in Motor Vehicles account.
(ii) Purchases of machinery entered in Purchases account.
(iii) Sale of £250 to C. Phillips completely omitted from books.
(iv) Sale to A. Henriques entered in A. Henry's account.
(A) ii and iii
(B) i and ii
(C) iii and iv
(D) i and iv.

29.1. Show the journal entries necessary to correct the following errors:

(i)   A sale of goods £678 to J. Harris had been entered in J. Hart's account.
(ii)   The purchase of a machine on credit from L. Pyle for £4,390 had been completely omitted from our books.
(iii) The purchase of a motor van £3,800 had been entered in error in the Motor Expenses account.
(iv)   A sale of £221 to E. Fitzwilliam had been entered in the books, both debit and credit, as £212.
(v)   Commission received £257 had been entered in error in the Sales Account.
(vi)   A receipt of cash from T. Heath £77 had been entered on the credit side of the cash book and the debit side of T. Heath's account.
(vii) A purchase of goods £189 had been entered in error on the debit side of the drawings account.
(viii) Discounts Allowed £366 had been entered in error on the debit side of the Discounts Received account.

29.2A. Show the journal entries needed to correct the following errors:

(i)   Purchases £699 on credit from K. Ward had been entered in H. Wood's account.
(ii)   A cheque of £189 paid for advertisements had been entered in the cash column of the cash book instead of in the bank column.
(iii) Sale of goods £443 on credit to B. Gorton had been entered in error in B. Gorton's account.
(iv)   Purchase of goods on credit K. Isaacs £89 entered in two places in error as £99.
(v)   Cash paid to H. Moore £89 entered on the debit side of the cash book and the credit side of H. Moore's account.
(vi)   A sale of fittings £500 had been entered in the Sales Account.
(vii) Cash withdrawn from bank £100, had been entered in the cash column on the credit side of the cash book, and in the bank column on the debit side.
(viii) Purchase of goods £428 has been entered in error in the Fittings Account.

30

Suspense Accounts and Errors

In Chapter 29 errors were looked at where the trial balance totals were not thrown out of agreement. However, there are many errors which will mean that the trial balance will not 'balance'.

We can now look at some of these. It is assumed that there are no compensating errors.

1.   Incorrect additions, either totals too great or too small, in any account.

2.   Entering an item on only one side of the books. For instance, if the debit entry is made but not the credit entry, or a credit entry but no debit entry.

3.   Entering one figure on the debit side of the books but another figure on the credit side. For instance, if £80 for cash received from M. Brown is entered in the cash book, but £280 is entered in respect of it in Brown's account.

Every effort should be made to find the errors immediately, but especially in examinations it is assumed that for one reason or other this is not possible. Making this assumption, the trial balance totals should be made to agree with each other by inserting the amount of the difference between the two sides in a Suspense Account. This occurs in Exhibit 30.1 where there is a £40 difference.

Exhibit 30.1

Trial Balance as on 31 December 19-5

	Dr	Cr
	£	£
Totals after all the accounts have been listed	100,000	99,960
Suspense Account		40
	100,000	100,000

Suspense Account

		19-5	£
		Dec 31 Difference per trial balance	40

If the errors are not found before the final accounts are prepared, the balance of £40, being a credit balance, will be shown on the capital and liabilities side of the balance sheet. This, however, should never occur if the figure is a large one: the error must always be found. If the item is small, however, it may be added to current liabilities if it is a credit balance, or to current assets if it is a debit balance.

When the error(s) are found they must be corrected. For each correction an entry must be made in The Journal describing the correction.

Assume that the error of £40 as shown in Exhibit 30.1 is found in the following year on 31 March 19-6. The error was that the sales account was undercast by £40. The balance on the suspense account should now be cancelled. The sales account should be credited to increase the account that had been understated. The accounts will appear:

Suspense Account

19-6	£	19-5	£
Mar 31 Sales	40	Dec 31 Difference per trial balance	40

Sales

		19-6	£
		Mar 31 Suspense	40

This can be shown in journal form as:

The Journal

	Dr	Cr
19-6	£	£
Mar 31 Suspense	40	
Sales		40
Correction of undercasting of sales by £40 in last year's accounts		

We can now look at Exhibit 30.2 where the suspense account difference was caused by more than one error.

Exhibit 30.2

The trial balance at 31 December 19-7 showed a difference of £77, being a shortage on the debit side. A suspense account is opened, and the difference of £77 is entered on the debit side of the account.

On 28 February 19-8 all the errors from the previous year were found.

(*a*) A cheque of £150 paid to L. Bond had been correctly entered in the cash book, but had not been entered in Bond's account.

(*b*) The purchases account had been undercast by £20.

(*c*) A cheque of £93 received from K. Smith had been correctly entered in the cash book, but had not been entered in Smith's account.

These are corrected as follows:

Suspense Account

19-8		£	19-8		£
Jan 1	Balance b/fwd	77	Feb 28	L. Bond	150
Feb 28	K. Smith	93	,, 28	Purchases	20
		170			170

L. Bond

19-8		£
Feb 28	Suspense	150

Purchases

19-8		£
Feb 28	Suspense	20

K. Smith

			19-8		£
			Feb 28	Suspense	93

The Journal

		Dr	Cr
19-8		£	£
Feb 28	L. Bond	150	
	Suspense		150
	Cheque paid omitted from Bond's account		
Feb 28	Purchases	20	
	Suspense		20
	Undercasting of purchases by £20 in last year's accounts		
Feb 28	Suspense	93	
	K. Smith		93
	Cheque received omitted from Smith's account		

Only those errors which do throw the trial balance totals out of balance have to be corrected via the Suspense Account.

The Effect of Errors on Reported Profits

When errors are not discovered until a later period, it will often be found that the gross and/or net profits will have been incorrectly stated for the earlier period when the errors were made but had not been found.

Exhibit 30.3 shows a set of accounts in which errors have been made.

Exhibit 30.3

K. Black

Trading & Profit & Loss Account for the year ended 31 December 19-5

	£	£
Sales		8,000
Less Cost of Goods Sold:		
Opening Stock	500	
Add Purchases	6,100	
	6,600	
Less Closing Stock	700	5,900
Gross Profit		2,100
Add Discounts Received		250
		2,350
Less Expenses:		
Rent	200	
Insurance	120	
Lighting and Heating	180	
Depreciation	250	750
		1,600

Balance Sheet as at 31 December 19-5

	£	£
Fixed Assets		
Fixtures at cost	2,200	
Less Depreciation to date	800	1,400
Current Assets		
Stock	700	
Debtors	600	
Bank	340	
	1,640	
Less Current Liabilities		
Creditors	600	
Working Capital		1,040
Suspense Account		60
		2,500

Financed by:		
Capital		
Balance as at 1.1.19-5	1,800	
Add Net Profit	1,600	
	3,400	
Less Drawings	900	2,500
		2,500

Now suppose that there had only been one error found on 31 March 19-6, and that was that sales had been overcast £60. The correction appears as:

Suspense

19-6			£	19-6		£
Jan	1 Balance b/d		60	Mar 31 Sales		60

Sales

19-6		£
Mar 31 Sales		60

The Journal

		Dr	Cr
19-6		£	£
Mar 31 Sales		60	
	Suspense		60
Overcasting of sales by £60 in last year's accounts.			

If a statement of corrected net profit for the year ended 31 December 19-5 is drawn up it will be shown in Exhibit 30.4.

Exhibit 30.4

K. Black

Statement of Corrected Net Profit for the year ended 31 December 19-5

	£
Net profit per the accounts	1,600
Less Sales overcast	·60
Corrected net profit for the year	1,540

If instead there had been 4 errors in the accounts of K. Black, found on 31 March 19-6, their correction can now be seen. Assume that the net difference had also been £60.

(a) Sales overcast by £70

(b) Rent undercast by £40

(c) Cash received from a debtor entered in the Cash Book only £50

(d) A purchase of £59 is entered in the books, debit and credit entries, as £95

The entries in the suspense account, and the journal entries will be as follows:

Suspense

19-6		£	19-6		£
Jan 1	Balance b/d	60	Mar 31	Sales	70
Mar 31	Debtor	50	,, 31	Rent	40
		110			110

The Journal

		Dr	Cr
19-6		£	£
Mar 31	Sales	70	
	Suspense		70
	Sales overcast of £70 in 19-5		
Mar 31	Rent	40	
	Suspense		40
	Rent expense undercast by £40 in 19-5		
Mar 31	Suspense	50	
	Debtor's account		50
	Cash received omitted from debtor's account in 19-5		
Mar 31	Creditor's account	36	
	Purchases		36
	Credit purchase of £59 entered both as debit and credit as £95 in 19-5		

N.B. Note that (*d*), the correction of the understatement of purchases, does not pass through the suspense account.

Exhibit 30.5 shows the statement of corrected net profit.

Exhibit 30.5

K. Black

Statement of Corrected Net Profit for the year ended 31 December 19-5

		£
Net profit per the accounts		1,600
Add Purchases overstated		36
		1,636
Less Sales overcast	70	
Rent undercast	40	110
Corrected net profit for the year		1,526

Error (*c*), the cash not posted to a debtor's account, did not affect profit calculations.

Exercises

MC77 Errors are corrected via The Journal because
(A) It saves the book-keeper's time
(B) It saves entering them in the ledger
(C) It is much easier to do
(D) It provides a record explaining the double-entry entries.

MC78 Which of these errors would be disclosed by the Trial Balance?
(A) Cheque £95 from C. Smith entered in Smith's account as £59
(B) Selling expenses had been debited to Sales Account
(C) Credit sale of £300 entered in double entry accounts as £30
(D) A purchase of £250 was omitted entirely from the books.

MC79 If a trial balance totals do not agree, the difference must be entered in
(A) The Profit and Loss Account
(B) A Suspense Account
(C) A Nominal Account
(D) The Capital Account.

30.1. Your book-keeper extracted a trial balance on 31 December 19-4 which failed to agree by £330, a shortage on the credit side of the trial balance. A Suspense Account was opened for the difference.

In January 19-5 the following errors made in 19-4 were found:
(i) Sales day book had been undercast by £100.
(ii) Sales of £250 to J. Cantrell had been debited in error to J. Cochrane's account.
(iii) Rent account had been undercast by £70.
(iv) Discounts Received account had been undercast by £300.
(v) The sale of a motor vehicle at book value had been credited in error to Sales Account £360.

You are required to:
(a) Show the journal entries necessary to correct the errors.
(b) Draw up the suspense account after the errors described have been corrected.
(c) If the net profit had previously been calculated at £7,900 for the year ended 31 December 19-4, show the calculation of the corrected net profit.

30.2A. You have extracted a trial balance and drawn up accounts for the year ended 31 December 19-6. There was a shortage of £292 on the credit side of the trial balance, a suspense account being opened for that amount.

During 19-7 the following errors made in 19-6 were located:
(a) £55 received from sales of old Office Equipment has been entered in the sales account.–
(b) Purchases day book had been overcast by £60.+
(c) A private purchase of £115 had been included in the business purchases.
(d) Bank charges £38 entered in the cash book have not been posted to the bank charges account.
(e) A sale of goods to B. Cross £690 was correctly entered in the sales book but entered in the personal account as £960.

You are to:
(i) Show the requisite journal entries to correct the errors.
(ii) Write up the suspense account showing the correction of the errors.
(iii) The net profit originally calculated for 19-6 was £11,370. Show your calculation of the correct figure.

30.3. R. Blackett's trial balance, extracted at 30 April 19-2, failed to agree. In early May the following errors were discovered.

1. The total of the returns outward book £124 had not been posted to the ledger.
2. An invoice received from W. Dawson, £100, had been mislaid. Entries for this transaction had, therefore, not been made.
3. A payment for repairs to the motor van £36 had been entered in the vehicle repairs account as £30.
4. When balancing the account of R. Race in the ledger, the debit balance had been brought down in error as £26, instead of £62.

Required:
(*a*) (i) Journal entries, complete with suitable narrations, to correct each of the above errors.
  (ii) A suspense account indicating the nature and extent of the original difference in the books.
  (iii) The incorrect total of the trial balance credit column, given that the incorrect total of the debit column was £10,000.

Required:
(*b*) *Four* types of errors which do not affect the agreement of the trial balance, giving an example of each.

(Associated Examining Board 'O' level)

30.4A. Chi Knitwear Ltd. is an old fashioned firm with a hand-written set of books. A Trial Balance is extracted at the end of each month, and a profit and loss account and balance sheet are computed. This month however the trial balance will not balance, the credits exceeding debits by £1,536.

You are asked to help and after inspection of the ledgers discover the following errrors.

1. A balance of £87 on a debtors account has been omitted from the schedule of debtors, the total of which was entered as debtors in the trial balance.
2. A small piece of machinery purchased for £1,200 had been written off to repairs.
3. The receipts side of the cash book had been undercast by £720.
4. The total of one page of the sales day book had been carried forward as £8,154, whereas the correct amount was £8,514.
5. A credit note for £179 received from a supplier had been posted to the wrong side of his account.
6. An electricity bill in the sum of £152, not yet accrued for, is discovered in a filing tray.
7. Mr. Smith whose past debts to the company had been the subject of a provision, at last paid £731 to clear his account. His personal account has been credited but the cheque has not yet passed through the cash book.

You are required to:
(*a*) Write up the Suspense Account to clear the difference, and
(*b*) State the effect on the accounts of correcting each error.

(Association of Certified Accountants).

30.5. When Debbie Brown extracted her trial balance at 31 March 19-2 she found it did not agree. She opened a suspense account, prepared her trading and profit and loss account and drew up the following balance sheet:

	£	£	£		£	£
Fixed Assets				*Capital*		
Shop Fittings,				Balance 1 April		
cost	1,500			19-1	7,500	
Less Depreciation	300	1,200		*Add* Profit for		
				Year	5,497	
Delivery van, cost	3,200				12,997	
Less Depreciation	800	2,400	3,600			
				Less Drawings	5,000	7,997
Current Assets						
Stock		2,917		*Current Liabilities*		
Sundry Debtors		2,154		Sundry Creditors		1,888
Bank		1,095		*Suspense Account*		9
Cash		128	6,294			
			£9,894			£9,894

Subsequent checking of her records revealed the following errors which when corrected eliminated the Suspense Account:

1. A cheque for £260 for the purchase of a new display stand on 31 March had been entered correctly in the cash book but had been entered in Shop Fittings Account as £200.
2. A credit note from XY Suppliers Ltd. for £60 had been entered correctly in the returns outwards book but had been posted to XY's account as £66.
3. Bank charges £21 appeared in the cash book but had not been posted to the ledger.
4. An invoice for £139 for goods sold to Thompson had been correctly entered in the sales day book but had been posted to Thompson's account as £193.
5. The debit balance of £223 on Smith's account at 31 March 19-2 had been carried down as £253 and included in the trial balance at that figure.

You are required to:

(*a*) Write up the Suspense Account showing therein the necessary correcting entries;
(*b*) Prepare a statement showing the revised profit for the year;
(*c*) Prepare a corrected balance sheet.
(Association of Accounting Technicians).

30.6A. The draft final accounts for the year ended 31 March 19-9 of Blackheath Limited, car dealers, show a gross profit of £36,000 and net profit of £9,000.

After subsequent investigations the following discoveries were made:

(i) Discounts received in August 19-8 of £210 have been credited, in error, to purchases.

(ii) A debt of £300 due from P. Black to the company was written off as irrecoverable in the company's books in December 19-8. Since preparing the draft accounts, P. Black has settled the debt in full.

(iii) The company's main warehouse was burgled in June 19-8, when goods costing £20,000 were stolen. This amount has been shown in the draft accounts as an overhead item 'Loss due to burglary'. Although the insurance company denied liability originally, in the past day or two that decision has been changed and Blackheath Limited have been advised that £14,000 will be paid in settlement.

(iv) On 2 January 19-9, a car which had cost the company £1,800 was taken from the showrooms for the use of one of the company's sales representatives whilst on company business. In the showrooms, this car had had a £2,400 price label. Effect has not been given to this transfer in the books of the company, although the car was not included in the trading stock valuation at 31 March 19-9. The company provides for depreciation on motor vehicles at the rate of 25% of the cost of vehicles held at the end of each financial year.

(v) Goods bought and received from L. Ring on 30 March 19-9 at a cost of £1,200 were not recorded in the company's books of account until early April 19-9. Although they were unsold on 31 March 19-9, the goods in question were not included in the stock valuation at that date.

(vi) The company is hoping to market a new car accessory product in July 19-9. The new venture is to be launched with an advertising campaign commencing in April 19-9. The cost of this campaign is £5,000 and this has been debited in the company's profit and loss account for the year ended 31 March 19-9 and is included in current liabilities as a provision, notwithstanding the confident expectation that the new product will be a success.

(vii) On 31 March 19-9 the company paid an insurance premium of £600, the renewal being for the year commencing 1 April 19-9. This premium was included in the insurances of £1,100 debited in the draft profit and loss account.

Required:

(a) The journal entries necessary to adjust for items (iii), (iv) and (vi) above. Note: Narratives are required.

(b) A computation of the corrected gross profit and net profit for the year ended 31 March 19-9.

(Association of Certified Accountants).

31

Control Accounts

When all the accounts were kept in one ledger a trial balance could be extracted as a test of the arithmetical accuracy of the account. It must be remembered that certain errors were not revealed by such a trial balance. If the trial balance totals disagreed, the number of entries for such a small business being relatively few, the books could easily and quickly be checked so as to locate the errors. However, when the firm has grown and the accounting work has been so subdivided that there are several or many ledgers, a trial balance the totals of which did not agree could result in a great deal of unnecessary checking before the errors were found. What is required in fact is a type of trial balance for each ledger, and this requirement is met by the Control Account. Thus it is only the ledgers whose control accounts do not balance that need detailed checking to find errors.

The principle on which the control account is based is simple, and is as follows. If the opening balance of an account is known, together with information of the additions and deductions entered in the account, the closing balance can be calculated. Applying this to a complete ledger, the total of opening balances together with the additions and deductions during the period should give the total of closing balances. This can be illustrated by reference to a sales ledger:

	£
Total of Opening Balances, 1 January 19-6	3,000
Add total of entries which have increased the balances	9,500
	12,500
Less total of entries which have reduced the balances	8,000
Total of closing balances should be	4,500

Because totals are used the accounts are often known as Total Accounts. Thus a control account for a sales ledger could be known either as a Sales Ledger Control Account or as a Total Debtors

Account. Similarly, a control account for a purchases ledger could be known either as a Purchases Ledger Control Account or as a Total Creditors Account.

It must be emphasized that control accounts are not necessarily a part of the double entry system. They are merely arithmetical proofs performing the same function as a trial balance to a particular ledger.

It is usual to find them in the same form as an account, with the totals of the debit entries in the ledger on the left-hand side of the control account, and the totals of the various credit entries in the ledger on the right-hand side of the control account.

Exhibit 31.1 shows an example of a sales ledger control account for a ledger in which all the entries are arithmetically correct.

Exhibit 31.1

	£
Sales Ledger No. 3	
Debit balances on 1 January 19-6	1,894
Total credit sales for the month	10,290
Cheques received from customers in the months	7,284
Cash received from customers in the month	1,236
Returns Inwards from customers during the month	296
Debit balances on 31 January as extracted from the sales ledger	3,368

Sales Ledger Control

19-6		£	19-6		£
Jan	1 Balances b/f	1,894	Jan 31 Bank		7,284
,,	31 Sales	10,290	,, ,, Cash		1,236
			,, ,, Returns Inwards		296
			,, ,, Balances c/d		3,368
		12,184			12,184

On the other hand Exhibit 31.2 shows an example where an error is found to exist in a purchases ledger. The ledger will have to be checked in detail, the error found, and the control account then corrected.

Exhibit 31.2

	£
Purchases Ledger No. 2	
Credit balances on 1 January 19-6	3,890
Cheques paid to suppliers during the month	3,620
Returns outwards to suppliers in the month	95
Bought from suppliers in the month	4,936
Credit balances on 31 January as extracted from the purchases ledger	5,151

Purchases Ledger Control

19-6		£	19-6		£
Jan 31	Bank	3,620	Jan 1	Balances b/f	3,890
,, ,,	Returns Outwards	95	,, 31	Purchases	4,936
,, ,,	Balances c/d	5,151			
		8,866*			8,826*

*There is a £40 error in the purchases ledger.

Other Advantages of Control Accounts

Control accounts have merits other than that of locating errors. Normally the control accounts are under the charge of a responsible official, and fraud is made more difficult because transfers made (in an effort) to disguise frauds will have to pass the scrutiny of this person.

For management purposes the balances on the control account can always be taken to equal debtors and creditors without waiting for an extraction of individual balances. Management control is thereby aided, for the speed at which information is obtained is one of the prerequisities of efficient control.

Exhibit 31.3

Sales Book

Date	*Details*	*Total*	*Ledgers*		
			A–F	*G–O*	*P–Z*
19-6		£	£	£	£
Feb 1	J. Archer	58	58		
,, 3	G. Gaunt	103		103	
,, 4	T. Brown	116	116		
,, 8	C. Dunn	205	205		
,, 10	A. Smith	16			16
,, 12	P. Smith	114			114
,, 15	D. Owen	88		88	
,, 18	B. Blake	17	17		
,, 22	T. Green	1,396		1,396	
,, 27	C. Males	48		48	
		2,161	396	1,635	130

The Sources of Information for Control Accounts

To obtain the totals of entries made in the various ledgers, analytical journals and cash books are often used. Thus a firm with sales ledgers split on an alphabetical basis might have a sales book as per Exhibit

31.3. The totals of the A – F column will be the total sales figures for the sales ledger A – F control account, the total of the G – O column for the G – O control account and so on.

In electronic or machine accounting the control account is usually built in as an automatic by-product of the system.

Other Transfers

Transfers to bad debts accounts will have to be recorded in the sales ledger control account as they involve entries in the sales ledgers.

Similarly, a contra account whereby the same firm is both a supplier and a customer, and inter-indebtedness is set off, will also need entering in the control accounts. An example of this follows: G. Carter has supplied the firm with £880 goods, and the firm has sold him £600 goods. In the firm's books the £600 owing by him is set off against the amount owing to him, leaving a net amount owing to Carter of £280.

Sales Ledger
G. Carter

	£		
Sales	600		

Purchases Ledger
G. Carter

			£
		Purchases	880

The set-off now takes place.

Sales Ledger
G. Carter

	£		£
Sales	600	Set-off: Purchases Ledger	600

Purchases Ledger
G. Carter

	£		£
Set-off: Sales Ledger	600	Purchases	880
Balance c/d	280		
	880		880
		Balance b/d	280

The transfer of the £600 will therefore appear on the credit side of the sales ledger control account and on the debit side of the purchases ledger control account.

Exhibit 31.4 shows a worked example of a more complicated control account.

Exhibit 31.4

19-6		£
Aug 1	Sales ledger – debit balances	3,816
,, 1	Sales ledger – credit balances	22
,, 31	Transactions for the month:	
	Cash received	104
	Cheques received	6,239
	Sales	7,090
	Bad Debts written off	306
	Discounts allowed	298
	Returns inwards	164
	Cash refunded to a customer who had overpaid his account	37
	Dishonoured cheques	29
	At the end of the month:	
	Sales ledger – debit balances	3,879
	Sales ledger – credit balances	40

Sales Ledger Control Account

19-6		£	19-6		£
Aug 1	Balances b/d	3,816	Aug 1	Balances b/d	22
,, 31	Sales	7,090	,, 31	Cash	104
,, ,,	Cash refunded	37	,, ,,	Bank	6,239
,, ,,	Cash; dishonoured		,, ,,	Bad debts	306
	cheques	29	,, ,,	Discounts allowed	298
,, ,,	Balances c/d	40	,, ,,	Returns inwards	164
			,, ,,	Balances c/d	3,879
		11,012			11,012

Control Accounts as Part of Double Entry

The control accounts may be treated as being an integral part of the double entry system, the balances of the control accounts being taken for the purpose of extracting a trial balance. In this case the personal accounts are being used as subsidiary records.

Self-Balancing Ledgers and Adjustment Accounts

Because ledgers which have a control account system are proved to be correct as far as the double entry is concerned they are sometimes called self-balancing ledgers. The control accounts where such terminology is in use are then often called 'Adjustment Accounts'.

Exercises

MC80 The balance carried down on a Sales Ledger Control Account is
(A) The total of sales
(B) The total of purchases
(C) The total of the creditors
(D) The total of the debtors.

MC81 Given opening debtors of £11,500, Sales £48,000 and receipts from debtors £45,000, the closing debtors should total
(A) £8,500
(B) £14,500
(C) £83,500
(D) £18,500.

MC82 In a Sales Ledger Control Account the Bad Debts written off should be shown in the account
(A) As a debit
(B) As a credit
(C) Both as a debit and as a credit
(D) As a balance carried down.

31.1. You are required to prepare a sales ledger control account from the following for the month of May:

19-6	£
May 1 Sales Ledger Balances	4,936
Totals for May:	
Sales Journal	49,916
Returns Inwards Journal	1,139
Cheques and Cash received from customers	46,490
Discounts allowed	1,455
May 31 Sales Ledger Balances	5,768

31.2. You are required to prepare a purchases ledger control account from the following for the month of June. The balance of the account is to be taken as the amount of creditors as on 30 June.

19-6	£
June 1 Purchases Ledger Balances	3,676
Totals for June:	
Purchases Journal	42,257
Returns Outwards Journal	1,098
Cheques paid to suppliers	38,765
Discounts received from suppliers	887
June 30 Purchases Ledger Balances	?

31.3A. From the following information you are required to prepare a sales ledger control account for the month of April and bring down the balance of the account at 30 April.

19-1		£
April 1	Sales ledger balances	4,850
April 30	Sales day book	49,640
	Bad debts written off	150
	Cheques received from debtors	48,280
	Discounts allowed	2,500
	Dishonoured cheques	130
	Goods returned by customers	1,200
	Balance in sales ledger off-set against credit balances in purchase ledger	290

(Joint Matriculation Board 'O' level)

31.4A. From such of the following information as is required prepare the sales ledger control account for the month of April 19-7:

	£
Cheques received from debtors	11,270
Cash discounts allowed	940
Cash discounts received	290
Amounts owing by debtors 1 April 19-7	31,500
Goods sold on credit	15,100
Debtors cheques returned by their banks unpaid	1,100
Interest charged on debtors' overdue debts	150
Returns inwards	750
Returns outwards	810
Bad debts written off	190

(Associated Examining Board 'O' level)

31.5. The trial balance of Queen and Square Ltd. revealed a difference in the books. In order that the error(s) could be located it was decided to prepare purchases and sales ledger control accounts.

From the following prepare the control accounts and show where an error may have been made:

19-6		£
Jan 1	Purchases Ledger Balances	11,874
	Sales Ledger Balances	19,744
	Totals for the year 19-6:	
	Purchases Journal	154,562
	Sales Journal	199,662
	Returns Outwards Journal	2,648
	Returns Inwards Journal	4,556
	Cheques paid to suppliers	146,100
	Petty Cash paid to suppliers	78
	Cheques and Cash received from customers	185,960
	Discounts allowed	5,830
	Discounts received	2,134
	Bad Debts written off	396
	Customers' cheques dishonoured	30
	Balances on the Sales Ledger set off against balances in the Purchases Ledger	1,036
Dec 31	The list of balances from the purchases ledger shows a total of £14,530 and that from the sales ledger a total of £21,658.	

31.6. Zee Bee Limited sold a considerable number of customers. This required that its sales ledger be split alphabetically to control its balances.

The following accounting information related to sales ledgers A – C and D – G for the month of August 19-8.

Closing balances 31 July 19-8:

		£
Dr. balances	A – C	7,940
,,	D – G	11,250
Cr. balances	A – C	170
,,	D – G	940
Credit sales	A – C	8,470
,,	D – G	19,380
Cash & cheques	A – C	4,500
received	D – G	7,770
Bad debts written off	A – C	190
Discounts allowed	A – C	709
	D – G	1,140
Returns inward	A – C	530
,,	D – G	320
Dishonoured cheques	D – G	920
Interest charged	A – C	170
on overdue accounts	D – G	90

One customer, Denby Ltd., had gone into liquidation. Fortunately an associated company, Asmar & Co., agreed to take over its debt of £1,170 during August. The control accounts were adjusted.

The closing credit balances 31 August 19-8 were, A – C £230 and D – G £590.

Required:

1. Prepare sales ledger control accounts for sales ledgers A – C and D – G for the month of August 19-8.
2. What can be deduced from the control accounts A – C and D – G regarding the accuracy of the ledgers A – C and D – G? The net totals of the individual ledger accounts on 31 August 19-8 were:

A – C	£11,651
D – G	£19,990

(Associated Examining Board 'O' level).

31.7A. The draft balance sheet at 31 March 19-9 of Tom Brown Limited included the following items:

	£
Purchases ledger control account	24,782 net balance
Sales ledger control account	37,354 net balance

These control account figures however did not agree with the position at 31 March 19-9 as shown by the lists of balances extracted from the individual creditors' and debtors' accounts, but the trial balance was agreed and the draft balance sheet balances.

The list of purchases ledger balances at 31 March 19-9 included the following debit balances:

	£
G. Brook	167
K. River	89

The list of sales ledger balances at 31 March 19-9 included the following credit balances:

	£
L. Bridge	642
S. Tunnel	914

Subsequent investigations revealed the following accounting errors:

(i)   The sales day book for December 19-8 was overcast by £1,500.

(ii) A credit note for goods costing £160 returned to the supplier, T. Street, in September 19-8, was not recorded in the company's books, but the stock records have been adjusted correctly. According to the list of balances T. Street is owed £790 at 31 March 19-9.

(iii) A cheque for £900 received from a customer, P. Bridger Limited, in February 19-9, was credited, in error, to L. Bridge.
Note: The account of P. Bridger Limited in the sales ledger shows a debit balance at 31 March 19-9 of £960.

(iv) In February 19-9, a debt due from T. Wood to the company of £600 was written off as a bad debt. Although the debt has been written off in T. Wood's personal account, no adjustment for this has been made in the relevant control account.

(v)   A payment of £420 to J. King, supplier, in June 19-8, was debited in the purchases account. The invoices making up this amount were correctly entered in the purchase day book.

Required:

(a) A computation of the corrected balances at 31 March 19-9 of the purchases ledger control account and the sales ledger control account.

(b) An extract of the balance sheet at 31 March 19-9 of Tom Brown Limited showing the inclusion of the purchases ledger balances and sales ledger balances at 31 March 19-9.

(c) Explain the importance of control accounts in a modern accounting system.

(Association of Certified Accountants)

31.8. The Balances extracted from the records of Perrod and Company at 31 December 19-8 were as follows:

	£
Premises (cost)	7,000
Capital	8,440
Drawings	1,935
Provision for depreciation of office equipment at 1 January 19-8	480
Debtors' Control Account	1,891
Creditors' Control Account	2,130
Stock at 1 Janaury 19-8	1,200
Purchases	9,480
Sales	14,003
Returns inwards	310
Office equipment (cost) (balance at 1 January 19-8)	1,600
Wages	1,540
Commission	160
Discount allowed	210
Discount received	121
Bank (credit balance)	980
Cash in hand	56
Heating and Lighting	375
Postage and Stationery	224
Bad Debts	68

A preliminary trial balance was prepared, but, although no arithmetical errors were made, the trial balance did not balance. In seeking the reasons for the difference, the following facts emerged.

(i) *Debtors' Control Account*

    (a) No entry had been made in the control account in respect of the debts written off as bad;

    (b) A cheque paid by a debtor for £110 had been returned on 31 December 19-8 by the bank marked 'return to drawer'. An entry had been made in both the bank account and the debtors' account for this, but no entry had been made in the control account.

    (c) Sales on credit of £97 to A. Jones had been correctly entered in his account but nothing had been entered in the control account.

    (d) M. Smith had been allowed a cash discount of £43, but no corresponding entry had appeared in the control account.

(ii) *Creditors' Control Account*

This exceeded the balance of the individual creditors' accounts by £12. The difference was caused by:

    (a) Goods returned to R. Hardy costing £69 had been entered correctly in the control account, but no entry had been made in Mr. Hardy's account.

    (b) An invoice for £56 had been incorrectly entered in the control account as £65.

    (c) Two credit balances of £45 and £27 had been omitted from the list extracted from the creditors' ledger.

(iii) Some office equipment which had cost £240 had been debited to the purchase account.

(iv) The wages (£1,540) included £320 of personal drawings by the owner of the business.

(v) The provision for depreciation of office equipment had been credited in 19-7 with straight line depreciation of 10%, i.e. £160 but the depreciation should have been charged at 12½% per annum.

(vi) The account for stationery (£224) included £45 of personal notepaper for the owner.

(vii) The returns inwards account had been credited with £90 for some goods returned to a creditor.

Required:

(a) Prepare the Debtors' and Creditors' Control Accounts taking into account where appropriate the facts ascertained in (i) and (ii) above.

(b) Prepare journal entries to correct the errors and omissions enumerated in (iii) to (vii) above.

(c) Given that Perrod and Company's stock at 31 December 19-8 was valued at £1,400 and the depreciation on office equipment for the year was £230, prepare a Balance Sheet as at 31 December 19-8, showing clearly the net profit for the year.

(Note: A Trading Profit and Loss Account is NOT required).

(Association of Certified Accountants).

32

Introduction to Accounting Ratios

Mark-up and Margin

The purchase and sale of a good may be shown as

Cost Price + Profit = Selling Price.

The profit when expressed as a fraction, or percentage, of the cost price is known as the mark-up.

The profit when expressed as a fraction, or percentage, of the selling price is known as the margin.

$$\text{Cost Price} + \text{Profit} = \text{Selling Price.}$$
$$\pounds4 \quad + \quad \pounds1 \quad = \quad \pounds5.$$

$$\text{Mark-up} = \frac{\text{Profit}}{\text{Cost Price}} \text{ as a fraction, or if required as a percentage}$$

$$\text{multiply by} \frac{100}{1}$$

$$= \frac{\pounds1}{\pounds4} = \frac{1}{4}, \text{ or } \frac{1}{4} \times \frac{100}{1} = 25 \text{ per cent.}$$

$$\text{Margin} = \frac{\text{Profit}}{\text{Selling Price}} \text{ as a fraction, or if required as a}$$

$$\text{percentage multiply by} \frac{100}{1}$$

$$= \frac{\pounds1}{\pounds5} = \frac{1}{5}, \text{ or } \frac{1}{5} \times \frac{100}{1} = 20 \text{ per cent.}$$

The following illustrations[1] of the deduction of missing information assume that the rate of mark-ups and margins are constant, in other words the goods dealt in by the firm have uniform margins and mark-ups and they do not vary between one good and another. It also ignores wastages and pilferages of goods, also the fact that the market value of some goods may be below cost and therefore need to be taken

---

1. The horizontal style of accounts will be used in this chapter, simply because it is less confusing when showing illustrations of missing figures.

into stock at the lower figure. These items will need to be the subject of separate adjustments.

1. The following figures are for the year 19-5:

	£
Stock 1.1.19-5	400
Stock 31.12.19-5	600
Purchases	5,200

A uniform rate of mark-up of 20 per cent is applied.
Find the gross profit and the sales figure.

Trading Account

	£		£
Stock 1.1.19-5	400	Sales	?
Add Purchases	5,200		
	5,600		
Less Stock 31.12.19-5	600		
Cost of goods sold	5,000		
Gross profit	?		

Answer:
It is known that: Cost of goods sold + Profit = Sales
and also that: Cost of goods sold + Percentage Mark-up = Sales
The following
figures are also
known: £5,000 + 20 per cent = Sales
After doing the
arithmetic: £5,000 + £1,000 = £6,000
    The trading account can be completed by inserting the gross profit £1,000 and £6,000 for Sales.

2. Another firm has the following figures for 19-6:

	£
Stock 1.1.19-6	500
Stock 31.12.19-6	800
Sales	6,400

A uniform rate of margin of 25 per cent is in use.
Find the gross profit and the figure of purchases.

Trading Account

	£		£
Stock 1.1.19-6	500	Sales	6,400
Add Purchases	?		
Less Stock 31.12.19-6	800		
Cost of goods sold	?		
Gross Profit	?		
	6,400		6,400

Answer: Cost of goods sold + Gross Profit = Sales
Therefore   Sales   − Gross Profit = Cost of Goods Sold
           Sales   − 25 per cent
                 Margin   = Cost of Goods Sold
      £6,400   − £1,600   = £4,800

Now the following figures are known:

	£
Stock 1.1.19-6	500
Add Purchases (1)	?
(2)	?
Less Stock 31.12.19-6	800
Cost of goods sold	4,800

The two missing figures are found by normal arithmetical deduction:

No. (2) less £800 = £4,800
Therefore No. (2) = £5,600
So that: £500 opening stock   +   No. (1) = £5,600
Therefore No. (1) = £5,100

The completed trading account can now be shown:

Trading Account

	£		£
Stock 1.1.19-6	500	Sales	6,400
Add Purchases	5,100		
	5,600		
Less Stock 31.12.19-6	800		
Cost of goods sold	4,800		
Gross Profit	1,600		
	6,400		6,400

This technique is found very useful by retail stores when estimating the amount to be bought if a certain sales target is to be achieved. Alternatively, stock levels or sales figures can be estimated given information as to purchases and opening stock figures.

The Relationship Between Mark-Up and Margin

As both of these figures refer to the same profit, but expressed as a fraction or a percentage of different figures, there is bound to be a relationship. If one is known as a fraction, the other can soon be found.

If the mark-up is known, to find margin take the same numerator to be numerator of the margin, then for the denominator of the margin take the total of the mark-up's denominator plus the numerator. An example can now be shown:

Mark-up	Margin
$\dfrac{1}{4}$	$\dfrac{1}{4+1} = \dfrac{1}{5}$
$\dfrac{2}{11}$	$\dfrac{2}{11+2} = \dfrac{2}{13}$

If the margin is known, to find the mark-up take the same numerator to be the numerator of the mark-up, then for the denominator of the mark-up take the figure of the margin's denominator less the numerator:

Margin	Mark-up
$\dfrac{1}{6}$	$\dfrac{1}{6-1} = \dfrac{1}{5}$
$\dfrac{3}{13}$	$\dfrac{3}{13-3} = \dfrac{3}{10}$

Manager's Commission

Managers of businesses are very often remunerated by a basic salary plus a percentage of profits. It is quite common to find the percentage expressed not as a percentage of profits before such commission has been deducted, but as percentage of the amount remaining after deduction of the commission.

For example, assume that profits before the manager's commission was deducted amounted to £8,400, and that the manager was entitled to 5 per cent of the profits remaining after such commission was deducted. If 5 per cent of £8,400 was taken, this amounts to £420, and the profits remaining would amount to £7,980. However, 5 per

cent of £7,980 amounts to £399 so that the answer of £420 is wrong.
The formula to be used to arrive at the correct answer is:

$$\frac{\text{Percentage commission}}{100 + \text{Percentage commission}} \times \text{Profits before commission.}$$

In the above problem this would be used as follows:

$$\frac{5}{100 + 5} \times £8,400 = £400 \text{ manager's commission.}$$

The profits remaining are £8,000 and as £400 represents 5 per cent of it the answer is verified.

Commonly Used Accounting Ratios

There are some ratios that are in common use for the purpose of comparing one period's results against those of a previous period. Two of those most in use are the ratio of gross profit to sales, and the rate of turnover or stockturn.

(a) Gross Profit as Percentage of Sales

The basic formula is:

$$\frac{\text{Gross profit}}{\text{Sales}} \times \frac{100}{1} = \text{Gross profit as percentage of sales.}$$

Put another way, this represents the amount of gross profit for every £100 of sales. If the answer turned out to be 15 per cent, this would mean that for every £100 of sales £15 gross profit was made before any expenses were paid.

This ratio is used as a test of the profitability of the sales. Just because the sales are increased does not of itself mean that the gross profit will increase. The trading accounts in Exhibit 32.1 illustrates this.

Exhibit 32.1

Trading Accounts for the year ended 31 December

	19-6 £	19-7 £		19-6 £	19-7 £
Stock	500	900	Sales	7,000	8,000
Purchases	6,000	7,200			
	6,500	8,100			
Less Stock	900	1,100			
Cost of goods sold	5,600	7,000			
Gross Profit	1,400	1,000			
	7,000	8,000		7,000	8,000

In the year 19-6 the gross profit as a percentage of sales was:

$$\frac{1,400}{7,000} \times \frac{100}{1} = 20 \text{ per cent.}$$

In the year 19-7 it became:

$$\frac{1,000}{8,000} \times \frac{100}{1} = 12\frac{1}{2} \text{ per cent.}$$

Thus sales had increased, but as the gross profit percentage had fallen by a relatively greater amount the actual gross profit has fallen.

There can be many reasons for such a fall in the gross profit percentage. Perhaps the goods being sold have cost more but the selling price of the goods has not risen to the same extent. Maybe, in order to boost sales, reductions have been made in the selling price of goods. There could be a difference in the composition of types of goods sold, called the sales-mix, between this year and last, with different product lines carrying different rates of gross profit per £100 of sales. Alternatively there may have been a greater wastage or pilferage of goods. These are only some of the possible reasons for the decrease. The idea of calculating the ratio is to highlight the fact that the profitability per £100 of sales has changed, and so promote an inquiry as to why and how such a change is taking place.

As the figure of sales less returns inwards is also known as turnover, the ratio is also known as the gross profit percentage on turnover.

(b) Stockturn or Rate of Turnover

This is another commonly used ratio, and is expressed in the formula:

$$\frac{\text{Cost of goods sold}}{\text{Average stock}} = \frac{\text{Number of times stock is turned over within the period}}{}$$

Ideally, the average stock held should be calculated by taking a large number of readings of stock over the accounting year, then dividing the totals of the figures obtained by the number of readings. For instance, monthly stock figures added up then divided by twelve. It is a well-known statistical law that the greater the sample of figures taken the smaller will be the error contained in the answer.

However, it is quite common, especially in examinations or in cases where no other information is available, to calculate the average stock as the opening stock plus the closing stock and the answer divided by two. The statistical limitations of taking only two figures when calculating an average must be clearly borne in mind.

Using the figures in Exhibit 32.1:

$$19\text{-}6 \quad \frac{5,600}{(500+900) \div 2} = \frac{5,600}{700} = 8 \text{ times per annum.}$$

$$19\text{-}7 \quad \frac{7,000}{(900+1,100) \div 2} = \frac{7,000}{1,000} = 7 \text{ times per annum.}$$

In terms of periods of time, in the year 19-6 a rate of 8 times per annum means that goods on average are held 12 months ÷ 8 = 1.5 months before they are sold.

For 19-7 goods are held on average for 12 months ÷ 7 = 1.7 months approximately before they are sold.

When the rate of stockturn is falling it can be due to such causes as a slowing down of sales activity, or to keeping a higher figure of stock than is really necessary. The ratio does not prove anything by itself, it merely prompts inquiries as to why it should be changing.

Exercises

MC83 If cost price is £90 and selling price is £120, then
(i)   Mark-up is 25 per cent
(ii) Margin is 33⅓ per cent
(iii) Margin is 25 per cent
(iv) Mark-up is 33⅓ per cent
(A) i and ii
(B) i and iii
(C) iii and iv
(D) ii and iv.

MC84 Given cost of goods sold £16,800 and margin of 20 per cent, then sales figure is
(A) £20,160
(B) £13,600
(C) £21,000
(D) None of these.

MC85 If opening stock is £3,000, closing stock £5,000, Sales £40,000 and margin 20 per cent, then stockturn is
(A) 8 times
(B) 7½ times
(C) 5 times
(D) 6 times.

32.1. R. Stubbs is a trader who sells all of his goods at 25 per cent above cost. His books give the following information at 31 December 19-5:

	£
Stock 1 January 19-5	9,872
Stock 31 January 19-5	12,620
Sales for year	60,000

You are required to:
(a) Ascertain cost of goods sold.
(b) Show the value of purchases during the year.
(c) Calculate the profit made by Stubbs.
  Show your answer in the form of a trading account.

32.2A. C. White gives you the following information as at 30 June 19-7:

	£
Stock 1 July 19-6	6,000
Purchases	54,000

White's mark-up is 50 per cent on 'cost of goods sold'. His average stock during the year was £12,000.

Draw up a trading and profit and loss account for the year ended 30 June 19-7.

(a) Calculate the closing stock as at 30 June 19-7.

(b) State the total amount of profit and loss expenditure White must not exceed if he is to maintain a *net* profit on sales of 10 per cent.

32.3. J. Green's business has a rate of turnover of 7 times. Average stock is £12,600. Trade discount allowed is 33⅓ per cent off all selling prices. Expenses are 66⅔ per cent of gross profit.

You are to calculate:

(a) Cost of goods sold. (b) Gross Profit. (c) Turnover. (d) Total Expenses. (e) Net Profit.

32.4A. The following figures relate to the retail business of J. Clarke for the month of May 19-8. Goods which are on sale fall into two categories, A and B.

	Category A	Category B
Sales to the public at manufacturer's recommended list price	£6,000	£14,000
Trade discount allowed to retailers	20%	25%
Total expenses as a percentage of sales	10%	10%
Annual rate of stock turnover	12	20

Calculate for each category:

(a) Cost of Goods sold. (b) Gross Profit. (c) Total expenses. (d) Net Profit. (e) Average stock at cost, assuming that sales are distributed evenly over the year, and that there are twelve equal months in the year.

32.5. The following information was available on Unitsales Ltd.

	19-6	19-7	19-8
	£	£	£
Opening Stock			
Purchases	85,000		
Closing Stock	5,000		
Sales		140,000	
Gross Profit	25,000		
Variable expenses			18,900
Fixed expenses	5,500	5,000	
Net profit			9,100

For 19-6:
1. Gross profit was 20% of sales.
2. Variable expenses were 10% of sales.
3. All purchases cost £1 per unit and stocks were valued at £1 per unit.

For 19-7:
1. The purchase price of units increased by 10%, but the volume bought increased by 20% compared with 19-6.
2. The closing stock of 8,000 units were bought in 19-7.
3. Variable expenses amount to 13% of sales.

For 19-8:
1. The net profit/sales ratio was 1% greater than the 19-7 figure.
2. Fixed expenses increased by £1,000 on the 19-7 figure.
3. The number of units purchased was 90,000 at the 19-7 purchase price.

Required:
Draw a table the same as the one above. Use the information given to make the necessary calculations and complete the table.
(Associated Examining Board 'O' level)

32.6A. Trading Account for the year ended 31 December 19-1.

	£		£
Stock 1 January 19-1	3,000	Sales	60,000
Purchases	47,000		
	50,000		
Stock 31 December 19-1	4,500		
Cost of sales	45,500		
Gross profit	14,500		
	60,000		60,000

R. Sheldon presents you with the trading account set out above. He always calculates his selling price by adding 33⅓% of cost on to the cost price.
(a) If he has adhered strictly to the statement above, what should be the percentage of gross profit to sales?
(b) Calculate his actual percentage of gross profit to sales.
(c) Give two reasons for the difference between the figures you have calculated above.
(d) His suppliers are proposing to increase their prices by 5%, but R. Sheldon considers that he would be unwise to increase his selling price. To obtain some impression of the effect on gross profit if his costs should be increased by 5% he asks you to reconstruct his trading account to show the gross profit if the increase had applied from 1 January 19-1.
(e) Using the figures given in the trading account at the beginning of the question, calculate R. Sheldon's rate of stock turnover.
(f) R. Sheldon's expenses amount to 10% of his sales. Calculate his net profit for the year ended 31 December 19-1.
(g) If all expenses remained unchanged, but suppliers of stock increased their prices by 5% as in (d) above, calculate the percentage reduction in the amount of net profit which R. Sheldon's accounts would have shown.
(University of London 'O' level).

33

Single Entry and Incomplete Records

For every small shopkeeper, market stall or other small business to keep its books using a full double-entry system would be ridiculous. First of all, a large number of the owners of such firms would not know how to write up double-entry records, even if they wanted to.

It is far more likely that they would enter down details of a transaction once only, that is why we would call it single-entry. Also many of them would have failed to record every transaction, and these therefore would be incomplete − the reason why we would call these 'incomplete records'.

It is perhaps only fair to remember that accounting is after all supposed to be an aid to management, it is not something to be done as an end in itself. Therefore, many small firms, especially retail stores, can have all the information they want by merely keeping a cash book and having some form of record, not necessarily in double entry form, of their debtors and creditors.

Probably the way to start is to recall that, barring an introduction of extra cash or resources into the firm, the only way that capital can be increased is by making profits. Therefore, the most elementary way of calculating profits is by comparing capital at the end of last period with that at the end of this period. If it is known that the capital at the end of 19-4 was £2,000 and that at the end of 19-5 it has grown to £3,000, and that there have been no drawings during the period, nor has there been any fresh introduction of capital, the net profit must therefore be £3,000 − £2,000 = £1,000. If on the other hand the drawings had been £700, the profits must have been £1,700 calculated thus:

Last year's Capital + Profits − Drawings = this year's Capital
£2,000 +   ?   − £700   =   £3,000

Filling in the missing figure by normal arithmetical deduction:

£2,00 + £1,700 − £700 = £3,000.

Exhibit 33.1 shows the calculation of profit where insufficient information is available to draft a trading and profit and loss account, only information of assets and liabilities being known.

Exhibit 33.1

H. Taylor provides information as to his assets and liabilities at certain dates.

At 31 December 19-5. *Assets:* Motor van £1,000; Fixtures £700; Stock £850; Debtors £950; Bank £1,100; Cash £100. *Liabilities:* Creditors £200; Loan from J. Ogden £600.

At 31 December 19-6. *Assets:* Motor van (after depreciation) £800; Fixtures (after depreciation) £630; Stock £990; Debtors £1,240; Bank £1,700; Cash £200. *Liabilities:* Creditors £300; Loan from J. Ogden £400; Drawings were £900.

First of all a Statement of Affairs is drawn up as at 31 December 19-5. This is the name given to what would have been called a balance sheet if it had been drawn up from a set of records. The capital is the difference between the assets and liabilities.

Statement of Affairs as at 31 December 19-5

	£	£
Fixed Assets		
Motor Van		1,000
Fixtures		700
		1,700
Current Assets		
Stock	850	
Debtors	950	
Bank	1,100	
Cash	100	
	3,000	
Less Current Liabilities		
Creditors	200	
Working Capital		2,800
		4,500
Financed by		
Capital (difference)		3,900
Long Term Liability		
Loan from J. Ogden		600
		4,500

A statement of affairs is now drafted up at the end of 19-6. The formula of Opening Capital + Profit − Drawings = Closing Capital is then used to deduce the figure of profit.

Statement of Affairs as at 31 December 19-6

	£	£
Fixed Assets		
Motor Van		800
Fixtures		630
		1,430
Current Assets		
Stock	990	
Debtors	1,240	
Bank	1,700	
Cash	200	
	4,130	
Less Current Liabilities		
Creditors	300	3,830
		5,260
Financed by:		
Capital		
Balance at 1.1.19-6	3,900	
Add Net Profit (C)	?	
(B)	?	
Less Drawings	900 (A)	?
Long Term Loan		
Loan from J. Ogden		400

Deduction of Net Profit.
Opening Capital + Net Profit − Drawings = Closing Capital. Finding the missing figures (A) (B) and (C) by deduction,
(A) is the figure is needed to make the balance sheet totals equal, i.e. £4,860.
(B) is therefore £4,860 + £900 = £5,760.
(C) is therefore £5,760 − £3,900 = £1,860.
To check:

		£		
Capital		3,900		
Add Net Profit	(C)	1,860		
	(B)	5,760		
Less Drawings		900	(A)	4,860

Obviously, this method of calculating profit is very unsatisfactory as it is much more informative when a trading and profit and loss account can be drawn up. Therefore, whenever possible the comparisons of capital method of ascertaining profit should be avoided and a full set of final accounts drawn up from the available records. When doing this it must be remembered that the principles of calculating profit are still those as described in the compilation of a double entry trading and profit and loss account. Assume that there are two businesses identical in every way as to sales, purchases, expenses, assets and liabilities, the only difference being that one proprietor keeps a full double entry set of books while the other keeps his on a single entry basis. Yet when each of them draws up his final accounts they should be identical in every way. Exhibit 33.2 shows the method for drawing up final accounts from single entry records.

Exhibit 33.2

The accountant discerns the following details of transactions for J. Frank's retail store for the year ended 31 December 19-5:

1. The sales are mostly on a credit basis. No records of sales have been made, but £10,000 has been received, £9,500 by cheque and £500 by cash, from persons to whom goods have been sold.

2. Amount paid by cheque to suppliers during the year = £7,200.

3. Expenses paid during the year: By cheque, Rent £200, General Expenses £180; by cash, Rent £50.

4. J. Frank took £10 cash per week (for 52 weeks) as drawings.

5. Other information is available:

	At 31.12.19-4	At 31.12.19-5
	£	£
Debtors	1,100	1,320
Creditors for goods	400	650
Rent Owing	–	50
Bank Balance	1,130	3,050
Cash Balance	80	10
Stock	1,590	1,700

6. The only fixed asset consists of fixtures which were valued at 31 December 19-4 at £800. These are to be depreciated at 10 per cent per annum.

The first step is to draw up a statement of affairs as at 31 December 19-4.

Statement of Affairs as at 31 December 19-4

	£	£
Fixed Assets		
Fixtures		800
Current Assets		
Stock	1,590	
Debtors	1,100	
Bank	1,130	
Cash	80	
	3,900	
Less Current Liabilities		
Creditors	400	
Working Capital		3,500
		4,300
Financed by:		
Capital (difference)		4,300
		4,300

All of these opening figures are then taken into account when drawing up the final accounts for 19-5.

Next a cash and bank summary is drawn up, followed by the final accounts.

	Cash	Bank		Cash	Bank
	£	£		£	£
Balances 31.12.19-4	80	1,130	Suppliers		7,200
Receipts from debtors	500	9,500	Rent	50	200
			General Expenses		180
			Drawings	520	
			Balances 31.12.19-5	10	3,050
	580	10,630		580	10,630

J. Franks
Trading and Profit and Loss Account for the year ended 31 December 19-5

	£	£
Sales (note 2)		10,220
Less Cost of Goods Sold:		
Stock at 1.1.19-5	1,590	
Add Purchases (note 1)	7,450	
	9,040	
Less Stock at 31.12.19-5	1,700	7,340
Gross Profit		2,880
Less Expenses:		
Rent (note 3)	300	
General Expenses	180	
Depreciation: Fixtures	80	560
Net Profit		2,320

Note 1. In double entry, purchases means the goods that have been bought in the period irrespective of whether they have been paid for or not during the period. The figure of payments to suppliers must therefore be adjusted to find the figures of purchases.

	£
Paid during the year	7,200
Less payments made, but which were for goods which were purchases in a previous year (creditors 31.12.19-4)	400
	6,800
Add purchases made in this year, but for which payment has not yet been made (creditors 31.12.19-5)	650
Goods bought in this year, i.e. purchases	7,450

The same answer could have been obtained if the information had been shown in the form of a total creditors account, the figure of purchases being the amount required to make the account totals agree.

Total Creditors

	£		£
Cash paid to suppliers	7,200	Balances b/f	400
Balances c/d	650	Purchases (missing figures)	7,450
	7,850		7,850

Note 2. The sales figure will only equal receipts where all the sales are for cash. Therefore, the receipts figures need adjusting to find sales. This can be done by constructing a total debtors account, the sales figures being the one needed to make the totals agree.

Total Debtors

	£		£
Balances b/f	1,100	Receipts: Cash	500
		Cheque	9,500
Sales (missing figures)	10,220	Balances c/d	1,320
	11,320		11,320

Note 3: Expenses are those consumed during the year irrespective of when payment is made. A rent account can be drawn up, the missing figure being that of rent for the year.

Rent Account

	£		£
Cheques	200	Rent (missing figure)	300
Cash	50		
Accrued c/d	50		
	300		300

The balance sheet can now be drawn up as in Exhibit 33.3.

Exhibit 33.3

Balance Sheet as at 31 December 19-5

	£	£	£
Fixed Assets			
Fixtures at 1.1.19-5		800	
Less Depreciation		80	720
Current Assets			
Stock		1,700	
Debtors		1,320	
Bank		3,050	
Cash		10	
		6,080	
Less Current Liabilities			
Creditors	650		
Rent Owing	50	700	
Working Capital			5,380
			6,100
Financed by:			
Capital			
Balance 1.1.19-5 (per Opening Statement of Affairs)			4,300
Add Net Profit			2,320
			6,620
Less Drawings			520
			6,100

Incomplete Records and Missing Figures

In practice, part of the information relating to cash receipts or payments is often missing. If the missing information is in respect of one type of payment, then it is normal to assume that the missing figure is the amount required to make both totals agree in the cash column of the cash and bank summary. This does not happen with bank items owing to the fact that another copy of the bank statement can always be obtained from the bank. Exhibit 33.4 shows an example when the drawings figure is unknown, Exhibit 33.5 is an example where the receipts from debtors had not been recorded.

Exhibit 33.4

The following information of cash and bank receipts and payments is available:

	Cash	Bank
	£	£
Cash paid into the bank during the year	5,500	
Receipts from debtors	7,250	800
Paid to suppliers	320	4,930
Drawings during the year	?	—
Expenses paid	150	900
Balances at 1.1.19-5	35	1,200
Balances at 31.12.19-5	50	1,670

	Cash	Bank		Cash	Bank
	£	£		£	£
Balances 1.1.19-5	35	1,200	Banking C	5,500	
Received from debtors	7,250	800	Suppliers	320	4,930
Bankings C		5,500	Expenses	150	900
			Drawings	?	
			Balances 31.12.19-5	50	1,670
	7,285	7,500		7,285	7,500

The amount needed to make the two sides of the cash columns agree is £1,265. Therefore, this is taken as the figure of drawings.

Exhibit 33.5

Information of cash and bank transactions is available as follows:

	Cash	Bank
	£	£
Receipts from debtors	?	6,080
Cash withdrawn from the bank for business use (this is the amount which is used besides cash receipts from debtors to pay drawings and expenses)		920
Paid to suppliers		5,800
Expenses paid	640	230
Drawings	1,180	315
Balances 1.1.19-5	40	1,560
Balance 31.12.19-5	70	375

	Cash	Bank		Cash	Bank
	£	£		£	£
Balances 1.1.19-5	40	1,560	Suppliers		5,800
Received from debtors	?	6,080	Expenses	640	230
Withdrawn from			Withdrawn from		
Bank C	920		Bank C		920
			Drawings	1,180	315
			Balances 31.12.19-5	70	375
	1,890	7,640		1,890	7,640

Receipts from debtors is, therefore, the amount needed to make each side of the cash column agree, £930.

It must be emphasized that balancing figures are acceptable only when all the other figures have been verified. Should for instance a cash expense be omitted when cash received from debtors is being calculated, then this would result in an understatement not only of expenses but also ultimately of sales.

Where there are Two Missing Pieces of Information

If both cash drawings and cash receipts from debtors were not known it would not be possible to deduce both of these figures. The only source lying open would be to estimate whichever figure was more capable of being accurately assessed, use this as a known figure, then deduce the other figure. However, this is a most unsatisfactory position as both of the figures are no more than pure estimates, the accuracy of each one relying entirely upon the accuracy of the other.

Goods Stolen or Lost by Fire etc.

When goods are stolen, destroyed by fire, or lost in some other way, then the value of them will have to be calculated. This could be needed to substantiate an insurance claim or to settle problems concerning taxation etc.

If the stock had been properly valued immediately before the fire, burglary etc, then the stock loss would obviously be known. Also if a full and detailed system of stock records were kept, then the value would also be known. However, as the occurrence of fires or burglaries cannot be foreseen, and not many businesses keep full and proper stock records, the stock loss will have to be calculated in some other way.

The methods described in this chapter and chapter 32 are used instead. The only difference is that instead of computing closing stock at a year end, for example, the closing stock will be that as at immediately before the fire consumed it or it was stolen.

Two exhibits 33.6 and 33.7 will now be looked at. The first exhibit will be a very simple case, where figures of purchases and sales are known and all goods are sold at a uniform profit ration. The second exhibit is rather more complicated. Horizontal style accounts will be used for the sake of simplicity of illustration.

Exhibit 33.6

J. Collins lost the whole of his stock by fire on 17 March 19-9. The last time that a stocktaking had been done was on 31 December 19-8, the last balance sheet date, when it was £1,950 at cost. Purchases from then to 17 March 19-9 amounted to £6,870 and Sales for the period were £9,600. All sales were made at a uniform profit margin of 20 per cent.

First, the Trading Accounting can be drawn up with the known figures included. Then the missing figures can be deduced afterwards.

J. Collins
Trading Account for the period 1 January 19-9 to 17 March 19-9

		£		£
Opening Stock		1,950	Sales	9,600
Add Purchases		6,870		
		8,820		
Less Closing Stock	(C)	?		
Cost of Goods Sold	(B)	?		
Gross profit	(A)	?		
		9,600		9,600

Now the missing figures can be deduced.

It is known that the gross profit margin is 20 per cent, therefore Gross Profit (A) is 20% of £9,600 = £1,920.

Now (B) ? + (A) £1,920 = £9,600, so that (B) is difference, i.e. £7,680.

Now that (B) is known (C) can be deduced, £8,820 − (C) ? = £7,680, so (C) is difference, i.e. £1,140.

The figure for goods destroyed by fire, at cost, is therefore £1,140.

Exhibit 33.7

T. Scott had the whole of his stock stolen from his warehouse on the night of 20 August 19-6. Also destroyed was his sales and purchases journals, but the sales and purchases ledgers were salvaged. The following facts are known:

(i) Stock was known at the last balance sheet date, 31 March 19£6, to be £6,480 at cost.

(ii) Receipts from debtors during the period 1 April to 20 August 19-6 amounted to £31,745. Debtors were: at 31 March 19-6 £14,278, at 20 August 19-6 £12,333.

(iii) Payments to creditors during the period 1 April to 20 August 19-6 amounted to £17,720. Creditors were: at 31 March 19-6 £7,633, at 20 August 19-6 £6,289.

(iv) The margin on sales has been constant at 25 per cent. Before we can start to construct a Trading Account for the period, we need to find out the figures of Sales and of Purchases. These can be found by drawing up Total Debtors' and Total Creditors' Accounts sales and purchases figures being the differences on the accounts.

Total Creditors

		£			£
Cash and Bank		17,270	Balances	b/fwd	7,633
Balances	c/d	6,289	Purchases (difference)		15,926
		23,559			23,559

Total Debtors

		£			£
Balances	b/fwd	14,278	Cash and Bank		31,745
Sales (difference)		29,800	Balances	c/d	12,333
		44,078			44,078

The Trading Account can now show the figures already known.

Trading Account for the period 1 April to 20 August 19-6

		£		£
Opening Stock		12,480	Sales	29,800
Add Purchases		15,926		
		28,406		
Less Closing Stock	(C)	?		
Cost of Goods Sold	(B)	?		
Gross Profit	(A)	?		
		29,800		29,800

Gross Profit can be found, as the margin on sales is known to be 25%, therefore (A) = 25% of £29,800 = £7,450.

Cost of Goods Sold (B) ? + Gross Profit £7,450 = £29,800 therefore (B) is £22,350.

£28,406 − (C) ? = (B) £22,350, therefore C is £6,056.

The figure for cost of goods stolen is therefore £6,056.

Exercises

MC86 Given last year's Capital as £7,450, this year's Capital as £9,800 and Drawings as £4,500, then Profit must have been
(A) £2,150
(B) £5,450
(C) £6,850
(D) £7,250.

MC87 If creditors at 1 January 19-3 were £2,500 creditors at 31 December 19-3 £4,200 and payments to creditors £32,000, then purchases for 19-3 are
(A) £30,300
(B) £33,700
(C) £31,600
(D) None of these.

MC88 Given opening capital of £16,500, closing capital as £11,350 and drawings were £3,300, then
(A) Loss for the year was £1,850
(B) Profit for the year was £1,850
(C) Loss for the year was £8,450
(D) Profit for the year was £8,450.

33.1. B. Arkwright started in business on 1 January 19-5 with £10,000 in a bank account. Unfortunately he did not keep proper books of account.

He is forced to submit a calculation of profit for the year ended 31 December 19-5 to the Inspector of Taxes. He ascertains that at 31 December 19-5 he had stock valued at cost £3,950, a motor van which had cost £2,800 during the year and which had depreciated by £550, debtors of £4,970, expenses prepaid of £170, bank balance £2,564, cash balance £55, trade creditors £1,030, and expenses owing £470.

His drawings were: cash £100 per week for 50 weeks, cheque payments £673.

Draw up statements to show the profit or loss for the year.

33.2A. J. Kirkwood is a dealer who has not kept proper books of account. At 31 August 19-6 his state of affairs was as follows:

	£
Cash	115
Bank Balance	2,209
Fixtures	4,000
Stock	16,740
Debtors	11,890
Creditors	9,052
Motor Van (at valuation)	3,000

During the year to 31 August 19-7 his drawings amounted to £7,560. Winnings from a football pool £2,800 were put into the business. Extra fixtures were bought for £2,000.

At 31 August 19-7 his assets and liabilities were: Cash £84, Bank Overdraft £165, Stock £21,491, Creditors for goods £6,002, Creditors for expenses £236, Fixtures to be depreciated £600, Motor Van to be valued at £2,500, Debtors £15,821, Pre-paid Expenses £72.

Draw up a statement showing the profit or loss made by Kirkwood for the year ended 31 August 19-7.

33.3. Following is a summary of Kelly's bank account for the year ended 31 December 19-7:

	£		£
Balance 1.1.19-7	405	Payments to creditors	
Receipts from debtors	37,936	for goods	29,487
Balance 31.12.19-7	602	Rent	1,650
		Rates	890
		Sundry Expenses	375
		Drawings	6,541
	38,943		38,943

All of the business takings have been paid into the bank with the exception of £9,630. Out of this, Kelly has paid wages of £5,472, drawings of £1,164 and purchase of goods £2,994.

The following additional information is available:

	31.12.19-6	31.12.19-7
Stock	13,862	15,144
Creditors for goods	5,624	7,389
Debtors for goods	9,031	8,624
Rates Prepaid	210	225
Rent Owing	150	—
Fixtures at valuation	2,500	2,250

You are to draw up a set of final accounts for the year ended 31 December 19-7. Show all of your workings.

33.4A. J. Evans has kept records of his business transactions in a single entry form, but he did not realise that he had to record cash drawings. His bank account for the year 19-4 is as follows:

	£		£
Balance 1.1.19-4	1,890	Cash withdrawn from bank	5,400
Receipts from debtors	44,656	Trade Creditors	31,695
Loan from T. Hughes	2,000	Rent	2,750
		Rates	1,316
		Drawings	3,095
		Sundry Expenses	1,642
		Balance 31.12.19-4	2,648
	48,546		48,546

Records of cash paid were, Sundry Expenses £122, Trade Creditors £642. Cash Sales amounted to £698.

The following information is also available:

	31.12.19-3	31.12.19-4
	£	£
Cash in Hand	48	93
Trade Creditors	4,896	5,091
Debtors	6,013	7,132
Rent Owing	–	250
Rates in Advance	282	312
Motor Van (at valuation)	2,800	2,400
Stock	11,163	13,021

You are to draw up a Trading and Profit and Loss Account for the year ended 31 December 19-4, and a Balance Sheet as at that date. Show all of your workings.

33.5. T. Malden buys goods on credit and sell exclusively for immediate cash. He carries on his business from a market stall rented from the local authority.

He does not keep any formal accounts, but the following information has been collected from records which he has made available.

	1 January 19-1	31 December 19-1
	£	£
Stock	300	450
Creditors	180	70
Cash at bank	450	370

	£
Payments to suppliers for stock during year	3,000
Payments to local authority for stall rent	550
December's rent due but unpaid	50
Private drawings during year	2,000
Cost of stock stolen and not covered by insurance	300
Payments for wrapping paper, etc.	40
Wrapping paper account due but unpaid	5
Cash takings during year	5,510

It is known that all cash takings have been paid into the bank, and that all payments and withdrawals have been made by cheque. There have been no transactions other than those indicated above.

Prepare T. Malden's Trading and Profit and Loss Account for the year ended 31 December 19-1 and a Balance Sheet as at that date.

(University of London 'O' level)

33.6A. D. Quox, a retailer, did not keep proper books of account, but he was able to supply his accountant with the following information on 1 April 19-8:

	£
Trade debtors	2,400
Bank	7,709
Cash	401
Fixtures and fittings	2,500
Freehold premises	15,500
Trade creditors	2,362
Stock	5,000

Further information was provided on transactions during the year ended 31 March 19-9:

	Cash £	Bank £		Cash £	Bank £
Receipts from goods sold	28,450		Payments to suppliers of goods		17,500
Interest from private investment		108	Cash paid into bank	24,400	
Cash receipts paid into bank		24,400	Wages and salaries payments	2,900	
			Rates		590
			Advertising		140
			Insurance		150
			Drawings	150	4,500
			Repairs and decorations	10	375
			Carriage outwards	170	—

Notes

(*a*) Fixtures and fittings were to be depreciated by 10% of the book value at the beginning of the year.

(*b*) Insurance had been paid for the period from 1 April 19-8 till 30 September 19-9.

(*c*) £150 was still owing for wages.

(*d*) Discounts allowed for the year were £1,564.

(*e*) At 31 March 19-9 the following balances were provided:

Stock	£4,700
Trade debtors	£2,386
Trade creditors	£4,562

Required:

1. A calculation of the capital of the business at 1 April 19-8,
2. A calculation of the cash and bank balances at 31 March 19-9,
3. A trading and profit and loss account for the year ended 31 March 19-9 and a balance sheet as at that date.

(Associated Examining Board 'O' level)

33.7. The following is a summary of the bank statements of Lockhart, a trader, for the year ending 31 May 19-1.

Bank Statements

	Paid £	Received £	Balance £
1 June 19-0			500
Trade creditors	18,700		
Rent and rates	700		
Purchase of fixtures	600		
General expenses	1,600		
Drawings	4,500		
Cash sales banked		20,000	
Credit sales banked		4,000	
Proceeds on sale of fixtures (net book value £400)		300	
31 May 19-1 Balance overdrawn			(1,300)

The following additional information is available.

(i) All takings from cash sales were banked with the exception of £4,000, out of which Lockhart paid wages of £3,000 and retained the balance for his own use.

(ii) Discounts received and allowed from trade creditors and debtors were £1,000 and £700, respectively.

(iii) An examination of the cheque book and bank paying-in book revealed that a cheque for £400 was written on 31 May 19-1 for the payment of suppliers and that a cheque from a customer for £500 was banked on 31 May 19-1. Lockhart had ignored this information and neither item appeared on the bank statement until 5 June 19-1.

(iv) Lockhart disclosed the following information.

	31 May 19-0 £	31 May 19-1 £
Stock	1,500	1,700
Trade creditors	1,800	1,900
Trade debtors	2,300	2,100
Rates paid in advance	200	250
General expenses creditors	100	300
Fixtures (at valuation)	1,500	1,600

Prepare the trading and profit and loss account for Lockhart for the year ending 31 May 19-1 and a balance sheet as at that date.

(Joint Matriculation Board 'A' level)

33.8A. A. Highton is in business as a general retailer. He does not keep a full set of accounting records; however it has been possible to extract the following details from the few records that are available:

Balances as at:	1 April 19-1	31 March 19-2
	£	£
Freehold Land and Buildings, at cost	10,000	10,000
Motor Vehicles (cost £3,000)	2,250	
Stock, at cost	3,500	4,000
Trade Debtors	500	1,000
Prepayment – Motor Vehicles Expenses	200	300
– Property Insurance	50	100
Cash at Bank	550	950
Cash in Hand	100	450
Loan from Highton's father	10,000	
Trade Creditors	1,500	1,800
Accrual – Electricity	200	400
– Motor Vehicle Expenses	200	100

Extract from a rough Cash Book for the year to 31 March 19-2

RECEIPTS	£
Cash Sales	80,400
PAYMENTS	**£**
Cash Purchases	17,000
Drawings	7,000
General Shop Expenses	100
Telephone	100
Wages	3,000

Extract from the Bank Pass Sheets for the year to 31 March 19-2

RECEIPTS	£
Cash Banked	52,850
Cheques from Trade Debtors	8,750
PAYMENTS	**£**
Cheques to Suppliers	47,200
Loan Repayment (including interest)	10,100
Electricity	400
Motor Vehicle Expenses	1,000
Property Insurance	150
Rates	300
Telephone	300
Drawings	1,750

Note: Depreciation is to be provided on the motor vehicle at a rate of 25% per annum on cost.

You are required to:

Prepare a Trading, and Profit and Loss Account for the year to 31 March 19-2, and a Balance Sheet as at that date.

(Association of Accounting Technicians).

33.9. Philip Gold is a retailer in motor car accessories. Despite professional advice he does not maintain a full accounting system. He argues that if all cash transactions are dealt with through his bank account, and the bank does its job properly, then his annual accounts and particularly the reported profit figure for tax assessment are relatively easy to effect. You have been asked to prepare certain accounts from his bank statements and other business transactions in order to ascertain his profit performance and financial status in respect of the year ended 31st July 19-1. The following information is obtained.

(i) His current assets as at 31st July 19-0 and 31st July 19-1 were as follows:

	19-0	19-1
	£	£
Trading stock at or below cost	4,230	3,560
Trade debtors	3,760	2,310
Advance payments – rates	75	90
Bank balance	–	1,190

(ii) His current liabilities as at 31st July 19-0 and 31st July 19-1 were as follows:

	19-0	19-1
	£	£
Trade creditors	3,390	3,920
Accrued payments – electricity	50	70
Bank overdraft	2,100	–

(iii) Business transactions for the year ended 31st July 19-1 all effected through his bank account:

	£
Shop assistant's wages	3,400
Suppliers of accessories	25,140
Rent, rates and electricity	1,010
Other operating overheads	746
Interest-free loan from relative	2,500

(iv) Accessories costing £600 were withdrawn from the business by Gold for his own usage.

(v) Mark-up on accessories is 40 per cent on cost.

(vi) Shop fixtures and fittings at cost as at 31st July 19-0 were £2,900 and one year later £4,100. No fixed assets were sold during the year.

Accumulated depreciation as at 31st July 19-0 was £870. The annual depreciation expense is at the rate of 10 per cent based on the cost of the assets at the year end and still held in the business.

(vii) The source of all cash received was from trade debtors, except for the loan from the relative, and all cash received has been banked in the business, except for withdrawals of £5,200 by Gold.

Required:

(a) A summary of the business bank account for the year ended 31st July 19-1.

(b) A business trading and profit and loss account for the year ended 31st July 19-1 and balance sheet as at that date.

(Institute of Chartered Secretaries and Administrators).

33.10A. John Snow is the sole distribution agent in the Branton area for Diamond floor tiles. Under an agreement with the manufacturers, John Snow purchases the Diamond floor tiles at a trade discount of 20% off list price and annually in May receives an agency commission of 1% of his purchases for the year ended on the previous 31 March.

For several years, John Snow has obtained a gross profit of 40% on all sales. In a burglary in January 19-1 John Snow lost stock costing £4,000 as well as many of his accounting records. However, after careful investigations, the following information has been obtained covering the year ended 31 March 19-1:

(i) Assets and liabilities at 31 March 19-0, were as follows:

	£
Buildings: at cost	10,000
provision for depreciation	6,000
Motor vehicles: at cost	5,000
provision for depreciation	2,000
Stock: at cost	3,200
Trade debtors (for sales)	6,300
Agency commission due	300
Prepayments (trade expenses)	120
Balance at bank in hand	4,310
Trade creditors	4,200
Accrued expenses (vehicle expenses)	230

(ii) John Snow has been notified that he will receive an agency commission of £440 on 1 May 19-1.

(iii) Stock, at cost, at 31 March 19-1 was valued at £3,000 more than a year previously.

(iv) In October 19-0 stock costing £1,000 was damaged by dampness and had to be scrapped as worthless.

(v) Trade creditors at 31 March 19-1 related entirely to goods received whose list prices totalled £9,500.

(vi) Discounts allowed amounts to £1,620 whilst discounts received were £1,200.

(vii) Trade expenses prepaid at 31 March 19-1 totalled £80.

(viii) Vehicle expenses for the year ended 31 March 19-1 amount to £7,020.

(ix) Trade debtors (for sales) at 31 March 19-1 were £6,700.

(x) All receipts are passed through the bank account.

(xi) Depreciation is provided annually at the following rates:

Buildings 5% on cost;
Motor vehicles 20% on cost.

(xii) Commissions received are paid direct to the bank account.

(xiii) In addition to the payments for purchases, the bank payments were:

	£
Vehicle expenses	6,720
Drawings	4,300
Trade expenses	7,360

(xiv) John Snow is not insured against loss of stock owing to burglary or damage to stock caused by dampness.

Required:

John Snow's trading and profit and loss account for the year ended 31 March 19-1 and a balance sheet at that date.

(Association of Certified Accountants).

33.11. David Denton set up in business as a plumber a year ago, and he has asked you to act as his accountant. His instructions to you are in the form of the following letter.

Dear Henry,

I was pleased when you agreed to act as my accountant and look forward to your first visit to check my records. The proposed fee of £250 p.a. is acceptable. I regret that the paperwork for the work done during the year is incomplete. I started my business on 1 January last, and put £6,500 into a business bank account on that date. I brought my van into the firm at that time, and reckon that it was worth £3,600 then. I think it will last another three years after the end of the first year of business use.

I have drawn £90 per week from the business bank account during the year. In my trade it is difficult to take a holiday, but my wife managed to get away for a while. The travel agents bill for £280 was paid out of the business account. I bought the lease of the yard and office for £6,500. The lease has ten years to run, and the rent is only £300 a year payable in advance on the anniversary of the date of purchase, which was 1 April. I borrowed £4,000 on that day from Aunt Jane to help pay for the lease. I have agreed to pay her 10% interest per annum, but have been too busy to do anything about this yet.

I was lucky enough to meet Miss Prism shortly before I set up on my own, and she has worked for me as an office organiser right from the start. She is paid a salary of £3,000 p.a. All the bills for the year have been carefully preserved in a tool box, and we analysed them last week. The materials I have bought cost me £9,600, but I reckon there was £580 worth left in the yard on 31 December. I have not paid for them all yet, I think we owed £714 to the suppliers on 31 December. I was surprised to see that I had spent £4,800 on plumbing equipment, but it should last me five years or so. Electricity bills received up to 30 September came to £1,122; but motor expenses were £912, and general expenses £1,349 for the year. The insurance premium for the year to 31 March next was £800. All these have been paid by cheque but Miss Prism has lost the rate demand. I expect the Local Authority will send a reminder soon since I have not yet paid. I seem to remember that rates came to £180 for the year to 31 March next.

Miss Prism sent out bills to my customers for work done, but some of them are very slow to pay. Altogether the charges made were £29,863, but only £25,613 had been received by 31 December. Miss Prism thinks that 10% of the remaining bills are not likely to be paid. Other customers for jobs too small to bill have paid £3,418 in cash for work done, but I only managed to bank £2,600 of this money. I used £400 of the difference to pay the family's grocery bills, and Miss Prism used the rest for general expenses, except for £123 which was left over in a drawer in the office on 31 December.

Kinds regards,
Yours sincerely,
David.

You are required to draw up a Profit and Loss Account for the year ended 31 December, and a Balance Sheet as at that date.

(Association of Certified Accountants)

33.12A. Since commencing business several years ago as a cloth dealer, Tom Smith has relied on annual receipts and payments accounts for assessing progress. These accounts have been prepared from his business bank account through which all business receipts and payments are passed.

Tom Smith's receipts and payments account for the year ended 31 March 19-0 is as follows:

	£		£
Opening balance	1,680	Drawings	6,300
Sales receipts	42,310	Purchases payments	37,700
Proceeds of sale of		Motor van expenses	2,900
grandfather clock	870	Workshop: rent	700
Loan from John Scott	5,000	rates	570
Closing balance	1,510	Wages – John Jones	3,200
	£51,370		£51,370

Additional information:

(a) The grandfather clock sold during the year ended 31 March 19-0 was a legacy received by Tom Smith from the estate of his late father.

(b) The loan from John Scott was received on 1 January 19-0; interest is payable on the loan at the rate of 10% per annum.

(c) In May 19-0 Tom Smith received from his suppliers a special commission of 5% of the cost of purchases during the year ended 31 March 19-0.

(d) On 1 October 19-9, Tom Smith engaged John Jones as a salesman. In addition to his wages, Jones receives a bonus of 2% of the business's sales during the period of his employment; the bonus is payable on 1 April and 1 October in respect of the immediately preceding six month's period.
Note: It can be assumed that sales have been, at a uniform level throughout the year ended 31 March 19-0.

(e) In addition to the items mentioned above, the assets and liabilities of Tom Smith were as follows:

At 31 March	19-9	19-0
	£	£
Motor van, at cost	4,000	4,000
Stock in trade, at cost	5,000	8,000
Trade debtors	4,600	12,290
Motor vehicle expenses prepaid	–	100
Workshop rent accrued due	–	200
Trade creditors	2,900	2,200

(f) It can be assumed that the opening and closing balances in the above receipts and payments account require no adjustment for the purposes of Tom Smith's accounts.

(g) As from 1 April 19-9, it has been decided to provide for depreciation on the motor van annually at the rate of 20% of the cost.

Required:
The trading and profit and loss account for the year ended 31 March 19-0, and a balance sheet at that date of Tom Smith.
(Association of Certified Accountants)

33.13. Walter Parsons is in business as a sole trader. On 14 February 19-0, his warehouse caught fire and was destroyed together with his entire stock in trade. His financial year ends on 31 December and from his records the following information is available: –

Goods purchased since 31 December 19-9 to the date of the fire amounted to £2,440. Of these, goods costing £110 were not delivered to Parsons until after the fire. Sales for the same period amounted to £3,280 and all these goods were delivered by Parsons to his customers, before the fire took place.

Parsons' latest Trading Account was as follows: –

Trading Account for the year ended 31 December 19-9

	Dr. £		Cr. £
To Stock 1 January 19-9	2,180	By Sales	15,000
Add Purchases	10,870		
	13,050		
Less Stock 31 December 19-9	1,800		
Cost of Goods Sold	11,250		
Gross Profit	3,750		
	£15,000		£15,000

Parsons confirms that the percentage of Gross Profit to Sales during 19-0 was the same as that for the year 19-9.

Required:

From the above information calculate the value – at cost price – of the goods destroyed in the fire. (Calculations must be shown.)

(London Chamber of Commerce and Industry)

33.14A. The following is the Trading Account of William Martin, a sole trader.

Trading Account for the year ended 31 December 19-1

	Dr. £		Cr. £
To Stock 1 January 19-1	3,200	By Sales	24,000
Purchases	17,700		
	20,900		
Less Stock 31 December 19-1	2,900		
Cost of Goods Sold	18,000		
Gross Profit	6,000		
	24,000		24,000

During the night of 4 June, 19-2 Martin's warehouse was broken into and his entire stock in trade was stolen except for a small quantity of goods in an office. The value – at cost price – of the goods which were not stolen was £190.

The following information is available from Martin's records.

Purchases   1 January 19-2 to 4 June 19-2 £6,400
             Of this total goods costing £240 had *not* been delivered by 4 June
             19-2.

Sales   1 January 19-2 to 4 June 19-2 £8,280
             All the goods sold had been delivered from the warehouse by the
             close of business on 4 June 19-2.

Required:

Calculate the value, at *cost price,* of the goods actually stolen.
Calculations *must be shown*.

Note:

Assume that the percentage of gross profit to Sales is the same for 19-2 as
it was for 19-1.

(London Chamber of Commerce and Industry)

34

Receipts and Payments Accounts and Income and Expenditure Accounts

Clubs, associations and other non-profit making organizations do not have trading and profit and loss accounts drawn up for them, as their principal function is not trading or profit making. They are run to further the promotion of an activity or group of activities, such as playing football or engaging in cultural activities. The kind of final accounts prepared by these organizations are either Receipts and Payments Accounts or Income and Expenditure Accounts.

Receipts and payments accounts are merely a summary of the cash book for the period. Exhibit 34.1 is an example.

Exhibit 34.1

The Homers Running Club

Receipts and Payments Account for the year ended 31 December 19-5

Receipts	£	Payments	£
Bank Balance 1.1.19-5	236	Groundsman's wages	728
Subscriptions received for		Upkeep of sports stadium	296
19-5	1,148	Committee expenses	58
Rent from sub-letting ground	116	Printing and stationery	33
		Bank Balance 31.12.19-5	385
	1,500		1,500

However, when the organization owns assets and has liabilities, the receipts and payments account is an unsatisfactory way of drawing up accounts as it merely shows the cash position. What is required is a balance sheet, and an account showing whether or not the association's capital is being increased. In a commercial firm the latter information would be obtained from a profit and loss account. In a non-profit-making organization it is calculated in an account called the income and expenditure account. In fact the income and expenditure account follows all the basic rules of profit and loss accounts. Thus expenditure consists of those costs consumed during the period and income is the revenue earned in the period. Where income exceeds expenditure the difference is called 'Surplus of Income over Expenditure'. Where expenditure exceeds income the difference is called 'Excess of Expenditure over Income'.

There is, however, one qualification to the fact that normally such an organization would not have a trading or profit and loss account. This is where the organization has carried out an activity deliberately so as to make a profit to help finance the main activities. Running a bar so as to make a profit would be an example of this, or having dances. For this profit-aimed activity a trading or profit and loss account may be drawn up, the profit or loss being transferred to the income and expenditure account.

If the books had been kept on a double entry basis, the income and expenditure account and balance sheet would be prepared in the same manner as the profit and loss account and the balance sheet of a commercial firm, only the titles of the accounts and terms like 'surplus' or 'excess' being different. It is perhaps more usual to find that the records have been kept in a single entry form. In this case the starting point is that as described in the last chapter, namely the drafting of an opening statement of affairs followed by a Cash Book Summary. If a receipts and payments account exists then this is in fact a cash book summary. The preparation of the income and expenditure account and the balance sheet then follows the normal single entry fashion. Exhibit 34.2 shows the preparation on such a basis.

Exhibit 34.2

Long Lane Football Club

Receipts and Payments Account for the year ended 31 December 19-6

Receipts		£	Payments	£
Bank Balance 1.1.19-6		524	Payment for bar supplies	3,962
Subscriptions received for:			Wages:	
	19-5 (arrears)	55	Groundsman and assistant	939
	19-6	1,236	Barman	624
	19-7 (in advance)	40	Bar Expenses	234
Bar Sales		5,628	Repairs to stands	119
Donations Received		120	Ground upkeep	229
			Secretary's expenses	138
			Transport Costs	305
			Bank Balance 31.12.19-6	1,053
		7,603		7,603

The treasurer of the Long Lane Football Club has prepared a receipts and payments account, but members have complained about the inadequacy of such an account. He therefore asks an accountant to prepare a trading account for the bar, and an income and expenditure account and a balance sheet. The treasurer gives the accountant a copy of the receipts and payments account together with information of assets and liabilities at the beginning and end of the year:

Notes:

1.

	31.12.19-5	31.12.19-6
	£	£
Stocks in the bar − at cost	496	558
Owing for bar supplies	294	340
Bar expenses owing	25	36
Transport costs	−	65

2. The land and football stands were valued at 31 December 19-5 at: land £4,000; football stands £2,000; the stands are to be depreciated by 10 per cent per annum.

3. The equipment at 31 December 19-5 was valued at £550, and is to be depreciated at 20 per cent per annum.

4. Subscriptions owing by members amounted to £55 on 31 December 19-5, and £66 on 31 December 19-6.

From this information the accountant drew up the accounts and statements that follow.

Working of purchases and bar expenses figures:

Purchases Control

	£		£
Cash	3,962	Balances (creditors) b/f	294
Balances c/d	340	Trading Account (difference)	4,008
	4,302		4,302

Bar Expenses

	£		£
Cash	234	Balance b/f	25
Balance c/d	36	Trading Account (difference)	245
	270		270

Statement of Affairs as at 31 December 19-5

	£	£	£
Fixed Assets			
Land			4,000
Stands			2,000
Equipment			550
			6,550
Current Assets			
Stock in the Bar		496	
Debtors for Subscriptions		55	
Cash at Bank		524	
		1,075	
Less Current Liabilities			
Creditors	294		
Bar Expenses Owing	25	319	
Working Capital			756
			7,306
Financed by:			
Accumulated Fund (difference)			7,306
			7,306

Long Lane Football Club
Bar Trading Account for the year ended 31 December 19-6

	£	£
Sales		5,628
Less Cost of Goods Sold:		
Stock 1.1.19-6	496	
Add Purchases	4,008	
	4,504	
Less Stock 31.12.19-6	558	3,946
Gross Profit		1,682
Less: Bar Expenses	245	
Barman's Wages	624	869
Net Profit to Income & Expenditure Account		813

Income & Expenditure Account for the year ended 31 December 19-6

	£	£	£
Income			
Subscriptions for 19-6			1,302
Profit from the bar			813
Donations Received			120
			2,235
Less Expenditure			
Wages – Groundsman and Assistant		939	
Repairs to Stands		119	
Ground Upkeep		229	
Secretary's Expenses		138	
Transport Costs		370	
Depreciation			
Stands	200		
Equipment	110	310	2,105
Surplus of Income over Expenditure			130

Workings on transport costs and subscriptions received figures:
Transport Costs

	£		£
Cash	305	Income and Expenditure	
Accrued c/d	65	Account	370
	370		370

Subscriptions Received

	£		£
Balance (debtors) b/f	55	Cash 19-5	55
Income and Expenditure		19-6	1,236
Account (difference)	1,302	19-7	40
Balance (in advance) c/d	40	Balance (owing) c/d	66
	1,397		1,397

It will be noted that subscriptions received in advance are carried down as a credit balance to the following period.

The Long Lane Football Club
Balance Sheet as at 31 December 19-6

	£	£	£
Fixed Assets			
Land at valuation			4,000
Pavilion at valuation		2,000	
Less Depreciation		200	1,800
Equipment at valuation		550	
Less Depreciation		110	440
			6,240
Current Assets			
Stock of Bar Supplies		558	
Debtors for Subscriptions		66	
Cash at Bank		1,053	
		1,677	
Less Current Liabilities			
Creditors for Bar Supplies	340		
Bar Expenses Owing	36		
Transport Costs Owing	65		
Subscriptions Received in Advance	40	481	
Working Capital			1,196
			7,436
Financed by:			
Accumulated Fund			
Balance as at 1.1.19-6			7,306
Add Surplus of Income over Expenditure			130
			7,436

Life Membership

In some clubs and societies members can make a payment for life membership. This means that by paying a fairly substantial amount now the member can enjoy the facilities of the club for the rest of his life.

Such a receipt should not be treated as Income in the Income and Expenditure Account solely in the year in which the member paid the money. It should be credited to a Life Membership Account, and transfers should be made from that account to the credit of the Income and Expenditure Account of an appropriate amount annually.

Exactly what is meant by an appropriate amount is decided by the committee of the club or society. The usual basis is to establish, on average, how long members will continue to use the benefits of the club. To take an extreme case, if a club was in existence which could not be joined until one achieved the age of 70, then the expected number of years' use of the club on average per member would be relatively few. Another club, such as a golf club, where a fair proportion of the members joined when reasonably young, and where the game is capable of being played by members until and during old age, would expect a much higher average of years of use per member. The simple matter is that the club should decide for itself.

In an examination the candidate has to follow the instructions set for him by the examiner. The credit balance remaining on the account, after the transfer of the agreed amount has been made to the credit of the Income and Expenditure Account, should be shown on the Balance Sheet as a liability. It is, after all, the liability of the club to provide amenities for the member without any further payment by him.

Entrance Fees

In quite a lot of clubs, one has to pay certain fees on application for membership. Such fees are called entrance fees. They are paid quite apart from the usual monthly or quarterly subscription.

Such a receipt should not be treated as Income in the Income and Expenditure Account solely in the year in which the member is admitted. It should be credited to Entrance Fees Account and transfers should be made from that account to the Income and Expenditure Account by an appropriate amount annually, such amounts being decided by the committee of the club or society.

Outstanding Subscriptions and the Prudence Concept

The treatment of subscriptions owing has so far followed the normal procedures as applied to debtors in a commercial firm. However, as most treasurers of associations are fully aware, many members who owe subscriptions leave the association and never pay the amounts owing. This is far more prevalent than with debtors of a commercial firm. It can perhaps be partly explained by the fact that a commercial firm would normally sue for unpaid debts, whereas associations rarely sue for unpaid subscriptions. To bring in an unpaid subscriptions as assets therefore contravenes the prudence concept which tends to understate assets rather than overstate them. With many clubs therefore, unpaid subscriptions are ignored in the income and expenditure account and balance sheet. If they are eventually paid they are then brought in as income in the year of receipt irrespective of the period covered by the subscriptions.

In examinations, the student should bring debtors for subscriptions into account unles he is given instructions to the contrary.

Exercises

MC89 A Receipts and Payments Account is one
(A) Which is accompanied by a balance sheet
(B) In which the profit is calculated
(C) In which the opening and closing cash balances are shown
(D) In which the surplus of income over expenditure is calculated.

MC90 Instead of a Capital Account a club has
(A) An Accumulated Fund
(B) An Income and Expenditure Account
(C) A Balance Sheet
(D) A Bar Trading Account.

34.1. A summary of the Uppertown Football Club is shown below. From it, and the additional information, you are to construct an Income and Expenditure Account for the year ended 31 December 19-4, and a Balance Sheet as at that date.

Cash Book Summary

	£		£
Balance 1.1.19-4	180	Purchase of equipment	125
Collections at matches	1,650	Rent for football pitch	300
Profit on sale of refreshments	315	Printing and Stationery	65
		Secretary's expenses	144
		Repairs to equipment	46
		Groundsman's wages	520
		Miscellaneous expenses	66
		Balance 31.12.19-4	879
	2,145		2,145

Further information:
(i) At 1.1.19-4 equipment was valued at £500.
(ii) Depreciate all equipment 20 per cent for the year 19-4.
(iii) At 31.12.19-4 rent paid in advance was £60.
(iv) At 31.12.19-4 there was £33 owing for printing.

34.2A. The assets and liabilities of the Parkside Cricket Club at 30 September 19-1 were: premises £250,000; subscriptions in arrears £48; equipment £3,200; bank £1,896; bar stocks £920; subscriptions in advance £29; creditors for bar supplies £340; accumulated fund £255,695.

Receipts and payments for the year ended 30 September 19-2 were:

Receipts – subscriptions £694 (including £42 owing from last year); bar takings £7,200; socials and dances £320; sub-letting of cricket ground £200;

Payments – equipment £1,000; ground maintenance £1,260; rates £1,200; creditors for bar supplies £2,980; light and heat £220; insurance £86; general expenses £104.

At the end of September 19-2, the following further information was available.

1. Subscriptions not received from year ended 30 September 19-1 are to be written off.
2. Depreciate equipment by £200.
3. Creditors for bar supplies £786.
4. Subscriptions in arrears £45.
5. Light and heat owing £30.
6. Insurance prepaid £14.
7. Bar stocks £821.

Required:
(a) For the year ended 30 September 19-2:
   (i) an account showing the net profit or loss on the bar;
   (ii) the income and expenditure account.
   Note. A balance sheet is *not* required.
(b) A statement of the main difference between a non-commercial organisation and a business firm. How is this difference reflected in their respective final accounts?

(Associated Examining Board 'O' level)

34.3. On 1 January 19-1 the Tigers Rugby Club had fixed assets of a club house, £20,000, and a motor mower, £60 (cost £600).

The current assets and liabilities were:

	1 January 19-1	31 December 19-1
	£	£
Bar stock	450	600
Bar creditors	300	550
Rates paid in advance	100	120
Subscriptions in arrears	200	350
Subscriptions paid one year in advance	50	80
Cash in hand and at bank	620	1,735

A summary of the receipts and payments for the year ended 31 December 19-1 was as follows:

Receipts	£	Payments	£
Members' subscriptions	1,700	Rent of ground	600
(including £160 for 19-0)		Balls, shirts, etc.	310
Sales from dance tickets	1,500	Groundsman's fees	400
Bar takings	8,000	Referees' expenses	150
		Travelling expenses	1,000
		Bar stock	5,350
		Dance expenses	700
		Rates	300
		Stationery	120
		Sundry bar expenses	280
		Insurance	75
		New motor mower	800

You are required to prepare:

(a) A statement calculating the accumulated fund as at 1 January 19-1,

(b) (i) A bar account

(ii) A subscription account

(iii) An income and expenditure account, showing the profit or loss on dances, for the year ended 31 December 19-1,

(c) The balance sheet as at 31 December 19-1,

The following information should be taken into account:

(1) Subscriptions in arrears for more than one year are to be written off.

(2) Expenditure on balls, shirts, etc., is to be written off in year of purchase.

(3) Depreciation of the mower is to be calculated at 10% per annum. The new mower was purchased 1 January 19-1 at a cost of £850, less £50 trade-in allowance for the old mower.

(Joint Matriculation Board 'O' level).

34.4. The treasurer of the City Sports Club has produced the following receipts and payments account for the year ended 31 December 19-7:

Receipts	£	Payments	£
Balance at bank 1 January 19-7	1,298	Coffee supplies bought	1,456
Subscriptions received	3,790	Wages of attendants and	
Profits and dances	186	cleaners	1,776
Profit on exhibition	112	Rent of rooms	887
Coffee bar takings	2,798	New equipment bought	565
Sale of equipment	66	Travelling expenses of teams	673
		Balance at bank 31 December	
		19-7	2,893
	8,250		8,250

Notes:

(a) Coffee bar stocks were valued: 31 December 19-6 £59, 31 December 19-7 £103. There was nothing owing for coffee bar stocks on either of these dates.

(b) On 1 January 19-7 the club's equipment was valued at £2,788. Included in this figure, valued at £77, was the equipment sold during the year for £66.

(c) The amount to be charged for depreciation of equipment for the year is £279. This is in addition to the loss on equipment sold during the year.

(d) Subscriptions owing by members 31 December 19-6 nil, at 31 December 19-7 £29.

You are required to:
(i) Draw up the coffee bar trading account for the year ended 31 December 19-7. For this purpose £650 of the wages is to be charged to this account, the remainder will be charged in the income and expenditure account.
(ii) Calculate the accumulated fund as at 1 January 19-7.
(iii) Draw up the income and expenditure account for the year ended 31 December 19-7, and a balance sheet as at 31 December 19-7.

34.5A. The following trial balance of Haven Golf Club was extracted from the books as on 31 December 19-8:

	Dr £	Cr £
Clubhouse	21,000	
Equipment	6,809	
Profits from raffles		4,980
Subscriptions received		18,760
Wages of bar staff	2,809	
Bar stocks 1 January 19-8	1,764	
Bar purchases and sales	11,658	17,973
Greenkeepers' wages	7,698	
Golf professional's salary	6,000	
General expenses	580	
Cash at bank	1,570	
Accumulated fund at 1 January 19-8		18,175
	59,888	59,888

Notes:
(a) Bar purchases and sales were on a cash basis. Bar stocks at 31 December 19-8 were valued at £989.
(b) Subscriptions paid in advance by members at 31 December 19-8 amounted to £180.
(c) Provide for depreciation of equipment £760.

You are required to:
(i) Draw up the Bar trading account for the year ended 31 December 19-8.
(ii) Draw up the Income and expenditure account for the year ended 31 December 19-8, and a Balance Sheet as at 31 December 19-8.

34.6. The following receipts and payments account for the year ended 31 March 19-1 for the Green Bank Sports Club has been prepared by the treasurer, Andrew Swann:

Receipts	£	Payments	£
Balances brought forward		Painting of Clubhouse	580
1 April 19-0:		Maintenance of grounds	1,310
Cash in hand	196	Bar steward's salary	5,800
Bank current account	5,250	Insurances	240
Members subscriptions:		General expenses	1,100
Ordinary	1,575	Building society investment	
Life	800	account	1,500
Annual dinner – ticket sales	560	Secretary's honorarium	200
Bar takings	21,790	Annual dinner – expenses	610
		New furniture and fittings	1,870
		Bar purchases	13,100
		Rent of clubhouse	520
		Balances carried forward	
		31 March 19-1:	
		Bank current account	3,102
		Cash in hand	239
	£30,171		£30,171

The following additional information has been given:

(i) Ordinary membership subscriptions.

          £

Received in advance at 31 March 19-0   200

The subscriptions received during the year ended 31 March 19-1 included £150 in advance for the following year.

(ii) A life membership scheme was introduced on 1 April 19-9; under the scheme life membership subscriptions are £100 and are appointed to revenue over a ten year period.

      Life membership subscriptions totalling £1,100 were received during the first year of the scheme.

(iii) The club's building society investment account balance at 31 March 19-0 was £2,676; during the year ended 31 March 19-1 interest of £278 was credited to the account.

(iv) All the furniture and fittings in the club's accounts at 31 March 19-0 were bought in January 19-8 at a total cost of £8,000; it is the club's policy to provide depreciation annually on fixed assets at 10% of the cost of such assets held at the relevant year end.

(v) Other assets and liabilities of the club were:

At 31 March	19-0	19-1
	£	£
Bar stocks	1,860	2,110
Insurance prepaid	70	40
Rent accrued due	130	140
Bar purchases creditors	370	460

Required:

(a) The bar trading and profit and loss account for the year ended 31 March 19-1.

(b) The club's income and expenditure account for the year ended 31 March 19-1 and a balance sheet at that date.

(c) Outline the advantages and disadvantages of receipts and payments accounts for organisations such as the Green Bank Sports Club.

(Association of Certified Accountants)

34.7A. The following is the Receipts and Payments Account of the Listorn Social Club for the year ended 31 October 19-1.

Receipts	£	Payments	£
Cash in hand at 1 Nov. 19-0	408	Printing, Stationery & Stamps	4,930
Balance at bank at 1 Nov. 19-0	5,236	Wages	15,062
		Rent and Rates	8,160
		Heat, Light Cleaning etc.	5,440
Annual subscriptions	28,764	Cost of Entertainments	3,468
Entrance Fees	3,196	Purchases for Catering	8,024
Sale of Tickets for Entertainments	6,120	Honorarium to Secretary	1,700
Hire of Hall	8,500	Purchase of Refrigeration Equipment	3,264
Receipts from Catering	9,690	Purchase of 3,000 shares in Starn Ltd.	3,536
		Cash in hand at 31 Oct. 19-1	340
		Bal. at Bank at 31 Oct. 19-1	7,990
	£61,914		£61,914

On 31 October 19-0 the Club held Furniture and Equipment valued at £12,750 and at that date subscriptions unpaid amounted to £918 while those paid in advance amounted to £612. Also at that date Rates had been paid in advance to the extent of £544 and there was owing in respect of Catering purchases £1,020.

At 31 October 19-1, Subscriptions in arrears were £1,122 and those received in advance amounted to £408, and there was £3,332 owing in respect of Catering purchases. At that date there was a stock of Stationery and Stamps on hand valued at £714. The amount paid during the year for Rates was £1,360 and this was a payment on account of the total rates for the year ending 31 January 19-2 which were £2,040; and depreciation for the year in respect of the Furniture and Fittings amounted to £1,054.

You are required to prepare: an income and expenditure Account for the year ending 31 October 19-1, and a Balance Sheet as at that date.
(Association of Business Executives)

34.8. The following receipts and payments account for the year ended 31 October 19-0 has been prepared from the current account bank statements of the Country Cousins Sports Club:

19-9		£	19-0		£
Nov 1	Balance b/fwd	1,700	Oct 31	Clubhouse:	
19-0				Rates and insurance	380
Oct 31	Subscriptions	8,600		Decoration and	
	Bar takings	13,800		repairs	910
	Donations	1,168		Annual dinner –	
	Annual dinner –			Catering	650
	Sale of tickets	470		Bar purchases	9,200
				Stationery and	
				printing	248
				New sports equipment	2,463
				Hire of films	89
				Warden's salary	4,700
				Petty cash	94
				Balance c/fwd	7,004
		£25,738			£25,738

The following additional information has been given:

At 31 October	19-9	19-0
	£	£
Clubhouse, at cost	15,000	15,000
Bar stocks, at cost	1,840	2,360
Petty cash float	30	10
Bank deposit account	600	730
Subscriptions received in advance	210	360
Creditors for bar supplies	2,400	1,900

It has been decided to provide for depreciation annually on the clubhouse at the rate of 10% of cost and on the new sports equipment at the rate of $33\frac{1}{3}$% of cost.

The petty cash float is used exclusively for postages.

The only entry in the bank deposit account during the year ended 31 October 19-0 concerns interest.

One-quarter of the warden's salary and one-half of the clubhouse costs, including depreciation, are to be apportioned to the bar.

The donations received during the year ended 31 October 19-0 are for the new coaching bursary fund which will be utilised for the provision of training facilities for promising young sportsmen and sportswomen. It is expected to make the first award during 19-1.

Required:

(a) An account showing the profit or loss for the year ended 31 October 19-0 on the operation of the bar.

(b) An Income and Expenditure Account for the year ended 31 October 19-0 and a Balance Sheet at that date for the Country Cousins Sports Club.

(Association of Certified Accountants)

35

Manufacturing Accounts

The final accounts prepared so far have all been for firms whose function is limited to that of merchandising, i.e. the buying and selling of goods. Obviously there are many firms whose main activity is in the manufacture of goods for sale. For these firms a Manufacturing Account is prepared in addition to the trading and profit and loss accounts.

Because the costs in the manufacturing account are involved with production there is an obvious link with the costing records, and the concepts of the manufacturing account are in fact really costing concepts. It will therefore be necessary to first of all examine the main elements and division of cost as used in costing. These may be summarized in chart form as follows:

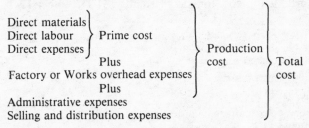

```
Direct materials ⎫
Direct labour    ⎬ Prime cost              ⎫
Direct expenses  ⎭                         ⎬ Production ⎫
              Plus                           cost      ⎬ Total
Factory or Works overhead expenses ⎪                   ⎪ cost
              Plus                 ⎭                    ⎪
Administrative expenses                                ⎪
Selling and distribution expenses                      ⎭
```

By 'direct' is meant that the materials, labour and expenses involved are traceable to the particular unit of goods being made, and that the trouble and labour involved in doing this are worthwhile. Labour such as that of a lathe operator will be direct labour, whereas that of a foreman who supervises many jobs cannot be easily traced down to each particular unit being produced and will accordingly be classified as indirect labour, forming part of the factory overhead expenses. The cost of direct materials will include the cost of carriage inwards on raw materials. Examples of direct expenses are the hire of special plant for a particular job, and royalties payable to inventors for use of a patent where a charge is levied on each unit produced.

Factory overhead expenses consist of all those expenses which occur in the factory where production is carried on, but which cannot easily be traced to the units being manufactured. Examples are wages of cleaners and crane drivers, rent and rates of the factory, depreciation of plant and machinery used in the factory, running of fork-lift trucks, factory power and lighting and heating.

Adminstration expenses consist of such items as managers' salaries, legal and accountancy charges, the depreciation of accounting machinery and secretarial salaries.

Selling and distribution expenses are items such as salesmen's salaries and commission, carriage outwards, depreciation of delivery vans, advertising and display expenses.

In the manufacturing account the production cost of goods completed during the accounting period is ascertained. This means that all the elements of Production cost, i.e. direct materials, direct labour, direct expenses and factory overhead expenses, are charged to the manufacturing account. All administration and selling and distribution expenses are charged to the profit and loss account. Note that the manufacturing account is concerned with the production cost of goods completed in the year irrespective of when work started on them. For this reason goods partly finished, known as work in progress, must be taken into account.

The necessary details required to draw up a manufacturing account can now be looked at. In the first example, Exhibit 35.1, it has been assumed that there was no work in progress, either at the beginning or end of the accounting period.

Exhibit 35.1
Details of production cost for the year ended 31 December 19-7:

	£
1 January 19-7, stock of raw materials	500
31 December 19-7, stock of raw materials	700
Raw materials purchased	8,000
Manufacturing (direct) wages	21,000
Royalties	150
Indirect wages	9,000
Rent of factory – excluding administration and selling and distribution blocks	440
Depreciation of plant and machinery in factory	400
General indirect expenses	310

The production cost of goods completed, when ascertained, is carried down to the trading account, taking the place where normally purchases are shown. As this is a manufacturing concern selling its own products there will not usually be a figure for the purchase of finished goods. Sometimes, however, if a firm has produced less than the customers have demanded, then the firm may well have bought an outside supply of finished goods. In this case, the trading account will have both a figure for purchases and for production cost of goods completed.

Manufacturing Account for the year ended 31 December 19-7

	£	£
Stock of Raw Materials 1.1.19-7		500
Add Purchases		8,000
		8,500
Less Stock of Raw Materials 31.12.19-7		700
Cost of Raw Materials Consumed		7,800
Manufacturing Wages		21,000
Royalties		150
Prime Cost		28,950
Factory Overhead Expenses		
Rent	440	
Indirect Wages	9,000	
General Expenses	310	
Depreciation of Plant and Machinery	400	10,150
Production Cost of Goods Completed c/d		39,100

When there is work in progress, i.e. goods only part completed at the beginning and end of an accounting period an adjustment is needed. To find the production cost of goods completed in the period the value of work in progress at the beginning must be brought into account as it will be work (provided it is not a job such as building a ship which will take more than a year) which is completed within the accounting period. On the other hand, work in progress at the end of the period must be carried forward to the next period, as it is completed within the next period. To do this, the value of work in progress at the beginning is added to the total production cost for the period, and the closing work in progress is deducted. An example is shown in Exhibit 35.2.

Exhibit 35.2

	£
1 January 19-7, Stock of raw materials	800
31 December 19-7, Stock of raw materials	1,050
1 January 19-7, Work in progress	350
31 December 19-7, Work in progress	420
Year to 31 December 19-7:	
Wages: Direct	3,960
Indirect	2,550
Purchase of raw materials	8,700
Fuel and power	990
Direct expenses	140
Lubricants	300
Carriage inwards on raw materials	200
Rent of factory	720
Depreciation of factory plant and machinery	420
Internal transport expenses	180
Insurance of factory buildings and plant	150
General factory expenses	330

Manufacturing Account for the year ended 31 December 19-7

	£	£
Stock of raw materials 1.1.19-7		800
Add Purchases		8,700
,, Carriage inwards		200
		9,700
Less Stock of raw materials 31.12.19-7		1,050
Cost of raw materials consumed		8,650
Direct wages		3,960
Direct expenses		140
Prime cost		12,750
Factory Overhead Expenses		
Fuel and power	990	
Indirect wages	2,550	
Lubricants	300	
Rent	720	
Depreciation of plant	420	
Internal transport expenses	180	
Insurance	150	
General factory expenses	330	5,640
		18,390
Add Work in progress 1.1.19-7		350
		18,740
Less Work in progress 31.12.19-7		420
Production cost of goods completed c/d		18,320

The trading account is concerned with finished goods. If in the foregoing exhibit there had been £3,500 stock of finished goods at 1 January 19-7 and £4,400 at 31 December 19-7, and the sales of finished goods amounted to £25,000, then the trading account would appear:

Trading Account for the year 31 December 19-7

	£	£
Sales		25,000
Less Cost of Goods Sold:		
Stock of finished goods 1.1.19-7	3,500	
Add Production cost of goods completed b/d	18,320	
	21,820	
Less Stock of finished goods 31.12.19-7	4,400	17,420
Gross Profit c/d		7,580

The profit and loss account is then constructed in the normal way.

A complete worked example is now given. Note that in the profit and loss account the expenses have been separated so as to show whether they are administration expenses, selling and distribution expenses, or financial charges.

The trial balance Exhibit 35.3 has been extracted from the books of J. Jarvis, Toy Manufacturer, as on 31 December 19-7:

Exhibit 35.3

J. Jarvis
Trial balance as on 31 December 19-7

	Dr	Cr
	£	£
Stock of raw materials 1.1.19-7	2,100	
Stock of finished goods 1.1.19-7	3,890	
Work in progress 1.1.19-7	1,350	
Wages (direct £18,000; Factory indirect £14,500)	32,500	
Royalties	700	
Carriage inwards (on raw materials)	350	
Purchases of raw materials	37,000	
Productive machinery (cost £28,000)	23,000	
Accounting machinery (cost £2,000)	1,200	
General factory expenses	3,100	
Lighting	750	
Factory power	1,370	
Administrative salaries	4,400	
Salesmen's salaries	3,000	
Commission on sales	1,150	
Rent	1,200	
Insurance	420	
General administration expenses	1,340	
Bank charges	230	
Discounts allowed	480	
Carriage outwards	590	
Sales		100,000
Debtors and creditors	14,230	12,500
Bank	5,680	
Cash	150	
Drawings	2,000	
Capital as at 1.1.19-7		29,680
	142,180	142,180

Notes at 31.12.19-7:

1. Stock of raw materials £2,400, stock of finished goods £4,000, work in progress £1,500.

2. Lighting, and rent and insurance are to be apportioned: factory 5/6ths, administration 1/6th.

3. Depreciation on productive and accounting machinery at 10 per cent per annum on cost.

J. Jarvis
Manufacturing, Trading and Profit and Loss Account for the year ended
31 December 19-7

	£	£
Stock of raw materials 1.1.19-7		2,100
Add Purchases		37,000
,, Carriage inwards		350
		39,450
Less Stock raw materials 31.12.19-7		2,400
Cost of raw materials consumed		37,050
Direct labour		18,000
Royalties		700
Prime cost		55,750
Factory Overhead Expenses:		
General factory expenses	3,100	
Lighting 5/6ths	625	
Power	1,370	
Rent 5/6ths	1,000	
Insurance 5/6ths	350	
Depreciation of plant	2,800	
Indirect labour	14,500	23,745
		79,495
Add Work in progress 1.1.19-7		1,350
		80,845
Less Work in progress 31.12.19-7		1,500
Production cost of goods completed c/d		79,345
Sales		100,000
Less Cost of goods sold:		
Stock of finished goods 1.1.19-7	3,890	
Add Production cost of goods completed	79,345	
	83,235	
Less Stock of finished goods 31.12.19-7	4,000	79,235
Gross Profit		20,765
Administration Expenses		
Administrative salaries	4,400	
Rent 1/6th	200	
Insurance 1/6th	70	
General expenses	1,340	
Lighting 1/6th	125	
Depreciation of accounting machinery	200	6,335
Selling and Distribution Expenses		
Salesmens salaries	3,000	
Commission on sales	1,150	
Carriage outwards	590	4,740
Financial Charges		
Bank charges	230	
Discounts allowed	480	710	11,785
Net Profit		8,980

J. Jarvis
Balance Sheet as at 31 December 19-7

	£	£
Fixed Assets		
Productive Machinery at cost	28,000	
Less Depreciation to date	7,800	20,200
Accounting Machinery at cost	2,000	
Less Depreciation to date	1,000	1,000
		21,200
Current Assets		
Stock		
Raw Materials	2,400	
Finished Goods	4,000	
Work in Progress	1,500	
Debtors	14,230	
Bank	5,680	
Cash	150	
	27,960	
Less Current Liabilities		
Creditors	12,500	
Working Capital		15,460
		36,660
Financed by:		
Capital		
Balance as at 1.1.19-7		29,680
Add Net Profit		8,980
		38,660
Less Drawings		2,000
		36,660

Market Value of Goods Manufactured

The accounts of Jarvis, just illustrated, are subject to the limitation that the respective amounts of the gross profit which are attributable to the manufacturing side or to the selling side of the firm are not known. A technique is sometimes used to bring out this additional information. By this method the cost which would have been involved if the goods had been bought in their finished state instead of being manufactured by the firm is brought into account. This is credited to the manufacturing account and debited to the trading account so as to throw up two figures of gross profit instead of one. It should be pointed out that the net profit will remain unaffected. All that will have happened will be that the figure of £20,765 gross profit will be shown as two figures instead of one.

The accounts, in summarized form will appear:

Manufacturing, Trading and Profit and Loss Account for the year ended 31 December 19-7

	£	£
Market value of goods completed c/d		95,000
Less Production cost of goods completed (as before)		79,345
Gross profit on manufacture c/d		15,655
Sales		100,000
Stock of finished goods 1.1.19-7	3,890	
Add Market value of goods completed b/d	95,000	
	98,890	
Less Stock of finished goods 31.12.19-7	4,000	94,890
Gross profit on trading c/d		5,110
Gross Profit		
On manufacturing	15,655	
On trading	5,110	20,765

Exercises

MC91 Prime cost includes
(i)   Direct Labour
(ii) Factory overhead expenses
(iii) Direct Labour
(iv) Direct Expenses.
(A) i, ii and iii
(B) ii, iii and iv
(C) i, iii and iv
(D) i, ii and iv.

MC92 Work in Progress is the
(A) Value of finished goods on hand
(B) Value of Goods Produced
(C) Value of Partly Finished Goods
(D) Sales less Cost of Goods Sold.

MC93 Which of the following should be charged in the Profit and Loss Account
(A) Office Rent
(B) Work in Progress
(C) Direct Materials
(D) Carriage on Raw Materials.

MC94 Prime Cost is the total of
(A) Direct Materials + Works Overhead Expenses
(B) Direct Materials + Direct Labour + Direct Expenses
(C) Production Cost + Selling Expenses
(D) Administrative Expenses + Selling & Distribution Expense.

MC95 In the Manufacturing Account is calculated
(A) The Production Costs paid in the year
(B) The Total Cost of Goods Produced
(C) The Production Cost of Goods Completed in the period
(D) The Gross Profit on goods sold.

35.1. The following items have been extracted from the books of a manufacturing company for the year ended 31 December 19-0:

	£
Stock of raw materials, 1 January 19-0, at cost	6,500
Raw materials purchased	33,500
Stock of raw materials, 31 December 19-0, at cost	15,000
Work in progress 1 January 19-0	10,000
Work in progress 31 December 19-0	22,000
Finished goods 1 January 19-0	5,000
Finished goods 31 December 19-0	4,000
Sales	75,000
Carriage on purchase of raw materials	1,000
Rent and rates	2,000
Heating and lighting	3,600
Factory wages – direct wages 18,000	
indirect wages 7,000	25,000
Office salaries	3,000
Depreciation of plant and machinery	400

You are required to prepare a manufacturing, trading, and profit and loss account for the year ended 31 December 19-0. Rent and rates, and heating and lighting should be apportioned in the ratio three to factory expenses and one to office expenses respectively.
(Joint Matriculation Board 'O' level)

35.2A. From the following details you are to draw up a Manufacturing, Trading and Profit and Loss Account of B. Noone for the year ended 30 September 19-4.

	30.9.19-3	30.9.19-4
	£	£
Stocks of Raw Materials, at cost	8,460	10,970
Work in Progress	3,070	2,460
Finished Goods Stock	12,380	14,570

For the year:	£
Raw Materials Purchased	38,720
Manufacturing Wages	20,970
Factory Expenses	12,650
Depreciation:	
Plant and Machinery	7,560
Delivery Vans	3,040
Office Equipment	807
Factory Power	6,120
Advertising	5,080
Office and Administration Expenses	5,910
Salesmens' Salaries and Expenses	6,420
Delivery Van Expenses	5,890
Sales	134,610
Carriage Inwards	2,720

35.3. Prepare Manufacturing, Trading and Profit and Loss Accounts from the following balances of T. Jackson for the year ended 31 December 19-7.

	£
Stocks at 1 January 19-7:	
Raw Materials	18,450
Work in Progress	23,600
Finished Goods	17,470
Purchases: Raw Materials	64,300
Carriage on Raw Materials	1,605
Direct Labour	65,810
Office Salaries	16,920
Rent	2,700
Office Lighting and Heating	5,760
Depreciation: Works Machinery	8,300
Office Equipment	1,950
Sales	200,600
Factory Fuel & Power	5,920

Rent is to be apportioned: Factory ⅔rds: Office ⅓. Stocks at 31 December 19-7 were: Raw Materials £20,210, Work in Progress £17,390, Finished Goods £21,485.

35.4A. Arthur Price, an engineer, ran a manufacturing business, but he did not keep proper books of account. He was able to provide the following information on his activities for the year ended 30 June 19-9.

	£
Balance as at 1 July 19-8	
Creditors for raw materials	15,000
Debtors for finished units	22,500
Stock of finished units	27,000
Maintenance wages owing	1,000
Payments	
To creditors for raw materials	60,000
Direct manufacturing wages	31,500
Factory heating and lighting	2,500
Factory maintenance wages	12,000
Factory rent and rates	2,000
Direct manufacturing expenses	4,000
Repairs to manufacturing machinery	5,000
Receipts:	
From debtors for finished units sold	196,000
Balances as at 30 June 19-9	
Creditors for raw materials	20,000
Debtors for finished units	20,500
Stock of finished units	31,000

The finished units produced during the year were transferred to the warehouse at factory cost. There was no work-in-progress.

Of the raw materials purchased during the year, ninetenths were consumed by the factory. There was no opening stock of raw materials.

Depreciation on machinery for the year was estimated to be £9,500.

Required:
For the year ended 30 June 19-9, prepare
(*a*) a manufacturing account showing clearly prime cost and factory cost of goods produced;
(*b*) a trading account.

(Associated Examining Board 'O' level)

35.5. D. Saunders is a manufacturer. His trial balance at 31 December 19-6 is as follows:

	£	£
Delivery Van Expenses	2,500	
Lighting and Heating: Factory	2,859	
Office	1,110	
Manufacturing Wages	45,470	
General Expenses: Office	3,816	
Factory	5,640	
Salesmen: Commission	7,860	
Purchase of Raw Materials	39,054	
Rent: Factory	4,800	
Office	2,200	
Machinery (cost £50,000)	32,500	
Office Equipment (cost £15,000)	11,000	
Office Salaries	6,285	
Debtors	28,370	
Creditors		19,450
Bank	13,337	
Sales		136,500
Premises (Cost £50,000)	40,000	
Stocks at 31 December 19-5:		
Raw Materials	8,565	
Finished Goods	29,480	
Drawings	8,560	
Capital		137,456
	293,406	293,406

Prepare the Manufacturing, Trading and Profit and Loss Accounts for the year ended 31 December 19-6 and a Balance Sheet as at that date. Give effect to the following adjustments:
1. Stocks at 31 December 19-6, Raw Materials £9,050, Finished Goods £31,200. There is no Work in Progress.
2. Depreciate Machinery £2,000, Office Equipment £1,500, Premises £1,000.
3. Manufacturing Wages due but unpaid at 31 December 19-6 £305, Office Rent prepaid £108.

35.6A. B. Owens has a manufacturing business. His trial balance as on 31 December 19-7 was as follows:

	£	£
Carriage Outwards	7,038	
Rent: Office	990	
Factory	4,850	
Office Machinery (cost £6,000)	4,200	
Bank		14,360
Debtors	28,972	
Sales		184,715
Machinery (cost £50,000)	28,000	
Salaries to Salesmen	8,570	
Raw Material Purchases	57,245	
Sundry Expenses: Factory	1,362	
Office	898	
Creditors		15,477
Stocks at 31 December 19-6:		
Raw Materials	15,872	
Finished Goods	51,897	
Office Salaries	8,416	
Manufacturing Wages	64,371	
Lighting and Heating: Office	1,475	
Factory	4,896	
Drawings	9,900	
Capital		84,400
	298,952	298,952

You are to draw up a Manufacturing, Trading and Profit and Loss Account for the year ended 31 December 19-7, and a Balance Sheet as on that date. Give effect to the following adjustments:

(*a*) Depreciate Machinery £5,000, Office Machinery £800.
(*b*) The following were due but unpaid at 31 December 19-7, Carriage Outwards £188, Lighting and Heating: − Office £125, Factory £488.
(*c*) The factory rent had been prepaid £250 at 31 December 19-7.
(*d*) Stocks at 31 December 19-7, Raw Materials £13,820, Finished Goods £56,842.

36

Departmental Accounts

Accounting information varies in its usefulness. For a retail store with five departments, it is obviously better to know that the store has made £10,000 gross profit than to be completely ignorant of this fact. The figure of £10,000 gross profit unfortunately does not give the owners the insight into the business necessary to control it much more effectively. What would be far more meaningful would be the knowledge of the amount of gross profit or loss for each department. Assume that the gross profits and losses for the departments were as follows:

Department	Gross profit	Gross loss
	£	£
A	4,000	
B	3,000	
C	5,000	
D		8,000
E	6,000	
	18,000	8,000

Gross profit of the firm, £10,000.

Ignoring the overhead expenses for the sake of simplicity, although in practice they should never be ignored, can any conclusions be drawn from the above? It may well appear that if department D was closed down then the store would make £18,000 gross profit instead of £10,000. This could equally well be true or false depending on circumstances. Department D may be deliberately run at a loss so that its cheap selling prices may attract customers who, when they come to the store, also buy goods in addition from departments A, B, C and E. If department D were closed down perhaps most of the customers would not come to the store at all. In this case all the other departments would only have small gross profits because of the falls in sales and if this happened the gross profits might well be – departments: A £1,000, B £500, C £2,500 and E £2,000, a total of £6,000. Therefore department D operating at a loss because of cheap prices would have increased the gross profit of the firm.

The converse could, however, hold true. If department D were closed down the sales in the other departments might rise. Department D could be a wine and spirits department at the entrance to the store through which all customers have to walk to the other departments. Teetotallers may therefore avoid the store because they would not like to be seen going into a department where alcohol was being sold. To close down the department, leaving it merely as an access route to the other departments, may result in higher sales in these other departments because the teetotallers who had previously shunned the store might now become customers. The effect on the existing non-teetotal customers could also be considered as well as the possibility of the re-location of the wine and spirits department.

Accounting information therefore seldom tells all the story. It serves as one measure, but there are other non-accounting factors to be considered before a relevant decision for action can be made.

The various pros and cons of the actions to be taken to increase the overall profitability of the business cannot therefore be efficiently considered until the departmental gross profits or losses are known. It must not be thought that departmental accounts refer only to departmental stores. They refer to the various facets of a business. Consider the simple case of a barber who does shaving and haircutting. He may find that the profit from shaving is very small, and that if he discontinues shaving he will earn more from extra haircutting because he does not have to turn customers away because of lack of time. The principle of departmental accounts is concerned just as much with the small barber's shop as with a large department store. The reputation of many a successful businessman has been built up on his ability to utilize the departmental account principle to guide his actions to increase the profitability of a firm. The lesson still has to be learned by many medium-sized and small firms. It is one of accounting's greatest, and simplest, aids to business efficiency.

Expenses

The expenses of the firm are often split between the various departments, and the net profit for each department then calculated. Each expense is divided between the departments on what is considered to be the most logical basis. This will differ considerably between businesses. An example of a Trading and Profit and Loss Account drawn up in such a manner is shown in Exhibit 36.1.

Exhibit 36.1

Northern Stores have three departments in their store:

	(a) Jewellery	(b) Ladies hairdressing	(c) Clothing
	£	£	£
Stock of goods or materials, 1 January 19-8	2,000	1,500	3,000
Purchases	11,000	3,000	15,000
Stock of goods or materials, 31 December 19-8	3,000	2,500	4,000
Sales and work done	18,000	9,000	27,000
Wages of assistants in each department	2,800	5,000	6,000

The following expenses cannot be traced to any particular department:

	£
Rent	3,500
Administration expenses	4,800
Air conditioning and lighting	2,000
General expenses	1,200

It is decided to apportion rent together with air conditioning and lighting in accordance with the floor space occupied by each department. These were taken up in the ratios of (a) one-fifth, (b) half, (c) three-tenths. Administration expenses and general expenses are to be split in the ratio of sales and work done.

The Northern Stores

Trading and Profit and Loss Account for the year ended 31 December 19-8

	(a) Jewellery		(b) Hairdressing		(c) Clothing	
	£	£	£	£	£	£
Sales and Work Done		18,000		9,000		27,000
Cost of Goods or Materials:						
Stock 1.1.19-8	2,000		1,500		3,000	
Add Purchases	11,000		3,000		15,000	
	13,000		4,500		18,000	
Less Stock 31.12.19-8	3,000	10,000	2,500	2,000	4,000	14,000
Gross Profit		8,000		7,000		13,000
Less Expenses:						
Wages	2,800		5,000		6,000	
Rent	700		1,750		1,050	
Administration expenses	1,600		800		2,400	
Air conditioning and lighting	400		1,000		600	
General expenses	400	5,900	200	8,750	600	10,650
Net Profit/Loss		2,100		(1,750)		2,350

This way of calculating net profits and losses seems to imply a precision that is lacking in fact, and would often lead to an interpretation that the hairdressing department has lost £1,750 this year, and that this amount would be saved if the department was closed down. It has already been stated that different departments are very often dependent on one another, therefore it will be realized that this would not necessarily be the case. The calculation of net profits and losses are also dependent on arbitrary division of overhead expenses. It is by no means obvious that the overheads of department (*b*) would be avoided if it were closed down. Assuming that the sales staff of the department could be discharged without compensation, then £5,000 would be saved in wages. The other overhead expenses shown under department (*b*) would not, however, necessarily disappear. The rent may still be payable in full even though the department were closed down. The administration expenses may turn out to be only slightly down, say from £4,800 to £4,600, a saving of £200; air conditioning and lighting down to £1,500, a saving of £500; general expenses down to £1,100, a saving of £100. Therefore the department, when open, costs an additional £5,800 compared with when the department is closed. This is made up as follows:

	£
Administration expenses	200
Air conditioning and lighting	500
General expenses	100
Wages	5,000
	5,800

But when open, assuming this year is typical, the department makes £7,000 gross profit. The firm is therefore £1,200 a year better off when the department is open than when it is closed, subject to certain assumptions. These are:

(*a*) That the remaining departments could not be profitably expanded into the space vacated to give greater proportionate benefits than the hairdressing department.

(*b*) That a new type of department which would be more profitable than hairdressing could not be set up.

(*c*) That the department could not be leased to another firm at a more profitable figure than that shown by hairdressing.

There are also other factors which, though not easily seen in an accounting context, are still extremely pertinent. They are concerned with the possible loss of confidence in the firm by customers generally; what appears to be an ailing business does not usually attract good customers. Also the effect on the remaining staff should not be ignored. The fear that the dismissal of the hairdressing staff may mirror what is also going to happen to themselves may result in the loss of staff, especially the most competent members who could easily find work elsewhere, and so the general quality of the staff may decline with serious consequences for the firm.

A far less misleading method of drafting departmental accounts is by showing costs which are in the nature of direct costs allocated entirely to the department, and which would not be payable if the department was closed down, in the first section of the Trading and Profit and Loss Account. The second section is left to cover those expenses which need arbitrary apportionment or which would still be payable on the closing of the department. The surpluses brought down from the first section represent the 'contribution' that each department makes to cover the expenses and profit. The contributions can thus be seen to be the results of activities which are under a person's control, in this case the departmental managers concerned. The sales revenue has been generated by the workforce, etc., all under their control, and the costs charged have been under their control, so that the surpluses earned (or deficits incurred) are affected by the degree of their control. The other costs in the second section are not, however, under their control. The departmental managers cannot directly affect to any great extent the costs of rent or of air conditioning and lighting, so that the contributions from the sections of the business must more than cover all these expenses if the business is to earn a profit. From the figures given in Exhibit 36.1 the accounts would appear as shown in Exhibit 36.2.

Exhibit 36.2

The Northern Stores

Trading and Profit and Loss Account for the year ended 31 December 19-8

	(a) Jewellery		(b) Hairdressing		(c) Clothing	
	£	£	£	£	£	£
Sales and work done		18,000		9,000		27,000
Less Cost of goods or materials:						
Stock 1.1.19-8	2,000		1,500		3,000	
Add Purchases	11,000		3,000		15,000	
	13,000		4,500		18,000	
Less Stock 31.12.19-8	3,000		2,500		4,000	
	10,000		2,000		14,000	
Wages	2,800	12,800	5,000	7,000	6,000	20,000
Surpluses c/d		5,200		2,000		7,000

All Departments

		£
Surpluses b/d:		
Jewellery	5,200	
Hairdressing	2,000	
Clothing	7,000	14,200
Less:		
Rent and rates	3,500	
Administration expenses	4,800	
Air conditioning and lighting	2,000	
General expenses	1,200	11,500
Net Profit		2,700

None the less, frustrating though it may be, in examinations students must answer the questions as set, and not give their own interpretations of what the question should be. Therefore if an examiner gives details of the methods of apportionment of expenses, then he is really looking for an answer in the same style as Exhibit 36.1.

The Balance Sheet

The Balance Sheet does not usually show assets and liabilities split between different departments.

Inter-departmental Transfers

Purchases made for one department may be subsequently sold in another department. In such a case the items should be deducted from the figure for Purchases of the original purchasing department, and added to the figure for Purchases for the subsequent selling department.

Exercises

MC96 Departmental accounts
(A) Have to be drawn up in a firm with departments
(B) Tell us which departments should be shut down
(C) Give us information to highlight each department's progress.

MC97 The best method of departmental accounts is
(A) To allocate expenses in proportion to sales
(B) To charge against each department its controllable costs
(C) To charge all expenses between the departments.

36.1. From the following you are to draw up the Trading Account for Charnley's Department Store from the following for the year ended 31 December 19-8.

Stocks:	1.1.19-8	31.12.19-8
	£	£
Electrical Department	6,080	7,920
Furniture Department	17,298	16,150
Leisure Goods Department	14,370	22,395

Sales for the year:	£
Electrical Department	29,840
Furniture Department	73,060
Leisure Goods Department	39,581

Purchases for the year:	
Electrical Department	18,195
Furniture Department	54,632
Leisure Goods Department	27,388

36.2. J. Spratt is the producer of a shop selling books, periodicals, newspapers and children's games and toys. For the purposes of his accounts he wishes the business to be divided into two departments:

Department A   Books, periodicals and newspapers.
Department B   Games, toys and fancy goods.

The following balances have been extracted from his nominal ledger at 31 March 19-6:

	Dr	Cr
	£	£
Sales Department A		15,000
Sales Department B		10,000
Stocks Department A, 1 April 19-5	250	
Stocks Department B, 1 April 19-5	200	
Purchases Department A	11,800	
Purchases Department B	8,200	
Wages of sales assistants Department A	1,000	
Wages of sales assistants Department B	750	
Newspapers delivery wages	150	
General office salaries	750	
Rates	130	
Fire insurance – buildings	50	
Lighting and air conditioning	120	
Repairs to premises	25	
Internal telephone	25	
Cleaning	30	
Accountancy and audit charges	120	
General office expenses	60	

Stocks at 31 March 19-6 were valued at:
Department A   £300
Department B   £150

The proportion of the total floor area occupied by each department was:

Department A   One-fifth
Department B   Four-fifths

Prepare J. Spratt's Trading and Profit and Loss Account for the year ended 31 March 19-6, apportioning the overhead expenses, where necessary, to show the Department profit or loss. The apportionment should be made by using the methods as shown:

Area − Rates, Fire Insurance, Lighting and Air Conditioning, Repairs, Telephone, Cleaning; Turnover − General Office Salaries, Accountancy, General Office Expenses.

36.3A. From the following list of balances you are required to prepare a departmental trading and profit and loss account in columnar form for the year ended 31 March 19-0, in respect of the business carried on under the name of Ivor's Superstores:

		£	£
Rent and rates			4,200
Delivery expenses			2,400
Commission			3,840
Insurance			900
Purchases:	Dept. A	52,800	
	B	43,600	
	C	34,800	
			131,200
Discounts received			1,968
Salaries and wages			31,500
Advertising			1,944
Sales:	Dept. A	80,000	
	B	64,000	
	C	48,000	
			192,000
Depreciation			2,940
Opening Stock:	Dept. A	14,600	
	B	11,240	
	C	9,120	
			34,960
Administration and general expenses			7,890
Closing stock:	Dept. A	12,400	
	B	8,654	
	C	9,746	
			30,800

Except as follows, expenses are to be apportioned equally between the departments.

Delivery expenses − proportionate to sales.
Commission − two per cent of sales.
Salaries and wages; Insurance − in the proportion of 6:5:4.
Discounts received − 1.5 per cent of purchases.

37

Columnar Day Books

Purchases Analysis Books

Provided firms finish up with the items needed for display in their final accounts, the actual manner in which they do it is completely up to them. Some firms use one book to record all items got on credit. These consist not only of the Purchases, but also of items such as Motor Expenses, Stationery, Fixed Assets, Carriage Inwards and so on. The idea is that all invoices for items which will not be paid for on the day that the item is received will be entered in this book. However, all of the various types of items are not simply lumped together, as the firm needs to know how much of the items were for Purchases, how much for Stationery, how much for Motor Expenses, etc., so that the relevant expense accounts can have the correct amount of expenses entered in them. This is achieved by having a set of analysis columns in the book, all of the items are entered in a Total Column, but then they are analysed as between the different sorts of expenses, etc.

Exhibit 37.1 shows such a Purchases Analysis book drawn up for a month from the following list of items got on credit:

19-5		£
May	1 Bought goods from D. Watson Ltd on credit	296
,,	3 Bought goods on credit from W. Donachie & Son	76
,,	5 Motor van repaired, received invoice from Barnes Motors Ltd	112
,,	6 Bought stationery from J. Corrigan	65
,,	8 Bought goods on credit from C. Bell Ltd	212
,,	10 Motor lorry serviced, received invoice from Barnes Motors Ltd	39
,,	13 Bought stationery on credit from A. Hartford & Co	35
,,	16 Bought goods on credit from M. Doyle Ltd	243
,,	20 Received invoice for carriage inwards on goods from G. Owen	58
,,	21 Bought goods on credit from B. Kidd & Son	135
,,	24 Bought goods on credit from K. Clements	122
,,	24 Received invoice for carriage inwards from Channon Haulage	37
,,	26 Bought goods on credit from C. Bell Ltd	111
,,	28 Bought stationery on credit from A. Hartford & Co.	49
,,	29 Bought goods on credit from B. Kidd & Son	249
,,	31 Received invoice for petrol for the month, to be paid for in June, from Barnes Motors Ltd	280

Exhibit 37.1

Purchases Analysis Book

Date	Name of Firm	PL Folio	Total	Purchases	Stationery	Motor Expenses	Carriage Inwards
19-5			£	£	£	£	£
May 1	D. Watson Ltd	129	296	296			
,, 3	W. Donachie & Son	27	76	76			
,, 5	Barnes Motors Ltd	55	112			112	
,, 6	J. Corrigan & Co	88	65		65		
,, 8	C. Bell Ltd	99	212	212			
,, 10	Barnes Motors Ltd	55	39			39	
,, 13	A. Hartford & Co	298	35		35		
,, 16	M. Doyle Ltd	187	243	243			
,, 20	G. Owen	222	58				58
,, 21	B. Kidd & Son	188	135	135			
,, 24	K. Clements	211	122	122			
,, 24	Channon Haulage	305	37				37
,, 26	C. Bell Ltd	99	111	111			
,, 28	A. Hartford & Co	298	49		49		
,, 29	B. Kidd & Son	188	249	249			
,, 31	Barnes Motors Ltd	55	280			280	
			2,119	1,444	149	431	95
				GL 77	GL 97	GL 156	GL 198

Exhibit 37.1 shows that the figure for each item is entered in the Total column, and is then also entered in the column for the particular type of expense. At the end of the month the arithmetical accuracy of the additions can be checked by comparing the total of the Total column with the sum of totals of all of the other columns. These two grand totals figures should equal each other. In this case 1,444 + 149 + 431 + 95 = 2,119. The total column will also be useful for Control Accounts; examined in Chapter 31.

It can be seen that the total of Purchases for the month of May was £1,444 and therefore this can be debited to the Purchases Account in the General Ledger; similarly the total of Stationery bought on credit in the month can be debited to the Stationery Account in the General Ledger and so on. The folio number of the page to which the relevant total has been debited is shown immediately under the total figure for each column, e.g. under the column for Purchases is GL 77, meaning that the item has been entered in the General Ledger page 77. The entries can now be shown:

General Ledger

Purchases Account Page 77

	£
19-5	
May 31 Purchases Analysis 105	1,444

Stationery Page 97

	£
19-5	
May 31 Purchases Analysis 105	149

Motor Expenses		Page 156

19-5	£	
May 31 Purchases Analysis		
105	431	

Carriage Inwards		Page 198

19-5	£	
May 31 Purchase Analysis		
105	95	

The individual accounts of the creditors, whether they be for goods or for expenses such as Stationery or Motor Expenses, can be kept together in a single Purchases Ledger. There is no need for the Purchases Ledger simply to have accounts only for creditors for Purchases. Perhaps there is a slight misuse of the name Purchases Ledger where this happens, but it is common practice amongst a lot of firms. Many firms will give it the more correct title of Bought Ledger.

To carry through the double entry involved with Exhibit 37.3 the Purchases Ledger is now shown.

Purchases Ledger

W. Donachie & Son			Page 27

	19-5		£
	May 3 Purchases	PB 105	76

Barnes Motors Ltd			Page 55

	19-5		£
	May 5 Purchases	PB 105	112
	,, 10 ,,	PB 105	39
	,, 31 ,,	PB 105	280

J. Corrigan & Co.			Page 88

	19-5		£
	May 6 Purchases	PB 105	65

C. Bell Ltd			Page 99

	19-5		£
	May 8 Purchases	PB 105	212
	,, 26 ,,	PB 105	111

D. Watson Ltd			Page 129

	19-5		£
	May 1 Purchases	PB 105	296

M. Doyle Ltd			Page 187
19-5			£
May 16 Purchases		PB 105	243

B. Kidd & Son			Page 188
19-5			£
May 21 Purchases		PB 105	135
,, 29 ,,		PB 105	249

K. Clements			Page 211
19-5			£
May 24 Purchases		PB 105	122

G. Owen			Page 222
19-5			£
May 20 Purchases		PB 105	58

A. Hartford & Co			Page 298
19-5			£
May 13 Purchases		PB 105	35
,, 28 ,,		PB 105	49

Channon Haulage			Page 305
19-5			£
May 24 Purchases		PB 105	37

The reader has just been shown how to draw up Purchases Analysis Books. The basic idea of having a total column, and analysing the items under various headings, can be carried one stage further. This could be the case where it was desired to ascertain the profits of a firm on a departmental basis.

In such a case the Purchases Analysis Books already described could have additional columns so that the purchase of goods for each department could be easily ascertained. Taking the Purchases Analysis Book per Exhibit 37.1, assume that the firm had three departments, Sports Department, Household Department and Electrical Department. Instead of one column for Purchases there could be three columns, each one headed with the title of a Department. When the invoices for purchases were being entered in the enlarged Purchases Analysis Book, the amount of each invoice could be split as between each department, and the relevant figures entered in each column. The total figure of all the three columns would represent the total for Purchases, but it would also be known how much of the Purchases were for each department. This would help when the final accounts were being drafted in a departmental fashion. The Purchases

Analysis Book per Exhibit 37.1 might appear instead as follows in Exhibit 37.2

Exhibit 37.4

Date 19-5		Name of Firm	Pl. Folio	Total	Sports Dept.	House-hold Dept.	Elec-trical Dept.	Station-ery	Motor Exps.	Carriage Inwards
		Purchases Analysis Book								**Page 105**
				£	£	£	£	£	£	£
May	1	D. Watson Ltd	129	296	80	216				
,,	3	W. Donachie & Son	27	76	76					
,,	5	Barnes Motors Ltd	55	112					112	
,,	6	J. Corrigan & Co	88	65				65		
,,	8	C. Bell Ltd	99	212	92		120			
,,	10	Barnes Motors Ltd	55	39					39	
,,	13	A. Hartford & Co	298	35				35		
,,	16	M. Doyle Ltd	187	243			243			
,,	20	G. Owen	222	58						58
,,	21	B. Kidd & Son	188	135	135					
,,	24	K. Clements	211	122	70		52			
,,	24	Channon Haulage	305	37						37
,,	26	C. Bell Ltd	99	111		111				
,,	28	A. Hartford & Co	298	49				49		
,,	29	B. Kidd & Son	188	249	60	103	86			
,,	31	Barnes Motors Ltd	55	280					280	
				2,119	513	430	501	149	431	95
					GL 77	GL 77	GL 77	GL 97	GL 156	GL 198

The Purchases Account in the General Ledger could also have three columns, so that the purchases for each department could be entered in separate columns. Then, when the Trading Account is drawn up the respective totals of each department could be transferred to it.

Of course, a Purchases Day Book could be kept, strictly for Purchases only, without the other expenses, such as Stationery, Motor Expenses and Carriage Inwards. In this case there would simply be the total column with an analysis column for each separate department's purchase.

With Purchases, the use of an analysis book with columns for other expenses is very useful. When looking at Sales, however, the need to split Sales between departments is not usually accompanied by the need to show analysis columns for other items of income. Involved in the expenditure of a firm are many items of expense besides Purchases. With income, the main part of income is represented by the Sales. The amount of transactions in such items as the selling of a fixed asset are relatively few. The Sales Analysis Book, or Columnar Sales Book as it might be called, therefore usually consists of the sales of goods only.

A columnar Sales Book for the same firm as in Exhibit 37.2 might appear as in Exhibit 37.3.

Exhibit 37.3

Columnar Sales Day Book

Date	Name of Firm	SL Folio	Total	Sports Dept.	Household Dept.	Electrical Dept.
19-5		£	£	£	£	£
May 1	N. Coward Ltd	87	190		190	
,, 5	L. Olivier	76	200	200		
,, 8	R. Colman & Co	157	307	102		205
,, 16	Aubrey Smith Ltd	209	480			480
,, 27	H. Marshall	123	222	110	45	67
,, 31	W. Pratt	66	1,800		800	1,000
			3,199	412	1,035	1,752
				GL 88	GL 88	GL 88

The Sales Account, and the Purchases Account, in the General Ledger could be in columnar form. From Exhibits 37.4 and 37.5 the Purchases and Sales Accounts would appear as:

General Ledger

Sales   page 88

19-5		Sports Dept. £	Household Dept. £	Electrical Dept. £
May 31	Credit Sales for the month	412	1,035	1,752

page 77   Purchases

19-5		Sports Dept. £	Household Dept. £	Electrical Dept. £
May 31	Credit Purchases for the month	513	430	501

The Purchases and Sales Accounts would then accumulate the figures for these items, so that when the final accounts were being drawn up the total figures for each department could be transferred to the Trading Account. There is, of course, nothing to stop a firm having one account for Purchases (Sports Dept.), another for Purchases (Household Dept.) and so on. The Stock Account could be kept in a columnar fashion as well, to aid the transfer of stock values to the respective departmental columns in the Trading Account.

The personal accounts in the Sales and Purchases Ledgers would not be in columnar form. As an instance of this, the personal account of W. Pratt in the Sales ledger would simply be debited with £1,800 in respect of the goods sold to him, there being no need to show the analysis between Household and Electrical Departments in his account. If the firm wanted to have columnar personal accounts then there is nothing to stop them keeping them, but this would not normally be the case.

Sales Analysis Books and VAT

All that would be needed would be an extra column for VAT. In the example that follows the debtors would be charged up with the gross amounts, whilst the VAT £184 would be credited to the VAT Account, and the Sales figures of £1,040, £410 and £390 credited to the Sales Account.

Columnar Sales Day Book

Date	Name of Firm	SL Folio	Total	VAT	Furniture Dept.	Hardware Dept.	General Dept.
19-4			£	£	£	£	£
May 1 H. Smedley		133	220	20	200		
,, 6 T. Sarson		297	528	48	210	100	170
,, 16 H. Hartley Ltd		444	286	26		110	150
,, 31 H. Walls		399	990	90	630	200	70
			2,024	184	1,040	410	390
				GL 65	GL 177	GL 177	GL 177

Books as Collection Points

We can see that the various Sales and Purchases Journals, and the ones for returns, are simply collection points for the data to be entered in the accounts of the double-entry system. There is nothing by law that says that, for instance, a Sales Journal has to be written up. What we could do is to look at the Sales Invoices and enter the debits in the customers' personal accounts from them. Then we could keep all the Sales Invoices together in a file. At the end of the month we could use an adding machine to add up the amounts of the Sales Invoices, and then enter that total to the credit of the Sales Account int he General Ledger.

That means that we would have done without the Sales Journal. As the debits in the customers' accounts are made, not by looking at the Sales Journal, but by looking at the Sales Invoices (we could say that these are 'slips' or paper), the system would be known as a 'slip' system. Such a system could lead to more errors being made and not being detected. It could also mean that book-keepers could more easily commit fraud as it would be more difficult for proprietors to see what was going on. The 'slip' system could also be used for Purchases and for Returns.

Exercises

37.1. C. Taylor, a wholesale dealer in electrical goods, has three departments: (a) Hi Fi, (b) TV, and (c) Sundries. The following is a summary of Taylor's Sales Invoices during the period 1 to 7 February 19-7:

	Customer	Invoice No.	Depart- ment	List price less trade discount	VAT	Total invoice price
				£	£	£
Feb 1	S. Markham	586	TV	2,600	260	2,860
2	F. Clarke	587	Hi Fi	1,800	180	1,980
3	C. Willis	588	TV	1,600	160	1,760
5	C. Mayall	589	Sundries	320	Nil	320
7	F. Clarke	590	TV	900	90	990
	S. Markham	591	Hi Fi	3,400	340	3,740

(a) Record the above transactions in a columnar book of original entry and post to the General Ledger in columnar form.

(b) Write up the Personal Accounts in the appropriate ledger.

N.B. – Do NOT balance off any of your ledger accounts.

*N.B. VAT was 10% rate

37.2. Enter up a Purchases Analysis Book with columns for the various expenses for M. Barber for the month from the following information on credit items.

19-6		£
July	1 Bought goods from L. Ogden	220
,,	3 Bought goods from E. Evans	390
,,	4 Received electricity bill (lighting & heating from North Electricity Board)	88
,,	5 Bought goods from H. Noone	110
,,	6 Motor lorry repaired, received bill from Kirk Motors	136
,,	8 Bought stationery from Avon Enterprises	77
,,	10 Motor van serviced, bill from Kirk Motors	55
,,	12 Gas bill received from North Gas Board (lighting & heating)	134
,,	15 Bought goods from A. Dodds	200
,,	17 Bought light bulbs (lighting & heating) from O. Aspinall	24
,,	18 Goods bought from J. Kelly	310
,,	19 Invoice for carriage inwards from D. Adams	85
,,	21 Bought stationery from J. Moore	60
,,	23 Goods bought from H. Noone	116
,,	27 Received invoice for carriage inwards from D. Flynn	62
,,	31 Invoice for motor spares supplied during the month received from Kirk Motors	185

37.3. Enter up the relevant accounts in the Purchases and General Ledgers from the Purchases Analysis Book you have completed for question 37.2.

38

Partnership Accounts: An Introduction

The final accounts so far described have, with the exception of income and expenditure accounts, been concerned with businesses each owned by one person. There must obviously come a time when it is desirable for more than one person to participate in the ownership of the business. It may be due to the fact that the amount of capital required cannot be provided by one person, or else that the experience and ability required to run the business cannot be found in any one person alone. Alternatively, many people just prefer to share the cares of ownership rather than bear all the burden themselves. Very often too there is a family relationship between the owners.

The form of business organization necessary to provide for more than one owner of a business formed with a view of profit is either that of a limited company or of a partnership. This chapter deals with partnerships, the governing act being the Partnership Act 1890. A partnership may be defined as an association of from two to twenty persons (except that there is no maximum limit for firms of accountants, solicitors, Stock Exchange members or other professional bodies which receive the approval of the Board of Trade for this purpose) carrying on business in common with a view of profit. A limited company would have to be formed if it was desired to have more than twenty owners.

With the exception of one special type of partner, known as a limited partner, each partner is liable to the full extent of his personal possessions for the whole of the debts of the partnership firm should the firm be unable to meet them. Barring limited partners, each partner would have to pay his share of any such deficiency. A limited partner is one who is registered under the provisions of the Limited Partnership Act 1907, and whose liability is limited to the amount of capital invested by him; he can lose that but his personal possessions cannot be taken to pay any debts of the firm. A limited partner may not however take part in the management of the partnership business. There must be at least one general partner in a limited partnership.

Persons can enter into partnership with one another without any form of written agreement. It is, however, wiser to have an agreement drawn up by a lawyer, as this will tend to lead to fewer possibilities of misunderstandings and disagreements between partners. Such a partnership deed or articles of partnership can contain as much, or as little, as the partners desire. It does not cover every eventuality. The usual accounting requirements covered can be listed:

1. The capital to be contributed by each partner.

2. The ratio in which profits (or losses) are to be shared.

3. The rate of interest, if any, to be given on capital before the profits are shared.

4. The rate of interest, if any, to be charged on partners' drawings.

5. Salaries to be paid to partners.

Some comments on the above are necessary.

(a) Ratio in Which Profits are to be Shared

It is often thought by students that profits should be shared in the same ratio as that in which capital is contributed. For example, suppose the capitals were Allen £2,000 and Beet £1,000, many people would share the profits in the rato of two-thirds to one-third, even though the work to be done by each partner is similar. A look at the division of the first few years' profits on such a basis would be:

Years	1	2	3	4	5	Total
	£	£	£	£	£	£
Net profits	1,800	2,400	3,000	3,000	3,600	
Shared:						
Allen ⅔	1,200	1,600	2,000	2,000	2,400	9,200
Beet ⅓	600	800	1,000	1,000	1,200	4,600

It can now be seen that Allen would receive £9,200, or £4,600 more than Beet. Equitably the difference between the two shares of profit in this case, as the duties of the partners are the same, should be adequate to compensate Allen for putting extra capital into the firm. It is obvious that £4,600 extra profits is far more than adequate for this purpose.

Consider too the position of capital ratio sharing of profits if one partner put in £99 and the other put in £1 as capital.

To overcome the difficulty of compensating for the investment of extra capital, the concept of interest on capital was devised.

(b) Interest on Capital

If the work to be done by each partner is of equal value but the capital contributed is unequal, it is equitable to grant interest on the partners' capitals. This interest is treated as a deduction prior to the calculation of profits and their distribution according to the profit-sharing ratio.

The rate of interest is a matter for agreement between the partners, but it should theoretically equal the return which they would have received if they had invested the capital elsewhere.

Taking Allen and Beet's firm again, but sharing the profits equally after charging 5 per cent per annum interest on capital, the division of profits would become:

Years	1	2	3	4	5	Total
	£	£	£	£	£	£
Net Profit	1,800	2,400	3,000	3,000	3,600	
Interest on Capitals						
Allen	100	100	100	100	100 =	500
Beet	50	50	50	50	50 =	250
Remainder shared:						
Allen ½	825	1,125	1,425	1,425	1,725 =	6,525
Beet ½	825	1,125	1,425	1,425	1,725 =	6,525

Summary	Allen	Beet
	£	£
Interest on Capital	500	250
Balance of Profits	6,525	6,525
	7,025	6,775

Allen has thus received £250 more than Beet this being adequate return (in the partners' estimation) for having invested an extra £1,000 in the firm for five years.

(c) Interest on Drawings

It is obviously in the best interests of the firm if cash is withdrawn from the firm by the partners in accordance with the two basic principles of: (1), as little as possible, and (2), as late as possible. The more cash that is left in the firm the more expansion can be financed, the greater the economies of having ample cash to take advantage of bargains and of not missing cash discounts because cash is not available and so on.

To deter the partners from taking out cash unnecessarily the concept can be used of charging the partners interest on each withdrawal, calculated from the date of withdrawal to the end of the financial year. The amount charged to them helps to swell the profits divisible between the partners.

The rate of interest should be sufficient to achieve this end without being unduly penal.

Suppose that Allen and Beet have decided to charge interest on drawings at 5 per cent per annum, and that their year end was 31 December. The following drawings are made:

Allen

Drawings		Interest	
			£
1 January	£100	£100 × 5% × 12 months =	5
1 March	£240	£240 × 5% × 10 months =	10
1 May	£120	£120 × 5% × 8 months =	4
1 July	£240	£240 × 5% × 6 months =	6
1 October	£80	£80 × 5% × 3 months =	1
		Interest charged to Allen =	26

Beet

Drawings		Interest	
			£
1 January	£60	£60 × 5% × 12 months =	3
1 August	£480	£480 × 5% × 5 months =	10
1 December	£240	£240 × 5% × 1 month =	1
		Interest charged to Beet =	14

(d) Salaries

A partner may have some particular responsibility or extra task that the others have not got. It may in fact be of a temporary nature. To compensate him for this, it is best not to disturb the profit- and loss-sharing ratio. It is better to let him have a salary sufficient to compensate him for the extra tasks performed. This salary is deductible before arriving at the balance of profits to be shared in the profit-sharing ratio. A change in the profit- and loss-sharing ratio to compensate him would have meant bearing a larger share of any loss, hardly a fair means of compensation; or if there was only a small profit the extra amount received by him would be insufficient compensation, while if there was a large profit he may well be more than adequately compensated.

An Example of the Distribution of Profits

Taylor and Clarke are in partnership sharing profits and losses in the ratio of Taylor 3/5ths, Clarke 2/5ths. They are entitled to 5 per cent per annum interest on capitals, Taylor having £2,000 capital and Clarke £6,000. Clarke is to have a salary of £500. They charge interest on drawings, Taylor being charged £50 and Clarke £100. The net profit, before any distributions to the partners, amounted to £5,000 for the year ended 31 December 19-7.

	£	£	£
Net Profit			5,000
Add Charged for interest on drawings:			
Taylor		50	
Clarke		100	
			150
			5,150
Less Salary: Clarke		500	
Interest on Capital:			
Taylor	100		
Clarke	300		
		400	
			900
			4,250

	£	£
Balance of profits		
Shared:		
Taylor 3/5ths	2,550	
Clarke 2/5ths	1,700	
		4,250

The £5,000 net profits have therefore been shared:

	Taylor £	Clarke £
Balance of profits	2,550	1,700
Interest on Capital	100	300
Salary	–	500
	2,650	2,500
Less Interest on drawings	50	100
	2,600	2,400

£5,000

The Final Accounts

If the sales, stock and expenses of a partnership were exactly the same as that of a sole trader then the trading and profit and loss account would be identical with that as prepared for the sole trader. However, a partnership would have an extra section shown under the profit and loss account. This section is called the profit and loss appropriation account, and it is in this account that the distribution of profits is shown. The heading to the trading and profit and loss account does not include the words 'appropriation account'. It is purely an accounting custom not to include it in the heading.

The trading and profit and loss account of Taylor and Clarke from the details given would appear:

Taylor and Clarke

Trading and Profit and Loss Account for the year ended 31 December 19-7

Trading Account – same as for sole trader

£

Profit and Loss Account – same as for sole trader

	£	£	£
Net Profit			5,000
Interest on drawings:			
Taylor		50	
Clarke		100	150
Less:			5,150
Interest on capitals			
Taylor	100		
Clarke	300	400	
Salary: Clarke		500	900
			4,250
Balance of profits shared:			
Taylor ³⁄₅ ths		2,550	
Clarke ²⁄₅ ths		1,700	4,250

Fixed and Fluctuating Capital Accounts

There is a choice open in partnership accounts of:

(a) Fixed Capital Accounts Plus Current Accounts

The capital account for each partner remains year by year at the figure of capital put into the firm by the partners. The profits, interest on capital and the salaries to which the partner may be entitled are then credited to a separate current account for the partner, and the drawings and the interests on drawings are debited to it. The balance of the current account at the end of each financial year will then represent the amount of undrawn (or withdrawn) profits. A credit balance will be undrawn profits, while a debit balance will be drawings in excess of the profits to which the partner was entitled.

For Taylor and Clarke, capital and current accounts, assuming drawings of £2,000 each, will appear:

Taylor – Capital

			£
	Jan	1 Balance b/d	2,000

Clarke – Capital

			£
	Jan	1 Balance b/d	6,000

Taylor – Current Account

		£			£
Dec 31	Cash: Drawings	2,000	Dec 31	Profit and Loss Appropriation Account:	
,,	Profit and Loss Appropriation: Interest on Drawings	50		Interest on Capital	100
				Share of Profits	2,550
,, 31	Balance c/d	600			
		2,650			2,650
					£
	Jan	1 Balance b/d			600

Clarke – Current Account

		£			£
Dec 31	Cash: Drawings	2,000	Dec 31	Profit and Loss Appropriation Account:	
,, 31	Profit and Loss Appropriation: Interest on Drawings	100		Interest on Capital	300
				Share of Profits	1,700
,, 31	Balance c/d	400		Salary	500
		2,500			2,500
					£
	Jan	1 Balance b/d			400

Notice that the salary of Clarke was not paid to him, it was merely credited to his account. If in fact it was paid in addition to his drawings, the £500 cash paid would have been debited to the current account changing the £400 credit balance into a £100 debit balance.

(b) Fluctuating Capital Accounts

The distribution of profits would be credited to the capital account, and the drawings and interest on drawings debited. Therefore the balance on the capital account will change each year, i.e. it will fluctuate.

If Fluctuating Capital Accounts had been kept for Taylor and Clarke they would have appeared:

Taylor – Capital

	£			£
Dec 31 Cash: Drawings	2,000	Jan 1 Balance b/d		2,000
,, 31 Profit and Loss Appropriation Account:		Dec 31 Profit and Loss Appropriation Account:		
Interest on Drawings	50	Interest on Capital		100
,, 31 Balance c/d	2,600	Share of Profits		2,550
	4,650			4,650
		Jan 1 Balance b/d		2,600

Clarke – Capital

	£			£
Dec 31 Cash: Drawings	2,000	Jan 1 Balance b/d		6,000
,, 31 Profit and Loss Appropriation Account:		Dec 31 Profit and Loss Appropriation Account:		
Interest on Drawings	100	Interest on Capital		300
,, 31 Balance c/d	6,400	Salary		500
		Share of Profit		1,700
	8,500			8,500
		Jan 1 Balance b/d		6,400

Fixed Capital Accounts Preferred

The keeping of fixed capital accounts plus Current Accounts is considered preferable to fluctuating capital accounts. When partners are taking out greater amounts than the share of the profits that they are entitled to, this is shown up by a debit balance on the current account and so acts as a warning.

Where No Partnership Agreement Exists

Where no agreement exists, express or implied, Section 24 of the Partnership Act 1890 governs the situation. The accounting contents of this section states:

1. Profits and losses are to be shared equally.

2. There is to be no interest allowed on capital.

3. No interest is to be charged on drawings.

4. Salaries are not allowed.

5. If a partner puts a sum of money into a firm in excess of the capital he has agreed to subscribe, he is entitled to interest at the rate of 5 per cent per annum on such an advance.

This section applies where there is no agreement. There may be an agreement not by a partnership deed but in a letter, or it may be implied by conduct, for instance when a partner signs a balance sheet which shows profits shared in some other ratio than equally.

In some cases of disagreement as to whether agreement existed or not only the courts would be competent to decide.

The Balance Sheet

The capital part side of the balance sheet will appear:

Balance Sheet as at 31 December 19-7

		£	£
Capitals:	Taylor	2,000	
	Clarke	6,000	8,000

Current Accounts	Taylor	Clarke
	£	£
Interest on Capital	100	300
Share of profits	2,550	1,700
Salary	–	500
	2,650	2,500
Less Drawings	2,000	2,000
Interest on drawings	50	100
	600	400

1,000

If one of the current accounts had finished in debit, for instance if the current account of Clarke had finished up as £400 debit, the abbreviation Dr would appear and the balances would appear net in the totals column:

	Taylor	Clarke	
	£	£	£
Closing balance	600	400 *Dr*	200

If the net figure turned out to be a debit figure then this would be deducted from the total of the capital accounts.

Exercises

MC98 Does a partnership have to pay Interest on the partners' capitals?
(A) Yes
(B) Never
(C) Depends on agreement between partners
(D) Only if interest is charged on drawings.

MC99 Where there is no partnership agreement then profits and losses
(A) Must be shared in same proportion as capitals
(B) Must be shared equally
(C) Must be shared equally after adjusting for interest on capital
(D) None of these.

MC100 If it is required to maintain fixed capitals then the partners' shares of profits must be
(A) Debited to Capital Accounts
(B) Credited to Capital Accounts
(C) Debited to partners' Current Accounts
(D) Credited to partners' Current Accounts

38.1. Stephens, Owen and Jones are partners. They share profits and losses in the ratios of ⅖, ⅖ and ⅕ respectively.

For the year ended 31 December 19-6 their capital accounts remained fixed at the following amounts:

	£
Stephens	6,000
Owen	4,000
Jones	2,000

They have agreed to give each other 10 per cent interest per annum on their capital accounts.

In addition to the above, partnership salaries of £3,000 for Owen and £1,000 for Jones are to be charged.

The net profit of the partnership, before taking any of the above into account was £25,200.

You are required to draw up the appropriation account of the partnership for the year ended 31 December 19-6.

38.2. Draw up a profit and loss appropriation account for the year ended 31 December 19-7 and balance sheet extracts at that date, from the following:
(i) Net Profits £30,350.
(ii) Interest to be charged on capitals: Williams £2,000; Powell £1,500; Howe £900.
(iii) Interest to be charged on drawings: Williams £240; Powell £180; Howe £130.
(iv) Salaries to be credited: Powell £2,000; Howe £3,500.
(v) Profits to be shared: Williams 50%; Powell 30%; Howe 20%.
(vi) Current Accounts: Williams £1,860; Powell £946; Howe £717.
(vii) Capital Accounts: Williams £40,000; Powell £30,000; Howe £18,000.
(viii) Drawings: Williams £9,200; Powell £7,100; Howe £6,900.

38.3A. Dent, Bishop and White are in partnership. They share profits and losses in the ratio 3:2:1 respectively. Interest is charged on drawings at the rate of 10 per cent per annum and credited at the same rate in respect of the balances on the partners' capital accounts.

Bishop is to be credited with a salary of £2,000 per annum.

In the year to 31 December 19-4 the net profit of the firm was £50,400. The partners drawings of Dent £8,000; Bishop £7,200; White £4,800 were taken in two equal instalments by the partners on 1 April 19-4 and 1 October 19-4.

The balances of the partner's accounts at 31 December 19-3 were as follows:

(all credit balances)	Capital Accounts £	Current Accounts £
Dent	30,000	750
Bishop	28,000	1,340
White	16,000	220

You are required to:
(i) Prepare the firm's profit and loss appropriation account for the year ended 31 December 19-4,
(ii) Show how the partners' capital and current accounts are shown in the balance sheet as at 31 December 19-4.

38.4. Mendez and Marshall are in partnership sharing profits and losses equally. The following is their trial balance as at 30 June 19-6:

	Dr. £	Cr. £
Buildings (cost £75,000)	50,000	
Fixtures at cost	11,000	
Provision for Depreciation: Fixtures		3,300
Debtors	16,243	
Creditors		11,150
Cash at Bank	677	
Stock at 30 June 19-5	41,979	
Sales		123,650
Purchases	85,416	
Carriage Outwards	1,288	
Discounts Allowed	115	
Loan Interest: King	4,000	
Office Expenses	2,416	
Salaries and Wages	18,917	
Bad Debts	503	
Provision for Bad Debts		400
Loan from J. King		40,000
Capitals: Mendez		35,000
Marshall		29,500
Current Accounts: Mendez		1,306
Marshall		298
Drawings: Mendez	6,400	
Marshall	5,650	
	244,604	244,604

Prepare a trading and profit and loss appropriation account for the year ended 30 June 19-6, and a balance sheet as at that date.

(i) Stock, 30 June 19-6 £56,340.
(ii) Expenses to be accrued: Office Expenses £96; Wages £200.
(iii) Depreciate fixtures 10 per cent on reducing balance basis, buildings £1,000.
(iv) Reduce provision for bad debts to £320.
(v) Partnership salary: £800 to Mendez. Not yet entered.
(vi) Interest on drawings: Mendez £180; Marshall £120.
(vii) Interest on capital account balances at 10 per cent.

38.5. You are required to prepare a trading and profit and loss account for the year ended 31 December 19-5, and a balance sheet as at that date from the following:

Trial Balance as at 31 December 19-5

	Dr	Cr
	£	£
Drawings:		
Perkins	1,750	
Hodson	1,429	
Capital:		
Perkins		9,000
Hodson		4,800
Current accounts as at 1 January 19-5:		
Perkins		880
Hodson	120	
Motor vehicles (cost £2,500)	1,870	
Stock – 1 January 19-5	2,395	
Returns inwards and outwards	110	286
Sales		28,797
Purchases	19,463	
Wages and salaries	4,689	
Carriage inwards	216	
Delivery expenses	309	
Rent and rates	485	
Insurances	116	
Debtors and creditors	8,462	1,899
Cash in hand	180	
General expenses	204	
Loan – T. Farthingale		2,000
Discounts allowed and received	392	404
Motor expenses	635	
Cash at bank	5,241	
	48,066	48,066

Notes at 31 December 19-5:

1. Stock £5,623
2. Depreciate motors 10 per cent on reducing balance basis
3. Insurance prepaid £12
4. Rates owing £57

5. Included in salaries is a salary to Hodson for the year £300
6. Allow 5 per cent interest on capitals
7. Charge interest on drawings: Perkins £58; Hodson £39
8. Goods value £75 have been taken by Perkins for his own use, no entry having been in the books
9. Profit shared: Hodson 2/5ths; Perkins 3/5ths (calculations to nearest £)
10. Loan interest owing £140
11. Make a provision for bad debts £320.

38.6A. Oscar and Felix are in partnership. They share profits on the ratio: Oscar 60 per cent; Felix 40 per cent. The following trial balance was extracted as at 31 March 19-6:

	Dr. £	Cr. £
Office Equipment at cost	6,500	
Motor Vehicles at cost	9,200	
Provisions for depreciation at 31.3.19-5:		
Motor Vehicles		3,680
Office Equipment		1,950
Stock 31 March 19-5	24,970	
Debtors and Creditors	20,960	16,275
Cash at Bank	615	
Cash in Hand	140	
Sales		90,370
Purchases	71,630	
Salaries	8,417	
Office Expenses	1,370	
Discounts Allowed	563	
Current Accounts at 31.3.19-5:		
Oscar		1,379
Felix		1,211
Capital Accounts: Oscar		27,000
Felix		12,000
Drawings: Oscar	5,500	
Felix	4,000	
	153,865	153,865

Draw up a set of final accounts for the year ended 31 March 19-6 for the partnership. The following notes are applicable at 31 March 19-6.
(i) Stock 31 March 19-6 £27,340.
(ii) Office Expenses owing £110.
(iii) Provide for depreciation: Motors 20 per cent of cost, Office Equipment 10 per cent of cost.
(iv) Charge Interest on capitals at 10 per cent.
(v) Charge Interest on drawings: Oscar £180; Felix £210.

38.7A. Menzies, Whitlam and Gough share profits and losses in the ratios 5:3:2 respectively. Their trial balance as at 30 September 19-5 was as follows:

	Dr. £	Cr. £
Sales		210,500
Returns Inwards	6,800	
Purchases	137,190	
Carriage Inwards	1,500	
Stock 30 September 19-4	42,850	
Discounts Allowed	110	
Salaries and Wages	18,296	
Bad Debts	1,234	
Provision for Bad Debts 30.9.19-4		800
General Expenses	945	
Rent and Rates	2,565	
Postages	2,450	
Motor Expenses	3,940	
Motor Vans at cost	12,500	
Office Equipment at cost	8,400	
Provisions for Depreciation at 30.9.19-4:		
Motor Vans		4,200
Office Equipment		2,700
Creditors		24,356
Debtors	37,178	
Cash at Bank	666	
Drawings: Menzies	12,610	
Whitlam	8,417	
Gough	6,216	
Current Accounts: Menzies		1,390
Whitlam	153	
Gough		2,074
Capital Accounts: Menzies		30,000
Whitlam		16,000
Gough		12,000
	304,020	304,020

Draw up a set of final accounts for the year ended 30 September 19-5. The following notes are relevant at 30 September 19-5:

(i) Stock 30 September 19-5 £51,060.
(ii) Rates in advance £120; Stock of postage stamps £190.
(iii) Increase provision for bad debts to £870.
(iv) Salaries: Whitlam £1,200; Gough £700. Not yet recorded.
(v) Interest on Drawings: Menzies £170; Whitlam £110; Gough £120.
(vi) Interest on Capitals at 10 per cent.
(vii) Depreciate Motor Vans £2,500, Office Equipment £1,680.

39

Goodwill

When a firm has been in existence for some time, then if the owner(s) wanted to sell the business, they may well be able to obtain more for the business as a going concern than they would if the assets shown on the Balance Sheet were sold separately. To simplify matters, imagine that a man has a small engineering works, of which he was the orginator, and that the business was started by him some twenty years ago. He now wishes to sell the business. If sold separately, the assets on the balance sheet would fetch a total of £40,000, being £12,000 for machinery, £25,000 for premises and the stock £3,000. As a complete going concern a purchaser may be willing to pay a total of £50,000 for it. The extra £10,000 that the purchaser will pay over and above the total saleable values of the identifiable assets is known in accounting as goodwill. This is a technical term used in accounting, it must not be confused with the meaning of goodwill in ordinary language usage.

The reasons why the purchaser would be willing to pay £10,000 for goodwill are not always capable of being identified with precision, nor is it often possible to place any particular value on any of the reasons which have induced him to make this offer. One fact only is obvious, and that is that no rational person would be willing to pay a higher figure for the entire going concern than he would pay for buying the identifiable assets separately, unless the expected rate of return on the purchase money spent was greater in the case of the entire going concern. While it is not possible to list all of the factors which induce purchasers to pay for goodwill, it may be useful to examine some possible motives.

(*a*) The business may have enjoyed some form of monopoly, either nationally or locally. There may not be sufficient trade for two such engineering firms to be carried on profitably. If the purchaser buys this firm then no one may set up in competition with him. On the other hand, if he buys the other assets separately and sets up his own firm, then the original business will still be for sale and the owner may well fix a price that will induce someone to buy it. Many prospective entrants would therefore be prepared to pay an extra amount in the hope of preserving the monopoly position. The monopoly may possibly be due to some form of governmental licence not otherwise easily available.

(b) The purchaser could continue to trade under the same name as that of the original firm. The fact that the firm was well known could mean that new customers would be attracted for this reason alone. The seller would probably introduce the purchaser to his customers. The establishment of a nucleus of customers is something that many new firms would be willing to pay for, as full profits could be earned from the very start of the business instead of waiting until a large enought body of customers is built up. There could be profitable contracts that were capable of being taken over only by the purchaser of the firm.

(c) The value of the labour force, including management skills other than that of the retiring proprietor. The possession of a skilled labour force, including that of management, is an asset that Balance Sheets do not disclose. To recruit and train a suitable labour force is often costly in money and effort, and the purchaser of a going concern would obviously normally be in a position to take over most of the labour force.

(d) The possession of trade marks and patents. These may have cost the original owner little or nothing, not be shown on the Balance Sheet, and could be unsaleable unless the business is sold as a going concern.

(e) The location of the business premises may be more valuable if a particular type of business is carried on rather than if the premises were sold to any other kind of business firm.

(f) The costs of research and development which have brought about cheaper manufacturing methods or a better product may not have been capitalized, but may have been charged as revenue expenditure in the periods when the expenditure was incurred. For any new firm starting up it could well cost a considerable amount of money to achieve the same results.

The amount which someone is prepared to pay for goodwill therefore depends on their view of the future profits which will accrue to the business due to the factors mentioned, or similar assets difficult to identify. The seller of the business will want to show these additional assets to their best advantage, while the buyer will discount those that he feels are inappropriate or over-stressed. The figure actually paid for goodwill will therefore often be a compromise.

The economic state of the country, and whether or not a boom or a recession is in the offing, together with the effects of a credit squeeze or of reflation, plus the relative position of the particular industry, trade or profession, will all affect people's judgements of future profits. In addition the shortage of funds or relatively easy access to finance for such a purchase will, together with the factors already mentioned, lead to marked differences of money paid for goodwill of similar firms at different points in time.

There are also instances where the amount that could be obtained for an entire going concern is less than if all the assets were sold separately. This, contrary to many a person's guess is not 'badwill', as this is just not an accounting term, but would in fact be negative goodwill. The owner would, if he was a rational man, sell all the assets separately, but it does not always hold true. The owner may well have a pride in his work, or a sense of duty to the community, and may elect to sell only to those who would carry on in the same tradition despite the fact that higher offers for the assets had been made. Someone who has to sell his business quickly may also be forced to accept less than he would wish. In accounting it is well to remember that figures themselves only tell part of the story.

Methods of Valuing Goodwill

Custom plays a large part in the valuation of goodwill in many sorts of businesses. Goodwill exists sometimes only because of custom, because if a somewhat more scientific approach was used in certain cases it would be seen that there was no justification for a figure being paid for goodwill. However, justification or not, goodwill exists where the purchaser is willing to pay for it.

The mere calculation of a figure for goodwill does not mean that someone will be willing to pay this amount for it. As with the striking of any bargain there is no certainty until the price is agreed.

A very important factor to take into account in the valuation of goodwill is based on the 'momentum' theory of goodwill. This can be stated to be that the profits accruing to a firm from the possession of the goodwill at a point in time will lose momentum, and will be gradually replaced by profits accruing from new goodwill created later on. Thus the old goodwill fades away or loses momentum, it does not last for ever, and new goodwill is gradually created. Therefore in a business goodwill may always exist, but it will very rarely be either of the same value or composed of the same factors.

Some of the methods used in goodwill valuation can now be looked at. The rule of thumb approach can be seen in particular in methods (i), (ii) and (iii) which follow. However, the accountant's role has often been not necessarily to find any 'true' figure which could be validated in some way, but has instead been to find an 'acceptable' figure, one which the parties to a transaction would accept as the basis for settlement. In particular trades, industries and professions, these methods while not necessarily 'true' have certainly been acceptable as the basis for negotiations.

(i)   In more than one type of retail business it has been the custom to value goodwill at the average weekly sales for the past year multiplied by a given figure. The given figure will, of course, differ as between different types of businesses, and often changes gradually in the same types of businesses in the long term.

(ii) With many professional firms, such as accountants in public practice, it is the custom to value goodwill as being the gross annual fees times a given number. For instance, what is termed a two years' purchase of a firm with gross fees of £6,000 means goodwill = 2 × £6,000 = £12,000.

(iii) The average net annual profit for a specified past number of years multiplied by an agreed number. This is often said to be x years purchase of the net profits.

(iv) The super-profits basis.

(a) The Traditional View

The net profits are taken as not representing a realistic view of the 'true' profits of the firm. For a sole trader, no charge has been made for his services when calculating net profit, yet obviously he is working in the business just as is any other employee. If the net profit is shown as £5,000, can he say that he is better off by £5,000 than he would otherwise have been? The answer must be negative, since if he had not owned a business he could have been earning money from some other employment. Also, if he had not invested his money in the business he could have invested it somewhere else. If these two factors are taken into account, the amount by which he would have been better off is given the name of 'super-profit'.

Exhibit 39.1

Hawks, a chemist, has a shop from which he makes annual net profits of £4,300. The amount of his capital invested in the business was £10,000. If he had invested it elsewhere in something where the element of risk was identical he would have expected a 5 per cent return per annum. If, instead of working for himself, he had in fact taken a post as a chemist he would have earned a salary of £1,800 per annum.

	£	£
Annual net profits		4,300
Less Remuneration for similar work	1,800	
,, Interest on capital invested £10,000 at 5 per cent	500	2,300
Annual Super-profits		2,000

If it is expected that super-profits can be earned for each of the next five years, then the value of the goodwill is the value of receiving £2,000 extra for each of the next five years.

Sometimes the goodwill is calculated as x years purchase of the super-profits. If this were an eight-year purchase of super-profits of £5,000, then the goodwill would be stated to be worth £40,000.

(b) The Discounted Momentum Value Method

The momentum theory of goodwill has already been discussed briefly. The benefits to be gained from goodwill purchased fall as that goodwill gradually ceases to exist, while other benefits are gained from new goodwill created by the new firm. The principle may be further illustrated by reference to the fact that old customers die or may leave the firm, and new ones coming along to replace them are likely to be due to the efforts of the new proprietors. Therefore when buying a business the goodwill should be assessed as follows:

(i)   Estimate the profits that will accrue from the firm if the existing business is taken over.

(ii)   Estimate the profits that would be made if, instead of buying the existing business, identical assets are bought (other than the goodwill) and the firm starts from scratch.

The difference in the profits to be earned will therefore be as a result of the incidence of the goodwill.

Exhibit 39.2

Years	Estimated profits if existing business taken over	Estimated profits if new business set up	Excess profits caused by goodwill taken over
	£	£	£
1	10,000	4,000	6,000
2	11,000	6,000	5,000
3	11,500	8,500	3,000
4	12,000	11,000	1,000
5	12,000	12,000	–
(and later years will show no difference in profits)			
			15,000

Sole Trader's Books

It would not be normal for goodwill to be entered in a sole trader's books unless he had actually bought it. Therefore the very existence of goodwill in the Balance Sheet would result in the assumption that the sole trader had bought the business from someone previously and was not himself the founder of the business.

Partnership Books

The partners may make any specific agreement between themselves concerning goodwill. There is no limit as to the ways that they may devise to value it or to enter it in the books, or to make adjusting entries in the books without opening a Goodwill Account. Whatever they agree will therefore take precedence over anything written in this chapter.

However, failing any agreement to the contrary, it is possible to state that a partner in a firm will own a share in the goodwill in the same ratio which he shares profits. Thus if A take one-quarter of the profits, then he will be the owner of one-quarter of the goodwill. This will hold true whether or not a Goodwill Account is in existence. Should a new partner be introduced who will take a share of one-third of the profits, he will, subject to there being any contrary agreement, be the owner of one-third of the goodwill. It is therefore essential that he should either pay something for goodwill when he enters the firm, or else an amount should be charged to his Capital Account.

This can probably be seen more clearly if a simple example is taken. A and B are in partnership sharing profits one-half each. A new partner, C, is admitted and A, B and C will now take one-third share of the profits, and therefore each will now own one-third of the goodwill. As A and B used to own one-half of the goodwill each they have therefore given part of the asset to C. A few months later the business is sold to a large company and £30,000 is obtained for goodwill. A, B and C will thus receive £10,000 each for their respective shares of the goodwill. If C had not been charged for goodwill, or had paid nothing for it, then A and B would have surrendered part of their ownership of the firm to C and received nothing in return.

Any change in profit sharing will, unless specifically agreed to the contrary, mean that the ownership of the goodwill will also change. As some partners give up their share, or part of their share, of an asset while other partners gain, it is therefore essential that some payment or adjustment be made whenever profit sharing is altered. This will take place whenever any of the following events occur:

1. There is a change in the profit-sharing ratios of existing partners.

2. A new partner is introduced.

3. A partner dies or retires.

In all these cases the whole of the goodwill is not sold. Only in (2) is part of the goodwill sold or charged to an outsider. In (3) the goodwill may be bought by the remaining partners, this is not necessarily the same figure that could be obtained by sale to an outsider. In the case of (2) it is usually assumed that if a new partner is to pay £1,000 to the old partners in satisfaction for a one-quarter share of the goodwill, then the entire goodwill is worth £4,000. The reasoning behind this is that if one-quarter could be sold for £1,000 then the total price would be in the same ratio, i.e. 25 per cent equals £1,000, therefore 100 per cent equals £4,000. This is very often just not true. A relatively higher price may be obtainable from someone who was to be a senior partner than from someone who was to be a junior partner. Thus a one-quarter share of the goodwill might fetch £1,000, but a three-quarters' share of the goodwill might fetch (say) £5,000 because of the factors of prestige and control that a senior partnership would give to the purchaser.

Similarly, with the retirement or death of a partner the amount payable to him or his representatives may not be directly proportional to the total value of goodwill. Circumstances vary widely, but personal relationships and other factors will affect the sum paid.

The question of the value to be placed on goodwill in all of these cases is therefore one of agreement between the partners, and is not necessarily equal to the total saleable value.

Goodwill Accounts and Partnerships

Unlike a sole trader, a partnership may therefore have a Goodwill Account opened in its books even though the goodwill has never been purchased from an outside source. For instance, a Goodwill Account may be opened just because the partners have changed profit-sharing ratios even though they were the partners that were the founders of the firm, and had not therefore ever paid anything to an outsider for goodwill.

With some of the methods used a Goodwill Account is opened, whereas in others adjustments are made without the use of a Goodwill Account. It is not always advantageous to open a Goodwill Account. The mere existence of a Goodwill Account in the Balance Sheet may influence some prospective purchaser of the business, or of part of the business, in a way that was not intended when the Goodwill Account was opened. If a Goodwill Account showed a balance of £10,000 and the partners wanted to sell goodwill for £30,000, the purchaser's decision may be affected. He may have been quite content to pay £30,000 if a Goodwill Account had never existed, but he is now in the position of being asked to pay £30,000 for something which had been valued at £10,000 x years ago. On the other hand, suppose that the Goodwill Account was shown at £10,000 but that the price asked for it was only £4,000. Both of these cases may well put doubts into the mind of the purchaser that would never have existed if a Goodwill Account had never been shown. On the other hand, a lender of money may be happy to see the firm's belief in its goodwill valuation stated as an asset in the Balance Sheet. Business decisions can never be divorced from behavioural patterns. A feeling of 'he gave X £1,000 for it a year ago, why should I give £2,000 for it now?' is very often totally irrational, and would not exist if in fact the buyer never knew that the seller had bought it for that amount.

1. Where there is a change in the Profit-sharing Ratios of Existing Partners

This will normally occur when the effective contributions made by the partners in terms of skill or effort have changed in some way. A partner's contribution may be reduced because of ill-health or old age, or because he is now engaged in some other activity outside the partnership firm. A partner's contribution may have increased because of greater effort or skill compared with when he first joined the firm. The partners will then have to mutually agree to the new profit-sharing ratios. Lack of agreement could mean that the firm would have to be dissolved.

Taking the same basic data, the two methods used whereby (*a*) a Goodwill Account is opened, and (*b*) adjustments are made without the use of a Goodwill Account, can now be illustrated.

Exhibit 39.3

E, F and G have been in business for ten years. They have always shared profits equally. No Goodwill Account has ever existed in the books. On 31 December 19-6 they agree that G will take only a one-fifth share of the profits as from 1 January 19-7, this being due to the fact that he will be devoting less of his time to the business in future. E and F will then each take two-fifths of the profits. The summarized Balance Sheet of the business on 31 December 19-6 appears as follows:

Balance Sheet as at 31 December 19-6

	£		£
Capitals: E	3,000		
F	1,800	Net Assets	7,000
G	2,200		
	7,000		7,000

The partners agree that the goodwill should be valued at £3,000.

(a) Goodwill account opened. A Goodwill Account is opened and the total value of goodwill is debited to it. The credit entries are made in the partner's Capital Accounts, being the total value of goodwill divided between the partners in their old profit-sharing ratio.

The Balance Sheet items before and after the adjustments will appear as:

	Before	After		Before	After
	£	£		£	£
Capitals: E	3,000	4,000	Goodwill	–	3,000
F	1,800	2,800			
G	2,200	3,200	Other Assets	7,000	7,000
	7,000	10,000		7,000	10,000

(b) Goodwill account not opened. The effect of the change of ownership of goodwill may be shown in the following form:

Before		After		Loss or Gain	Action Required
	£		£		
E One-third	1,000	Two-fifths	1,200	Gain £200	Debit E's Capital Account £200
F One-third	1,000	Two-fifths	1,200	Gain £200	Debit F's Capital Account £200
G One-third	1,000	One-fifth	600	Loss £400	Credit G's Capital Account £400
	3,000		3,000		

The column headed 'Action Required' shows that a partner who has gained goodwill because of the change must be charged for it by having his Capital Account debited with the value of the gain. A partner who has lost goodwill must be compensated for it by having his Capital Account credited.

The Balance Sheet items before and after the adjustments will therefore appear as:

	Before	After		Before	After
	£	£		£	£
Capitals: E	3,000	2,800	Net Assets	7,000	7,000
F	1,800	1,600			
G	2,200	2,600			
	7,000	7,000		7,000	7,000

It would appear at first sight that there is some disparity between the use of methods (*a*) and (*b*). Suppose however that very shortly after the above adjustments the business is sold, the time element being so short that there has been no change in the value of goodwill. If the other assets are sold for £7,000 and the goodwill for £3,000, then in method (*a*) the £10,000 would be exactly sufficient to pay the amounts due to the partners according to their Capital Accounts. In the method (*b*) the Capital Accounts total £7,000 and so the cash received from the sale of the other assets would be exactly enough to pay for those amounts due to the partners. In addition the goodwill has been sold for £3,000, and this sum can now be paid to the partners in the ratio which they owned goodwill, i.e. E two-fifths, £1,200, F two-fifths, £1,200 and G one-fifth, £600. This means that in total each would receive: E £2,800 + £1,200 = £4,000; F £1,600 + £1,200 = £2,800; and G £2,600 + £600 = £3,200. These can be seen to be the same amounts as those paid under method (*a*). The two methods therefore bring about the same end result, the only difference being that one method utilizes a Goodwill Account whereas the other method avoids it.

2. A New Partner is Introduced

On the introduction of a new partner, unless he takes over the share of a retiring or deceased partner, then obviously the share of the profits taken by each of the partners must change. If A is taking two-thirds of the profits and B one-third, then with the introduction of C, the old partners must give up a share of the profits to him. They can do this by either (*a*) giving up the same proportion of their share of the profits so that the comparative ratios in which they share profits remain the same as before, or else (*b*) the sharing of profits becomes such that the relative profit-sharing ratios of the old partners change as between the new firm and the old firm.

If (*a*) applies, then with the advent of C the profits shared could become any of the following:

Some Possible Solutions

	A	B	C
1	½	¼	¼
2	²/₅	¹/₅	²/₅
3	⁴/₇	²/₇	¹/₇
4	⁴/₉	²/₉	³/₉

A used to have two-thirds of the profit and B one-third of the profit. A therefore always had a share of the profits which was twice as great as that of B. In all of the above solutions A still takes twice as much as B, irrespective of whatever C takes.

On the other hand, if the ratios became A one-third, B one-third and C one-third, then A would have ceased taking twice as much profits as B. This has been referred to as (*b*).

Where (*a*) applies the only adjustments needed are those between C and the old partnership to compensate for C taking over part of the goodwill. If (*b*) applies, then there will still be adjustments necessary for the goodwill taken over by C, but there will also be adjustments necessary for the change in the relative shares of goodwill held by the old partners.

(a) No Change in the Old Partners' Relative Shares of Profits. The three basic methods in use have been designed to meet the particular wishes of the partners. Each one is used to meet a particular situation. Thus method (i) is suitable where the old partners want to be paid in cash privately, and (ii) applies where the cash is to be retained in the business, whereas (iii) will be used where an adjustment only is required, in all probability because the incoming partner has insufficient cash to pay separately for goodwill.

(i) The new partner pays a sum to the old partners privately which they share in their old profit-sharing ratios. Sometimes the money is paid into the business, only to be drawn out immediately, this is merely being a contra in the Cash Book.

(ii) The new partner pays cash into the business. This is debited to the Cash Book, then credited to the old partners' Capital Accounts in their old profit-sharing ratios.

(iii) A Goodwill Account is opened in which the total estimated value of goodwill is debited, and the credits are made in the old partner's Capital Accounts in their old profit-sharing ratios. No cash is paid in by the new partner specifically for goodwill. Any cash he does pay in, is in respect of capital and will therefore be credited to this Capital Account.

(b) Where the Old Partners' Relative Shares of Profits Change with the Introduction of a New Partner. The introduction of a new partner often takes place because of some fundamental change in the business, and it is often found that the relative shares of profits taken by the old partners need adjusting to preserve an equitable division of the profits to be made in the future. Either the partner will pay a premium for his share of the goodwill, or else an adjustment will be made to charge his Capital Account without any cash being paid by him.

(i) The New Partner Pays a Premium for a Share of Goodwill. Unless otherwise agreed, the assumption is that the total value of goodwill is directly proportionate to the amount paid by the new partner for the share taken by him. If a new partner pays £1,200 for a one-fifth share of the profits, then goodwill is taken to be £6,000. A sum of £800 for a one-quarter share of the profits would therefore be taken to imply a total value of £3,200 for goodwill.

It must be stressed that where a Goodwill Account had been in existence in the old partnership showing the full value of goodwill then the old partners will have been credited with their respective shares, and the following adjustments would not be applicable. These two methods are therefore dependent on adjustments for goodwill rather than the opening of a Goodwill Account.

Exhibit 39.4

Partners, J, K, L and M share profits in the ratio 2:3:4:1 respectively. (In other words, there are $2 + 3 + 4 + 1$ parts = 10 parts in all, so that J takes two-tenths, K three-tenths, L four-tenths and M one-tenth of the profits.) A new partner N is to be introduced, to pay £1,000 as a premium for his share of the goodwill. The profits will now be shared between J, K, L, M and N in the ratios 2:1:2:2:1 respectively (8 parts in all). The effect of the changes in the ownership of goodwill is now shown in the form of a table. As £1,000 has been paid for one-eighth of the goodwill, the total goodwill is taken as £8,000.

Before			After		Loss or Gain	Action Required
		£		£		
J	Two-tenths	1,600	Two-eighths	2,000	Gain £400	Debit J's Capital Account £400
K	Three-tenths	2,400	One-eighth	1,000	Loss £1,400	Credit K's Capital Account £1,400
L	Four-tenths	3,200	Two-eighths	2,000	Loss £1,200	Credit L's Capital Account £1,200
M	One-tenth	800	Two-eighths	2,000	Gain £1,200	Debit M's Capital Account £1,200
N	–	–	One-eighth	1,000	Gain £1,000	Debit N's Capital Account £1,000
		8,000		8,000		

K and L are the partners who have given up part of their ownership of goodwill. They are therefore compensated by having their Capital Accounts increased, while the partners who have gained are charged, i.e. debited, with the goodwill taken over. The debit in N's Capital Account will be cancelled by the credit entry made when he actually pays in the premium of £1,000 as arranged. Thus the new partner will have paid for his share of the goodwill, while the others will have had their claims against the assets of the firm, i.e. their Capital Accounts, adjusted accordingly.

(ii) The New Partner Does Not Pay a Premium for Goodwill.
Assuming that the facts were the same as in Exhibit 39.2, but that the new partner N was not to actually pay an amount specifically for goodwill yet the total value of goodwill was taken as £8,000, then the entries would be exactly the same as already shown. The only difference would be that the debit entry in N's Capital Account would not be cancelled out by an equal credit by an amount paid in specifically for the purpose. If N paid in £3,000 into the business, then the £1,000 debit for goodwill would reduce his capital to £2,000. Likewise if he only paid in £400 his Capital Account would show a debit balance of £600 until his share of the profits became sufficient to transform this into a normal credit balance.

3. A Partner Retires or Dies

When a partner leaves the firm, then he, or his personal representatives, will agree with the old partners as to how this shall be arranged. Perhaps the partnership deed will contain provisions for such an event, and if so this will normally be observed. Otherwise a new agreement will be arrived at. It would of course, be normal for any agreement to take the course that the retiring partner was entitled to have his share of the goodwill credited to his Capital Account in his profit-sharing ratio. He could leave the amount due to him as a loan to the partnership, or else all or part of it be repaid to him either immediately or be repaid by instalments.

It could well be the case that a new partner takes over the retiring partner's share, all transactions being between him and the retiring partner, the other partners not interfering in any way. The only point that can be made with any certainty is that if the partners cannot agree as to the manner in which any settlement is to be made, then the partnership will have to be dissolved. In this case the procedures are outlined in volume 2.

Many students are needlessly upset in examinations, because sometimes the examiner sets a question involving partnership goodwill in which the procedures to be carried out are quite unlike anything the student has ever seen before. It must be borne in mind that the partners can agree to payments or adjustments for goodwill in a manner decided by themselves. It does not have to bear any relationship to normal practice; it is purely a matter for agreement. Therefore the examiner is imagining such a situation, and the instructions the examination candidates are given are in accordance with such an imaginary agreement. If the student complies with the instructions he is therefore answering the question in the way required by the examiner.

Depreciation of Goodwill

Opinion has always been split between two main schools of thought. One school considered that purchased goodwill should be written off directly and should not be maintained as an asset. The other school took the view that goodwill should be depreciated through the profit and loss account year by year over its useful life.

A Company's Books

In January 1985 Statement of Standard Accounting Practice No. 22 (SSAP 22) 'Accounting for Goodwill' was issued. This relates to companies and groups of companies.

A brief summary of SSAP 22 is as follows:

1. Purchased goodwill should normally be eliminated immediately as an asset from the books on acquisition.

2. In some companies, where special needs are appropriate, the purchased goodwill can be 'amortised' (i.e. depreciated) year by year over its useful economic life.

3. Goodwill which has not been bought, but has been created within the company (inherent goodwill) should never be brought into the books at all.

4. Where there is 'negative goodwill' — see page 375 — this should be added to the reserves in the balance sheet of the company.

Exercises

MC101 You are to buy an existing business which has assets valued at buildings £50,000, motor vehicles £15,000, fixtures £5,000 and stock £40,000. You are to pay £140,000 for the business. This means that
(A) You are paying £40,000 for Goodwill
(B) Buildings are costing you £30,000 more than their value
(C) You are paying £30,000 for Goodwill
(D) You have made an arithmetical mistake.

MC102 Which of the following would *not* be considered to be a part of Goodwill
(A) There is a first-class labour force
(B) The firm has a good reputation
(C) The firm owns its own buildings
(D) The firm has a lot of regular customers.

MC103 Normally, a partner will own a share in the goodwill
(A) In same ratio as Profits shared
(B) In same ratio as Current Accounts
(C) In same ratio as Capital Accounts
(D) Equally.

39.1. The partners have always shared their profits in the ratios of X 4: Y 3: Y 1. They are to alter their profit ratios to X 3: Y 5: Z 2. The last balance sheet before the change was:

Balance Sheet as at 31 December 19-7

	£
Net Assets (not including goodwill)	14,000
	14,000
Capitals:	
X	6,000
Y	4,800
Z	3,200
	14,000

The partners agree to bring in goodwill, being valued at £12,000 on the change.

Show the balance sheets on 1 January 19-8 after goodwill has been taken into account if.

(*a*) Goodwill account was opened.

(*b*) Goodwill account was not opened.

39.2A. The partners are to change their profit ratios as shown:

	Old Ratio	New Ratio
A	2	3
B	3	4
C	4	3
D	1	2

They decide to bring in a goodwill amount of £18,000 on the change. The last balance sheet before any element of goodwill has been introduced was:

Balance Sheet as at 30 June 19-8

	£
Net Assets (not including Goodwill)	18,800
	18,800
Capitals:	
A	7,000
B	3,200
C	5,000
D	3,600
	18,800

Show the balance sheets on 1 July 19-8 after necessary adjustments have been made if:

(*a*) Goodwill account was opened.

(*b*) Goodwill account was not opened.

39.3. X and Y are in partnership, sharing profits and losses equally. They decide to admit Z. By agreement, goodwill valued at £6,000 is to be introduced into the business books. Z is required to provide capital equal to that of Y after he has been credited with his share of goodwill. The new profit sharing ratio is to be 4:3:3 respectively for X, Y and Z.

The Balance Sheet before admission of Z showed:

	£
Fixed and Current Assets	15,000
Cash	2,000
	17,000
Capital X	8,000
Capital Y	4,000
Current Liabilities	5,000
	17,000

Show:
(a) Journal Entries for admission of Z.
(b) Opening Balance Sheet of new business.
(c) Journal entries for writing off the goodwill which the new partners decided to do soon after the start of the new business.

39.4. A, B and C are in partnership sharing profits and losses in the ratios of 5:4:1 respectively. Their Capital Accounts show credit balances of A £3,000, B £5,000 and C £4,000.

Two new partners are introduced, D and E. The profits are now to be shared: A 3; B 4; C 2; D 2; E 1. D is to pay in £3,000 for his share of the goodwill but E has insufficient cash to pay immediately.

No Goodwill Account is to be opened. Show the Capital Accounts for all of the partners after D has paid for his share of the goodwill.

39.5A. L, M and S are in partnership. They shared profits in the ratio 2:5:3. It is decided to admit R. It is agreed that goodwill was worth £10,000, but that this is not to be brought into the business records. R will bring £4,000 cash into the business for capital. The new profit sharing ratio is to be L 3: M 4: S 2: R 1.

The Balance Sheet before R was introduced was as follows:

	£
Assets (other than cash)	11,000
Cash	2,500
	13,500
Capitals: L	3,000
M	5,000
S	4,000
Creditors	1,500
	13,500

Show:
(a) The entries in the Capital Accounts of L, M, S and R, the accounts to be in columnar form.
(b) The balance sheet after R has been introduced.

40

Partnership Accounts Continued: Revaluation of Assets

Revaluation of Assets

It has been shown in Chapter 39 that adjustments or payments are required for goodwill in a partnership when a new partner is introduced, the partners change their relative profit-sharing ratios, or a partner retires or dies. Similarly, on each of those occasions the other assets may need to be revalued. Unless there is some agreement to the contrary, if the business is sold and the sale price of the assets exceeds their book values, then the resultant profit is shared between the partners in their profit- and loss-sharing ratios. Similarly, a loss would be borne by them in the same ratios. It is therefore essential that the assets on the Balance Sheet are not markedly out of touch with reality when any changes in partnerships occur. Exhibit 40.1 illustrates the necessity for the revaluation of assets.

Exhibit 40.1

The summarized Balance Sheet of a partnership business is as follows:

Balance Sheet as at 31 December 19-6

	£
Property (at cost)	2,000
Machinery (at cost *less* depreciation)	3,500
Stock	1,500
Debtors	3,000
Bank	2,000
	12,000
Capitals: J	4,000
K	3,000
L	5,000
	12,000

J, K and L started the business thirty years previously. They had always shared profits equally, but from 1 January 19-7 it was to change to J three-sevenths, K three-sevents and L one-seventh. No revaluation of the assets took place. Six months later business was sold because of friction between J and K. Because of the nature of the business the assets have to be realized separately and there is no goodwill. The firm had been extremely fortunate in the choice of its premises thirty years ago, they were now sold for £23,000, a profit of £21,000. With the machinery the firm had been negligent in not realizing that obsolescence had greatly reduced its value and the sale realized only £350 − a loss of £3,150. The stock was sold for £1,500. The debtors included a debt of £2,100 from Long Ltd which had to be written off as a bad debt, all the other debts being realized in full. In fact it was L who had strongly recommended that Long Ltd was acceptable as a customer. None of the realized prices had been affected to any marked extent by events of the previous six months.

The profit on the premises £21,000 is divided as to J three-sevenths, £9,000, K three-sevenths, £9,000, and L one-seventh, £3,000. L's chagrin can be understood when it can be stated that if the partnership assets had been sold more than six months previously, then his share would have been one-third, £7,000 instead of £3,000.

The loss on the machinery is £3,150, shared J three-sevenths, £1,350, K three-sevenths, £1,350, and L one-seventh, £450. As the obsolescence factor is traceable back to more than six months ago, then L's advantage is not an equitable one.

The loss on debtors of £2,100 can be largely traceable to L's action in recommending an uncreditworthy customer. Yet the loss is shared: J three-sevenths, £900, K three-sevenths, £900 and L one-seventh, only £300.

The need for the assets to be revalued upon some change in the basis of the partnership is therefore obvious. The revised agreed values are amended quite simply. A Revaluation Account is opened, any increase in asset values being credited to it and the corresponding debits being in the asset accounts, while any reductions in asset values are debited to the Revaluation Account and credited to the asset accounts. If the increases exceed the reductions, then there is said to be a profit on revaluation, such a profit being shared by the old partners in their old profit-sharing ratio, the credit entries being made in the partners' Capital Accounts. The converse applies for a loss on revaluation. An illustration is now given in Exhibit 40.2.

Exhibit 40.2

The following is the summarized Balance Sheet of R, S and T who shared profits and losses in the ratios 3:2:1 respectively.

From 1 January 19-8 the profit-sharing ratios are to be altered to R 2:S 4:T 1. The following assets are to be revalued in the following amounts − Premises £7,000, Fixtures £1,800, Motor vehicles £1,300, and Stock to £1,500. The accounts needed to show the revaluation are as follows:

Balance Sheet as at 31 December 19-7

	£
Premises (at cost)	4,500
Motor Vehicles (at cost *less* depreciation)	1,500
Fixtures (at cost *less* depreciation)	2,000
Stock	1,800
Debtors	1,600
Bank	600
	12,000
Capitals: R	4,000
S	5,000
T	3,000
	12,000

Revaluation

	£	£		£
Assets reduced in value:			Assets increased in value:	
Fixtures		200	Premises	2,500
Motor Vehicles		200		
Stock		300		
Profit on Revaluation carried to Capital Accounts				
	£			
R three-sixths	900			
S two-sixths	600			
T one-sixth	300	1,800		
		2,500		2,500

Premises

	£		£
Balance b/fwd	4,500		
Revaluation: Increase	2,500	Balance c/d	7,000
	7,000		7,000
Balance b/d	7,000		

Fixtures

	£		£
Balance b/fwd	2,000	Revaluation: Reduction	200
		Balance c/d	1,800
	2,000		2,000
Balance b/d	1,800		

Motor Vehicles

	£		£
Balance b/fwd	1,500	Revaluation: Reduction	200
		Balance c/d	1,300
	1,500		1,500
Balance b/d	1,300		

Stock

	£		£
Balance f/fwd	1,800	Revaluation: Reduction	300
		Balance c/d	1,500
	1,800		1,800
Balance b/d	1,500		

Capital: R

	£		£
		Balance b/fwd	4,000
Balance c/d	4,900	Revaluation: Share of profit	900
	4,900		4,900
		Balance b/d	4,900

Capital: S

	£		£
		Balance b/fwd	5,000
Balance c/d	5,600	Revaluation: Share of profit	600
	5,600		5,600
		Balance b/d	5,600

Capital: T

	£		£
Balance c/d	3,300	Balance b/fwd	3,000
		Revaluation: Share of	
		profit	300
	3,300		3,300
		Balance b/d	3,300

The balances brought down are those used to start the recording of transactions for the following period.

Exercises

MC104 Assets can be revalued in a partnership change because
(A) The law insists upon it
(B) It helps prevent injustice to some partners
(C) Inflation affects all values.

MC105 Any loss on revaluation is
(A) Credited to old partners in old profit sharing ratios
(B) Credited to new partners in new profit sharing ratios
(C) Debited to old partners in old profit sharing ratios
(D) Debited to new partners in new profit sharing ratios.

40.1.   **Hughes, Allen and Elliott**
Balance Sheet as at 31 December 19-5

	£
Buildings at cost	8,000
Motor Vehicles (at cost *less* depreciation)	3,550
Office Fittings (at cost *less* depreciation)	1,310
Stock	2,040
Debtors	4,530
Bank	1,390
	20,820
Capitals:	£
Hughes	9,560
Allen	6,420
Elliott	4,840
	20,820

The above partners have always shared profits and losses in the ratio: Hughes 5: Allen 3: Elliott 2.

From 1 January the assets were to be revalued as the profit sharing ratios are to be altered soon. The following assets are to be revalued to the figures shown: Building £17,500, Motor Vehicles £2,600, Stock £1,890, Office Fittings £1,090.
(i) You are required to show all the ledger accounts necessary to record the revaluation.
(ii) Draw up a balance sheet as at 1 January 19-6.

40.2A. Avon and Brown have been in partnership for many years sharing profits and losses in the ratio of 3:2 respectively. The following was their Balance Sheet as at 31 December 19-6.

	£
Goodwill	2,000
Plant & Machinery	1,800
Stock	1,960
Debtors	2,130
Cash at Bank	90
	£7,980

	£
Capital: Avon	4,000
Brown	3,000
	7,000
Sundry Creditors	980
	£7,980

On 1 January 19-7, they decided to admit Charles as a partner on the condition that he contributed £2,000 as his Capital but that the plant and machinery and stock should be revalued at £2,000 and £1,900 respectively, the other assets, excepting goodwill, remaining at their present book values. The goodwill was agreed to be valueless.

You are require to show:
(a) The ledger entries dealing with the above in the following accounts:
   (i) Goodwill Account,
   (ii) Revaluation Accounts,
   (iii) Capital Accounts;
(b) The Balance Sheet of the partnership immediately after the admission of Charles.

40.3. Fitton, Ball and Davies share profits in the ratio of 4:3:3 respectively. They decide to admit Noone as a partner, when profits will be shared Fitton 4: Ball 3: Davies 3: Noone 2. The last balance sheet before admission of Noone, who paid in capital of £8,000 was:

Balance Sheet as at 31 March 19-9

	£
Premises	11,560
Machinery	3,980
Motor Vehicles	6,810
Fixtures	1,540
Stock	4,850
Debtors	3,260
Bank	1,600
	33,600

	£
Capitals:	
Fitton	18,000
Ball	9,600
Davies	6,000
	33,600

Upon admittance of Noone a goodwill account of £20,000 is to be opened. In addition the assets are to be revalued to: Premises £30,000, Machinery £3,700, Motor Vehicles £6,400, Fixtures £1,200, Stock £5,600.

You are to:
(a) Show the Revaluation Account and Capital Accounts recording the above.
(b) Draw up the balance sheet as on 1 April 19-9 after the above adjustments have been completed.

40.4A. Alan, Bob and Charles are in partnership sharing profits and losses in the ratio 3:2:1 respectively.

The Balance Sheet for the partnership as at 30 June 19-2 is as follows:

	£	£
Fixed Assets		
Premises		90,000
Plant		37,000
Vehicles		15,000
Fixtures		2,000
		144,000
Current Assets		
Stock	62,379	
Debtors	34,980	
Cash	760	98,119
		£242,119

	£	£
Capital		
Alan		85,000
Bob		65,000
Charles		35,000
		185,000
Current Account		
Alan	3,714	
Bob	(2,509)	
Charles	4,678	5,883
Loan – Charles		28,000
Current Liabilities		
Creditors		19,036
Bank Overdraft		4,200
		£242,119

Charles decides to retire from the business on 30 June 19-2, and Don is admitted as a partner on that date. The following matters are agreed:

1. Certain assets were revalued – Premises   £120,000
                                       – Plant   £35,000
                                         – Stock   £54,179
2. Provision is to be made for doubtful debts in the sum of £3,000.
3. Goodwill is to be recorded in the books on the day Charles retires in the sum of £42,000. The partners in the new firm do not wish to maintain a goodwill account so that amount is to be written back against the new partners' capital accounts.
4. Alan and Bob are to share profits in the same ratio as before, and Don is to have the same share of profits as Bob.
5. Charles is to take his car at its book value of £3,900 in part payment, and the balance of all he owed by the firm in cash except £20,000 which he is willing to leave as a loan account.
6. The partners in the new firm are to start on an equal footing so far as capital and current accounts are concerned. Don is to contribute cah to bring his capital and current accounts to the same amount as the original partner from the old firm who has the lower investment in the business.

      The original partner in the old firm who has the higher investment will draw out cash so that his capital and current account balances equal those of his new partners.

Required:

(a) Account for the above transactions, including Goodwill and retiring Partners Accounts.

(b) Draft a Balance Sheet for the partnership of Alan, Bob and Don as at 30 June 19-2.

(Association of Accounting Technicians)

41

An Introduction to the Final Accounts of Limited Liability Companies

The two main disadvantages of a partnership are that the number of owners cannot normally exceed twenty, and that their liability, barring limited partners, is not limited to the amount invested in the partnership but extends to the individual partners' private possessions. This means that the failure of the business could result in a partner losing both his share of the business assets and also part or all of his private assets as well.

The form of organization to which these two limitations do not apply are known as Limited Liability Companies. There are companies which have unlimited liability, but these are not dealt with in this volume. From this point any reference to a company means a limited liability company. The law governing these companies in the United Kingdom is the Companies Act 1985.

The capital of a limited company is divided into Shares. These can be of any denomination, such as £5 shares or £1 shares. To become a Member of a limited company, alternatively called a Shareholder, a person must buy one of more shares. He may either pay in full for the shares that he takes up, or else the shares may be partly paid for, the balance to be paid as and when the company may arrange. The liability of a member is limited to the shares that he holds, or where a share is only partly paid he is also liable to have to pay the amount owing by him on the shares. Thus, even if a company loses all its assets, a member's private possessions cannot be touched to pay the company's debts, other than in respect of the amount owing on partly paid shares.

Companies thus fulfil the need for the capitalization of a firm where the capital required is greater than that which twenty people can contribute, or where limited liability for all members is desired.

Private and Public Companies

There are two classes of company, the Private Company and the

Public Company. In fact, private companies outnumber public companies by a considerable number. In Section 1 of the Companies Act 1985 a public company is defined as one whose memorandum states that the company is a public company, and has registered as such. A public company must normally have an authorized capital of at least £50,000. Minimum membership is two, there is no maximum.

The name of a public company must either end if the words 'public limited company' or the abbreviation 'plc', or the Welsh equivalent if the registered office is situated in Wales.

Private companies are usually (but not always) smaller businesses, and may be formed by two or more persons. A private company is defined by the Act as a company which is not a public company. In fact the main difference, other than a private company can have authorized capitals less than £50,000, is that public companies are allowed to offer their shares for subscription by the public at large, whereas 'private companies' cannot do this. Therefore if you were to walk into a bank, or similar public place, and see a prospectus offering anyone the chance to take up shares in a company, then that company would be a 'public' company.

The day-to-day business of a company is not carried on by the shareholders. The possession of a share normally confers voting rights on the holder, who is then able to attend general meetings of the company. At one of these the shareholders will meet and will vote for Directors, these being the people who will be entrusted with the running of the business. At each Annual General Meeting the directors will have to report on their stewardship, and this report is accompanied by a set of Final Accounts for the year.

Share Capital

A shareholder of a limited company obtains his reward in the form of a share of the profits, known as a Dividend. The directors consider the amount of profits and decide on the amount of profits which are placed to reserves. Out of the profits remaining the directors then propose the payment of a certain amount of dividend to be paid. It is important to note that the shareholders cannot propose a higher dividend for themselves than that already proposed by the directors. They can however propose that a lesser dividend should be paid, although this action is very rare indeed. If the directors propose that no dividend be paid then the shareholders are powerless to alter the decision.

The decision by the directors as to the amount proposed as dividends is a very complex one and cannot be fully discussed here. Such points as government directives to reduce dividends, the effect of taxation, the availability of bank balances to pay the dividends, the possibility of take-over bids and so on will all be taken into account.

The dividend is usually expressed as a percentage. Ignoring income tax, a dividend of 10 per cent in Firm A on 500,000 Ordinary

Shares of £1 each will amount to £50,000, or a dividend of 6 per cent in Firm B on 200,000 Ordinary Shares of £2 each will amount to £24,000. A shareholder having 100 shares in each firm would receive £10 from Firm A and £12 from Firm B.

There are two main types of share, Preference Shares and Ordinary Shares. A preference share is one whose main characteristics is that it is entitled to a specified percentage rate of dividend before the ordinary shareholders receive anything. On the other hand the ordinary shares would be entitled to the remainder of the profits which have been appropriated for dividends.

For example, if a company had 10,000 5 per cent preference shares of £1 each and 20,000 ordinary shares of £1 each, then the dividends would be payable as in Exhibit 41.1.

Exhibit 41.1

Years	1	2	3	4	5
	£	£	£	£	£
Profits appropriated for Dividends	900	1,300	1,600	3,100	2,000
Preference Dividends (5%)	500	500	500	500	500
Ordinary Dividends	(2%) 400	(4%) 800	(5½%) 1,100	(13%) 2,600	(7½%) 1,500

There are two main types of preference share, these being Non-cumulative Preference Shares and Cumulative Preference Shares. A non-cumulative preference share is one which is entitled to a yearly percentage rate of dividend, and should the available profits be insufficient to cover the percentage dividend then the deficiency cannot be made good out of future years' profits. On the other hand, any deficiency on the part of cumulative preference shares can be carried forward as arrears, and such arrears are payable before the ordinary shares receive anything.

Illustrations of the two types of share should make this clearer: Exhibit 41.2: A company has 5,000 £1 ordinary shares and 2,000 5 per cent non-cumulative preference shares of £1 each. The profits available for dividends are: year 1 £150, year 2 £80, year 3 £250, year 4 £60, year 5 £500.

Year	1	2	3	4	5
	£	£	£	£	£
Profits	150	80	250	60	500
Preference Dividend (limited in years 2 and 4)	100	80	100	60	100
Dividends on Ordinary Shares	50	—	150	—	400

Exhibit 41.3: Assume that the preference shares in Exhibit 41.2 had been cumulative, the dividends would have been:

Year	1	2	3	4	5
	£	£	£	£	£
Profits	150	80	250	60	500
Preference Dividend	100	80	120*	60	140*
Dividends on Ordinary Shares	50	—	130	—	360

   *including arrears.

The total of the Share Capital which the company would be allowed to issue is known as the Authorized Share Capital, or alternatively as the Nominal Capital. The share capital actually issued to shareholders is known as the Issued Capital. Obviously, if the whole of the share capital which the company is allowed to issue has in fact been issued, then the authorized and the issued share capital will be the same figure.

Where only part of the amount payable on each share has been asked for, then the total amount asked for on all shares is known as the Called-up Capital. The Uncalled Capital is therefore that part of the amount payable on all the shares for which payment has not been requested. Calls in arrear relate to amounts requests (called for) but not yet received, while calls in advance relate to moneys received prior to payment being requested. Paid-up Capital will be that part of the capital which has actually been paid by shareholders.

An illustration should make this clearer. This is shown as Exhibit 41.4.

Exhibit 41.4

   (i) Better Enterprises Ltd was formed with the legal right to be able to issue 100,000 shares of £1 each.
   (ii) The company has actually issued 75,000 shares.
   (iii) None of the shares have yet been fully paid up. So far the company has made calls of 80p (£0.80) per share.
   (iv) All the calls have been paid by shareholders except for £200 owing from one shareholder.

(a) Authorised Normal Share Capital is (i) £100,000
(b) Issued Share Capital is (ii) £75,000.
(c) Called up Capital is (iii) 75,000 × £0.80 = £60,000.
(d) Calls in arrear amounted to (iv) £200.
(e) Paid-up Capital is (c) £60,000 less (d) £200 = £59,800.

Trading and Profit and Loss Accounts

From the viewpoint of the preparation of trading and profit and loss accounts, there are no differences as between public and private limited companies. The accounts now described are those purely for internal use by the company. Obviously, if a full copy of the trading and profit and loss accounts were given to each shareholder, the company's rivals could easily obtain a copy, and would then be in a position to learn about details of the company's trading which the company would prefer to keep secret. The Companies Act therefore states that only certain details of the trading and profit and loss account must be shown. Companies can, if they so wish, disclose more than the minimum information required by law, but it is simply a matter for the directors to decide whether or not it would be in the company's interest. A discussion of the minimum information required is contained in Volume 2.

The trading account of a limited company is no different from that of a sole trader or of a partnership. The profit and loss account also follows the same pattern as those of partnerships or sole traders except for some types of expense which are peculiar to limited companies. The two main expenses under this heading are:

1.   Directors' remuneration. This is obvious, since only in companies are directors found.

2.   Debenture interest. The term debenture is used when money is received on loan to the company and written acknowledgement is given, usually under seal. Thus a loan to a partnership is known as a loan, while usually a loan to a company is known as a debenture. The interest payable for the use of the money is an expense of the company, and is payable whether profits are made or not. This means that debenture interest is charged as an expense in the Profit and Loss Account itself. Contrast this with dividends which are dependent on profits having been made.

When a company is being formed there are expenses concerned with its incorporating such as stamp duties, legal expenses etc. Collectively these are known as preliminary expenses. Before 1981 these could be shown as an asset in the balance sheet, but they should now be written off as an expense immediately.

The Appropriation Account

Next under the profit and loss account is a section called, as it would also be in a partnership, the profit and loss appropriation account. The net profit is brought down from the profit and loss account, and in the appropriation account is shown the manner in which the profits are to be appropriated, i.e. how the profits are to be used.

First of all, if any of the profits are to be put to reserve then the transfer is shown. To transfer to a reserve means that the directors wish to indicate that that amount of profits is not to be considered as available for dividends in that year. The reserve may be specific, such as a Fixed Asset Replacement Reserve or it may be a General Reserve.

Out of the remainder of profits the dividends are proposed and the unused balance of profits is carried forward to the following year, where it goes to swell the profits then available for appropriation. It is very rare, assuming the firm has not been incurring losses, for there not to be any unappropriated balance of profits carried forward even if it is the policy of the firm to declare the greatest possible dividends, because dividends are normally proposed either as a whole percentage or to a one-half or one-quarter per cent. Arithmetically it is uncommon for the profits remaining after transfers to reserves to exactly equal such a figure.

Exhibit 41.5 shows the profit and loss appropriation account of a new business for its first three years of business.

Exhibit 41.5

I.D.O. Ltd has an Ordinary Share Capital of 40,000 ordinary shares of £1 each and 20,000 5 per cent preference shares of £1 each.

The net profits for the first three years of business ended 31 December are: 19-4 £5,967; 19-5 £7,864, and 19-6, £8,822.

Transfers to reserves are made as follows: 19-4 nil; 19-5, general reserve, £1,000, and 19-6, fixed assets replacement reserve, £2,250.

Dividends were proposed for each year on the preference shares and on the ordinary shares at: 19-4, 10 per cent; 19-5, 12½ per cent; 19-6, 15 per cent.

Profit and Loss Appropriation Accounts
(1) For the year ended 31 December 19-4

		£
Net Profit brought down		5,967
Less Proposed Dividends:		
Preference Dividend of 5%	1,000	
Ordinary Dividend of 10%	4,000	5,000
Balance carried forward to next year		967

(2) For the year ended 31 December 19-5

		£
Net Profit brought down		7,864
Add Balance brought forward		
from last year		967
		8,831
Less:		
Transfer to General Reserve	1,000	
Proposed Dividends:		
Preference Dividend of 5%	1,000	
Ordinary Dividend of 12½%	5,000	7,000
Balance carried forward to next year		1,831

(3) *For the year ended 31 December 19-6*

		£
Net Profit brought down		8,822
Add Balance brought forward from last year		1,831
		10,653
Less:		
Transfer to Fixed Assets Replacement Reserve	2,250	
Proposed Dividends:		
Preference Dividend of 5%	1,000	
Ordinary Dividend of 15%	6,000	9,250
		1,403

The Balance Sheet

Until the year 1981, a company could, *provided it disclosed the necessary information,* draw up its Balance Sheet and Profit and Loss Account for publication in any way that it wished. The 1985 Companies Act lays down the precise manner of display. As the regulations are quite detailed a study of them is best left until volume 2.

In this chapter the final accounts shown generally fit in with the requirements of the 1985 Companies Act without going into the detail required by the Act.

Now shown is a company balance sheet. See also the notes on the following page.

Balance Sheet as at 31 December 19-7

	Cost	Depreciation to date	Net
Fixed Assets	£	£	£
Buildings	15,000	6,000	9,000
Machinery	8,000	2,400	5,600
Motor Vehicles	4,000	1,600	2,400
	27,000	10,000	17,000
Current Assets			
Stock		6,000	
Debtors		3,000	
Bank		2,000	
		11,000	
Less Current Liabilities			
Proposed Dividend	1,000		
Creditors	3,000	4,000	
Working Capital			7,000
			24,000

Financed by:	£	£
Share Capital		
Authorized 20,000 shares of £1 each		20,000
Issued 12,000 Ordinary shares of £1 each, fully paid		12,000
Reserves		
Share premium	1,200	
General reserve	3,800	
Profit and Loss Account	1,000	
		6,000
		18,000
Debentures		
Six per cent Debentures		6,000
		24,000

Notes:

1.   Fixed assets should normally be shown either at cost or alternatively at some other valuation. In either case, the method chosen should be clearly stated.

2.   The total depreciation from date of purchase to the date of the balance sheet should be shown.

3.   The authorized share capital, where it is different from the issued share capital, is shown as a note.

4.   Reserves consist either of those unused profits remaining in the appropriation account, or transferred to a reserve account appropriately titled, e.g. General Reserve, Fixed Assets Replacement Reserve, etc. Volume 2 of this book will examine these in rather more detail. At this juncture all that needs to be said is that any account labelled as a reserve has originated by being charged as a debit in the appropriation account and credited to a reserve account with an appropriate title. These reserves are shown in the balance sheet after share capital under the heading of 'Reserves'.

   One reserve that is in fact not labelled with the word 'reserve' in its title is the Share Premium Account. For reasons which will be explained in Volume 2, shares can be issued for more than their face or nominal value. The excess of the price at which they are issued over the nominal value of the shares is credited to a Share Premium Account. This is then shown with the other reserves in the Balance Sheet.

5.   Where shares are only partly called up, then it is the amount actually called up that appears in the balance sheet and not the full amount.

6. The share capital and reserves should be totalled so as to show the book value of all the shares in the company.

Either the terms 'Shareholders' Funds' or 'Members' Equity' are often given to the total of share Capital plus Reserves.

Exercises

MC106 In a limited company which of the following are shown in the Appropriation Account?
(i) Debenture Interest
(ii) Proposed Dividend
(iii) Transfers to Reserves
(iv) Directors' Remuneration.
(A) i and ii
(B) ii and iii
(C) i and iv
(D) ii and iv.

MC107 The Issued Capital of a company is
(A) Always the same as the Authorised Capital
(B) The same as Preference Share Capital
(C) Equal to the reserves of the company
(D) None of the above.

MC108 A company wishes to pay out all available profits as dividends. Net Profit is £26,600. There are 20,000 8% Preference Shares of £1 each, and 50,000 Ordinary Shares of £1 each. £5,000 is to be transferred to General Reserve. What Ordinary dividends are to be paid, in percentage terms?
(A) 20 per cent
(B) 40 per cent
(C) 10 per cent
(D) 60 per cent.

41.1. After the preparation of the trading and profit and loss account the following balances remained in the books of A. Co. Ltd., at 31 December 19-6.

	£		£
Creditors	16,900	Depreciation on plant and	
Debenture interest owing	175	machinery	16,000
£1 ordinary shares fully paid	100,000	£1 5 per cent preference	
Trade expenses owing	3,075	shares fully paid	5,000
Cash	7,500	Debtors	18,900
Stock	25,000	Freehold premises	71,000
Profit and loss account	30,000	7 per cent debentures	5,000
		Plant and machinery	41,000
		Bank	12,750

The company had issued all its authorized ordinary share capital, but £5,000 of £1 5 per cent preference shares still remained unissued.

Required:
A balance sheet as at 31 December 19-6 clearly showing the following:
(*a*) fixed assets
(*b*) current assets
(*c*) working capital
(*d*) current liabilities
(*e*) shareholders' interest.

(Associated Examining Board 'O' level)

41.2A. A balance sheet is drawn up from the following as at 30 June 19-6:

	£
Issued Share Capital: Ordinary Shares £1 each	100,000
Authorised Share Capital: Ordinary Shares or £1 each	200,000
10 per cent Debentures	40,000
Buildings at cost	105,000
Motor Vehicles at cost	62,500
Fixtures at cost	11,500
Profit and Loss Account	5,163
Fixed Assets Replacement Reserve	8,000
Stock	16,210
Debtors	14,175
General Reserve	6,000
Creditors	9,120
Proposed Divided	5,000
Depreciation to date: Motor Vehicles	15,350
Premises	22,000
Fixtures	3,750
Bank (balancing figure for you to ascertain)	?

41.3. The following information was available on Z Ltd. for the year ended 31 March 19-7.

Authorized Capital
100,000 £1 ordinary shares
250,000 9 per cent £1 preference shares

Issued Capital
800,000 £1 ordinary shares fully paid

Revenue profits earned for the year
£252,000

Dividends paid
Interim of 6 per cent of the nominal share value
Final of 9 per cent of the nominal share value

Profit and loss appropriation account
Credit balance 1 April 19-6 £340,000

1. From the above information calculate:
(*a*) The total dividend paid by the company.
(*b*) The dividend paid per share (in pence).
(*c*) The profits earned during the year per share (in pence).
2. Prepare the company's profit and loss appropriation account for the year ended 31 March 19-7, given that the directors had decided to transfer £100,000 to general reserve.

(Associated Examining Board 'O' level)

41.4A. Conrad & Co. Ltd. is a small private company with capital of £75,000 in shares of £1 each. 50,000 £1 shares have been issued and are fully paid at a premium of 10%.

The following balances have been taken from the books on 31 December 19-8:

	£		£
Capital	50,000	Premises (cost £50,000)	35,000
Share premium	5,000	Machinery	30,000
Retained profits	7,900	Delivery vans	10,000
Creditors	2,500	Stock	5,000
Provision for depreciation:		Debtors	3,000
Machinery	10,000	Bank	5,000
Vans	8,000	Cash	50
Provision for doubtful debts	150	Payments in advance	500
Unpaid dividends	5,000		
	88,550		88,550

Set out the Balance Sheet in the long or vertical form indicating clearly (a) the working capital, (b) the net worth and (c) the capital employed.

(University of London 'O' level)

41.5.

(a) The following terms usually appear in the final accounts of a limited company:
  (i) interim dividend,
  (ii) authorised capital,
  (iii) general reserve,
  (iv) share premium account.

Required:

An explanation of the meaning of each of the above terms.

(b) The following information has been obtained from the books of Drayfuss Ltd:

Authorised capital	100,000 8% £1 preference shares
	400,000 50p ordinary shares
Profit and loss account balance	
1 April 19-8	*cr* £355,000
General Reserve	£105,000
Issued capital	80,000 8% £1 preference shares (fully paid)
	250,000 50p ordinary shares (fully paid)
Net trading profit for the year	
to 31 March 19-9	£95,000.

The preference share interim dividend of 4% had been paid and the final dividend of 4% had been proposed by the directors.

No ordinary share interim dividend had been declated, but the directors proposed a final dividend of 15p per share.

The directors agreed to transfer to general reserve £150,000.

Required:

The profit and loss appropriation account for the year ended 31 March 19-9.

(Ignore taxation).

(Associated Examining Board 'O' level)

41.6A. The following information was available on P. Co. Ltd., for the year ended 31 August 19-9, after the trading and profit and loss account had been prepared.

Issued Capital	£	Authorised Capital	£
250,000 10p Ordinary shares	25,000	500,000 10p Ordinary shares	50,000
100,000 £1 10% Preference shares	100,000	100,000 £1 10% Preference shares	100,000
Trade creditors	9,700	Cash	2,575
Profit and loss account cr.		Bank	10,000
balance	41,200	Stock	61,350
Freehold premises (at cost)	73,000	Trade expenses owing	
Plant and machinery (at cost)	49,000	31 August 19-9	350
Share premium account	15,000	8% Debentures – issued by	
Provision for depreciation		P. Co. Ltd.	10,000
on plant and machinery	11,370	Fixtures and fittings (at cost)	8,800
		Trade debtors	10,895
		Provision for depreciation on	
		fixtures and fittings	3,000

(a) The stock valuation at 31 August 19-9 included £7,350 of obsolete stock. The obsolete stock should now be written off.

(b) Insurance of £250 had been paid in advance, but no adjustment had been made in the profit and loss account for this item.

(c) A 10% preference dividend had been proposed, but no entry had been made.

Required:

A balance sheet as at 31 August 19-9 incorporating the necessary adjustments to correct the errors made. It is important that the balance sheet should be presented in good form including appropriate sub-headings and sub-totals.

(Associated Examining Board 'O' level)

41.7. The following balances were extracted from the books of H. Lindas Ltd. on 31 March 19-1, after the completion of the trading and profit and loss accounts:

	£
Stock at 31 March 19-1	7,000
Debtors	3,000
Bank overdraft	2,000
Creditors	9,000
Cash	100
Premises (at cost)	17,000
Machinery (at cost) 1 April 19-8	7,000
Motor Vans (at cost) 1 April 19-8	5,000
Goodwill	10,000

You are required to prepare a balance sheet as at 31 March 19-1 using the above balances and the following information:

(a) The company was formed and commenced business 3 years previously on 1 April 19-8, with an authorised share capital of 50,000 ordinary shares of £1 each.

(b) 20,000 shares each fully paid were issued at a premium of 10p per share.

(c) The company made the the following net profits during its three years of trading:

March 19-9	£2,000
March 19-0	£3,000
March 19-1	£6,000

No dividends had been declared or paid and all but £2,000 of the profits had been transferred to a general reserve account.

(d) Depreciation had been provided each year on the original cost at the rate of 10% per annum on machinery and 20% per annum on motor vans.

(Joint Matriculation Board 'O' level)

41.8A. The following balances, at 1 January 19-2, were taken from the books of Leo Johnson & Company Ltd. which had an authorised capital of 50,000 ordinary shares of £1 each.

Issued share capital 33,000 ordinary shares of £1 each, fully paid; motor vans £3,935; premises £26,000; creditors £10,065; debtors £8,600; balance at bank £4,901; stock £6,629; profit and loss account credit balance £3,700; proposed dividend for 19-1 £3,300.

Required:
(a) The balance sheet of Leo Johnson & Company Ltd. at 1 January 19-2, in a form which shows clearly the shareholders' funds and the working capital.

During the month of January 19-2, some of the company's transactions were:

(1) paid the month's wages £1,320, by cheque;
(2) sent W. Gallagher, a creditor, a cheque for £176 in full settlement of his account for £200;
(3) an old delivery van, book value £325, was sold for £300 cash;
(4) paid ordinary share dividend, £3,300 by cheque.

Required:
(b) A tabulated statement, as shown below, giving the effect of each of the above transactions on current assets, working capital and on the profit and loss account balance. The first one has been done for you, as an example.

		Effect on	
Transaction	current assets	working capital	profit/loss balance
(1)	bank minus £1,320 therefore current assets minus £1,320	current assets minus £1,320 therefore working capital minus £1,320	wages plus £1,320 therefore profit/ loss balance minus £1,320

Required:
(c) An explanation of the importance of working capital.

(Associated Examining Board 'O' level)

41.9. Mr. Bearbull was considering investing funds in either buying shares in Zeta Ltd., or investing in a bank. He obtained the following information regarding balances in the books of Zeta Ltd. as at 30 June 19-8:

	£
Freehold land and buildings (at cost)	370,000
Provision for depreciation on plant & machinery	155,000
Provision for bad debts	1,400
Bank overdraft	126,500
14% Secured debentures	100,000
Cash balances	25,250
Plant and machinery at cost	400,000
Provision for depreciation on motor vehicles	38,750
Stocks: valued at cost	225,500
Trade debtors	78,900
Trade creditors	51,000
Proposed final dividend – ordinary shares	30,000
Motor vehicles at cost	70,500
Profit and loss account	117,500 cr.

Additional information was available as follows:

(a) Authorised capital:

> 500,000 £1 ordinary shares
> 300,000 £1 9% Preference shares

> 300,000 of the ordinary shares had been issued at £1.50 per share fully paid

> 100,000 of the preference shares had been issued at £1 per share fully paid

(b) The interim ordinary dividend had been paid at 2p per share.

(c) Mr. Bearbull was advised that his capital of £10,000 could buy 7,000 ordinary shares in Zeta Ltd. Altneratively he could place his capital in a bank to earn 9% interest per annum.

Required:

1. A balance sheet for Zeta Ltd. as at 30 June 19-8, using appropriate classifications of assets and liabilities.

2. A calculation to show Mr. Bearbull's alternative returns on capital assuming that ordinary dividends and interest rates remain unchanged for the next 12 months.

(Associated Examining Board 'O' level)

41.10A. The following balances were extracted from the books of J. Green and Company Limited after completion of the Manufacturing Account for the year ended 31 December 19-8.

	£	£
Premises (at cost)	100,000	
Share Capital (Authorised and fully paid):		
120,000 Ordinary shares at £1 each		120,000
20,000 8% Preference shares at £1 each		20,000
Trade Debtors and Creditors	20,400	16,800
Undistributed Profit (1 January 19-8)		25,200
Sales		184,600
Administration Expenses	13,800	
Selling and Distribution Expenses	32,600	
10% Debentures		10,000
Cost of Goods Manufactured	128,600	
General Reserve		12,000
Plant and Machinery (at cost)	60,000	
Depreciation of Plant and Machinery:		
Accumulated Provision		18,800
Charge for 19-8		6,000
Interim Preference Dividend paid	800	
Interim Ordinary Dividend paid	6,000	
Debenture Interest paid	500	
Bank	17,300	
Stocks:		
Finished Goods (1 January 19-8)	17,400	
Raw Materials (31 December 19-8)	11,800	
Work in Progress (31 December 19-8)	4,200	
	£413,400	£413,400

You are required to prepare Trading and Profit and Loss Accounts for the year ended 31 December 19-8 and a Balance Sheet as at that date after incorporating the following information.

(a) Stock of finished goods a 31 December 19-8 was valued at £22,000.

(b) Provision should be made for payment of
    (i)   the balance of debenture interest,
    (ii) a final dividend of 20% on ordinary shares,
    (iii) the balance of the preference share dividend.

(c) The General Reserve is to be increased by £4,000.

(Joint Matriculation Board 'O' level)

41.11. The Barr Trading Co. Ltd. is registered with an authorised capital of £1,500,000 divided into 500,000 10% preference shares of £1 each and 1,000,000 ordinary shares of £1 each.

After completion of the Trading and Profit and Loss Account for the year ended 31 May 19-2 the following balances remain in the books:

	£'000s	£'000s
Preference share capital (fully paid)		500
Ordinary share capital (fully paid)		900
Profit and Loss Account balance brought forward		10
General reserve		50
Net profit for the year ended 31 May 19-2		300
Premises (at cost)	1,250	
Delivery vans (at cost)	125	
Provision for depreciation of delivery vans		35
Fixtures and fittings (at cost)	60	
Provision for depreciation of fixtures and fittings		20
Cash in hand and at bank	314	
Trade debtors	27	
Provision for doubtful debts		1
Creditors		12
Stocks	50	
Payments in advance	2	
	£1,828	£1,828

The directors propose to pay the preference dividend, a dividend of 20% to the ordinary shareholders and transfer £50,000 to general reserve.

Prepare the profit and loss appropriation account for the company and set out a Balance Sheet after these proposals have been agreed, but before the dividends are paid.

To obtain full marks your Balance Sheet should be set out in the vertical or columnar form, showing clearly the working capital.

(University of London 'O' level)

41.12A. Backwater Ltd. has an authorised share capital of
    50,000 ordinary shares of £1 each, and
    10,000 10% preference shares of £1 each.

The company had issued 30,000 ordinary shares fully paid and all the preference shares at £1 each. The balances in the books for the year ended 31 December 19-9 were as follows:

		£
Wages and salaries		17,000
Office expenses		700
Plant and machinery (at cost)		10,000
Fixtures and fittings (at cost)		2,000
Stock at 1 January 19-9		20,000
Profit and loss account at 1 January 19-9		13,000 (CR)
Depreciation to date:		
Plant and machinery	4,000	
Fixtures and fittings	500	
		4,500
Rates		800
Carriage inwards		300
Insurance		200
Purchases (less returns)		40,000
Sales (less returns)		90,000
Discounts allowed		100
Discounts received		500
Bad debts written off		400
Creditors		26,000
Debtors		25,000
Provision for bad debts		500
Freehold premises (at cost)		43,000
Cash in hand		3,000
Bank (debit)		12,000

You are required to prepare the company's trading and profit and loss account for the year ended 31 December 19-9, and a balance sheet as at that date taking into account the adjustments required by the following information.

(a) Stock at 31 December 19-9 = £5,000.

(b) The dividend to preference shareholders is to be paid but there is to be no dividend to ordinary shareholders.

(c) Provide for depreciation as follows:
plant and machinery 10% on cost
fixtures and fittings 5% on cost

(d) Rates for the year are £600.

(Joint Matriculation Board 'O' level)

42

Purchase of Existing Partnership and Sole Traders' Businesses

Quite frequently an existing partnership or sole trader's business is taken over as a going concern. At this juncture several methods of how this is done can be considered:

(i) An individual purchases the business of a sole trader.
(ii) A partnership acquires the business of a sole trader.
(iii) Existing businesses of sole traders join together to form a partnership.
(iv) A limited company takes over the business of a sole trader or partnership.

It must not be thought that because the assets bought are shown in the selling firm's books at one value, that the purchaser(s) must record the assets taken over in its own books at the same value. The values shown in the books of the purchaser(s) are those values at which they are buying the assets, such values being frequently quite different than those shown in the selling firm's books. As an instance of this, the selling firm may have bought premises many years ago for £10,000, but they may now be worth £50,000. The purchaser buying the premises will obviously have to pay £50,000, and it is therefore this value that is recorded in the books of the purchaser(s). Alternatively, the value at which it is recorded in the books of the purchaser(s) may be less than that shown in the selling firm's books. Where the total purchase consideration exceeds the total value of the indentifiable assets then such excess is the goodwill. Should the total purchase consideration be less than the values of the identifiable assets, then the difference would be entered in a Capital Reserve Account.

It is easier to start with the takeover of the simplest sort of business unit, that of a sole trader. Some of the Balance Sheets shown will be deliberately simplified so that the principles involved are not hidden behind a mass of complicated calculations.

To illustrate the takeover of a business, given varying circumstances, the same business will be assumed to be taken over in different ways. The balance sheet of this business is that of A. Brown, Exhibit 42.1.

Exhibit 42.1

A. Brown
Balance Sheet as at 31 December 19-6

	£
Fixtures	30,000
Stock	8,000
Debtors	7,000
Bank	1,000
	46,000
	£
Capital	43,000
Creditors	3,000
	46,000

(a) An individual purchases business of sole trader.

(i) Assume that the assets and liabilities of A. Brown, with the exception of the bank balance, are taken over by D. Towers. He is to take over the assets and liabilities at the valuations as shown. The price to be paid is £52,000. The opening balance sheet of Towers will be as in Exhibit 42.2.

Exhibit 42.2

D. Towers
Balance Sheet as at 1 January 19-7

	£
Goodwill	10,000
Fixtures	30,000
Stock	8,000
Debtors	7,000
	55,000
	£
Capital	52,000
Creditors	3,000
	55,000

As £52,000 had been paid for net assets (assets less liabilities) valued at £30,000 + £8,000 + £7,000 − £3,000 = £42,000, the excess £10,000 represents the amount paid for goodwill.

(ii) Suppose that, instead of the information just given, the same amount had been paid by Towers, but the assets were taken over at a value of Fixtures £37,000; Stock £7,500; Debtors £6,500, the opening balance sheet of D. Towers would have been as in Exhibit 42.3.

Exhibit 42.3

D. Towers
Balance Sheet as at 1 January 19-7

	£
Goodwill	4,000
Fixtures	37,000
Stock	7,500
Debtors	6,500
	55,000

	£
Capital	52,000
Creditors	3,000
	55,000

As £52,000 had been paid for net assets valued at £37,000 + £7,500 + £6,500 − £3,000 = £48,000, the excess £4,000 represents the amount paid for goodwill. The other assets are shown at their value to the purchaser, Towers.

(b) Partnership acquires business of a sole trader

Assume instead that the business of Brown had been taken over by M. Ukridge and D. Allen. The partners are to introduce £30,000 each as capital. The price to be paid for the net assets, other than the bank balance, is £52,000. The purchasers placed the following values on the assets taken over: Fixtures £40,000; Stock £7,000; Debtors £6,000.

The opening balance sheet of Ukridge and Allen will be as in Exhibit 42.4.

Exhibit 42.4

M. Ukridge & D. Allen
Balance Sheet as at 1 January 19-7

	£
Goodwill	2,000
Fixtures	40,000
Stock	7,000
Debtors	6,000
Bank	8,000
	63,000

	£
Capitals:	
M. Ukridge	30,000
D. Allen	30,000
	60,000
Creditors	3,000
	63,000

The sum of £52,000 has been paid for net assets of £40,000 + £7,000 + £6,000 − £3,000 = £50,000. This makes goodwill be the excess of £2,000.

The bank balance is made up of £30,000 + £30,000 introduced by the partners, less £52,000 paid to Brown = £8,000.

(c) Amalgamation of Existing Sole Traders

Now assume that Brown was to enter into partnership with T. Owens whose last balance sheet was as shown in Exhibit 42.5.

Exhibit 42.5

T. Owens
Balance Sheet as at 31 December 19-6

	£
Premises	20,000
Fixtures	5,000
Stock	6,000
Debtors	9,000
Bank	2,000
	42,000
	£
Capital	37,000
Creditors	5,000
	42,000

(i) If the two traders were to amalgamate all their business assets and liabilities, at the values as shown, the opening balance sheet of the partnership would be as in Exhibit 42.6.

Exhibit 42.6

A. Brown & T. Owens
Balance Sheet as at 1 January 19-7

	£
Premises	20,000
Fixtures	35,000
Stock	14,000
Debtors	16,000
Bank	3,000
	88,000
Capitals:	£
Brown	43,000
Owens	37,000
Creditors	8,000
	88,000

(ii) Suppose that instead of both parties agreeing to amalgamation at the asset values as shown, the following values had been agreed to:

Owen's premises to be valued at £25,000, and his stock at £5,500. Other items as per last balance sheet, Brown's fixtures to be valued at £33,000, his stock at £7,200 and debtors at £6,400. It is also to be taken that Brown has goodwill, value £7,000, whereas Owen's goodwill was considered valueless. Other items as per last balance sheet.

The opening balance sheet will be at the revised figures, and is shown as Exhibit 42.7.

Exhibit 42.7

A. Brown & T. Owen
Balance Sheet as at 1 January 19-7

	£
Goodwill	7,000
Premises	25,000
Fixtures	38,000
Stock	12,700
Debtors	15,400
Bank	3,000
	101,100

	£
Capitals:	
Brown	51,600
Owen	41,500
Creditors	8,000
	101,100

Brown's capital can be seen to be £43,000 + £3,000 (fixtures) − £800 (stock) − 600 (debtors) + £7,000 (goodwill) = £51,600.

Owen's capital is £37,000 + £5,000 (premises) − £500 (stock) = £41,500.

(d) Limited Company acquires business of sole trader

More complicated examples will be examined in volume two. In this volume only an elementary treatment will be considered.

Before the acquisition the balance sheet of D. Lucas Ltd was as shown in Exhibit 42.8.

Exhibit 42.8.

D. Lucas Ltd.

Balance Sheet as at 31 December 19-6

	£
Fixtures	36,000
Stock	23,000
Debtors	14,000
Bank	6,000
	79,000
Share Capital:	£
Preference Shares	20,000
Ordinary Shares	40,000
Profit and Loss	8,000
Creditors	11,000
	79,000

(i) Assume that Brown's business had been acquired, except for the bank balance, goodwill being valued at £8,000 and the other assets and liabilities at balance sheet values. Lucas Ltd is to issue an extra 32,000 £1 ordinary shares at par and 18,000 £1 preference shares at par – to Brown, in full settlement of the £50,000 net assets taken over.

Exhibit 42.9 shows the balance sheet of the company before and after the acquisition.

Exhibit 42.9

Lucas Ltd.

Balance Sheets

	Before	+ or –	After
	£		£
Goodwill	–	+ 8,000	8,000
Fixtures	36,000	+ 30,000	66,000
Stock	23,000	+ 8,000	31,000
Debtors	14,000	+ 7,000	21,000
Bank	6,000		6,000
	79,000		132,000

	Before	+ or –	After
	£		£
Share Capital:			
Preference	20,000	+ 18,000	38,000
Ordinary	40,000	+ 32,000	72,000
Profit & Loss	8,000		8,000
Creditors	11,000	+ 3,000	14,000
	79,000		132,000

(ii) If instead we assume that the business of Brown was acquired as follows:

The purchase price to be satisfied by Brown being given £5,000 cash and to issue to him an extra 50,000 ordinary shares at par and £10,000 debentures at par. The assets taken over to be valued at Fixtures £28,000; Stock £7,500; Debtors £6,500. The bank balance is not taken over.

Exhibit 42.10 shows the balance sheet of the company after the acquisition.

Exhibit 42.10

Lucas Ltd.
Balance Sheets

	Before £	+ or −	After £
Goodwill	–	+ 26,000	26,000
Fixtures	36,000	+ 28,000	64,000
Stock	23,000	+ 7,500	30,500
Debtors	14,000	+ 6,500	20,500
Bank	6,000	− 5,000	1,000
	79,000		142,000

	Before £	+ or −	After £
Share Capital:			
Preference	20,000		20,000
Ordinary	40,000	+ 50,000	90,000
Debentures		+ 10,000	10,000
Profit & Loss	8,000		8,000
Creditors	11,000	+ 3,000	14,000
	79,000		142,000

Goodwill is calculated: Purchase consideration is made up of ordinary shares £50,000 + debentures £10,000 + bank £5,000 = £65,000.

Nets assets bought are: Fixtures £28,000 + Stock £7,500 + Debtors £6,500 − Creditors £3,000 = £39,000.

Therefore Goodwill is £65,000 − £39,000 = £26,000.

Business Purchase Account

In this chapter, to economise on space and descriptions, only the balance sheets have been shown. However, in the books of the purchaser the purchase of a business should pass through a 'Business Purchase Account'.

This would be as follows:

Business Purchase Account

Debit	*Credit*
Each liability taken over.	Each asset taken over at
Vendor: net amount of	values placed on it,
purchase price.	including Goodwill.

Vendor's Account (Name of seller/s)

Debit	*Credit*
Bank (or Share Capital)	Amount to be paid
Amount paid	for business

Various Asset Accounts

Debit
Business Purchase (value placed
on asset taken over)

Various Liability Accounts

Credit
Amount of liability
taken over

Bank (or Share Capital)

Credit
Amount paid to Vendor.

Exercises

42.1.

C. Allen
Balance Sheet as at 31 December 19-4

	£
Premises	21,000
Stock	9,600
Debtors	6,300
Bank	1,700
	38,600

	£
Capital	31,800
Creditors	6,800
	38,600

(i) The business of Allen is taken over by S. Walters in its entirety. The assets are deemed to be worth the balance sheet values as shown. The price paid by Walters is £40,000. Show the opening balance sheet of Walters.

(ii) Suppose instead that R. Jones had taken over Allen's business. He does not take over the bank balance, and values premises at £28,000 and stock at £9,200. The price paid by him is £46,000. Show the opening balance sheet of Jones.

42.2A. I. Dodgem's balance sheet on 31 December 19-8 was as follows:

	£
Premises	55,000
Plant and machinery at cost	
less depreciation	21,000
Fixtures and fittings at cost *less* depreciation	4,000
Stock	17,000
Trade debtors	9,500
Cash	4,500
	£111,000

	£
Capital	87,000
Trade creditors	8,000
Bank overdraft	15,800
Expenses owing	200
	£111,000

An opportunity had arisen for Dodgem to acquire the business of A. Swing who was retiring.

A. Swing
Balance Sheet as at 31 December 19-8

	£
Premises	25,000
Plant	9,000
Motor Vehicle	3,500
Stock	11,000
Trade debtors	6,000
Bank	8,000
Cash	500
	£63,000
Capital	54,000
Trade Creditors	9,000
	63,000

Dodgem agreed to take over Swing's premises, plant, stock, trade debtors and trade creditors.

For the purpose of his own records Dodgem valued the premises at £35,000, plant at £6,000 and stock at £8,000.

The agreed purchase price was £50,000 and in order to finance the purchase Dodgem had obtained a fixed loan for 5 years from his bank, for one half of the purchase price on the condition that he contributed the same amount from his own private resources in cash. The purchase price was paid on 1 January 19-9.

Dodgem also decided to scrap some of his oldest plant and machinery which cost £9,000 with depreciation to date £8,000. This was sold for scrap for £300 cash on 1 January 19-9. On the same date he bought some new plant for £4,000, paying in cash.

Required:
(1) The purchase of business account in I. Dodgem's books.
(2) I. Dodgem's balance sheet as at 1 January 19-9 after all the above transactions have been completed.

(Associated Examining Board 'O' level)

42.3. (*a*) On 31 May 19-2 T. Roberts' Balance Sheet was as follows:

	£
Premises	80,000
Stock	5,000
Debtors	4,000
Cash and bank	2,450
	£91,450

	£
Capital	90,000
Creditors	1,450
	£91,450

On 1 June 19-2 W. Deakins, who had £120,000 in his business account, bought the business as a going concern for £110,000, taking over all liabilities and assets except cash and bank, at T. Roberts' valuation.

Set out W. Deakins' Balance Sheet on 1 June 19-2.

(*b*) Smith and Williams were in partnership sharing profit and loss equally. Their Balance Sheet on 31 May 19-2 was as follows:

	£
Premises	80,000
Stock	14,000
Debtors	4,000
Bank	2,000
	£100,000

	£
Capital Smith	50,000
Williams	50,000
	£100,000

Vernon was admitted as a partner from 1 June 19-2, bringing in £50,000 in cash. £40,000 of this cash was used immediately to purchase additional fixtures and fittings. However, before admitting Vernon the original partners agreed that the business was worth £140,000 as a going concern. The partners also agreed that for the time being the accounts should represent the full value of the business as a going concern.

Set out the opening Balance Sheet of the new partnership.

(*c*) Outline *one* method of dealing with the goodwill of the business when the proprietors decide to eliminate it from the accounts.

(University of London 'O' level)

42.4A. T. Smith, R. Wilkins and R. Yarrow were three small haulage contractors.

Their assets and liabilities on 31 May 19-1 were as follows:

	Smith	Wilkins	Yarrow
	£	£	£
Premises	13,000	15,000	8,000
Vehicles	10,000	18,000	6,000
Equipment	4,000	8,000	3,000
Debtors	1,300	1,800	600
Balance in bank	1,400	2,700	800
	29,700	45,500	18,400
Creditors	400	1,250	180
Capital	29,300	44,250	18,220
	29,700	45,500	18,400

The three decided to amalgamate into one partnership, which took over all assets and liabilities.

An independent valuer agreed the book values of all fixed assets, but considered a provision for doubtful debts should be made in each case as follows:

Smith	1% of debtors
Wilkins	2% of debtors
Yarrow	£200

He valued the businesses as going concerns as follows:

	£
Smith	35,000
Wilkins	50,000
Yarrow	25,000

(a) The new partnership came into existence on 1 June 19-1. Set out the opening Balance Sheet on that date.

(b) On 2 June 19-1 it was agreed to sell the premises which had belonged to Yarrow and to operate from the other two depots. Yarrow insisted that as the property had belonged to him he should receive the proceeds of the sale for his private purposes. Explain whether or not Yarrow is justified in his claim.

(University of London 'O' level)

42.5. A small private company is formed to take over the manufacturing business of John Crofton. The company will be known as John Crofton (Successor) Ltd.

The Company has an authorised capital of £100,000 divided into shares of 50p each. All the shares are issued and fully paid, including a premium of 10p per share. Fees and expenses paid in forming the new company amounted to £500.

The company took over all assets and liabilities with effect from 1 April 19-9, paying immediately a purchase price of £90,000.

The tangible assets taken over were valued as follows:

	£
Premises	30,000
Machinery and plant	15,000
Vehicles	13,000
Stocks	3,170
Debtors	2,400 (book value £3,000)

The liabilities taken over amounted to £4,000.

The company immediately bought new machinery at a cost of £20,000. One half of this price was paid immediately, the remainder will be paid during July 19-9.

Additional stocks were bought on credit for £5,400.

Set out (in long form) the opening Balance Sheet of John Crofton (Successor) Ltd. as at 1 April 19-9.

(University of London 'O' level)

42.6A. Spectrum Ltd. is a private company with an authorised capital of £700,000 divided into shares of £1 each. 500,000 shares have been issued and are fully paid. The company has been formed to acquire small retail shops and establish a chain of outlets.

The company made offers to three sole traders and purchased the businesses run by Red, Yellow and Blue.

The assets acquired, liabilities taken over, and prices paid are listed below:

	Red £	Yellow £	Blue £
Premises	75,000	80,000	90,000
Delivery vans	7,000	—	10,000
Furniture & fittings	12,000	13,000	13,000
Stock	8,000	7,000	12,000
Creditors	6,000	8,000	7,000
Purchase price	120,000	130,000	150,000

The company also purchased a warehouse to be used as a central distribution store for £60,000. This has been paid.

Preliminary expenses (formation expenses) of £15,000 have also been paid.

The company took over the three shops outlined above and started trading on 1 January 19-2.

Approaches have also been made to Green for the purchase of his business for £100,000. Green has accepted the offer and the company will take over in the near future the following assets and liabilities:

	£
Premises	70,000
Stock	18,000
Creditors	3,000

The transaction had not been completed on 1 January 19-2 and Green was still running his own business.

(a) Prepare the opening Balance Sheet of Spectrum Ltd. as at 1 January 19-2.
(b) How would you advise Spectrum Ltd. to finance the purchase of Green's business when the deal is completed?

(University of London 'O' level)

43

Funds Flow Statements:
An Introduction

A profit and loss account discloses the net profit (or loss) resulting from the business during a period. A balance sheet simply lists the balances remaining after the profit and loss account has been prepared. The balance sheet balances will however normally be quite different from those of last year's balance sheet. A funds flow statement endeavours to show the connection between the items in the two successive balance sheets. Whereas the profit and loss account will disclose the result of trading etc., the funds statement gives information as to the other types of activity which have occurred during the period, e.g. what fixed assets have been bought or sold, what loans have been obtained etc.

Further information from various forms of funds statements would enable the answers to be found such as:

> Why has the bank balance fallen?
> Where have the profits gone to?
> Why has the working capital increased?

In 1975 Statement of Standard Accounting Practice (SSAP 10 – see Chapter 10) was issued. All companies, except very small ones, have to prepare a 'Statement of Sources and Application of Funds'. In the SSAP 10 'funds' are working capital, although elsewhere there has been a wider interpretation of the meaning of 'funds'. In volume 2 SSAP 10 will be examined in detail. The present chapter looks at simple funds statements, without restricting itself to the 'working capital' definition of funds.

For this simple approach the definition of funds will be that of 'resources' as defined in Chapter 1 when the accounting equation was introduced.

Before actually performing the mechanics of constructing simple funds statements it must be stressed that:

(i) The statement supplements the information given in the Profit and Loss Account and Balance Sheet,

(ii) The funds statement is a period statement which shows the main changes which have taken place in the financial structure of the business as a result of *all* activities, i.e. not just the trading activities.

(iii) The technique used when preparing the statement is the comparison of two successive balance sheets to bring out the changes which have taken place in the period in between. Illustrations are now given of a sole trader's business.

Balance Sheet (1st date)		*Balance Sheet (2nd date)*	
	£		£
Premises	8,000	Premises	8,000
Stock	10,000	Stock	13,000
Bank	2,000	Bank	2,000
	20,000		23,000
		Capital	20,000
Capital	20,000	Creditors	3,000
			£23,000

At date 1 the funds supplied by the owner are represented by the resources of Premises, Stock and Bank, totalling £20,000.

Stock £3,000 is then bought on credit so that the balance sheet is changed to that shown of the 2nd date.

By comparing balance sheet 1 with balance sheet 2 it can be seen that the increase in stocks was financed by the credit allowed by the creditors. The Funds Statement can now be prepared.

Statement of Source and Application of Funds
for period from 1st date to 2nd date

	£
Source of Funds	
Creditors	3,000
Application of Funds	
Increase in Stock	3,000

Before the 3rd date £2,000 of the stock is sold on credit for £3,400. Then before the 4th date £1,500 was received from debtors and £1,200 of it is used to pay creditors.

Balance Sheet (3rd date)			*Balance Sheet (4th date)*		
	£	£		£	£
Premises		8,000	Premises		8,000
Stock		11,000	Stock		11,000
Debtors		3,400	Debtors		1,900
Bank		2,000	Bank		2,300
		24,400			23,200
Capital:	20,000		Capital:		21,400
Add Profit	1,400	21,400			
Creditors		3,000	Creditors		1,800
		24,400			23,200

By comparing balance sheet 2 and 3, it can be seen that stock has been reduced by £2,000 and the sale produced funds of that amount plus a further £1,400 in profit. This source of £3,400 is represented by a increase in debtors of the same amount. The second funds statement will accordingly show this.

By comparing balance sheet 3 and 4 it can be seen that debtors have provided funds of £1,500, represented partly by an increase in cash and partly by a reduction in creditors. The third funds statement will reveal that situation.

Statement of Source and Application of Funds for period 2nd date to 3rd date	£
Source of Funds	
Profit	1,400
Decrease in stock	2,000
	3,400
Application of Funds	
Increase in debtors	3,400

Statement of Source and Application of Funds for period 3rd date to 4th date	£
Source of Funds	
Decrease in debtors	1,500
Application of Funds	
Increase in bank	300
Decrease in creditors	1,200
	1,500

Adjustments Needed to Net Profit

When net profit is included as a source of funds, we usually have to adjust the net profit figure to take account of items included which do not involve a flow of funds. This will be illustrated by reference to balance sheets at 5th date and 6th date.

On the day that the balance sheet at the 5th date is being drawn up, extra Capital of £3,000 cash is brought in by the owner, and Fixtures are bought for £1,600, payment being made immediately.

Between then and the 6th date £3,200 stock is sold for £5,000 cash and the Fixtures are to be depreciated by £80. For the period the profit is therefore £1,800 − £80 = £1,720.

Balance Sheet (5th date)		£
Premises		8,000
Fixtures		1,600
Stock		11,000
Debtors		1,900
Bank		3,700
		26,200
Capital	21,400	
Add Cash Introduced	3,000	24,400
Creditors		1,800
		26,200

Balance Sheet (6th date)		£
Premises		8,000
Fixtures	1,600	
Less Depreciation	80	1,520
Stock		7,800
Debtors		1,900
Bank		8,700
		27,920
Capital	24,400	
Add Net Profit	1,720	26,120
Creditors		1,800
		27,920

When drawing up the Funds Statement for the period from date 4 to date 5 the purchase of Fixtures £1,600 will be shown as an application of funds. In the following period, date 5 to date 6, £80 is shown as depreciation of Fixtures and accordingly has also been deducted in calculating net profit. However the purchase of Fixtures in the previous period has already been treated as an application of Funds. As this has already been counted, Depreciation should not also be counted as an outflow of funds. To get to the correct figure of profit as a source of funds, the depreciation figure should accordingly be added back to the net profit figure.

Statement of Source and Application of Funds for period 4th date to 5th date		Statement of Source and Application of Funds for period 5th date to 6th date	
	£		
Source of Funds			£
Capital Introduced	3,000	Source of Funds	
		Net Profit	1,720
Application of Funds		Add Depreciation	80
Fixtures bought	1,600		
Increase in bank	1,400	Total generated from	
		operations	1,800
	3,000	Decrease in stock	3,200
			5,000
		Application of Funds	
		Increase in Bank	5,000
			5,000

Similarly, there are other non-cash items which would need adjusting to the net profit figure. These could be such items as provisions for bad debts or a book loss on the sale of a fixed asset. These can now be considered.

Between the 6th date and the 7th date £3,000 stock is sold for £5,100 to various customers on credit. As on the 7th date it is decided to make a provision for bad debts of £140. It is also decided to write off another £80 depreciation from fixtures. The net profit for the period will therefore be calculated as £5,100 − £3,000 = £2,100 less provision for bad debts £140 and depreciation £80 = £1,880.

Between the 7th date and the 8th date, the Premises were sold for £7,750, proceeds being received immediately. The £250 loss on sale was written off to profit and loss. Stock costing £2,300 was sold for £3,950 on credit. £1,100 is paid off amounts owing to creditors. For this period another £80 depreciation is to be written off fixtures. The net profit is therefore £3,950 − £2,300 = £1,650 less loss on premises £250 and depreciation £80 = £1,320. Note that the provision for bad debts has remained at £140.

	Balance Sheet (7th date)		
			£
Premises			8,000
Fixtures		1,520	
Less Depreciation		80	1,440
Stock			4,800
Debtors		7,000	
Less Provision		140	6,860
Bank			8,700
			29,800
Capital		26,120	
Add Net Profit		1,880	28,000
Creditors			1,800
			29,800

	Balance Sheet (8th date)		
			£
Fixtures		1,440	
Less Depreciation		80	1,360
Stock			2,500
Debtors		10,950	
Less Provision		140	10,810
Bank			15,350
			30,020
Capital		28,000	
Add Net Profit		1,320	29,320
Creditors			700
			30,020

Statement of Source and Application of Funds for period 6th date to 7th date

		£
Source of Funds		
Net Profit		1,880
Add Depreciation	80	
,, Provision for Bad Debts	140	220
Total Generated from Operation		2,100
Decrease in Stock		3,000
		5,100
Application of Funds		
Increase in Debtors		5,100

Statement of Source and Application of Funds for period 7th date to 8th date

		£
Source of Funds		
Net Profit		1,320
Add Depreciation	80	
,, Loss on Premises	250	330
Total Generated from Operations		1,650
Sale of Premises		7,750
Decrease in Stock		2,300
		11,700
Application of Funds		
Increase in Bank		6,650
Increase in Debtors		3,950
Decrease in Creditors		1,100
		11,700

Alternative Presentation

In chapter 11 the proposition that an accountant is a communicator was examined. Funds flow statements can be used to help communicate accounting information to those who are not well versed in Accounting, so that they may gain a better understanding of the financial statements.

Exhibit 43.1 gives two consecutive balance sheets of a business.

Exhibit 43.1

<table>
<tr><td colspan="3">A. Jackson
Balance Sheet as at
31 December 19-5</td><td colspan="3">A. Jackson
Balance Sheet as at
31 December 19-6</td></tr>
<tr><td></td><td>£</td><td>£</td><td></td><td>£</td><td>£</td></tr>
<tr><td>Fixed Assets</td><td></td><td></td><td>Fixed Assets</td><td></td><td></td></tr>
<tr><td>Premises at cost</td><td></td><td>50,000</td><td>Premises at cost</td><td></td><td>57,500</td></tr>
<tr><td>Motor Vehicles at
cost</td><td>24,000</td><td></td><td>Motor Vehicles at
cost</td><td>24,000</td><td></td></tr>
<tr><td>Less Depreciation</td><td>6,000</td><td>18,000</td><td>Less Depreciation</td><td>7,200</td><td>16,800</td></tr>
<tr><td></td><td></td><td>68,000</td><td></td><td></td><td>74,300</td></tr>
<tr><td>Current Assets</td><td></td><td></td><td>Current Assets</td><td></td><td></td></tr>
<tr><td>Stock</td><td>27,500</td><td></td><td>Stock</td><td>46,500</td><td></td></tr>
<tr><td>Debtors</td><td>15,700</td><td></td><td>Debtors</td><td>13,150</td><td>59,650</td></tr>
<tr><td>Bank</td><td>8,200</td><td>51,400</td><td></td><td></td><td></td></tr>
<tr><td></td><td></td><td></td><td></td><td></td><td>133,950</td></tr>
<tr><td></td><td></td><td>119,400</td><td></td><td></td><td></td></tr>
<tr><td></td><td></td><td></td><td>Capital</td><td></td><td></td></tr>
<tr><td></td><td></td><td></td><td>Balance at 1.1.19-6</td><td></td><td>113,100</td></tr>
<tr><td>Capital</td><td></td><td></td><td>Add Net Profit</td><td></td><td>17,500</td></tr>
<tr><td>Balance at 1.1.19-5</td><td></td><td>108,800</td><td></td><td></td><td></td></tr>
<tr><td>Add Net Profit</td><td></td><td>12,800</td><td></td><td></td><td>130,600</td></tr>
<tr><td></td><td></td><td></td><td>Less Drawings</td><td></td><td>9,200</td></tr>
<tr><td></td><td></td><td>121,600</td><td></td><td></td><td>121,400</td></tr>
<tr><td>Less Drawings</td><td></td><td>8,500</td><td></td><td></td><td></td></tr>
<tr><td></td><td></td><td>113,100</td><td>Current Liabilities</td><td></td><td></td></tr>
<tr><td>Current Liabilities</td><td></td><td></td><td>Creditors</td><td>4,250</td><td></td></tr>
<tr><td>Creditors</td><td></td><td>6,300</td><td>Bank Overdraft</td><td>8,300</td><td>12,550</td></tr>
<tr><td></td><td></td><td>119,400</td><td></td><td></td><td>133,950</td></tr>
</table>

A. Jackson asks his accountant to explain

(a) Why he now has a bank overdraft when last year he had money in the bank, and has run the business at a profit?

(b) Why his working capital has decreased during the year.

The accountant might draft his fund flow statements as follows:

	(a)

A. Jackson
Statement of Source and Application of Funds for the year ended 31 December 19-6

	£
Source of Funds	
Net Profit	17,500
Add Depreciation	1,200
Total Generated from Operations	18,700
Reduction in Debtors	2,550
	21,250
Application of Funds	
Drawings	9,200
Extra Premises bought	7,500
Increase in Stock	19,000
Decrease in Creditors	2,050	37,750
Reduction in Bank Funds	(16,500)
Bank Balance 31.12.19-5	8,200
Bank Overdraft 31.12.19-6	8,300	16,500

	(b)

A. Jackson
Statement of Source and Application of Funds for the year ended 31 December 19-6

	£	£
Source of Funds		
Net Profit		17,500
Add Depreciation		1,200
		18,700
Application of Funds		
Purchase of Extra Premises	7,500	
Drawings	9,200	16,700
		2,000
Increase/(Decrease) in Working Capital		
Increase in Stock	19,000	
Decrease in Debtors	(2,550)	
Decrease in Creditors	2,050	
Decrease in Bank	(16,500)	
		2,000

Exercises

43.1. The following Balance Sheets relate to a business run by T. Welldone.

Balance Sheet as at 31 December 19-6

		£		£
Fixed Assets		20,000	Capital	34,000
Current assets:			Creditors	2,000
Stock	4,000			
Debtors	1,000			
Bank	11,000			
		16,000		
		36,000		36,000

Balance Sheet as at 31 December 19-7

		£		£
Fixed Assets		35,000	Capital	40,000
Current assets:			Loan	5,000
Stock	13,000		Creditors	6,000
Debtors	2,000			
Bank	1,000			
		16,000		
		51,000		51,000

Mr. Welldone considers that he has not done well, as his money
bank has fallen from £11,000 to £1,000, in spite of the fact that h
borrowed £5,000 and left £6,000 of his profit in the business.

(a) Set out a statement to show Mr. Welldone how the money has been spe.

(b) Comment on Mr. Welldone's judgement of his success based upon the
balance in the bank.

(University of London 'O' level)

43.2A.

Robert Taylor

Balance Sheet as at 31 December 19-6

	£		£
Premises	20,000	Capital 1 January 19-6	25,000
Fixtures	4,000	Add net profit	5,000
Stock	3,000		
Debtors	1,000		30,000
Cash in bank	1,000	Less drawings	3,000
Cash in hand	300		
			27,000
		Trade creditors	2,300
	29,300		29,300

Balance Sheet as at 31 December 19-7

	£		£
Premises	20,000	Capital 1 January 19-7	27,000
Fixtures	3,000	Add net profit	3,000
Stock	6,000		
Debtors	3,500		30,000
Cash in hand	100	Less drawings	4,000
			26,000
		Trade creditors	5,000
		Bank overdraft	1,600
	32,600		32,600

Study the Balance Sheets shown above.

(a) Calculate the working capital on 31 December 19-6 and on 31 December
19-7.

(b) Calculate the percentage of net profit on capital at the beginning of each
year.

(c) Comment on the changes which have taken place in the figures for net
profit and drawings.

(d) Explain why it has become necessary to raise an overdraft during 19-7
and, paying attention to and comparing the figures for debtors, creditors,
stock and cash, comment briefly on the state of the business.

(University of London 'O' level)

43.3. The Balance Sheets of a sole trader for two successive years are given below. You are required to calculate the variation in working capital and to explain how the variation has arisen.

Balance Sheets — as on 31 December

	19-3 £	19-4 £		19-3 £	19-4 £
Land and Premises (cost £3,000)	2,600	2,340	Capital Account: 1 January	4,200	4,700
Plant and Machinery (cost £2,000)	1,500	—	*Add* Net Profit for the year	1,800	2,200
(cost £3,000)	—	2,300		6,000	6,900
Stocks	660	630	Deduct Drawings	1,300	1,500
Trade Debtors	1,780	1,260		4,700	5,400
Bank	—	710	Trade Creditors	1,200	840
			Bank Overdraft	640	—
			Loan (repayable December 19-0)	—	1,000
	6,540	7,240		6,540	7,240

43.4A.

John Flynn
Balance Sheets as at 31 December

	19-8 £	19-9 £		19-8 £	19-9 £
Buildings	5,000	5,000	Capital at 1 January	15,500	16,100
Fixtures less depreciation	1,800	2,000	Add Cash Introduced	—	2,500
Motor less depreciation	2,890	5,470	,, Net Profit for year	6,800	7,900
Stock	3,000	8,410		22,300	26,500
Debtors	4,860	5,970	Less Drawings	6,200	7,800
Bank	3,100	—		16,100	18,700
Cash	350	150	Creditors	2,900	2,040
			Bank Overdraft	—	1,260
			Loan (repayable 19-5)	2,000	5,000
	21,000	27,000		21,000	27,000

From the balance sheets above draw up a statement showing how the variation in working capital has arisen. Fixtures bought during the year amounted to £400, and a motor was bought for £4,000.

44

The Calculation of Wages and Salaries Payable to Employees

In the U.K. wages are generally taken to be the earnings paid on a weekly basis to employees, whilst salaries are those paid on a monthly basis.

The earnings of employees, whether paid monthly or weekly, are subject to various deductions. These can consist of the following items.

(1) Income Tax. In the U.K. the wages and salaries of all employees are liable to have income tax deducted from them. This does not mean that everyone will pay Income Tax, but that if Income Tax is found to be payable then the employer will deduct the tax from the employee's wages or salary.

Each person in the U.K. is allowed to set various personal reliefs against the amount earned to see if he/she is liable to pay Income Tax. The reliefs given for each person depend upon his or her personal circumstances. Extra relief is given to a man who is married, as compared to a single man; further extra relief will be given for factors such as having dependent relatives, and so on. The reliefs given are changed from time to time by Parliament. Most students will know of the 'Budget' which is presented to Parliament by the Chancellor of the Exchequer, in which such changes are announced. After discussion by Parliament, and subject to possible changes there, the changes will be incorporated into a Finance Act. This means that, for instance, a single man earning a given amount might pay Income Tax, whereas a married man who is eligible for extra reliefs might earn the same amount and pay no Income Tax at all.

Once the reliefs have been deducted from the earnings, any excess of the earnings above that figure will have to suffer Income Tax being levied on it. As the rates of Income Tax change regularly, all that can be given here are the basic principles; the rates given are for purposes of illustration only. A further complication arises because the rate of tax increases in steps when the excess of the earnings exceeds certain figures.

For instance, assume that the rate of Income Tax are (on the amount actually exceeding the reliefs for each person):

On the first £1,000   Income Tax at 20 per cent
On the next £5,000   Income Tax at 30 per cent
On the remainder   Income Tax at 50 per cent

The Income Tax payable by each of four persons can now be looked at.

Miss Jones earns £1,500 per annum. Her personal reliefs amount to £1,700. Income Tax payable = Nil.

Mr Bland earns £4,000 per annum. His personal reliefs are £3,400. He therefore has £600 of his earnings on which he will have to pay Income Tax. As the rate on the first £1,000 taxable is 20 per cent, then he will pay £600 × 20 per cent = £120.

Mrs Hugo earns £6,500 per annum. She has personal reliefs amounting to £2,700. She will therefore pay Income Tax on the excess of £3,800. This will amount to:

On the first £1,000 tax at 20 per cent	=	200
On the remaining £2,800 tax at 30 per cent	=	840
Total Income Tax		£1,040

Mr Pleasance has a salary of £10,000 per annum. His personal reliefs amount to £3,560. He will therefore pay Income Tax on the excess of £6,440. This will amount to:

On the first £1,000 tax at 20 per cent	=	200
On the next £5,000 tax at 30 per cent	=	1,500
On the next £440 tax at 50 per cent	=	220
Total Income Tax		£1,920

The actual deduction of the Income Tax from the earnings of the employee is made by the employer. The tax is commonly called P.A.Y.E. tax, which represents the initial letters for Pay As You Earn. The amount of reliefs to which each employee is entitled is communicated to the employer in the form of a Notice of Coding, on which a code number is stated. The code number is then used in conjunction with special tax tables to show the amount of the tax deductible from the employee's earnings.

So far the amount of tax payable by anyone has been looked at on an annual basis. However, P.A.Y.E. means precisely that: it involves paying the tax as the earnings are calculated on each pay date, weekly or monthly, and not waiting until after the end of the year to pay the bill. The code numbers and the tax tables supplied to the employer by the Inland Revenue are so worked out that this is possible. It is outside the scope of this book to examine in detail how this is done. However, in the case of the three people already listed who will have to pay Income Tax, if we assume that Mrs Hugo is paid weekly, then from each week's wage she will have to pay one week's tax, in her case £1,040 ÷ 52 = £20. If Mr Bland and Mr Pleasance are paid on a monthly basis, then Mr Bland will have to pay £120 ÷ 12 = £10 per month, and Mr Pleasance £1,920 ÷ 12 = £160 per month.

It may well have crossed the reader's mind that, for many people, the year's earnings are not known in advance, and that the total amount payable, divided neatly into weekly or monthly figures, would not be known until the year was finished. The operation of the P.A.Y.E. system automatically allows for this problem. A book on Income Tax should be studied if the reader would like to investigate further how this is carried out.

(2) In the U.K. employees are also liable to pay National Insurance contributions. The deduction of these is carried out by the employer at the same time as the P.A.Y.E. Income Tax deductions are effected. The payment of such National Insurance contributions is to ensure that the payer will be able to claim benefits from the State, if and when he is in a position to claim, such as unemployment benefit, sickness benefits, retirement pension and so on.

There is a lower limit for each employee below which no National Insurance is payable at all, and there is also a top limit, earnings above this amount being disregarded for National Insurance. These limits are changed by Parliament, usually annually. Any figures given in this book are by way of illustration only.

If it is assumed that the lower limit of earnings eligible for National Insurance contributions is £1,000, and that the top limit is £10,000, and that the rate of National Insurance payable by the employee is 5 per cent, then the following contributions would be made:

Mrs Jones: part-time cleaner, earns £900 per annum. National Insurance contribution nil.

Miss Hardcastle, earnings £3,000 per annum. National Insurance contribution £3,000 × 5 per cent = £150. The fact that there is a lower limit of £1,000 does not mean that the first £1,000 of the earnings are free of National Insurance contributions, but simply that anyone earning less than £1,000 will not pay any. Someone earning £1,100 would pay National Insurance of £1,100 × 5 per cent = £55.

Mr Evergreen earns £12,000 per annum. He would pay at the rate of 5 per cent on £10,000 only = £500.

As with the P.A.Y.E. Income Tax, the National Insurance contribution is payable per week or per month.

It should be noted that in the U.K. part of the National Insurance contributions are in respect of a supplement to the retirement pension. This supplement to the pension is based on the amount actually earned by the person during the years he was paying towards this supplement, and on the number of years he actually paid contributions. The more he earned, the more he would pay in contributions, and he would therefore get a bigger supplement than someone earning less and contributing less.

However, it was recognized when the scheme was started that some firms had special superannuation funds (dealt with later in this chapter), so that the employees in those firms would not necessarily wish to have an extra supplement from the State on top of their State retirement pension. At the same time they would therefore not want to pay as much in National Insurance as the man who wanted such a supplement. These firms were therefore given the right to 'opt out', and employees in these firms pay a lower percentage of their earnings in National Insurance contributions.

(3) Superannuation contributions. Many firms have superannuation schemes. These are schemes whereby the employee will receive a pension on retiring from the firm, plus, very often, a lump sum payment in cash. They also usually include benefits which will be paid to an employee's spouse if the employee dies before reaching retirement age.

Some of these schemes are non-contributory. This means that the firm pays for these benefits for its employees without deducting anything from the employee's earnings. The other schemes are contributory schemes whereby the employee will pay a part of the cost of the scheme by an agreed deduction from his earnings. The actual percentages paid by employees will vary from firm to firm. In addition the firm will pay part of the cost of the scheme without any cost to the employee. With the advent of the State scheme for a supplement to the retirement pension some firms opted out of the State supplement scheme, so that their employees rely on the firm's superannuation scheme instead. They still qualify for the basic State retirement pension, it will only be the supplement that they will not receive. Other firms carry on their own superannuation scheme and are also in the State and the benefits from their firm's superannuation scheme on top as well.

Normally the contributions of employees to the superannuation schemes of their firms are tax deductible. This means that the part of their earnings taken as their contribution to the firm's scheme will escape Income Tax. This is not so with the contribution to any part of the State National Insurance scheme at the time that this book is being written.

Calculation of Net Wages/Salary Payable

Two illustrations of the calculation of the net pay to be made to various employees can now be looked at.

		£
(A) G. Jarvis:	Gross Earning for the week ended 8 May 19-4	100
	Income Tax: found by consulting tax tables and employee's code number	12
	National Insurance 5%	

G. Jarvis: Payslip Week ended 8 May 19-4

	£	£
Gross pay for the week		100
Less Income Tax	12	
,, National Insurance	5	17
Net Pay		83

		£
(B) H. Reddish:	Gross earnings for the month of May 19-4	800
	Income Tax (from tax tables)	150
	Superannuation: 6% of gross pay	
	National Insurance 5% of gross pay	

H. Reddish: Payslip Month ended 31 May 19-4

	£	£
Gross pay for the month		800
Less Income tax	150	
,, Superannuation	48	
,, National Insurance	40	238
Net Pay		562

National Insurance: Employer's Contribution

Besides the amount of the National Insurance which has to be suffered by the employee, the employer also has to pay a percentage based on the employee's pay as the firm's own contribution. This expense is suffered by the firm; it has no recourse against its employee. The percentage which the firm will have to pay varies as Parliament amend it to deal with the changing economic climate of the country. In this book it will be treated as though it is 10 per cent, but this figure is simply for illustration purposes. It does, however, at the time that this book is being written, equate to the approximate proportion which the employer pays as compared with that paid by the employee, the latter being about one-half of that suffered by the employer.

The entry of salaries and wages in the books of a firm can now be seen. A firm owned by H. Offerton has one employee, whose name is F. Edgeley. For the month of June 19-3 the payslip made out for Edgeley has appeared as:

F. Edgeley: Payslip month ended 30 June 19-3

		£
Gross Pay for the month		600
Less Income Tax	90	
,, National Insurance 5%	30	120
Net Pay		480

Additional to this, the firm will also have to pay its own share of the National Insurance contribution for Edgeley. This will be 10 per cent of £600 = £60. Therefore to employ Edgeley in the firm for this month has cost the firm the amount of his gross pay £600, plus £60 National Insurance, a total of £660. This means that when the firm draws up its Profit and Loss Account, the charge for the employment of this person for the month should be £660.

The firm has however acted as a collector of taxes and National Insurance on behalf of the government, and it will have to pay over to the government's agent, which is the Inland Revenue, the amount collected on its behalf. If it is assumed that the £90 deducted from pay for Income Tax, and the £30 deducted for National Insurance, are paid to the Inland Revenue on 30 June 19-3, then the cash book will appear as:

Cash Book (bank columns)

Dr		Cr	
		19-3	£
		Jun 30 Wages (cheque to Edgeley)	480
		,, ,, Inland Revenue (see below)*	180
*Made up of: Income Tax P.A.Y.E.	90		
National Insurance (employee's part)	30		
National Insurance (employer's part)	60		
	180		

In a firm as small as the one illustrated, both the figure of £480 and the £180 could be posted to a 'Wages and National Insurance Account', to give a total for the monthy of £660. In a larger firm such payments would be best posted to separate accounts for National Insurance and for P.A.Y.E. Income Tax, transfers then being made when the final accounts are drawn up.

Exercises

44.1. H. Smith is employed by a firm of carpenters at a rate of £1.50 per hour. During the week to 18 May 19-5 he worked his basic week of 40 hours. The Income Tax due on his wages was £8, and he is also liable to pay National Insurance contributions of 5 per cent. Calculate his net wages.

44.2. B. Charles is employed as an undertaker's assistant. His basic working week consists of 40 hours, paid at the rate of £2 per hour. For hours worked in excess of this he is paid at the rate of 1½ times his basic earnings. In the week ended 12 March 19-6 he worked 60 hours. Up to £40 a week he pays no Income Tax, but he pays it at the rate of 30 per cent for all earnings above that figure. He is liable to pay National Insurance at the rate of 5 per cent. Calculate his net wages.

44.3. B. Croft has a job as a car salesman. He is paid a basic salary of £200 per month, with a commission extra of 2 per cent on the value of his car sales. During the month of April 19-6 he sells £30,000 worth of cars. He pays Income Tax at the rate of 30 per cent on all earnings above £100 per month. He also pays National Insurance at the rate of 5 per cent on the first £500 of his monthly earnings, paying nothing on earnings above that figure. Calculate his net pay for the month.

44.4A. T, Penketh is an accountant with a firm of bookmakers. He has a salary of £500 per month, but he also has a bonus dependent on the firm's profits. The bonus for the month was £200. He pays National Insurance at the rate of 5 per cent on his gross earnings up to a maximum of £600 per month, there being no contribution for earnings above that figure. He pays Income Tax at the rate of thirty per cent on his earnings between £100 and £300 per month, and at the rate of 50 per cent on all earnings above that figure. However, before calculating earnings on which he has to pay Income Tax, he is allowed to deduct the amount of superannuation payable by him which is at the rate of 10 per cent on gross earnings. Calculate his net pay for the month.

44.5A. R. Kennedy is a security van driver. He has a wage of £100 per week, and danger money of £1 per hour in addition for every hour he spends in transporting gold bullion. During the week ended 16 June 19-3 he spends 20 hours taking gold bullion to London Airport. He pays Income Tax at the rate of 25 per cent on all his earnings above £80 per week. He pays National Insurance at the rate of 5 per cent on gross earnings. Calculate his net wage for the week.

44.6A. V. Mevagissey is a director of a company. She has a salary of £500 per month. She pays superannuation at the rate of 5 per cent. She also pays National Insurance at the rate of 5 per cent of gross earnings. Her Income Tax, due on gross salary less superannuation, is at the rate of 30 per cent after her personal reliefs for the month, other than superannuation, of £300 have been deducted. Calculate her net pay for the month.

45

An Introduction to the Analysis and Interpretation of Accounting Statements

Throughout the book there have been quite a few references to such items as the use of Accounting Ratios (see chapter 32), or to the fact that accounts do not disclose all the information about a business (see chapter 10). For students who will not carry their study of Accounting beyond the coverage of this book, further work is called for in some of their syllabuses. The topics omitted so far can now be dealt with. Volume 2 will consider analysis and interpretation in much more detail.

Fixed and Variable Expenses

Some expenses will remain constant whether activity increases or falls, at least within a given range of change of activity. These expenses are called 'fixed expenses'. An example of this would be the rent of a shop which would remain at the same figure, whether sales increased 10 per cent or fell 10 per cent. The same would remain true of such things as rates, fire insurance and so on.

Wages of shop assistants could also remain constant in such a case. If, for instance, the shop employed two assistants then it would probably keep the same two assistants, on the same wages, whether sales increased or fell by 10 per cent.

Of course, such 'fixed expenses' can only be viewed as fixed in the short term. If sales doubled then the business might well need a larger shop or more assistants. A larger shop would almost certainly mean higher rates, higher fire insurance and so on, and with more assistants the total wage bill would be larger.

'Variable' expenses on the other hand will change with swings in activity. Suppose that wrapping materials are used in the shop, then it could well be that an increase in sales of 10 per cent may see 10 per cent more wrapping materials used. Similary an increase of 10 per cent of sales, if all sales are despatched by parcel post, could well see delivery charges increase by 10 per cent.

Some expenses could be part fixed and part variable. Suppose that because of an increase in sales of 10 per cent, that telephone calls made increased by 10 per cent. With telephone bills the cost falls into two parts, one for the rent of the phone and the second part corresponding to the actual number of calls made. The rent would not change in such a case, and therefore this part of telephone expense would be 'fixed' whereas the calls cost could increase by 10 per cent.

This means that the effect of a percentage change in activity could have a more/or less percentage change in net profit, because the fixed expenses (within that range of activity) may not alter.

Exhibit 45.1 shows the change in net profit in business (A) which has a low proportion of its expenses as 'fixed' expenses, whereas in business (B) the 'fixed' expenses are a relatively high proportion of its expenses.

Exhibit 45.1

Business (A)

			(i) If sales fell 10%		(ii) If sales rose 10%	
			£		£	
Sales		50,000	45,000		55,000	
Less Cost of Goods Sold		30,000	27,000		33,000	
Gross Profit		20,000	18,000		22,000	
Less Expenses:						
Fixed	3,000		3,000		3,000	
Variable	13,000	16,000	11,700	14,700	14,300	17,300
Net Profit		4,000		3,300		4,700

Business (B)

			(i) If sales fell 10%		(ii) If sales rose 10%	
			£		£	
Sales		50,000	45,000		55,000	
Less Cost of Goods Sold		30,000	27,000		33,000	
Gross Profit		20,000	18,000		22,000	
Less Expenses:						
Fixed	12,000		12,000		12,000	
Variable	4,000	16,000	3,600	15,600	4,400	16,400
Net Profit		4,000		2,400		5,600

The comparison of percentage changes in net profit therefore works out as follows:

	(A)	(B)

Decrease of 10% in sales

$$\frac{\text{Reduction in profit}}{\text{Original profit}} \times \frac{100}{1} \quad \frac{700}{4,000} \times \frac{100}{1} = 17.5\% \quad \frac{1,600}{4,000} \times \frac{100}{1} = 40\%$$

Increase of 10% in sales

$$\frac{\text{Increase in profit}}{\text{Original profit}} \times \frac{100}{1} \quad \frac{700}{4,000} \times \frac{100}{1} = 17.5\% \quad \frac{1,600}{4,000} \times \frac{100}{1} = 40\%$$

It can be seen that a change in activity in business (B) which has a higher fixed expense content, will result in greater percentage changes in profit, 40% in (B) compared with 17.5% in (A).

Rate of Return of Net Profit on Capital Employed

In chapter 22 it was stated that the term 'Capital Employed' had not been standardised. In this chapter the average of the capital account will be used, i.e. (Opening Balance + Closing Balance) ÷ 2.

In business (C) and (D) in Exhibit 45.2 the same amount of net profits have been made, but capitals employed are different.

Exhibit 45.2
Balance Sheets

	(C) £	(D) £
Fixed + Current Assets − Current Liabilities	10,000	16,000
Capital Accounts:		
Opening Balance	8,000	14,000
Add Net Profits	3,600	3,600
	11,600	17,600
Less Drawings	1,600	1,600
	10,000	16,000

Return on Capital Employed is:

(C) $\dfrac{3,600}{(8,000+10,000) \div 2} \times \dfrac{100}{1} = 40\%$

(D) $\dfrac{3,600}{(14,000+16,000) \div 2} \times \dfrac{100}{1} = 24\%$

The ratio illustrates that what is important is not simply how much profit has been made but how well the capital has been employed. Business (C) has made far better use of its capital, achieving a return of £40 net profit for every £100 invested, whereas (D) has received only a net profit of £24 per £100.

Profitability and Liquidity

The return of profit on capital employed gives an overall picture of profitability. It cannot always be assumed, however, that profitability is everything that is desirable. Page 1 of this volume stresses that accounting is needed, not just to calculate profitability, but also to know whether or not the business will be able to meet its commitments as they fall due.

The two main measures of liquidity are the Current Ratio and the Acid Test Ratio.

Current Ratio $=$ $\dfrac{\text{Current Assets}}{\text{Current Liabilities}}$

This compares assets which will become liquid in approximately 12 months with liabilities which will be due for payment in the same period.

Acid Test Ratio $=$ $\dfrac{\text{Current Assets} - \text{Stock}}{\text{Current Liabilities}}$

This shows that provided creditors and debtors are paid at approximately the same time, a view might be made as to whether the business has sufficient liquid resources to meet its current liabilities.

Exhibit 45.3 shows how two businesses may have a similar profitability, yet their liquidity positions may be quite different.

Exhibit 45.3

	(E)		(F)	
Fixed Assets		40,000		70,000
Current Assets				
Stock	30,000		50,000	
Debtors	45,000		9,000	
Bank	15,000		1,000	
	90,000		60,000	
Less Current Liabilities	30,000	60,000	30,000	30,000
		100,000		100,000
Capital				
Opening Capital		80,000		80,000
Add Net Profit		36,000		36,000
		116,000		116,000
Less Drawings		16,000		16,000
		100,000		100,000

(Note: Sales for both E and F amounted to 144,000)

Profitability: This is the same for both businesses.

Net Profit as a percentage of sales $= \dfrac{36,000}{144,000} \times \dfrac{100}{1} = 25\%$

Net Profit as a percentage of capital employed

$= \dfrac{36,000}{(80,000 + 100,000) \div 2} \times \dfrac{100}{1} = 40\%$

However, there is a vast difference in the liquidity of the two businesses.

Working Capital ratios (E) = $\dfrac{90,000}{30,000}$ = 3 : (F) = $\dfrac{60,000}{30,000}$ = 2

this looks adequate on the face of it, but the acid test ratio reveals that (F) is in distress, as it will probably find it difficult to pay its current liabilities on time.

Acid Test ratio (E) = $\dfrac{60,000}{30,000}$ = 2 : (F) = $\dfrac{10,000}{30,000}$ = 0.33

Therefore, for a business to be profitable is not enough, it should also be adequately liquid as well.

Trend Figures

In examinations a student is often given just one year's accounting figures and asked to comment on them. Obviously, lack of space on an examination paper may preclude several year's figures being given, also the student lacks the time to prepare a comprehensive survey of several year's accounts.

In real life, however, it would be extremely stupid for anyone to base decisions on just one year's accounts, if more information was available. What is important for a business is not just what, say, accounting ratios are for one year, but what the trend has been.

Given two similar types of businesses G and H, both having existed for 5 years, if both of them had exactly the same ratios in year 5, are they both exactly desirable as investments? Given one year's accounts it may appear so, but if one had all the 5 year's figures it may not give the same picture, as Exhibit 45.4 illustrates.

Exhibit 45.4

		Years				
		1	2	3	4	5 (current)
Gross Profit as % of Sales	G	40	38	36	35	34
	H	30	32	33	33	34
Net Profit as % of Sales	G	15	13	12	12	11
	H	10	10	10	11	11
Net Profit as % Capital Employed	G	13	12	11	11	10
	H	8	8	9	9	10
Liquidity Ratio	G	3	2.8	2.6	2.3	2.0
	H	1.5	1.7	1.8	1.9	2.0

From these figures G appears to be the worst investment for the future, as the trend appears to be downwards. If the trend for G is continued it could be in a very dangerous financial situation in a year or two. Business H, on the other hand, is strengthening its position all the time.

Of course, it would be ridiculous to assert that H *will* continue on an upward trend. One would have to know much more about the business to be able to judge whether or not that could be true.

However, given all other desirable information, trend figures would be an extra important indicator.

Limitations of Accounting Statements

Final accounts are only partial information. They show the reader of them, in financial terms, what has happened *in the past*. This is better than having no information at all, but one needs to know much more.

First, it is impossible to sensibly compare two businesses which are completely unlike one another. To compare a supermarket's figures with those of a chemical factory would be rather pointless. It would be like comparing a lion with a lizard.

Second, there are a whole lot of factors that the past accounts do not disclose. The desire to keep to the money measurement concept, and the desire to be objective, both dealt with in chapter 10, exclude a great deal of desirable information. Some typical desirable information can be listed, *beware,* the list is *indicative* rather than exhaustive.

(a) What are the future plans of the business? Without this an investment in a busines would be sheer guesswork.

(b) Has the firm got good quality staff?

(c) Is the business situated in a location desirable for such a business? A ship-building business situated a long way up a river which was becoming unnavigable, to use an extreme example, could soon be in trouble.

(d) What is its position as compared with its competitors? A business manufacturing a single product, which has a foreign competitor which has just invented a much improved product which will capture the whole market, is obviously in for a bad time.

(e) Will future government regulations affect it? Suppose that a business which is an importer of goods from Country X, which is outside the E.E.C., finds that the E.E.C. is to ban all imports from Country X?

(f) Is its plant and machinery obsolete? If so, the business may not have sufficient funds to be able to replace it.

(g) Is the business of a high-risk type or in a relatively stable industry?

(h) Has the business got good customers? A business selling largely to Country Y, which is getting into trouble because of shortage of foreign exchange, could soon lose most of its trade. Also if one customer was responsible for, say, 60 per cent of sales, then the loss of that one customer would be calamitous.

(i) Has the business got good suppliers of its needs? A business in wholesaling could, for example, be forced to close down if manufacturers decided to sell direct to the general public.

(j) Problems concerned with the effects of distortion of accounting figures caused by inflation (or deflation) are contained in volume 2.

The reader can now see that the list would have to be an extremely long one if it was intended to cover all possibilities.

APPENDIX I

Examination Techniques

As an author I can now change my writing style here into that of the first person singular, as I want to put across to you a message about examinations, and I want you to feel that I am writing this for you as an individual rather than simply as one of the considerable number of people who have read the technical part of the book.

When you think about it, you have spent a lot of hours trying to master such things as double entry, balance sheets, suspense accounts and goodness knows what else. Learning accounting/bookkeeping does demand a lot of discipline and practice. Compared with the many hours learning the stuff, most students spend very little time actually considering in detail how to tackle the examination. You are probably one of them, and I would like you to take some time away from your revision of the various topics in the syllabus, and instead I want you to think about the examination.

Let me start by saying that if you want to understand anything about examinations then you have got to understand examiners, so let us look together at what these peculiar creatures get up to in an examination. The first thing is that when they set an examination they are looking at it on the basis that they want good students to get a pass mark. Obviously anyone who doesn't achieve the pass mark will fail, but the object of the exercise is to find those who will pass rather than to find the failures. This means that if you have done your work properly, and if you are not sitting for an examination well above your intellectual capabilities, then you should manage to get a pass mark. By now you are probably falling asleep, but it was important to stress that before I could get down to the details of setting about the task.

There are, however, quite a large number of students who will fail, not because they haven't put in enough hours on their studies, not because they are unintelligent, but simply because they throw away marks unecessarily by poor examination technique. If you can read the rest of this piece, and then say honestly that you wouldn't have committed at least one of the mistakes that I am going to mention, then you are certainly well outside the ordinary range of students.

Before thinking about the examination paper itself, let us think about how you are going to get to the examination room. If it is at your own college then you have no problems as to how you will get there. On the other hand it may be at an external centre. Do you know exactly where the place is? If not, you had better have a trip there if possible. How are you going to get there? If you are going by bus or train do you know which bus or train to catch? Will it be the rush hour when it may well take you much longer than mid-day? Quite a large proportion of students lose their way on their way to the examination room, or else arrive, breathless and flustered, at the very last minute. They then start off the attempt at the examination in a somewhat nervous state, a recipe for disaster for a lot of students. So plan how you are going to get there, and give yourself enough time.

Last minute learning of stuff for your examination will be of little use to you. The last few days before the examination should not be spent in cramming. You can look at past examination papers and rework some of them. This is totally different from trying to cram new facts into your head. On the way to the exam don't read textbooks, try reading the newspaper or something similar.

* This is probably the first examination you will have taken in
* bookkeeping/Accounting. At this level the examiner is very much
* concerned with your practical ability in the subject. Accounting is
* a practical subject, and your practical competence is about to be
* tested. The examiner will therefore expect the answers to be neat
* and well set out. Untidy work with figures spread over the sheet
* in a haphazard way, badly written figures, and columns of figures
* in which the vertical columns are not set down in straight lines,
* will incur the examiner's displeasure.
*   Really, what you should say to yourself is: 'Suppose I was in
* charge of an office, doing this type of book-keeping work, what
* would I say if one of my assistants put on my desk a sheet of
* paper with book-keeping entries on it written in the same manner
* as my own efforts in attempting this examination question?'. Just
* look at some of the work you have done in the past in book-
* keeping. Would you have told your assistant to go back and do
* the work again because it is untidy? If you would say that about
* your own work then why should the examiner think any
* different.
*   Anyone who works in Accounting knows full well that
* untidy work leads to completely unnecessary errors. Therefore
* the examiner insisting on clear, tidy, well laid-out work is not
* being Victorian in approach, he/she wants to ensure that you are
* not going to mess up the work of an Accounting department.
* Imagine going to the Savings Bank and the manager says to you
* 'We don't know whether you've got £5 in the account or £5,000.
* You see the work of our clerks is so untidy that we can never sort
* out exactly how much is in anybody's account.' I would guess
* that you wouldn't want to put a lot of money into an account at
* that bank. How would you feel if someone took you to court for
* not paying a debt of £100 when in fact you owed them nothing?
* All of this sort of thing would happen all the time if we simply
* allowed people to keep untidy accounts. The examiner is there to
* ensure that the person to whom he gives a certificate will be
* worthy of it, and will not continually mess up the work of any
* firm at which he/she may work in the future.
*   I can imagine quite a few of you groaning at all of this, and if
* you don't want to pass the examination then please give up
* reading here. If you do want to pass, and your work is untidy,

then what can you do about it? Well, the answer is simple enough: start right now to be neat and orderly in your work. Quite a lot of students have said to me over the years 'I may be giving you untidy work now, but when I actually get in the exam room I will then do my work neatly enough.' This is as near impossible as anything can be. You cannot suddenly be able to do accounting work neatly, and certainly not when you are under the stress and strain of an examination. Even the neatest worker may well find that in an examination that his/her work may not be of its usual standard because of the fact that nervousness will see them make mistakes. If this is true, then if you are an untidy worker now your work in an examination is likely to be even more untidy. Have I convinced you yet?

The next thing is that work should not only be neat and well laid out. Headings should always be given, and any dates needed should be inserted. The test you should apply is to imagine that you are a partner in a firm of professional accountants and you are away on holiday for a few weeks. During that time your assistants have completed all sorts of work including reports, drafting final accounts, various forms of other computations and so on. All of this work is deposited on your desk while you are away. When you return you look at each item in the pile of stuff awaiting your attention. Suppose the first item is a Trading and Profit and Loss Account for the year ended 31 December 19-5 in respect of J. King, one of your clients. When you looked at it you could see that it was a Trading and Profit and Loss Account, but that you didn't know for which client, nor did you know which year it was for. Would you be annoyed with your staff? – of course you would. So therefore in an examination why should the examiner accept as a piece of your work a Trading and Profit and Loss Account answer without the name of the business on top, the fact that it was a Trading and Profit and Loss Account also written across the top, and in addition the period covered by it? Similarly a bank reconciliation statement should also state that fact and show the date and the name of the client. If proper headings are not given you will lose a lot of marks, even though the actual calculations of the gross and net profits are correct. Always therefore put in the headings properly; don't wait until your examination to start this correct practice.

If you have now got the right attitude about setting out your work, we must now look at the way in which you should tackle the examination paper when the time comes. One of the troubles about bookkeeping/accounting examinations is that the student is expected to do a lot of work in a relatively short time. I have personally campaigned against this attitude, but the tradition is of long-standing and I am therefore afraid that you are stuck with it. It will be the same for every other student taking your examination, so it is not unfair as far as any one student is concerned. Working at speed does bring about various disadvantages, and makes the way you tackle the examination of even greater importance than for examinations where the pace is more leisurely.

Very approximately, the marks allotted to each question will give you some idea as to how long you should take over the question. At this level quite a few of the papers are of 2 hours' duration. This means 100 possible marks for 120 minutes work. If your arithmetic is any good you will be able to see that to work out how long a question should take, the thing to do is to take the number of marks for the question and add one-fifth of that figure to equal minutes available. For example, a question with 30 marks should take 30 + one-fifth of 30 = 30 + 6 = 36 minutes, or a question worth 10 marks should take 10 + one-fifth of 10 = 10 + 2 = 12 minutes. In a 3-hour examination the easiest way to calculate it is to double the number given for marks and then subtract one-tenth of that total, so that a 25-mark question should take 25 × 2 = 50 less one-tenth, i.e. 5 = 45 minutes, or a 10-mark question should take 10 × 2 = 20 less one-tenth 2 = 18 minutes. Get used to working out, for your particular examination, how long questions should take.

However, the calculation of minutes to be spent on each question is an approximate one. If you are working in an examination room and you are beating the clock − for instance in a 2-hour examination − if, after half an hour you have attempted questions with a possible total of 30 marks, then you will feel more confident, as in that amount of time on a strict apportionment of marks as already described, you will have been expected to have attempted questions with a total of possible marks of 25. If, on the other hand, you have spent half an hour and are still struggling only part way through a long question worth 20 marks altogether, then it would not be surprising if you were becoming rather anxious. In fact examiners usually set what might be called 'warm-up' questions. These are usually fairly short, and not very difficult, questions and the examiner will expect you to tackle these questions first of all. You will probably be able to do these questions in less time than the time normally allocated. The examiner is trying to be kind to you. He knows that there is a certain amount of nervousness on the part of a student taking an examination, and he will want to give you the chance to calm down by letting you tackle these short, relatively easy questions, first of all, and generally settle down to your work.

	£
Opening Stock	4,000
Add Purchases	11,500
	15,500
Less Closing Stock	3,800
	12,700

One golden rule which should always be observed is 'show all of your workings'. Suppose for instance you have been asked to work out the Cost of Goods Sold, not simply as part of a Trading Account but for some other reason. On a scrap of paper you work out the answers above.

You put down the answer as £12,700. The scrap of paper with your workings on it is then crumpled up by you and thrown in the waste-paper basket as you leave the room. You may have noticed in reading this that in fact the answer should have been 11,700 and not 12,700, as the arithmetic was incorrect. The examiner may well have allocated say, 4 marks for this bit of the question. What will he do when he simply sees your answer as £12,700? Will he say: 'I should imagine that the candidate mis-added to the extent of £1,000, and as I am not unduly penalising for arithmetic, I will give the candidate 3½ marks.' I'm afraid the examiner cannot do this; the candidate has got the answer wrong, there is no supporting evidence, and so the examiner gives marks as nil. If you had only attached the workings to your answer, then I have no doubt that you would have got 3½ marks at least.

On the other hand, do not expect that these 'warm-up' questions will be numbered 1 and 2 on your examination paper. Most accounting examinations start off with a rather long-winded question, worth quite a lot of marks, as question number 1 on the paper. Over the years I have advised students not to tackle these questions first. A lot of students are fascinated by the fact that such a question is number 1, that it is worth a lot of marks, and their thinking runs: 'If I do this question first, and make a good job of it, then I am well on the way to passing the examination.' I do not deny that a speedy and successful attempt at such a question would probably lead to a pass. The trouble is that this doesn't usually happen, and many students have told me afterwards that their failure could be put down to simply ignoring this advice. What happens very often, is that the student starts off on such a question, things don't go very well, a few mistakes are made, the student then looks at the clock and see that he/she is not 'beating the clock' in terms of possible marks, and then panic descends on him/her. Leaving that question very hastily the student then proceeds to the next question, which normally might have been well attempted, but because of the state of mind a hash is made of that one as well, and so you may fail an examination which you had every right to think you could pass.

As this stage there are not usually many essay-type questions. Before I discuss these I want you to look at two questions set recently at this stage. Having done that visualise carefully what you would write in answer to them. Here they are:

(a) You are employed as a book-keeper by G. Jones, a trader. State briefly what use you would make of the following documents in relation to your book-keeping records.

(i) A bank statement.

(ii) A credit note received to correct an overcharge on an invoice.

(iii) A paying-in slip.

(iv) Petty cash voucher.

(b) Explain the term 'depreciation'. Name and describe briefly two methods of providing for depreciation of fixed assets.

Now we can test whether or not you would have made a reasonably good attempt at the questions. With question (a) a lot of students would have written down what a bank statement is, what a paying-in slip is, what a petty cash voucher is and so on. Marks gained by you for an answer like that would be . . . nil. Why is this? Well you simply have not read the question properly. The question asked what USE you would make of the documents, and not instead to describe what the documents were. The bank statement would be used to check against the bank column in the cash book or cash records to see that the bank's entries and your own were in accordance with one another, with a bank reconciliation statement being drawn up to reconcile the two sets of records. The petty cash voucher would be used as a basis for entering up the payments columns in the petty cash book. Therefore the USE of the items was asked for, not the DESCRIPTIONS of the items.

Let us see if you have done better on question (b). Would you have written down how to calculate two methods of depreciation, probably the reducing balance method and the straight line method? But have you remembered that the question also asked you to EXPLAIN THE TERM DEPRECIATION? In other words, what is depreciation generally. A fair number of students will have omitted that part of the question. My own guess is that far more students would have made a rather poor attempt at question (a) rather than question (b). In both cases the questions should have been read very carefully, and it is good practice to underline the key words in a question. If you had set out to underline the key words, to get at the core of the question, then you would have underlined the word USE as one of the keywords in question (a), and consequently have not been guilty of writing about descriptions of things instead of describing to what USE these things are put.

Many students, over the years, have asked me 'What happens if my balance sheet doesn't balance?'. The answer is to leave the question, not to look for error(s) at that juncture, and to tackle the next question. One of the reasons for this is contained in the next paragraph which is concerned with making certain you attempt every question. You might spend 20 minutes to find the error, which might save you 1 mark. In that time you might have gained, say, 10 marks, if instead you had tackled the next question, for which you would not have had time if you had wasted it by searching for the error(s). That assumes that you actually find the error(s). Suppose you don't, you have spent 20 minutes looking for it, have not found it, so how do you feel now? The answer is, of course, quite terrible. You may then make an even bigger mess of the rest of the paper than you would have done if you had simply ignored the fact that the balance sheet did not balance. In any case, it is quite possible to get, say, 29 marks out of 30 even though the balance sheet does not balance. The error may be a very minor case for which the examiner deducts one mark only. Of course, if you have finished all of the questions, then by all means spend the rest of your time tracing the error and correcting it. Be certain, however, that your corrections are carried out neatly, as untidy crossings-out can result in the loss of marks. So, sometimes, an error found can get back one mark, which is then lost again because the corrections make an untidy mess of your paper, and examiners usually do deduct marks, quite rightly so, for untidy work.

The last point which I want to get through to you is that you should attempt each and every question. On each question the first few marks are the easiest to get. For instance, on an essay question it is reasonably easy to get, say, the first 5 marks in a 20 mark question. Managing to produce a perfect answer to get the last 5 marks, from 15 to 20 total, is extremely difficult. This applies also to computational questions.

This means that, in an examination of, say, 5 questions with 20 marks possible for each question, there is not much point in tackling 3 questions only and trying to make a good job of each of them. The total possible marks would only be 60 marks, and if you had not achieved full marks for each question, in itself extremely unlikely, you could easily fall below the pass mark of (say) 50 marks. It is better to leave questions unfinished when your allotted time, calculated as shown earlier, has expired, and to then go on immediately to the other questions. It is so easy, especially in an accounting examination, to find that one has exceeded the time allowed for a question by a considerable margin. So, although you may find it difficult to persuade yourself to do so, move on to the next question when your time for a question has expired.

Over the years I have marked many thousands of examination scripts in Accounting. If only candidates had tackled the papers as I have advised, especially the last piece of advice, I would have been in the happy position of being able to recommend far many more pass certificates. So do not let the lack of examination technique spoil your chances, as so many people have in the past.

Finally, may I wish that your work gains the rewards that it deserves.

APPENDIX II

Answers to Multiple Choice Questions

1. (C)	2. (D)	3. (B)	4. (C)	5. (A)
6. (C)	7. (C)	8. (A)	9. (C)	10. (A)
11. (B)	12. (D)	13. (B)	14. (D)	15. (B)
16. (C)	17. (C)	18. (A)	19. (D)	20. (C)
21. (A)	22. (B)	23. (A)	24. (D)	25. (C)
26. (A)	27. (D)	28. (A)	29. (C)	30. (A)
31. (C)	32. (D)	33. (C)	34. (C)	35. (D)
36. (B)	37. (A)	38. (B)	39. (C)	40. (A)
41. (C)	42. (A)	43. (D)	44. (D)	45. (A)
46. (A)	47. (B)	48. (C)	49. (D)	50. (C)
51. (A)	52. (D)	53. (C)	54. (C)	55. (D)
56. (C)	57. (A)	58. (A)	59. (B)	60. (C)
61. (B)	62. (A)	63. (D)	64. (A)	65. (C)
66. (A)	67. (D)	68. (D)	69. (B)	70. (A)
71. (D)	72. (C)	73. (D)	74. (B)	75. (B)
76. (C)	77. (D)	78. (A)	79. (B)	80. (D)
81. (B)	82. (B)	83. (C)	84. (C)	85. (A)
86. (C)	87. (B)	88. (A)	89. (C)	90. (A)
91. (C)	92. (C)	93. (A)	94. (B)	95. (C)
96. (C)	97. (B)	98. (C)	99. (B)	100. (D)
101. (C)	102. (C)	103. (A)	104. (B)	105. (C)
106. (B)	107. (D)	108. (B)		

Answers to Exercises

1.1 (a) 10,700
(b) 23,100
(c) 4,300
(d) 3,150
(e) 25,500
(f) 51,400.

1.3 (i) Asset
(ii) Liability
(iii) Asset
(iv) Asset
(v) Liability
(vi) Asset

1.5 Wrong: Assets: Loan from C. Smith; Creditors; Liabilities: Stock of Goods; Debtors.

1.7 Assets: Motor 2,000; Premises 5,000; Stock 1,000; Bank 700; Cash 100 = total 8,800: Liabilities: Loan from Bevan 3,000; Creditors 400 = total 3,400. Capital 8,800 − 3,400 = 5,400.

1.9 Assets: Fixtures 5,500, Motors 5,700, Stock 8,800, Debtors 4,950, Bank 1,250 = Total 26,200. Capital 23,750, Creditors 2,450.

1.11 (*a*) − Cash, − Creditors   (*e*) + Cash, + Loan
    (*b*) − Bank, + Fixtures   (*f*) + Bank, − Debtors
    (*c*) + Stock, + Creditors   (*g*) − Stock, − Creditors
    (*d*) + Cash, + Capital   (*h*) + Premises, − Bank.

1.13 Assets: Fixtures 4,500, Motor 4,200, Stock 5,720, Debtors 3,000, Bank 5,450, Cash 400 = Total 23,270. Capital 18,900, Loan 2,000, Creditors 2,370.

2.1 (*a*) Dr Motor Van, Cr Cash. (*b*) Dr Office Machinery, Cr J. Grant & Son. (*c*) Dr Cash, Cr Capital. (*d*) Dr Bank, Cr J. Beach. (*e*) Dr A. Barrett, Cr Cash.

2.2 (*a*) Dr Machinery, Cr A. Jackson & Son. (*b*) Dr A. Jackson & Son, Cr Machinery. (*c*) Dr Cash, Cr J. Brown. (*d*) Dr Bank, Cr J. Smith (Loan). (*e*) Dr Cash, Cr Office Machinery.

2.5 Capital Cr 1,000, Cash Dr 1,000 Cr 60 and 698, Speed & Sons Dr 698 Cr 698, Motor lorry Dr 698, Office machinery Dr 60.

2.6 Bank Dr 2,500, Cr 150 & 600 & 750 & 280, Capital Cr 2,500, Office furniture Dr 150, Cr 60, Machinery Dr 750 & 280, Planers Dr 750, Cr 750, Motor van Dr 600, J. Walker Dr 60, Cr 60, Cash Dr 60.

2.7 Cash Dr 2,000 & 75 & 100, Cr 1,800, Bank Dr 1,800 & 500, Cr 950 & 58 & 100, Capital Cr 2,000, Office furniture Dr 120, Cr 62, Betta Built Dr 62 & 58, Cr 120, Motor van Dr 950, Evans & Sons Cr 560, Works machinery Dr 560, Cr 75, J. Smith (Loan) Cr 500.

2.8 Cash Dr 500 & 400 & 200; Cr 350 & 50: Bank Dr 10,000 & 1,000 & 350 & 1,000 & 1,800; Cr 3,000 & 2,000: Phillips Garages Dr 2,000; Cr 3,600: R. Jones Dr 3,000; Cr 1,000 & 1,800 & 200: J. Saunders Ltd, Dr 200; Cr 700: Loan J. Hawkins Cr 400: Loan H. Thompson Cr 1,000: Motor Van Dr 3,000 & 3,600: Cr 3,000: Office Equipment Dr 700 & 50; Cr 200: Capital Cr 10,000 & 500.

3.1 (*a*) Dr Purchases, Cr Cash   (*d*) Dr Cash, Cr Motor van
    (*b*) Dr Purchases, Cr E. Flynn   (*e*) Dr Cash, Cr Sales.
    (*c*) Dr C. Grant, Cr Sales

3.2 (*a*) Dr H. Flynn, Cr Returns Out. (*b*) Dr Purchases, Cr P. Franklin. (*c*) Dr S. Mullings, Cr Sales. (*d*) Dr Returns In, Cr M. Patterson. (*e*) Dr Purchases, Cr Bank.

3.5 Totals − Purchases Dr 307, Sales Cr 89, Returns outwards Cr 15, C. Blake Dr 15, Cr 72, C. Foster Cr 90, Cash Dr 25, E. Rose Dr 64, A. Price Cr 145.

3.6 Totals – Cash Dr 597 Cr 173, Capital Cr 500, Purchases Dr 299, Sales Cr 97, Returns outwards Cr 47, E. Morgan Dr 116, Cr 116, A. Moses Dr 19 Cr 98, A. Knight Dr 55 Cr 55.

3.7 Totals – Cash Dr 1,028 Cr 955, Bank Dr 1,000 Cr 710, Purchases Dr 133, S. Holmes Dr 78 Cr 78, Capital Cr 1,000, Motor van Dr 500, Sales Cr 126, D. Moore Dr 98, Returns outwards Cr 18, Fixtures Dr 150, Kingston Equipt Co Dr 150 Cr 150, Watson (Loan) Cr 100.

3.8 Capital Cr 10,000 & 500: Bank Dr 10,000 & 250; Cr 1,070 & 2,600: Cash Dr 400 & 200 & 70 & 500; Cr 250 & 220 & 100: Purchases Dr 840 & 3,600 & 370 & 220: Sales Cr 200 & 180 & 220 & 190 & 320 & 70: Returns Inwards Dr 40 & 30: Returns Outwards Cr 140 & 110: Motor Van Dr 2,600: Office Furniture Dr 600 & 100: Cr 160: Loan from T. Cooper Cr 400: F. Jones Dr 140 & 1,070; Cr 840 & 370: S. Charles Dr 110; Cr 3,600: C. Moody Dr 180; Cr 40: J. Newman Dr 220: H. Morgan Dr 190; Cr 30: J. Peat Dr 320: Manchester Motors Dr 2,600; Cr 2,600: Faster Supplies Dr 160; Cr 600.

4.1 (a) Dr Rates, Cr Bank
(b) Dr Wages, Cr Cash
(c) Dr Bank, Cr Rent received
(d) Dr Bank, Cr Insurance
(e) Dr General expenses, Cr Cash.

4.2 (a) Dr Rent, Cr Cash
(b) Dr Purchases, Cr Cash
(c) Dr Bank, Cr Rates
(d) Dr General Expenses, Cr Bank
(e) Dr Cash, Cr Commissions Received
(f) Dr T. Jones, Cr Returns Out
(g) Dr Cash, Cr Sales
(h) Dr Office Fixtures, Cr Bank
(i) Dr Wages, Cr Cash
(j) Dr Drawings, Cr Cash

4.5 Totals – Bank Dr 1,200 Cr 289, Cash Dr 120 Cr 33, Purchases Dr 381, T. Parkin Cr 296, C. Moore Cr 85, Capital Cr 200, U. Surer (Loan) Cr 1,000, Motor van Dr 250, Sales Cr 105, Motor expenses Dr 15, Wages Dr 18, Insurance Dr 22, Commission Cr 15, Electricity Dr 17.

4.6 Totals – Bank Dr 2,005, Cr 450, Capital Cr 2,000, Purchases Dr 289, M. Mills Dr 23 Cr 175, Fixtures Dr 150, Cash Dr 275 Cr 203, S. Waites Cr 114, Rent Dr 15, Stationery Dr 27, Returns outwards Cr 23, Rent received Cr 5, U. Henry Dr 77, Sales Cr 352, Motor van Dr 300, Wages Dr 117, Drawings Dr 44.

4.7 Totals – Cash Dr 1,549 Cr 1,186, Capital Cr 1,500, Purchases Dr 421, Rent Dr 28, Bank Dr 1,000 Cr 689, Sales Cr 132, Linton Dr 54 Cr 14, Stationery Dr 15, Returns outwards Cr 17, A. Hanson Dr 296 Cr 296, S. Morgan Dr 29, Repairs Dr 18, Returns inwards Dr 14, Motor van Dr 395, Motor expenses Dr 15, Fixtures Dr 120, A. Webster Cr 120.

5.1 Balances: H. Harvey Dr 416, L. Masters Dr 621, N. Morgan −, J. Lindo −.

5.2 Balances: J. Young Cr 233, G. Norman Cr 686, L. Williams Cr 180, T. Harris −.

5.5 Balances: D. Williams Dr 58, J. Moore Dr 653, G. Grant Dr 89, F. Franklin −, A White −, H. Samuels Cr 219, P. Owen Cr 65, O. Oliver −.

6.1 *Trial Balance* − Drs: Cash 215, Purchases 459, Rent 30, Bank 96, Hughes 129, Spencer 26, Carriage 23; Crs: Capital 250, Sales 348, Mendes 130, Booth 186, Lowe 64. Totals: 978.

6.2 *Trial Balance* − Drs: Purchases 360, Bank 361, Cash 73, Wages 28, Lane 74, Shop fixtures 50, Motor van 400, Elliot 35; Crs: King Loan 60, Braham 134, Henriques 52, Capital 800, Sales 291, Returns outwards 44. Totals: 1,381.

6.3 *Trial Balance* − Drs: Bank 267, Cash 84, Purchases 871, Neita 57, Motor van 256, Motor expenses 17, Barnes 24, K. Lyn 71, Moores 65, Returns inwards 11, Drawings 34, Postages 4, Edgar 67; Crs: Capital 650, Jones 673, Sales 438, Returns outwards 67. Totals: 1,828.

7.1 *Trading:* Dr Purchases 14,629 *less* Closing Stock 2,548 Cr Sales 18,462, Dr Gross Profit 6,381. *Profit and Loss:* Dr Salaries 2,150, Motor expenses 520, Rent and rates 670, Insurance 111, General 105, Net profit 2,825.

7.2 *Trading:* Dr Purchases 23,803, *less* Stock 4,166, Gross profit 9,157, Cr Sales 28,794. *Profit and Loss:* Dr Salaries 3,164, Rent 854, Lighting 422, Insurance 105, Motor expenses 1,133, Trade expenses 506, Net profit 2,973.

8.1 *Assets:* Premises 1,500, Motors 1,200, Stock 2,548, Debtors 1,950, Bank 1,654, Cash 40. Totals: 8,892. Capital 5,424, *add* Net profit 2,825, *less* Drawings 895, 7,354. *Liabilities:* Creditors 1,538.

8.2 *Assets:* Buildings 50,000, Fixtures 1,000, Motors 5,500, Stock 4,166, Debtors 3,166, Bank 3,847. Totals: 67,679. Capital: 65,900, *add* Net profit 2,973, Drawings 2,400, Creditors 1,206.

9.1 Dr Purchases 33,333 − Returns Out 495 + Carriage In 670 − Closing Stock 7,489 = Cost of Goods Sold 26,019, Gross Profit 11,833, Cr Sales 38,742 − Returns In 890.

9.3 Dr Opening Stock 2,368 + Purchases 11,874 − Returns Out 322 + Carriage In 310 − Closing Stock 2,946 = Cost of Goods Sold 11,284. Gross Profit 7,111: Cr Sales 18,600 − Returns In 205. P/L Dr Salaries 3,862, Rent and Rates 304, Carriage Out 200, Insurance 78, Motor Expenses 664. Office Expenses 216, Lighting 166, General Expenses 314, Net Profit 1,307. Cr Gross Profit 7,111.
Balance Sheet: F.A. Premises 5,000, Fixtures 350, Motors 1,800, C.A. Stock 2,946, Debtors 3,896, Bank 482. Totals 14,474. Capital 12,636 + Net Profit 1,307 − Drawings 1,200 = 12,743 C.L. Creditors 1,731.

9.4 Dr Opening Stock 3,776 + Purchases 11,556 − Returns Out 355 + Carriage In 234 − Closing Stock 4,998, Gross Profit 7,947. Cr Sales 18,600 − Returns In 440. P/L Dr Salaries 2,447. Motor Expenses 664, Rent 576, Carriage Out 326, Sundries 1,202, Net Profit 2,732, Cr Gross Profit 7,947.
Balance Sheet F.A. Fixtures 600, Motors 2,400, C.A. Stock 4,998, Debtors 4,577, Bank 3,876, Cash 120, Totals 16,571. Capital 12,844 + Net Profit 2,732 − Drawings 2,050 = 13,526. C.L. Creditors 3,045.

13.1 Totals: Cash 363, Bank 731, Balances − Cash 184, Bank 454.

13.2 Totals: Cash 380, Bank 2,700, Balances − Cash 98, Bank 2,229.

14.1 Totals: Dr Discounts 32, Cash 407, Bank 6,871, Cr Discounts 10, Cash 407, Bank 6,871, Balances c/d Cash 93, Bank 4,195.
Discounts Allowed Dr 32: Discounts Received Cr 10.

14.2 Totals: Dr Discounts 89, Cash 580, Bank 7,552, Cr Discounts 48, Cash 580, Bank 7,552. Balances c/d Cash 123, Bank 4,833.
Discounts Received Cr 48, Discounts Allowed Dr 89.

14.3 Totals: Dr Discounts 33, Cash 309, Bank 5,918, Cr Discounts 39, Cash 309, Bank 5,918, Balances c/d Cash 84, Bank 5,030.
Discounts Received Cr 39, Discounts Allowed Dr 33.

15.1 Sales Journal Total 881.

15.3 Sales Journal Total 540, (1) 60 + (4) 120 + (8) 20 + (20) 180 + (31) 160.

16.1 Purchases Journal Total 2,770 (1) 450 + (3) 800 + (15) 600 + (20) 280 + (30) 640.

16.3 Purchases Journal Total 375, Sales Journal Total 393.

17.1 Purchases Journal Total 1,096, Returns Outwards Journal 46.

17.3 Totals: Sales Journal 1,062, Returns Inwards 54, Purchases Journal 644, Returns Outwards 48.

17.4 Totals: Sales Journal 2,213, Returns In Journal 122, Purchases Journal 2,996, Returns Out Journal 94.

18.1 (i) Invoice after Trade Discount 700 + VAT 70 = 770
(ii) Books of D. Wilson Ltd Sales G. Christie & Son Dr 770
Books of G. Christie & Son D. Wilson Ltd, Cr 770.

18.2 Sales Book totals Net 520: VAT 52.
General Ledger: Sales Cr 520; VAT Cr 52.
Sales Ledger: M. Sinclair & Co Dr 165; M. Brown & Associates Dr 286; A. Axton Ltd Dr 88; T. Christie Dr 33.

18.3 Sales Book totals Net 590; VAT 59.
Purchases Book totals Net 700; VAT 70.
Sales Ledger: Dr B. Davies & Co 165; C. Grant Ltd 242 and 154; B. Karloff 88.
Purchases Ledger: Cr G. Cooper & Son 440; J. Wayne Ltd 209; B. Lugosi 55; S. Hayward 66.
General Ledger: Sales Cr 590: Purchases Dr 700: VAT Dr 700; Cr 59; Balance c/d 11.

19.1 STRAIGHT LINE 4,000 − 700 = 3,300 − 700 = 2,600 − 700 = 1,900 − 700 = 1,200 − 700 = 500.
REDUCING BALANCE 4,000 − 1,600 = 2,400 − 960 = 1,440 − 576 = 864 − 346 = 518 − 207 = 311.

19.2 STRAIGHT LINE 12,500 − 1,845 = 10,655 − 1,845 = 8,810 − 1,845 = 6,965 − 1,845 = 5,120.
REDUCING BALANCE 12,500 − 2,500 = 10,000 − 2,000 = 8,000 − 1,600 − 6,400 − 1,280 = 5,120.

19.3 STRAIGHT LINE 6,400 − 1,240 = 5,160 − 1,240 = 3,920 − 1,240 = 2,680 − 1,240 = 1,440 − 1,240 = 200.
REDUCING BALANCE 6,400 − 3,200 = 3,200 − 1,600 = 1,600 − 800 = 800 − 400 = 400 − 200 = 200.

19.7 Machines (A) 19-4 Cost 3,000 − Depreciation 19-4 300, 19-5 270, 19-6 243, (B) 19-5 Cost 2,000 − Depreciation 19-5 150, 19-6 185, (C) 19-6 Cost 1,000 − Depreciation 50. Total depreciation 19-6 243 + 185 + 50 = 478.

20.1 Motors vans Dr 3,800, Provision for depreciation Cr 620.

20.2 Machinery Dr 800, 1,000, 600, 200, Provision for depreciation −3, 80, −4, 145, −5, 240, −6, 255. *Balance Sheet:* −3,800 *less* 80, −4, 2,400 *less* 225, −5, 2,400 *less* 465, −6, 2,600 *less* 720.

20.3 Machinery Dr 640, 720, Fixtures Dr 100, 200, 50; Provision for: Depreciation machinery −5, 80, −6, 160, Depreciation fixtures −5, 30, −6, 32. *Balance Sheets:* −5, F 300 *less* 30, M 640 *less* 80, −6, F 350 *less* 62, M 1360 *less* 240.

20.4 Plant Dr −4, 900, 600, −6, 550, Cr −7, 900, Depreciation Dr −7, 675, Cr −4, 210, −5, 300, −6, 355, −7, 365. Disposals Dr Plant 900, Profit to Profit and Loss 50, Cr Depreciation 675, Cash 275. *Balance Sheet:* −4, 1,500 *less* 210, −5, 1,500 *less* 510, −6, 2,050 *less* 865, −7, 1,150 *less* 555.

20.5 Machinery Dr Bal b/f 52,590, Cash 2,480, Cr Disposals 2,800, Balance c/d 52,270, Office furniture Dr Balance b/f 2,860, Cash 320, Cr Balance c/d 3,180, Depreciation M. Dr Disposals 1,120, Balance c/d 29,777, Cr Balance b/f 25,670, Profit and Loss 5,227, Depreciation O.F. Dr Balance c/d 1,649, Cr Balance b/d 1,490, Profit and Loss 159. *Balance Sheet:* M. 52,270 *less* 29,777, O.F. 3,180 *less* 1,649. M. Disposals Dr M. 2,800, Cr Depn 1,120, Bank 800, P/Loss 880.

20.6 Red. Balance: (HT1) 800 *less* 160, 128, 102, 82, 66 = 262, (HT2) 860 *less* 172, 138, 110, 88 = 352, (HT3) 840 *less* 168, 134, 108 = 430, (HT4) 950 *less* 190, 152 = 608, (HT5) 980 *less* 196 = 784.
Straight Line: (HT1) 800 *less* 156×5 = 20, (HT2) 860 *less* 168×4 = 188, (HT3) 840 *less* 164×3 = 348, (HT4) 950 *less* 186×2 = 578, (HT5) 980 *less* 192 = 788.
Adjustments: Cr Prov for Dep A/c (HT1) 242, (HT2) 164, (HT3) 82, (HT4) 30, Dr Prov for Dep A/c (HT5) 4.
19-4 Depreciation: (HT1) nil, (HT3) 164, (HT4) 186, (HT5) 192, (HT6) 188, *loss* on (HT2) 128.

21.1 (i) Bad Debts Dr H. Gordon 110; D. Bellamy Ltd 64; J. Alderton 12; Provision c/d 220; Cr Profit and Loss 406.
(ii) 406.
(iii) Debtors 6,850 *less* Provision for Bad Debts 220.

21.2 (i) Bad Debts 19-6 Dr W. Best 85; S. Avon 140; Provision c/d 550: Cr Profit and Loss 775.
Bad Debts 19-7 Dr L. J. Friend 180; N. Kelly 60; A. Oliver 250; Provision c/d 600. Cr Provision b/d 550, Profit and Loss 540.
(ii) 19-6 Bad Debts 775: 19-7 Bad Debts 540.
(iii) 19-6 Debtors 40,500 *less* Provision for Bad Debts 550: 19-7 Debtors 47,300 *less* Provision for Bad Debts 600.

21.3 (i) Bad Debts Dr Various 540; Provision c/d 310: Cr Provision b/f 260; Profit and Loss 590.
(ii) Dr Bad Debts 590.
(iii) Debtors 6,200 *less* Provision for Bad Debts 310.

21.5 Balance Sheets are all same as for previous Method A answers.
(i) Bad Debts: Dr total 186, Cr Profit & Loss 186: Provision for Bad Debts Cr 220: Profit & Loss Dr 186, Provision for Bad Debts 220.
(ii) Charges to Profit & Loss: 19-6 Dr Bad Debts 225, Provision for Bad Debts 550: 19-7 Dr Bad Debts 490, Provision for Bad Debts 50.

22.1 Total Expenses to debit of P/L: Motor Expenses 772, Insurance 385, Stationery 2,040, Rates 880, To credit of P/L Rent Received 580.

22.3 Charges to P/L: Rates 1,229, Packing 5,499.

22.5 Sales 13,475 − Returns In 242 = 13,233 − C.G.S. Purchases 11,377 − Returns Out 268 + Carriage In 47 − Closing Stock 898 = 10,258, Gross Profit 2,975 + Discounts Received 210 + Rent 104 − Expenses: Wages 652, Motor Expenses 167, Office Expenses 104, Bad Debts 184, Insurance 20, Electricity 30, Loan Interest 42, Discounts Allowed 337, Rent 393, Depreciation of Motor 99 = Net Profit 1,261.

22.7 Sales 19,740 − C.G.S. Opening Stock 2,970 + Purchases 11,280 − Closing Stock 3,510 = 10,740, Gross Profit 9,000 + Discounts Received 360, − Expenses: Wages 2,670, Rent 880, Discounts Allowed 690, Van Running Costs 510, Bad Debts 870, Depreciation Office Furniture 180, Delivery Van 480 = Net Profit 3,080.
Balance Sheet: F.A. Office Furniture 1,440−180, Delivery Van 2,400−480, C.A. Stock 3,510, Debtors 4,920−330, Prepaid 140, Bank 1,140, Cash 210 − C.L. Creditors 2,490, Expenses Owing 150 = Working Capital 6,950, Totals 10,130. Financed by: Capital 9,900 + 3,080 − Drawings 2,850.

22.8 Sales 41,970 − Returns In 810 = 41,160 − C.G.S. Opening Stock 5,160 + Purchases 22,860 − Returns Out 570 − Closing Stock 4,290 = 23,160. Gross Profit 18,000 + Discounts Received 930 − Expenses: Wages 9,150, Rent 1,560, Carriage Out 2,160, General 470, Discounts Allowed 1,440, Provision for Bad Debts 150, Depreciation Fixtures 120, Van 300 = Net Profit 3,580.
Balance Sheet: F.A. Fixtures 1,200 − 120, Delivery Van 2,100 − 300 C.A. Stock 4,290, Debtors 11,910 − Provision 810, Prepaid 180. Cash 90 − C.L. Creditors 6,060, Expenses Owing 230, Bank Overdraft 4,350 = W.C. 5,020, Totals 7,900.
Capital 7,200 + Net Profit 3,580 − Drawings 2,880 = 7,900.

24.1 Capital (a) (c) (d) (f) (j) (l): Revenue: (b) (e) (g) (h) (i) (k).

24.3 Capital (i) (ii) (v).

24.5 (b): Capital (i) (ii) Machine part of (v) (vi)
Revenue: (iii) (iv) Drinks part of (v).

26.1 Cash at Bank 678 + Unpresented cheques 256 + Credit transfers 56 *less* Lodgement not recorded 115 = Balance per bank statement 875.

26.3 (a) To enter up Dr Walters 54, Cr Bank Charges 22, New balance c/d 1,863.
(b) Balance per C.B. 1,863 + Unpresented cheque 115 − Bankings not entered 427 = Balance per B.S. 1,551 or in a reverse fashion.

26.5(*a*) Balance per B.S. 924 − Unpresented cheques 194 = Balance per C.B. 730. Could have started from 760 or 988 balance, but obviously this way is easier.

(*b*) Unpresented cheques: Good 76, Burns 54, Kirk 148 = 278.

26.6(*a*) To enter up Dr Saunders 180, Cr Mercantile 200, Bank Charges 65, New balance c/d (overdraft) 4,007.

(*b*) Bank Overdraft per C.B. 4,007 + Bankings not entered 211 − Unpresented cheque 84 = Bank Overdraft per B.S. 4,134.

26.8 Uncorrected balance 17,397 + overstated cheque 45 + undercast total 200 − standing orders 1,152 & 150, bank charges 452 = Corrected Cash book balance 15,888.
B.R.S. Balance per C.B. (as corrected) 15,888 + unpresented cheques 1,435 − bankings not credited 1,620 − cheque debited in error 238 = Balance per B.S. 15,465.

27.1 *Trial Balance* − Drs: Discounts allowed 19, Cash 12, Bank 855, Benjamin 100, Duffy 48, Green 118, Pearson 67, Premises 2,000, Motor 750, Fixtures 600, Stock 1,289, Rent 15, Motor expenses 13, Drawings 20, Salaries 56, Rates 66, Purchases 344, Returns In 34. Crs: Discounts received 17, Harris 56, Gordon 38, Johnson 89, Best 72, Capital 5,598, Sales 527, Returns out 9. Totals 6,406.

27.2(i)	Motor Vehicles	Dr.	6,970	:	Kingston	Cr.	6,790
(ii)	Bad Debts	Dr.	34	:	H. Newman	Cr.	34
(iii)	Unique Offices	Dr.	490	:	Office Furniture	Cr.	490
(iv) (a)	Bank	Dr.	39	:	W. Charles	Cr.	39
(b)	Bad Debts	Dr.	111	:	W., Charles	Cr.	111
(v)	Drawings	Dr.	45	:	Purchases	Cr.	45
(vi)	Drawings	Dr.	76	:	Insurance	Cr.	76
(vii)	Machinery	Dr.	980	:	Systems Accelerated	Cr.	980

28.1 Receipts 100 + 78 = 178. Payments, Total 78, Motor Expenses 26, Post 17, Cleaning 11, Sundries 4, Ledger 20, Balance c/d 100.

28.2 Receipts 200 + 90 = 290. Payments, Total 90, Hotel 29, Post 20, Motor 12, Sundries 7, Ledger 22. Balance c/d 200.

29.1(i)	J. Harris	Dr.	678	:	J. Hart	Cr.	678
(ii)	Machinery	Dr.	4,390	:	L. Pyle	Cr.	4,390
(iii)	Motor Van	Dr.	3,800	:	Motor Expenses	Cr.	3,800
(iv)	E. Fitzwilliam	Dr.	9	:	Sales	Cr.	9
(v)	Sales	Dr.	257	:	Commissions Received	Cr.	257
(vi)	Cash	Dr.	154	:	T. Heath	Cr.	154
	needs double the amount.						
(vii)	Purchases	Dr.	189	:	Drawings	Cr.	189
(viii)	Discounts Allowed	Dr.	366	:	Discounts Received	Cr.	366

30.1 (*a*) (i) Suspense Dr 100, Sales Cr 100 (ii) Cantrell Dr 250, Cochrane Cr 250 (iii) Rent Dr 70, Suspense Cr 70, (iv) Suspense Dr 300, Discounts Received Cr 300 (v) Sales Dr 360, Motor Disposal Cr 360. (*b*) Suspense A/c Dr: Sales 100, Discounts Received 300 Cr: Balance b/f 330, Rent 70. (*c*) Net Profit per accounts 7,900 + Sales undercast 100 + Discounts undercast 300 − Rent 70 − Sales 360 = Corrected Net Profit 7,870.

30.3 (i) (1) Suspense Dr 124, Returns out Cr 124 (2) Purchases Dr 100. W. Dawson Cr 100 (3) Vehicle Dr 6, Suspense Cr 6 (4) R. Race Dr 36, Suspense Cr 36 (ii) Dr Returns Out 124, Cr Vehicles 6, Race 36, Balance (original error) 82 (iii) Total debit column 10,000 less suspense 82 = 9,918 original total.

30.5 (*a*) Suspense: Dr. X. Y. Suppliers 6, Thompson 54, Smith £30: Cr. Balance b/f 9, Shop Fittings 60, Bank Charges 21.
   (*b*) 5,497 − bank charges = 5,476 corrected profit.
   (*c*) F.A. Fittings 1,560 − 300 + Delivery Van 3,200 − 800 = 3,660 + C.A. Stock 2,917, Debtors 2,070, Bank 1,095, Cash 128 − C.L. Creditors 1,894 = Working Capital 4,316. Total 7,976, Capital 7,500 + Profit 5,476 − Drawings 5,000.

31.1 Dr Balance b/f 4,936, Sales Journal 49,916. toals 54,852. Cr Returns In 1,139, Cheques 46,490. Discounts 1,455, Balance c/d 5,768.

31.2 Dr Returns Out 1,098, Bank 38,765, Discounts 887, Balance c/d 5,183, Totals 45,933. Cr Balances b/f 3,676, Purchases 42,257.

31.5 Purchases Ledger Control: Drs Returns outwards 2,648, Cheques 146,100, Petty cash 78, Discounts received 2,134, Set-offs 1,036, Balances c/f 14,530 − Total: 166,526. Crs Balances b/f 11,874, Purchases 154,562. Total: 166,436. Difference between two sides 90.
Sales Ledger Control: Drs Balances b/f 19,744, Sales 199,962, Dishonoured cheque 30; Crs Returns inwards 4,556, Cheques 185,960, Discounts allowed 5,830, Bad debts 396, Set-offs 1,036, Balance c/f 21,658. Both totals are 219,436.

31.6 A−C figures shown first. Dr Balances b/f 7,940: 11,250, Sales 8,470: 19,380, Dishonoured cheques −: 920, Interest 170: 90, Debt taken over 1,170: −, Balances c/d 230: 590. Total A−C 17,980, D−G 32,230. Cr Balances b/d 170: 940, Cash 4,500: 7,770, Bad Debts 190: −, Discounts 709: 1,140, Returns In 530: 320, Debt taken over −: 1,170, Balances c/d 11,651: 19,990. An error exists in ledger A−C of 230 (17,980 − 17,750), and an error of 900 (32,230 − 31,330) in ledger D−G.

31.8 (a) Debtor Control: Dr Balances b/f 1,891, Cheque returned 110, Sales 97, Total 2,098. Cr Bad Debts 68, Discounts 43, Balances c/d 1,987. Creditor Control Dr Incorrect entry 9, Balances c/d 2,121: Cr Balances b/f 2,130.

    (b) (iii) Office Equipment Dr 240, Purchases Cr 240 (iv) Drawings Dr 320, Wages Cr 320 (v) Capital Dr 40, Depreciation Cr 40 (vi) Drawings Dr 45, Stationery Cr 45 (vii) Returns In Dr 90, Returns Out Cr 90.

    (c) F.A. Premises 7,000 + Office Equipment 1,840 − 750, C.A. Stock 1,400, Debtors 1,987, Cash 56 − C.L. Creditors 2,121, Bank Overdraft 980 = Working Capital 342. Totals 8,432. Capital 8,400 + Profit (by deduction) 2,332 − Drawings 2,300.

32.1 Dr Opening Stock 9,872 + Purchases 50,748 − Closing Stock 12,620 = C.G.S. 48,000, Gross Profit 12,000. Sales 60,000.

32.3 (a) We know that $\dfrac{\text{Cost of Goods Sold}}{\text{Average Stock}}$ = Rate of Turnover

    $\therefore$ substituting $\dfrac{x}{12{,}600} = 7$

    $\therefore x$ = Cost of Goods Sold = 88,200.

    (b) If margin is $33\frac{1}{3}\%$ then mark-up will be 50% Gross Profit is therefore 50% of 88,200 = 44,100.

    (c) Turnover is (a) + (b) = 88,200 + 44,100 = 132,300.

    (d) $66\frac{2}{3}\% \times 44{,}100 = 29{,}400$.

    (e) Gross Profit − Expenses = Net Profit = 14,700.

32.5

	19-6	19-7	19-8
Opening Stock	20,000	5,000	8,800
Purchases	85,000	112,200	99,000
Closing Stock	5,000	8,800	11,800
Sales	125,000	140,000	130,000
Gross Profit	25,000	31,600	34,000
Variable Expenses	12,500	18,200	18,900
Fixed Expenses	5,500	5,000	6,000
Net Profit	7,000	8,400	9,100

Workings
19-6
1. Gross Profit 20% of sales, therefore sales = 25,000 × 100/20 = 125,000.
2. Variable expenses 10% of sales = 10% × 125,000 = 12,500 Sales − Gross Profit = Cost of Goods Sold so 125,000 − 25,000 = Cost of Goods Sold 100,000. Opening Stock ? + Purchases 85,000 − Closing Stock 5,000 = Cost of Goods Sold 100,000. By deduction Opening Stock is 20,000.

19-7

1.   Purchases.

Same quantity as last year but a new price 85,000 + 10% = 93,500.
But increase in volume 20% so Purchases are 93,500 + 20% =
112,200.

Closing Stock 8,000 units at 1.10

Variable Expenses 140,000 × 13% = 18,200.

19-8

Purchases 90,000 × 1.10 = 99,000

Gross Profit = Net Profit 9,100 + Fixed Expenses 6,000 +
Variable Expenses 18,900 = 34,000

Net Profit for 19-7 as % on Sales = $\frac{8,400}{140,000} \times \frac{100}{1} = 6\%$

So for 19-8 Net Profit for 19-8 as % on Sales = 6 + 1 = 7%

As Net Profit = 9,100 the Sales can be calculated = $\frac{9,100}{7} \times 100$

= 130,000.

Sales 130,000 − Gross Profit 34,000 = 96,000 Cost of Goods Sold,
Opening Stock 8,800 + Purchases 99,000 − Closing Stock ? =
Cost of Goods Sold 96,000 so by deduction Closing Stock is
11,800.

33.1 F.A. 2,800 − 550, C.A. Stock 3,950, Debtors 4,970, Prepaid 170, Bank
2,564, Cash 55 − C.L. Creditors 1,030, Expenses Owing 470 = Working
Capital 10,209. Totals 12,459. Capital 10,000 + (C) ? = (B) ? − 5,673 =
(A) ? By deduction (A) = 12,459, (B) = 18,132, (C) = 8,132.

33.3 Sales 47,159 − C.G.S. Opening Stock 13,862 + Purchases 34,246 −
Closing Stock 15,144 = 32,964, Gross Profit 14,195, less Wages 5,472,
Rent 1,500, Rates 875, Sundries 375, Depreciation 250, = Net Profit
5,723. Balance Sheet: F.A. Fixtures 2,500 − 250, C.A. Stock 15,144,
Debtors 8,624, Prepaid 225 − C.L. Creditors 7,389, Bank Overdraft 602
= Working Capital 16,002. Totals 18,252. Capital 20,234 + Profit 5,723
− Drawings 7,705 = 18,252.

33.5 Sales 5,510 − C.G.S. Opening Stock 300 + Purchases 2,890 − Stock
Stolen 300 − Closing Stock 450 = 2,440, Gross Profit 3,070 − Expenses,
Rent 600, Paper 45, Cost of Stock Stolen 300 = Net Profit 2,125.
Balance Sheet: C.A. Stock 450, Bank 370 − C.L. Creditors 70, Rent
Owing 50, Paper Owing 5 = W.C. 695. Capital 570 + Profit 2,125 −
Drawings 2,000 = 695.

33.7 Sales 29,000 − C.G.S. Opening Stock 1,500 + Purchases 20,200 −
Closing Stock 1,700 = 20,000, Gross Profit 9,000 + Discounts Received
1,000 − Expenses, Wages 3,000, Rent 650, Discounts Allowed 700,
General 1,800, Loss on fixtures 100, Depreciation 100 = Net Profit
3,650. Balance Sheet: F.A. Fixtures 1,700 − 100, C.A. Stock 1,700,
Debtors 2,100, Prepaid 250, − C.L. Creditors 1,900, Accruals 300, Bank
Overdraft 1,200. W.C. = 650. Totals 2,250. Capital 4,100 + 3,650 −
5,500 = 2,250.

33.9 *(a)* Dr Loan 2,500, Debtors (missing figure) 37,486, − Drawings 5,200 = 32,286, Total 34, 786. Cr Overdraft b/f 2,100, Wages 3,400, Rent 1,010, Suppliers 25,140, Overheads 746, Fittings 1,200, Balance c/d 1,190.

(b) Sales 36,036 − C.G.S. Opening Stock 4,230 + Purchases 25,070 − Closing Stock 3,560 = 25,740, Gross Profit 10,296 − Expenses, Wages 3,400, Rent 1,015, Overheads 746, Depreciation 410 = Net Profit 4,725.Balance Sheet: F.A. Fixtures 4,100 − 1,280, C.A. Stock 3,560, Debtors 2,310, Prepaid 90, Bank 1,190 − C.L. Creditors 3,920, Expenses Owing 70 = W.C. 3,160. Totals 5,980. Capital 4,555 + Profit 4,725 − Drawings 5,800, Loan 2,500.

33.11 Work Done: Credit 29,863, Cash 3,418 = 33,281 − Expenses: Materials 9,020, Secretary 3,000, Rent 225, Rates 135, Insurance 600, Electricity 1,496, Motor 912, General 1,644, Loan Interest 300, Provision Bad Debts 425, Account Fee 250, Amortisation of Lease 487, Depreciation: Equipment 960, Van 900 = Net Profit 12,927. Balance Sheet: F.A. Lease 6,500 − 487. Equipment 4,800−960, Vehicle 3,600 − 900, C.A. Stock 580, Debtors 4,250 − 425, Prepaid 275, bank 6,084, Cash 123 − C.L. Creditors 714, Interest Owing 300, Accounts Fee 250, Rates Owing 135, Electricity Owing 374 = W.C. 9,114. Totals 21,667. Capital 10,100 + Net Profit 12,927 − Drawings 5,360 = 17,667 + Loan 4,000.

33.13 Dr Opening Stock 1,800 + Purchases 2,330 = 4,130 (D) − (C) ? = C.G.S. (B) ? + Gross Profit (A) ? = 3,280. G.P.% 25%. Therefore (A) is 820. By deduction (B) is 2,460 and (C) is 1,670, so 1,670 is Cost of Goods Destroyed by fire.

34.1 Income: Collections 1,650 + Profit on Refreshments 315 = 1,965 − Expenditure: Rent 240, Printing 98, Secretary 144, Repairs 46, Groundsman 520, Miscellaneous 66, Depreciation 125 = Surplus 726. Balance Sheet F.A. Equipment 625 − 125, C.A. Prepaid 60 + Cash 879 − C.L. Expenses Owing 33 = Working Capital 906 = Total 1,406. Accumulated Fund, Balance 680 + Surplus 726 = 1,406.

34.3 *(a)* 20,000 + (600−540) 60 + 450 + 100 + 200 + 620 − 300 − 50 = 21,080.

(b) (i) Takings 8,000 − Cost of Supplies, Opening Stock 450 + Purchases 5,600 − Closing Stock 600 = 5,450, Gross Profit 2,550 − Expenses 280 = Net Profit 2,270.

(ii) Dr Arrears b/f 200, I & E 1,860, Advances c/d 80, Total 2,140, Cr Advance b/f 50, Cash: Current 1,540, last year 160, Subs written off 40, Arrears c/d 350.

(iii) Income: Subs 1,860 − written off 40, Profit on Dance 800, Profit on Bar 2,270 = 4,890 − Expenditure Rent 600, Rates 280, Balls 310, Groundsman 400, Referee 150, Travelling 1,000, Stationery 120, Insurance 75, Loss on mower 10, Depreciation 85 = 3,030. Surplus 1,860.
F.A. House 20,000, Mower 850 − 85, C.A. Stock 600, Rates Prepaid 120, Subs Arrears 350, Cash & Bank 1,735 − C.L. Creditors 550, Subs in Advance 80 = Working Capital 2,175. Total 22,940. Accumulated Fund 21,080 + Surplus 1,860.

34.4 (i) Takings 2,798 – Cost of Supplies, Opening Stock 59 + Purchases 1,456 – Closing Stock 103 = 1,412, Gross Profit 1,386 – Wages 650 = Bar Profit 736.

(ii) 2,788 + 59 + 1,298 = 4,145.

(iii) Income: Subs 3,819, Bar Profit 736, Dance Profits 186, Exhibition Profit 112 = 3,853 – Expenditure Wages 1,126, Rent 887, Travelling 673, Depreciation 279, Loss on sales equipment 11 = 2,976 = Surplus 1,877.
F.A. Equipment 3,276 – 279, C.A. Bar Stock 103, Debtors 29, Bank 2,893. Total 6,022. Accumulated Fund 4,145 + Surplus 1,877.

34.6 (a) Sales 21,790 – Cost of Sales, Opening Stock 1,860 + Purchases 13,190 – Closing Stock 2,110 = Gross Profit 8,850 – Salary 5,800 = Net Profit 3,050.

(b) Income: Subs: Ordinary 1,625 + Life 190 = 1,815 + Bar Profit 3,050 + B.S. Interest 2,78 = 5,143 – Expenditure: Dinner (net cost) 50, Rent 530, Painting 580, Insurance 270, Depreciation 987, General 1,100, Maintenance 1,310, Honorarium 200 = 5,027 = Surplus 116.

(c) F.A. Fixtures 9,870 – 3,387, Investment 4,454, C.A. Stock 2,110, Prepaid 40, Bank 3,102, Cash 239 – C.L. Creditors 460, Accrued Expenses 140, Subs in Advance 150 = Working Capital 4,741, Total 15,678. Accumulated Fund 13,962 + Surplus 116 = 14,078, Life Fund 1,600.

34.8 (a) Sales 13,800 – Cost of Sales, Opening Stock 1,840 + Purchases 8,700 – Closing Stock 2,360 = 8,180, Gross Profit 5,620 – Salary 1,175, Clubhouse costs 1,395 = Net Profit 3,050.

(b) Income: Subs 8,450 + Bar Profit 3,050 + Interest 130 = 11,630 – Expenditure; Clubhouse costs (including depreciation) 1,395, Salary 3,525, Dinner 180, Depreciation 821, Hire of Films 89, Stationery 248, Postages 114 = 6,372 = Surplus 5,258. F.A. Clubhouse, 15,000 – 1,500 = 13,500, Sports Equipment 2,463 – 821 = 1,642. C.A. Stocks 2,360 + Bank 7,734, Cash 10 – C.L. Creditors 1,900, Subs in Advance 360 = Working Capital 7,844. Total 22,986. Accumulated Fund 16,560 + Surplus 5,258 + Coaching Fund 1,168.

35.1 Opening Stock R.M. 6,500, Purchases 33,500, Carriage 1,000, – Closing Stock R.M. 15,000 = Cost R.M. Consumed 26,000, Direct Labour 18,000 = Prime Cost 44,000, Overheads: Indirect Wages 7,000, Rent 1,500, Heating 2,700, Depreciation 400 = 55,600 + Opening W.I.P. 10,000 – Closing W.I.P. 22,000 = Production Cost of Goods Completed c/d 43,600. Sales 75,000, – C.G.S. Opening Stock 5,000 + Production Cost 43,600 – Closing Stock 4,000 = Gross Profit 30,400 – Expenses, Rent 500, Heating 900, Salaries 3,000 = Net Profit 26,000.

35.3 Opening Stock R.M. 18,450 + Purchases 64,300 + Carriage In 1,605 − Closing Stock R.M. 20,210 = Cost R.M. Consumed 64,145, Direct Labour 65,810 = Prime Cost 129,955 + Expenses, Rent 1,800, Fuel 5,920, Depreciation 8,300 + Opening W.I.P. 23,600 − Closing W.I.P. 17,390 = Production Cost c/d 152,185. Sales 200,600 − C.G.S. Opening Stock F.G. 17,470 + Production Cost 152,185 − Closing Stock F.G. 21,485 = Gross Profit 52,430 − Expenses: Salaries 16,920, Rent 900, Lighting 5,760, Depreciation 1,950 = Net Profit 26,900.

35.5 Opening Stock R.M. 8,565 + Purchases 39,054 − Closing Stock R.M. 9,050 = Cost R.M. Consumed 38,569, Wages 45,775 = Prime Cost 84,344 − Expenses: Lighting 2,859, General 5,640, Rent 4,800, Depreciation 2,000 = Production Cost c/d 99,643. Sales 136,500 − C.G.S. Opening Stock 29,480 + Production Cost b/d 99,643 − Closing Stock 31,200 = Gross Profit 38,577 − Expenses: Salaries 6,285, General 3,816, Rent 2,092, Heating 1,110, Commission 7,860, Van Expenses 2,500, Depreciation, Equipment 1,500, Premises 1,000 = Net Profit 12,414.
Balance Sheet: F.A. Premises 50,000 − 11,000, Machinery 50,000 − 19,500, Office Equipment 15,000 − 5,500, C.A. Stocks F.G. 31,200, R.M. 9,050, Debtors 28,370, Prepaid 108, Bank 13,337 − C.L. Creditors 19,450, Expenses Owing 305 = Working Capital 62,310. Total 141,310. Capital 137,456 + Net Profit 12,414 − Drawings 8,560.

36.1 Figures shown in order Electrical, Furniture, Leisure Goods. Sales 29,840: 73,060: 39,581 − Opening Stock 6,080: 17,298: 14,370 + Purchases 18,195: 54,632: 27,388 − Closing Stock 7,920: 16,150: 22,395, Gross Profit 13,485: 17,280: 20,218.

36.2 Figures shown Department A then B.
Sales 15,000: 10,000 − C.G.S. Opening Stock 250: 200, + Purchases 11,800: 8,200 − Closing Stock 300: 150 = Gross Profits 3,250: 1,750 − Expenses, Wages 1,000: 750, Delivery 150: − , Salaries 450: 300, Rates 26: 104, Insurance 10: 40, Lighting 24: 96, Repairs 5: 20, Telephone 5: 20, Cleaning 6: 24, Accounting 72: 48, General 36: 24, Net Profit 1,466: 324.

37.1 Columnar Sales Day Book: Total 11,650, VAT 1,030, Hi Fi 5,200, TV 5,100, Sundries 320. Ledger accounts obvious.

37.2 Purchases Analysis Book: Total 2,252, Purchases 1,346, Light 246, Motor 376, Stationery 137, Carriage In 147.

37.3 Debit each total to appropriate expense account. Ledger accounts obvious.

38.1 Net Profit 25,200 − Salaries (O) 3,000 (J) 1,000, Interest on Capitals (S) 600 (O) 400 (J) 200 = 20,000 shared (S) 8,000 (O) 8,000 (J) 4,000.

38.2 Net Profit 30,350 + Interest on Drawings (W) 240 (P) 180 (H) 130 − Interest on Capitals (W) 2,000 (P) 1,500 (H) 900; Salaries (P) 2,000 (H) 3,500 = 21,000 shared (W) 10,500 (P) 6,300 (H) 4,200.
Balance Sheet: Capitals (W) 40,000 (P) 30,000 (H) 18,000 = 88,000.
Current Accounts: Balances (W) 1,860 (P) 946 (H) 717 + Share of Profits (W) 10,500 (P) 6,300 (H) 4,200 + Salaries (P) 2,000 (H) 3,500 + Interest on Capital (W) 2,000 (P) 1,500 (H) 900 − Interest on Drawings (W) 240 (P) 180 (H) 130 − Drawings (W) 9,200 (P) 7,100 (H) 6,900 = Balances (W) 4,920 (P) 3,466 (H) 2,287 = 10,673.

38.4 Sales 123,650 − Cost of Goods Sold, Opening Stock 41,979 + Purchases 85,416 − Closing Stock 56,340 = 71,055, Gross Profit 52,595 + Reduction Provision B.D. 80 − Expenses: Salaries 19,117, Office 2,512, Carriage 1,288, Discounts 115, Bad Debts 503, Loan Interest 4,000, Depreciation Fixtures 770 Buildings 1,000 = Net Profit 23,370 + Interest on Drawings (Me) 180 (Ma) 120 − Interest on Capitals (Me) 3,500 (Ma) 2,950, Salary (Me) 800 = 16,420 shared (Me) 8,210 (Ma) 8,210.
Balance Sheet: F.A. Buildings 75,000 − 26,000, Fixtures 11,000 − 4,070, C.A. Stock 56,340, Debtors 16,243 − Provision 320. Bank 677 − C.L. Creditors 11,150 − Expenses Owing 296 = Working Capital 61,494. Totals 117,424.
Capitals (Me) 35,000 (Ma) 29,500 = 64,500. Current Accounts, Balance (Me) 1,306 (Ma) 298 + Interest on Capital (Me) 3,500 (Ma) 2,950, Salary (Me) 800, Balance of Profit (Me) 8,210 (Ma) 8,210 − Drawings (Me) 6,400 (Ma) 5,650 − Interest on Drawings (Me) 180 (Ma) 120 = 12,924, Loan 40,000.

38.5 Sales 28,797 − Returns In 110 = 28,687 − Cost of Goods Sold, Opening Stock 2,395 + Purchases 19,388 − Returns 286 + Carriage In 216 − Closing Stock 5,623 = 16,090 = Gross Profit 12,597 + Discounts 404 − Expenses: Wages 4,389, Rent 542, Insurance 104, Delivery 309, Motor 635, General 204, Loan Interest 140, Discounts 392, Depreciation 187, Provision B.D. 320 = Net Profit 5,779 + Interest on Drawings (P) 58 (H) 39 − Salary (H) 300 − Interest on Capital (P) 450 (H) 240 = 4,886 Shared (P) 2,932 (H) 1,954.
Balance Sheet: F.A. Motors 2,500 − 817, C.A. Stock 5,623, Debtors 8,462 − Provision 320, Prepaid 12, bank 5,241, Cash 180 − C.L. Creditors 1,899, Expenses Owing 197 = Working Capital 17,102, Totals 18,785. Capitals (P) 9,000 (H) 4,800 = 13,800. Current Accounts: Balances (P) 880 (H) 120) + Share of Profits (P) 2,932 (H) 1,954 + Interest on Capital (P) 450 (H) 240 − Drawings (P) 1,825 (H) 1,429 − Interest on Drawings (P) 58 (H) 39 = (P) 2,379 (H) 606 = 2,985, Loan 2,000.

39.1 (a)   Goodwill 12,000 + Other Assets 14,000 = 26,000. Capitals (X) 12,000; (Y) 9,300; (Z) 4,700.
   (b)   Net Assets 14,000. Capitals (X) 8,400: (Y) 3,300: (Z) 2,300.

39.3 (a) Goodwill Dr 6,000, Capitals Cr (X) 3,000 (Y) 3,000: Cash Dr 7,000, Capital Cr (Z) 7,000 (b) Goodwill 6,000 + Fixed & Current Assets 15,000 + Cash 9,000 = Total 30,000. Capitals (X) 11,000 (Y) 7,000 (Z) 7,000 + Current Liabilities 5,000. (c) Capitals Dr (X) 2,400 (Y) 1,800 (Z) 1,800: Goodwill Cr 6,000.

40.1 Revaluation: Dr Motors 950, Stock 150, Office Fittings 220, Profit: (H) 4,090 (A) 2,454 (E) 1,636 Cr Buildings 9,500. Capitals: Dr Balances c/d (H) 13,650 (A) 8,874 (E) 6,476 Cr Balances b/f (H) 9,560 (A) 6,420 (E) 4,840, Profit on Revaluation (H) 4,090 (A) 2,454 (E) 1,636.
Balance Sheet: F.A. Buildings 17,500, Motors 2,600, Fittings 1,090 = 21,190, C.A. Stock 1,890, Debtors 4,530, Bank 1,390 = Total 29,000. Capitals: (H) 13,650 (A) 8,874 (E) 6,476.

40.3 Revaluation: Dr Machinery 280, Motors 410, Fixtures 340, Profit (F) 15,264 (B) 11,448 (D) 11,448: Cr Premises 18,440, Stock 750. Goodwill 20,000. Capitals: Dr Balances c/d (F) 33,264 (B) 21,048 (D) 17,448 (N) 8,000 Cr. Balances b/f (F) 18,000 (B) 9,600 (D) 6,000. Profit on Revaluation (F) 15,264 (B) 11,448 (D) 11,448, Bank (N) 8,000.
Balance Sheet: F.A. Goodwill 20,000, Premises 30,000, Machinery 3,700, Motors 6,400, Fixtures 1,200, C.A. Stock 5,600, Debtors 3,260, Bank 9,600. Total 79,760. Capitals (F) 33,264 (B) 21,048 (D) 17,448 (N) 8,000.

41.1 F.A. Premises 71,000, Plant 41,000 − 16,000, C.A. Stock 25,000, Debtors 18,900, Bank 12,750, Cash 7,500 − C.L. Creditors 16,900 − Expenses Owing 3,250 = Working Capital 44,000. Totals 140,000. Share Capital (Authorised Note only) Issued Ordinary 100,000, Preference 5,000, Profit & Loss 30,000 = Shareholders' Interest 135,000 + Debentures 5,000.

41.3 (1)   (a)   6% + 9% = 15% of 800,000 = 120,000
      (b)   15% of £1 = 15 pence
      (c)   252,000/800,000 × 100 = 31.5 pence per share
   (2)   Balance b/f 340,000 + Net Profit 252,000 − General Reserve 100,000 − Dividend 120,000 = Balance c/f 372,000.

41.5 (a) see text. (b) Net Profit 95,000 + Balance b/f 355,000 − General Reserve 150,000 − Preference Dividends, interim 3,200, final 3,200, Ordinary Dividend 37,500 = Balance carried forward 256,100.

41.7 F.A. Goodwill 10,000, Premises 17,000, Machinery 7,000−2,100, Motors 5,000−3,000, C.A. Stock 7,000, Debtors 3,000, Cash 100 − C.L. Creditors 9,000, Bank Overdraft 2,000, Working Capital (900) = Total 33,000. Share Capital (Authorised as note) Issued 20,000. Reserves, Share Premium 2,000, General Reserve 2,000, Profit & Loss 9,000.

41.9 F.A. Land 370,000, Plant 400,000 − 155,000, Motors 70,500 − 38,750, C.A. Stock 225,500, Debtors 78,900 − 1,400, Cash 25,250 − C.L. Creditors 51,000, Overdraft 126,500, Proposed Dividend 30,000 = Working Capital 120,750 = Totals 767,500. Share Capital (Authorised note only) Issued, Ordinary 300,000, Preference 100,000, Reserves, Share Premium 150,000, Profit & Loss 117,500, Debentures 100,000. Returns: On Ordinary Shares 7,000 × £1 × 12% = 840 On other investment 900.

41.11 Net Profit b/d 300 + Balance b/f 10 = 310 − General Reserve 50, Preference Dividend 50, Ordinary Dividend 180 = Balance c/f 30. Balance Sheet: F.A. Premises 1,250, Vans 125 − 35, Fixtures 60 − 20. C.A. Stocks 50, Debtors 27 − 1, Prepaid 2, Cash 314 − C.L. Creditors 12, Proposed Dividends 230 = Working Capital 150 = Totals 1,530 (Authorised note only) Issued. Preference 500, Ordinary 900, Reserves, General 100, Profit & Loss 30.

42.1 Both balance sheets, S. Walters figures first. Goodwill 8,200: 9,300, Premises 21,000: 28,000, Stock 9,600: 9,200, Debtors 6,300: 6,300, Bank 1,700: −. Totals 46,800: 52,800. Capital 40,000: 46,000. Creditors 6,800: 6,800.

42.3 (a) Goodwill 22,450, Premises 80,000, Stock 5,000, Debtors 4,000, Bank 10,000, Totals 121,450, Capital 120,000, Creditors 1,450.
(b) Goodwill 40,000, Premises 80,000, Fixtures 40,000, Stock 14,000, Debtors 4,000, Bank 12,000, Totals 190,000. Capital (S) 70,000, (W) 70,000, (V) 50,000.
(c) See text.

42.5 F.A. Goodwill 30,430, Premises 30,000, Plant 35,000, Vehicles 13,000, C.A. Stocks 8,570, Debtors 3,000 − 600, Bank 14,100 − C.L. Creditors 14,000 = Working Capital 11,070 = Totals 119,500. Share Capital 100,000, Share Premium 20,000, Profit & Loss (500). Note − the 500 deficit on the Profit and Loss is the preliminary expenses written off.

43.1 (*a*) Source: Profits 6,000 + Increase in Creditors 4,000 + Loan 5,000 − Application, Increase in Stocks 9,000, Increase in Debtors 1,000, Fixed Assets bought 15,000 = (10,000). Reduction in bank funds 11,000 down to 1,000 = (10,000).

43.3 Source: Profit 2,200 + Depreciation 260 + 200 = Total Generated 2,660 + Loan 1,000 − Application, Drawings 1,500, Plant bought 1,000 = 1,160. Increase in Working Capital 600 to 1,760 = 1,160.

44.1 Gross Pay 60; Income Tax 8; National Insurance 3; Net Pay 49.

44.2 Gross Pay 140; Income Tax 30; National Insurance 7; Net Pay 103.

44.3 Gross Pay 800; Income Tax 210; National Insurance 25; Net Pay 565.

Index

Accounting Ratios, 287
Accounts, Classes of, 90
Accruals Concept, 83
Accrued Expenses, 183
Accrued Income, 186
Adjustment Accounts, 281
Advances, Partnerships, 367
Advance, Payments in, 184
Ageing Schedule, 173
Analysis of Accounts, 440
Appreciation, 147
Appropriation Accounts,
  – Companies, 400
  – Parnerships, 363
Assets:
  – Current, 65
  – Fixed, 65
  – Nature of, 2
  – Order in Balance Sheet, 66
Authorized Share Capital, 399

Bad Debts, 171
  – Provisions for, 172
  – Recovered, 177
Balance Sheets, 64
Balancing off Accounts, 42
Bank Cash Book, 257
Bank Giro Transfer, 235
Banking System, 93
Bank Overdraft, 110, 237
  – Reconciliation Statements, 234
  – Statement, 99
Bought Ledger, 122
Business Entity Concept, 83
Business Purchase, 412

Calls,
  – in Advance, 399
  – in Arrear, 399
Capital:
  – Authorized, 399
  – Called-up, 399
  – Employed, 191
  – Expenditure, 221
  – Invested, 191
  – Issued, 399
  – Uncalled, 399
  – Working, 191

Carriage:
  – Inwards, 70
  – Outwards, 70
Cash Book, The, 99
Cash Discounts, 105
Cheques, 93
Cheque Crossings, 95
Closing Stock, 56
Club Accounts, 318
Columnar Day Books, 351
Columnar Style, 188
Commission Errors, 261
Commission, Manager's, 290
Communication, 90
Company Accounts, 399
Compensating Errors, 261
Computers, 45, 89, 231
Concepts of Accounting, 80
Conservatism, 85
Consistency, 85
Contras, 101
Contribution, 347
Control Accounts, 277
Cost Concept, 82
Cost, Elements of, 331
Cost of Goods Sold, 54
Credit Control, 129
Credit Note, 125
Creditor, 3
Cumulative Preference Shares, 398
Current Accounts, 93
Current Asset, 65

Debentures, 400
  – Interest, 400
Debit Note, 127
Debtor, 4
Departmental Accounts, 343
Deposit Accounts, 93
Depreciation:
  – Causes of, 146
  – of Goodwill, 385
  – Nature of, 145
  – Provision for, 147, 165
  – Reducing Balance Method, 148
  – Straight Line Method, 148
Direct Expenses, 331
Directors' Fees, 400

Discounts:
— Allowed, 105
— Cash, 105
— Provision for, 177, 179
— Received, 105
— Trade, 117
Dishonoured Cheques, 238
Dividends, 397
Double Entry, Rules, 12, 34
Drawer, 94
Drawings Account,
— Interest on, 361
— Nature of, 37
— of Goods, 188
Dual Aspect Concept, 83

Entrance Fees, 323
Errors, 261
Examination Techniques, 446

Factoring, 130
Factory Overhead Expenses, 331
Final Accounts, 74
Fire Losses, 304
Fixed Assets, 65
Fixed Capitals, 364
Fixed Expenses, 440
Folio Columns, 102
Funds Flow Statements, 424

General Ledger, 88
Going Concern Concept, 82
Goods for own use, 188
Goodwill, 373
Gross Loss, 55
Gross Profit, 54
Gross Profit Percentage, 291

Impersonal Accounts, 90
Imprest Systems, 254
Income and Expenditure Accounts, 318
Income Tax, 433
Incomplete Records, 296
Interest on Advances, 367
— Capital, 360
— Drawings, 361
Invoice, 114
Internal Check, 128
Interpretation of Accounts, 440
Issued Share Capital, 399

Journal, The, 246

Liabilities:
— Nature of, 2
— Order in Balance Sheet, 66
Life Membership, 323

Limited Companies:
— Final Accounts, 399
— Liability, 396
— Partnerships, 359
Liquidity, 442
Loss:
— Gross, 55
— Net, 55
Losses by Theft, 304

Manager's Commission, 290
Manufacturing Accounts, 331
Margin, 287
Market Value, 337
Mark-up, 287
Materiality, 84
Members' Equity, 404
Modern Methods of Accounting, 228
Money Measurement Concept, 82

Narrative, 246
Narrative Style, 188
National Insurance, 435
Nominal Accounts, 90
— Ledger, 122
— Share Capital, 399
Notice of Coding, 434

Objectivity, 81
Omissions, Errors, 261
Opening Entries, 248
Ordinary Shares, 398
Original Entry, Errors, 262
Overdraft, 110, 237

Paid-up Capital, 399
Partnerships:
— Accounts, 359
— Advances, 367
— Agreements, 360
— Appropriation Accounts, 363
— Balance Sheet, 364
— Capital Accounts, 364
— Current Accounts, 364
— Interest on Capital, 360
— Interest on Drawings, 361
— Limited, 359
— Profit and Loss Accounts, 363
— Retirement, 384
— Revaluation of Assets, 388
— Salaries, 362
P.A.Y.E., 434
Payee, 94
Personal Accounts, 90
Petty Cash Books, 253
Posting, 102
Preference Shares, 397
Preliminary Expenses, 400

Prepaid Expenses, 184
Profitability, 442
Prime Cost, 331
Principle, Errors of, 261
Production Cost, 331
Profits:
 — Appropriation of, 363
 — Gross, 54
 — Net 54
Profit and Loss Account, 54
Provisions, for Bad Debts, 172
 — for Depreciation, 147, 165
 — for Discounts, 177, 179
Prudence, 85
Punched Cards, 230
Purchase of Businesses, 412
Purchases Account, 23
 — Analysis Books, 351
 — Book, 122
 — Day Book, 122
 — Journal, 89, 121
 — Ledger, 89, 122
 — Ledger Control Account, 278
 — Meaning of, 27
 — Returns Book, 128

Rate of Return, 442
Rate of Turnover, 292
Ratios, 287
Real Accounts, 90
Realisation Concept, 83
Receipts and Payment Accounts, 318
Reducing Balance Method, 148
Reserves, 400
Returns, 24
 — Inwards Book, 127
 — Inwards Journal, 125
 — Outwards Book, 128
 — Outwards Journal, 127
Revaluation of Assets, 388
Revenue Expenditure, 221

Salaries:
 — Calculations, 433
 — Partnerships, 362
Sales:
 — Account, 24
 — Analysis Books, 355
 — Book, 116
 — Day Book, 116
 — Invoice, 114
 — Journal, 89, 114
 — Ledger, 89, 115
 — Ledger Control Account, 277
 — Meaning of, 27
 — Returns Book, 127
Self Balancing Ledgers, 281
Shareholders Funds, 404

Share Premium Account, 403
Shares:
 — Classes of, 398
 — Ordinary, 398
 — Preference, 398
Single Entry, 296
S.S.A.P., 86, 385
Standing Orders, 236
Statement of Affairs, 297
Statement of Source and Application of Funds, 424
Statements of Standard Accounting Practice, 86, 385
Stock Account, 22, 57
 — Closing, 56
 — Valuation of, 56
Stockturn, 292
Statements, 129
Straight Line Method, 148
Subjectivity, 81
Superannuation, 436
Super Profits, 376
Suspense Account, 267

Total Cost,
 — Creditors Account, 278
 — Debtors Account, 277
Taxation:
 — Value Added Tax (VAT), 133
Trade Discount, 117
Trading Account, 54
Trend Figures, 444
Trial Balance, 49
 — Errors not revealed by, 261
 — Errors revealed by, 267

Uncalled Capital, 399
Unpresented Cheques, 235

Value Added Tax, 133
Variable Expenses, 440
V.A.T., 133
Vertical Accounts, 188

Wages Calculations, 433
Working Capital, 191
Works Overheads, 331
Work-in-Progress, 333